The New Testament

Also by C. K. Barrett and published by SPCK:

The Gospel according to St John (2nd edn)
Freedom and Obligation
Essays on Paul
Essays on John
The Gospel of John and Judaism

The New Testament Background
Selected Documents

Revised Edition

Edited, with Introductions and Notes, by

C. K. Barrett

First published in Great Britain 1956
Revised edition first published 1987
SPCK
Holy Trinity Church
Marylebone Road
London NW1 4DU

British Library Cataloguing in Publication Data

The New Testament background: selected
   documents.—Rev. ed.
   1.   Palestine—History—70 A.D.—
Sources
   I.   Barrett, C. K.
   933'.04   DS109.912

ISBN 0–281–04294–2

Typeset, printed and bound in Great Britain by
William Clowes Limited, Beccles and London

Contents

Acknowledgements   xvi
Introductions   xix
Abbreviations   xxii
The Sources   xxiii

I   The Roman Empire   I

Augustus and the Imperial Settlement   I
   1   *Res Gestae Divi Augusti* 12f., 24–7, 34f.   I
   2   Suetonius, *Augustus* 31   5
   3   Horace, *Carmen Saeculare*   6
   4   Virgil, *Eclogue* IV   8

Tiberius   10
   5   Suetonius, *Tiberius* 36   10
   6   Tacitus, *Annals* ii. 85   10
   7   Tacitus, *Annals* vi. 51   10

Gaius (Caligula)   11
   8   Josephus, *War* ii. 184–7, 192–203   11

Claudius   13
   9   Suetonius, *Claudius* 25   13
   10   Claudius, *An Ordinance*   14

Nero   15
   11   Tacitus, *Annals* xv. 44   15
   12   Suetonius, *Nero* 16   16
   13   Sulpicius Severus, *Chronicle* ii. 29   17
   14   Suetonius, *Nero* 57   17

Vespasian   18
   15   Tacitus, *Histories* ii. 4f.   18

Domitian   19
   16   Suetonius, *Domitian* 13   19
   17   Suetonius, *Domitian* 12   20
   18   Tacitus, *Agricola* 2   21
   19   Dio Cassius, *Epitome* 67. 14. 1–3   21

2   The Papyri   23

Preparation and Use of Papyrus   24
    20   Pliny, *Natural History* xiii. 68–83   24

Form and Style of Letter-writing in the Papyri   28
    21   P. Lond. 42. *A letter from wife to husband*   28
    22   P. Oxy. 292. *A letter of commendation*   29
    23   BGU 27. *A letter from brother to brother*   30
    24   *The Epistles of Diogenes*, 7. To Hicetas   30
    25   *The Epistles of Diogenes*, 45. To Perdiccas   31

Magical and Religious Papyri   31
    26   P. Oxy. 1211. *Articles for sacrifice*   32
    27   P. Tebt. 294. *The office of prophet*   32
    28   P. Oxy. 1148. *A question addressed to an oracle*   33
    29   P. Oxy. 1478. *A charm for victory*   33
    30   Paris Magical Papyrus, ll. 3007–3085. *Charms and*   34
         formulas
    31   P. Tebt. 276. *Astrology*   38

Papyri illustrating Social and Economic Conditions   38
    32   P. Tebt. 299. *Notice of birth*   39
    33   P. Oxy. 275. *Agreement of apprenticeship*   39
    34   BGU 1052. *A contract of marriage*   40
    35   P. Oxy. 744. *A letter from husband to wife*   40
    36   *Rev. Egypt.* 1919. *A letter from son to father*   41
    37   BGU 1103. *Deed of divorce*   41
    38   P. Tebt. 381. *A will*   42
    39   P. Oxy. 39. *Release from military service*   43
    40   P. Tebt. 300. *Notice of death*   43
    41   P. Cairo Zen. 59092. *A list of clothes*   43
    42   P. Tebt. 35. *Regulation of the price of myrrh*   44
    43   P. Oxy. 1439. *A toll receipt*   44
    44   P. Amh. 51. *Deed of sale of a house*   44
    45   P. Ryl. 175. *A complaint to the police*   45
    46   P. Hamb. i. 4. *Engagement to appear in court*   46
    47   P. Oxy. 37. *Minutes of legal proceedings*   46
    48   P. Lond. 1912. *Letter from the Emperor Claudius*   47

3   Inscriptions   51

The Gallio Inscription at Delphi   51
    49   *SIG* 3rd edn 801D. *Rescript of Claudius*   51

A Temple Inscription   53

    50   OGIS 598. *A Warning to Foreigners*   53

Synagogue Inscriptions   53

    51   *CIJ* 718. At Corinth   53
    52   *CIJ* 510 (= *CIG* 9909). At Rome   53
    53   *CIJ* 1404. At Jerusalem   54

Sacral Manumission   55

    54   *SIG* 2nd edn 845. At Delphi   55
    55   *CIJ* 683 (= *CIG* 2114bb). At Panticapaeum   56

Two Ossuaries at Talpioth   57

    56   'Iesous iou'   57
    57   'Iesous aloth'   57

4   The Philosophers and Poets   58

Heraclitus and the Logos   59

    58   Heraclitus, *Fragment* 1   59
    59   Heraclitus, *Fragment* 2   59
    60   Heraclitus, *Fragment* 31   60
    61   Heraclitus, *Fragment* 50   60

Plato: The Philosopher's Mission and the Doctrine of Ideas   60

    62   Plato, *Apology* 28D–30C   60
    63   Plato, *Republic* vii. 514A–517A   62

The Earlier Stoics   65

    64   Zeno, *Fragments* 175f.   66
    65   Zeno, *Fragment* 98   66
    66   Zeno, *Fragments* 162, 152   67
    67   Cleanthes, *Fragment* 537   67
    68   Chrysippus, *Fragment* 625   68
    69   Chrysippus, *Fragment* 1169   68
    70   Chrysippus, *Fragment* 1192   69
    71   Posidonius (*apud* Sextus Empiricus)   69
    72   Posidonius (*apud* Galen)   70

Stoic Ethics   70

    73   Epictetus, *Discourses* I, xvi. 1–8, 15–21   71
    74   Epictetus, *Discourses* II, viii. 9–14   72
    75   Epictetus, *Discourses* IV, i. 1–23, 128–31   72
    76   Marcus Aurelius, *To Himself* ii. 1   74
    77   Marcus Aurelius, *To Himself* iii. 7   75

78   Marcus Aurelius, *To Himself* iv. 7   75
79   Marcus Aurelius, *To Himself* vi. 54   76
80   Marcus Aurelius, *To Himself* viii. 34   76
81   Marcus Aurelius, *To Himself* xii. 35f.   76

Aristotle   77
82   Aristotle, *Nicomachean Ethics* V, iv. 7–12   77

Epicurus   78
83   Lucretius, *On the Nature of Things* i. 62–79   78
84   Epicurus, *Epistle to Menoeceus* 123ff., 127b–132   79

The Philosophic Missionary   81
85   Epictetus, *Discourses* III, xxii. 19–26   81
86   Philostratus, *Life of Apollonius* i. 17   82
87   Philostratus, *Life of Apollonius* iv. 20   83
88   Philostratus, *Life of Apollonius* v. 24   84
89   Apollonius of Tyana, *Epistle* iii   85

Poetic Comment   85
90   Aristophanes, *Clouds* 222–74   85
91   Aeschylus, *Eumenides* 752–807   88
92   Sophocles, *Antigone* 441–70   89
93   Euripides, *The Trojan Women* 634–83   90

5   Gnosis and Gnosticism   92

The Hermetic Literature   93
94   *Corpus Hermeticum* 1. *Poimandres* 1ff. Introduction   94
95   *Corpus Hermeticum* 1. *Poimandres* 4ff., 9. Cosmogony   95
96   *Corpus Hermeticum* 1. *Poimandres* 12–15. Archetypal   97
      Man and his Fall
97   *Corpus Hermeticum* 1. *Poimandres* 27ff. The Prophet's   98
      Mission
98   *Corpus Hermeticum* 1. *Poimandres* 30ff. The Sacrifice   99
      of Praise and Thanksgiving
99   *Corpus Hermeticum* 4. *The Bowl* 3–7   101
100   *Corpus Hermeticum* 13. *Concerning Rebirth* 1, 2   102

Coptic Texts from Nag Hammadi   103
101   *NHC* III. 70–90. *Eugnostos the Blessed*   103
102   *NHC* I. *The Gospel of Truth* 34–41   108
103   *NHC* II. *The Gospel of Thomas* 1–7, 24–7, 112–114   111

Mandaean Literature 114
104 *Right Ginza* II. 3 115
105 *Left Ginza* III. 19 118

6 Mystery Religions 120

The Myth 120
106 Plutarch, *Isis and Osiris* 12–19 121
107 Plutarch, *Isis and Osiris* 27 124
108 Eusebius, *Praeparatio Evangelica* II, ii. 22ff. 125

Initiation 125
109 Prudentius, *Peristephanon* x. 1011–50 126
110 Apuleius, *The Golden Ass (Metamorphoses)* xi. 22–6 127

Worship 130
111 Josephus, *Antiquities* xviii. 66–80 130
112 P. Paris 574. *A Mithras Liturgy* 132
113 *CIMRM* I. 423. *Dedication of a Mithraic chapel* 133
114 *CIMRM* I. 473. *A dedication in Rome* 134
115 *CIMRM* I. 523. *Record of a taurobolium* 134

7 Jewish History 135

The Maccabean Period 135
116 I *Maccabees* 1. 5–15 135
117 I *Maccabees* 1. 20–4 136
118 I *Maccabees* 1. 54–64 137
119 I *Maccabees* 2. 15–28 138
120 I *Maccabees* 3. 10–26 138
121 I *Maccabees* 4. 36–61 139
122 I *Maccabees* 8. 17–32 141
123 I *Maccabees* 11. 54–62 142

The High Priests 143
124 I *Maccabees* 14. 25–49 143
125 Josephus, *Antiquities* xiii. 372–6 145
126 Josephus, *Antiquities* xiv. 69–79 146

Herod the Great 148
127 Josephus, *War* i. 123–6 148
128 Josephus, *War* i. 199–207 149
129 Josephus, *War* I. 386f., 392b, 393a, 394, 396, 400 150

130   Josephus, *War* i. 401ff., 408, 417, 422   151
131   Josephus, *War* i. 429–33   152
132   Tacitus, *Histories* V. 4, 5, 8, 9. Impressions of a Gentile   153

Judaea under direct Roman Rule   155
133   Josephus, *War* ii. 111ff., 117   156
134   Josephus, *War* ii. 169–77   156

Pharisees, Sadducees, and Essenes   157
135   Josephus, *War* ii. 119f., 122, 137–42, 152f., 162–6   158
136   Philo, *Quod Omnis Probus Liber sit* 75–80   160
137   Philo, *De Vita Contemplativa* 1–3   161

The Jewish War of AD 66–70   162
138   Josephus, *War* ii. 254–6a., 258ff.   162
139   Josephus, *War* ii 271–8a   163
140   Josephus, *War* ii. 285–96   163
141   Josephus, *War* v. 362–74   165
142   Josephus, *War* vi. 392ff., 399–403a, 404–8   166
143   Josephus, *War* vii. 280–5, 295–6, 299, 315–16, 320–   168
       21, 333–6, 391–4, 400–401
144   Josephus, *War* vii. 216ff.   169

The Revolt of AD 132–5   170
145   Dio Cassius, *Roman History* lxix. 12ff.   170
146   Eusebius, *HE* IV, vi. 1–4   171
147   Eusebius, *HE* IV, viii. 4   172

The Dispersion   172
148   Josephus, *Antiquities* xiv. 110–118   173
149   Philo, *In Flaccum* 73ff.   174
150   Juvenal, *Satire* II. 10–16   175
151   Juvenal, *Satire* VI. 153–60, 542–7   175
152   Juvenal, *Satire* XIV. 96–106   176

8   Rabbinic Literature and Rabbinic Judaism   177

The Rabbis   177
153   *Aboth* I. 1ff.   177
154   *Aboth* I. 12–15   178
155   *Aboth* 2.1   179
156   *Aboth* 2. 8f.   180
157   *Aboth* 3. 14–17   181
158   *Aboth* 4. 1   182
159   *Yadaim* 4. 6, 7   183

The Literature 184

160 *Tosephta Sanhedrin* 7. 11 (p. 427) 185
161 *Siphre Numbers* 82, 83 (on *Numbers* 10.33, 34) 186
162 *Aboth* 2. 7 187
163 *Aboth* 3. 5 188
164 *Shabbath* 15. 1 188
165 *Aboth* 3. 18 189
166 *Sukkah* 2. 9 189
167 *Shabbath* 153a 189
168 *Nedarim* 9. 5 190
169 *Y. Baba Metzia* ii. 5. 8c 191
170 *Taanith* 3. 8 191

The Law 192

171 *Exodus Rabbah* 33. 1 192
172 *Siphre Numbers, Shelah,* 115, 35a 193
173 *Kiddushin* 30b 194

Feasts and Festivals 194

174 *Mekilta on Exodus* 31. 13 (109b) 194
175 *Tamid* 7. 4 195
176 *Shabbath* 7. 1f. 195
177 *Shabbath* 2. 7 196
178 *Pesahim* 10. 1, 3ff. 197
179 *Oholoth* 18. 7–10 198
180 *Pesahim* 68b 199
181 *Sukkah* 4. 1, 5–7, 9; 5. 1–3 200
182 *Yoma* 3. 8 202
183 *Yoma* 5. 1ff. 202
184 *Yoma* 6. 1, 2; 5. 4–7 203
185 *Yoma* 7.1 204
186 *Yoma* 8. 1 204

The Synagogue 204

187 *Benediction* 1 205
188 *Benediction* 2 205
189 *Benediction* 6 205
190 *Benediction* 7 205
191 *Benediction* 9 206
192 *Benediction* 10 206
193 *Benediction* 14 206
194 *The Qaddish Prayer* 206

Ḥaber and ʿAm ha-ʾaretz   206
   195   *Demai* 2. 2ff.   207
   196 . *Kelim* 1. 1, 2   208

Proselytes   208
   197   *Numbers Rabbah* 8. 3   208
   198   *Yebamoth* 47a, b   209

Heretics   210
   199   *Sanhedrin* 10. 1   210
   200   *Benediction* 12   211

Theology   211
   201   *Aboth* 3. 1   211
   202   *Aboth* 4. 2   211
   203   *Aboth* 4. 16f.   212
   204   *Aboth* 5. 10f.   212
   205   *Aboth* 5. 16   212
   206   *Aboth* 5. 20   213

Judicial Procedure   213
   207   *Sanhedrin* 4. 1, 3–5a; 5. 1   213
   208   *Sanhedrin* 7. 5   215
   209   *Sanhedrin* 6. 1–4   215

9   Qumran   218

The Community and its Story   218
   210   *Community Rule* (1QS) 5. 1—6. 8   219
   211   *Community Rule* (1QS) 8. 1–19   221
   212   *Damascus Rule* (CD) 1. 1—2. 13   223
   213   *Damascus Rule* (CD) 4. 2—6. 11   224
   214   *Damascus Rule* (CD) 10. 14—12. 6a   226

Faith and Practice   228
   215   *Community Rule* (1QS) 11. 2–22   229
   216   *Community Rule* (1QS) 6. 8b—7. 25   231
   217   *Hymns* (1QH) 1. 1–27a   234
   218   *Hymns* (1QH) 4. 22b–40   236
   219   *Hymns* (1QH) 6. 29–35   237
   220   *Hymns* (1QH) 11. 3–14   238

Biblical Exegesis   239
   221   *Commentary on Habakkuk* (1QpHab)   240

The War   246
  222   *War Rule* (1QM) 1. 1–12a   246
  223   *War Rule* (1QM) 5. 3—6. 17   247
  224   *War Rule* (1QM) 11. 1—12. 18   249

10 Philo   252

Philo's Faithfulness to the Law   252
  225   *De Migratione Abrahami* 89–93   253

His Philosophical Eclecticism   254
  226   *De Opificio Mundi* 15f.   254
  227   *Legum Allegoriae* 1. 70–73   255
  228   *De Opificio Mundi* 3, 8f.   257
  229   *De Opificio Mundi* 99f.   258

The Allegorical Method   259
  230   *De Posteritate Caini* 1–11   259

Etymological Arguments   261
  231   *De Abrahamo* 81ff.   261

Philo's Doctrine of the Logos and other intermediate Beings   262
  232   *Quis Rerum divinarum Heres?* 205f.   263
  233   *De Abrahamo* 119–22   264

Philo's own Religion and Ethics   265
  234   *Quis Rerum divinarum Heres?* 24–9   266
  235   *De Migratione Abrahami* 34f.   266
  236   *De Cherubin* 48f.   267
  237   *De Specialibus Legibus* i. 319f.   268

11 Josephus   269

Biographical Material   270
  238   Josephus, *Life* 7–12   270
  239   Josephus, *Life* 28f.   271
  240   Josephus, *War* iii. 392–408   272
  241   Josephus, *Life* 422–30   274

Josephus on John the Baptist, Jesus Christ, and James   275
  242   Josephus, *Antiquities* xviii. 116–19   276
  243   Josephus, *Antiquities* xviii. 63f.   277
  244   Josephus, *Antiquities* xx. 200   278

Josephus as Apologist   279
    245   Josephus, *Against Apion* i. 69–72   279
    246   Josephus, *Against Apion* ii. 79–85   280
    247   Josephus, *Against Apion* ii. 91–6   282
    248   Josephus, *Against Apion* ii. 164–71   283

Josephus as Interpreter of Scripture   284
    249   Josephus, *Antiquities* i. 27–39   284
    250   Josephus, *Antiquities* iii. 83–92   286
    251   Josephus, *Antiquities* viii. 111–121   287

12   Septuagint and Targum   290

The Traditional Origin of the Septuagint   292
    252   Philo, *De Vita Mosis* ii. 26–42   292
    253   *Epistle of Aristeas* 301–16   296

Selections from the Septuagint   298
    254   *Wisdom of Solomon* 7. 1—8. 1   299
    255   *Tobit* 4. 3–19   303
    256   *2 Maccabees* 7   306

Selections from Targums   309
    257   *Genesis* 1   309
    258   *Genesis* 22   311
    259   *Isaiah* 52. 13—53. 12   314

13   Apocalyptic   316

The Literary Forms of Apocalyptic   317
    260   *Daniel* 12   317
    261   *4 Ezra* 14. 1–17   318
    262   *1 Enoch* 1. 1f.   320
    263   *Psalms of Solomon* 2. 1–6, 24–35   320
    264   *4 Ezra* 11   322
    265   *4 Ezra* 13. 1–13   325
    266   *1 Enoch* 90. 28–42   326

The Essential Notions of Apocalyptic   328
    267   *4 Ezra* 7. 45–61   329
    268   *2 Baruch* 83. 4–9   330
    269   *Assumption of Moses* 10   331
    270   *Sibylline Oracles* iii. 767–808   333
    271   *2 Baruch* 25–30   335

272   *Psalms of Solomon* 17. 23–51   337
273   *Daniel* 7. 1–14   340
274   1 *Enoch* 48; 69. 26–9; 71. 14–17   341

Mysticism   344
275   1 *Enoch* 14   345
276   *Mishnah Hagigah* 2. 1   346
277   *Mishnah Megillah* 4. 10   346
278   *Tosephta Hagigah* 2. 3, 4   347
279   3 *Enoch* 11; 12   348
280   3 *Enoch* 16   349

Indexes

References   350
1   Old Testament   350
2   New Testament   351
3   Apocrypha and Pseudepigrapha   353
4   Josephus and Philo   354
5   Rabbinic Literature   355
6   Greek and Latin Authors   355
7   Patristic Writings   356

Names and Subjects   357

Acknowledgements

Thanks are due to the following for permission to reproduce copyright translations:

E. J. Brill: 101, 102, 103 (J. M. Robinson, *The Nag Hammadi Library*).

Cambridge University Press: 257, 258 (J. Bowker, *The Targums and Rabbinic Literature*).

T. and T. Clark and Charles Scribner's Sons: 13 (A. Roberts, *Sulpicius Severus*); 146, 147, 244 (A. C. McGiffert, *Eusebius: Ecclesiastical History*)—both in the series Nicene and Post-Nicene Christian Fathers.

Darton Longman and Todd Ltd and Doubleday and Co. Inc.: 279, 280 (J. H. Charlesworth, ed., *The Old Testament Pseudepigrapha*, I).

J. M. Dent and Sons Ltd and the Beacon Press: 64–72 (E. Bevan, *Later Greek Religion*).

The Egypt Exploration Society: 39 (B. P. Grenfell and A. S. Hunt, *Oxyrhynchus Papyri* I).

The Loeb Classical Library (William Heinemann Ltd and Harvard University Press): 3. (C. E. Bennett, *Horace*); 6, 7 (J. Jackson, *Tacitus: Annals*); 9, 12, 14, 16, 17 (J. C. Rolfe, *Suetonius*); 18 (W. Peterson, *Tacitus: Agricola*); 20 (H. Rackham, *Pliny*); 21–3, 26–9, 33–7, 41–8 (A. S. Hunt and C. C. Edgar, *Papyri*); 76–81 C. R. Haines, *Marcus Aurelius*); 86–9 (F. C. Conybeare, *Philostratus: The Life of Apollonius of Tyana, The Epistles of Apollonius, etc.*); 106–7 (F. C. Babbitt, *Plutarch*); 108 (E. H. Gifford, *Eusebius*); 110 (W. Adlington, rev. S. Gaselee, *Apuleius*); 136, 137, 149, 225–37, 252 (F. H. Colson and G. H. Whitater, *Philo*).

Macmillan and Co. Ltd: 49 (F. J. Foakes Jackson and K. Lake, *The Beginnings of Christianity*).

L. N. G. Montefiore: 169, 172, 173, 197 (C. G. Montefiore and H. Loewe, *A Rabbinic Anthology*).

John Murray (Publishers) Ltd: 15 (G. G. Ramsay, *The Histories of Tacitus*).

Oxford University Press (and the Clarendon Press): 1 (E. G. Hardy, *Monumentum Ancyranum*); 4 (J. Rhoades, *The Poems of Virgil*); 73, 74, 75, 85 (P. E. Matheson, *Epictetus: The Discourses and Manual*); 83 (Gilbert Murray, *Five Stages of Greek Religion*); 84 (C. Bailey, *Epicurus*); 104, 105 (W. Foerster and R. McL. Wilson, *Gnosis*); 116–23, 253–6, 261–72, 274 (R. H. Charles, ed., *The Apocrypha and Pseudepigrapha of the Old Testament*); 153–9, 162–6, 168, 170, 175–9, 181–6, 195, 199, 201–9, 276, 277 (H. Danby, *The Mishnah*); 259 (J. F. Stenning, *The Targum of Isaiah*); 275 (H. F. D. Sparks, *The Apocryphal Old Testament*).

Penguin Books Ltd: 210–24 (G. Vermes, *The Dead Sea Scrolls in English*).

The Singer's Prayer-Book Publication Committee: 187–93 (S. Singer, *The Authorised Daily Prayer Book*).

The Society of Biblical Literature and Scholars Press: 24, 25 (A. J. Malherbe, *The Cynic Epistles*).

The University of California: 31, 32, 38, 40 (B. P. Grenfell, A. S. Hunt and E. S. Goodspeed, *Tebtunis Papyri* II).

Other passages have been translated by the following:

10: F. de Zulueta (in *The Journal of Roman Studies*); 11: A. J. Church and W. J. Brodribb (*The Annals of Tacitus*); 30: A. Deissmann (*Light from the Ancient East*); 62, 63: B. Jowett (*The Dialogues of Plato*); 111: W. Whiston; 198: F. Gavin (*Jewish Antecedents of the Christian Sacraments*); 200: J. Jocz (*The Jewish People and Jesus Christ*); 2, 50–5, 58–61, 94–100, 109, 112, 113–15, 160, 167, 171, 174, 180, 242, 243: the Editor; 260, 273: the Revised Version of the Bible.

Introductions

To the First Edition

Some years ago I bought a copy of a small book by the late Paul Fiebig: *Die Umwelt des Neuen Testamentes: Religionsgeschichtliche und Geschichtliche Texte, in deutscher Übersetzung und mit Anmerkungen versehen, zum Verständnis des Neuen Testamentes* (Göttingen 1926). It occurred to me at once that a similar work would be of great use to English students of the New Testament. There are not a few books which describe the history and thought of the world in which the Church was born, but none (so far as I know) which offers the reader a selection of those original documents which alone can make this past world live. The undergraduate reading Theology at a university hears constantly of papyri and inscriptions, of philosophers and emperors, of Rabbis and apocalyptists, of writers such as Philo and Josephus, of soldiers such as Judas Maccabaeus and Titus, without perhaps knowing any of them at first hand. Even if he has read Classics before turning to Theology, his knowledge may not extend far beyond the borders of the Roman Empire, and the more respectable Greek and Latin philosophical and historical writers. He has probably not read the *Hermetica*, and he has certainly not read the Talmud. Most men will never read such works, and even the best men will read little of them while they are undergraduates: all therefore might well be grateful for an opportunity of consulting a selection of ancient literature, all of it relevant to the New Testament, but some of it not readily accessible.

My first thought was to translate, or at least imitate, Fiebig's book; but it soon appeared that his method—of taking New Testament topics and illustrating them—would not suit my purpose, for though I hoped to assist New Testament studies I did not wish to reduplicate but rather to make more intelligible the material already available in many excellent commentaries. The world of the first century (or thereabouts) is worth studying for its own sake, and when studied for its own sake it becomes even more valuable as the setting in which the Christian faith appeared. I therefore drew up a plan of my own, intended to cover as far as possible the period under review. That many gaps remain, and must inevitably remain, is very clear to me, but I hope that the book as a whole gives an accurate and fair (and not unreadable) account of the ancient world; at least, I have tried hard to understand sympathetically every author I have quoted.

The selection, arrangement, and annotation of the passages quoted have occupied a good deal of my leisure during the last few years. Now that at length the work has been completed, I hope it may prove useful not only to undergraduates reading Theology, who were in my mind at the beginning, but to many other classes of reader also, and especially to those who, in church or school, teach the New Testament.

My indebtedness to many translators is indicated in detail above; I have regularly checked their work, but it must not be assumed that I agree in every detail with all the versions I have quoted. As far as possible I have made consistent the capitalization, italicization, and spelling of transliterated words. I have also introduced consistency by indicating conjectural and explanatory supplements always by means of square brackets []; mere grammatical supplements, which are often necessary in translation from ancient languages, are not indicated.

Durham 1956   C. K. Barrett

To the Revised Edition

I am glad to think that there is some evidence that, in the thirty years since this book was first published, it has fulfilled some of the purposes I had in mind when I put it together, and mentioned in the Introduction to the First Edition. The need for a book of this kind is now greater than ever. A generation ago it could be assumed that many students of Theology had some acquaintance with classical literature; such an assumption would be very wide of the mark today. But the New Testament still speaks to us from its distant world, and the more clearly we see how strange it was to the world of the first century, yet spoke to that world with immediacy, power, and relevance, the more likely we are to see in our own world past its strangeness to its truth.

For a long time this collection has had a dated look. A little Qumran material crept into an Appendix; nothing was yet available of the Nag Hammadi texts. In the new edition these two sources find, I hope, not inadequate representation. I have taken the opportunity of making other additions, as well as a few omissions. For example, as I have continued to read Greek literature I have come to see the great tragedians as teachers about life, morals, destiny, and religion as profound as and more moving than the philosophers, and I have provided a small representation of their work. Again, it has seemed important to illustrate the ways in which Jews who were not Christians interpreted their Bible.

This Background book is now by no means the only one in the field. I have been glad to watch the appearance of others, and there has been none from which I have not learned. I hope, however, that this one may continue to be of service to a wide range of readers.

Durham 1986   C. K. Barrett

Abbreviations

BGU	Ägyptische Urkunden aus den königlichen Museen zu Berlin: Griechische Urkunden
CIG	*Corpus Inscriptionum Graecarum*
CIJ	*Corpus Inscriptionum Judaicarum*
CIL	*Corpus Inscriptionum Latinarum*
CIMRM	*Corpus Inscriptionum et Monumentorum Religionis Mithricae*
CIS	*Corpus Inscriptionum Semiticarum*
ETr.	English Translation
H&E	A. S. Hunt & C. C. Edgar, eds, *Select Papyri* (Loeb Library, 2 vols 1932, 1934)
HE	Eusebius, *Historia Ecclesiastica*
JTS	*Journal of Theological Studies*
NHC	Nag Hammadi Codex
OGIS	*Orientis Graecae Inscriptiones Selectae*
P. Amh.	The Amherst Papyri
P. Cairo Zen.	Zenon Papyri, ed. C. C. Edgar
P. Hamb.	Griechische Papyrusurkunden zu Hamburg
P. Lond.	Greek Papyri in the British Museum
P. Oxy.	Oxyrhynchus Papyri
P. Paris	Paris Papyrus
P. Ryl.	Catalogue of the Greek Papyri in the John Rylands Library, Manchester
P. Tebt.	The Tebtunis Papyri
Rev. Ég.	*Revue Égyptienne*
SIG	*Sylloge Inscriptionum Graecarum*

The Sources

It should be unnecessary to point out that these pages do not contain a complete account of the sources on which our knowledge of the ancient world is based. They are intended to convey a quantity of information that may be useful to those who are beginning the study of the subject and suggestions concerning what they may do next after they have made some use of this book. Perhaps the best general suggestion is that they should read more of the authors and texts quoted here and in particular that they should read some works through from beginning to end. I have kept in mind throughout the needs of the reader who knows no language but English.

The Roman Empire (ch. 1)

The story of the Roman Empire has long been familiar from well-known literary sources; in more recent times these have been supplemented by the use of evidence drawn from inscriptions, papyri, and coins.

The literary evidence is of different kinds, and of unequal value. Augustus's *Res Gestae*, though hardly an inspiring document, should not be missed; it is one of the few first-hand sources, drawn up by a leading actor in the story, and perhaps is none the worse for being as matter-of-fact as its author. The history of the whole period is told by Tacitus in the *Annals* and the *Histories*. It is not a perfect account, for it is tendentious, and parts of it have been lost; but even so it is a classical piece of historical writing, and on the whole Tacitus is faithful to his facts, though the interpretation he puts upon them is his own affair. Suetonius tells the same story in a different form and with less power in his books on the *Twelve Caesars*; there are other historians, such as Appian and Dio Cassius, whose works supplement those that have been mentioned but can for the present be deferred.

After reading Augustus himself and Tacitus, the student should look at the indirect literary evidence, the work of the literary men and philosophers of the period. Above all, Virgil claims attention, both in the *Aeneid*, which provides a religious and philosophical background for the achievements of Augustus and the greatness of Rome, and in the *Eclogues* and *Georgics*, which tell of the Italian's love for his native countryside. Other poets of the period take us for the most part into a different atmosphere; Horace, and still more Ovid, and satirists such as Martial and Juvenal, reflect the more sophisticated life of the city. Seneca may be read for practical Roman philosophy; interesting and often amusing glimpses of character and social custom under the Empire can be found in, for example, the works of Lucian, in *Trimalchio's Supper* (Petronius), and in the *Metamorphoses* (Apuleius).

For the use of papyri and inscriptions see below. The study of coins is a speciality which few can pursue at first hand; there is an excellent summary of the subject by H. Mattingly in the *Cambridge Ancient History* 12. 713–720. There is a striking example of its use in E. Stauffer's *Christ and the Caesars* (ETr. London 1955).

The Papyri (ch. 2)

The reader who wishes to see more of the daily life of the Empire revealed in the papyri cannot do better than use the volumes of A. S. Hunt and C. C. Edgar, referred to on p. 28. A smaller collection is that of G. Milligan, *Selections from the Greek Papyri* (Cambridge 1927). He may see how a special problem is illuminated by papyri in *Jews and Christians in Egypt* (by H. I. Bell, London and Oxford 1924); a more general account is given by N. Lewis, *Life in Egypt under Roman Rule* (Oxford 1983). When he has exhausted collections such as these he must turn to the full-scale publications of papyri, such as *The Oxyrhynchus Papyri*, of which the first volume appeared in 1898, the forty-eighth in 1981. Such a row of volumes may appear forbidding, but the contents are well tabulated and indexed, and it is easy to dip into them.

Inscriptions (ch. 3)

Inscriptions, unfortunately, are not so easily accessible; indeed, the reader who does not intend to use Latin and Greek can make very little headway with the subject. The most considerable collection of inscriptions provided with translations is perhaps that of the series *Monumenta Asiae Minoris Antiqua*. As its title implies, this series deals with only one part of the ancient world; but it serves as an excellent introduction. Further may be mentioned the very useful collections of W. Dittenberger (*Sylloge Inscriptionum Graecarum*, and *Orientis Graecae Inscriptiones Selectae*); and the four great *corpora—Corpus Inscriptionum Graecarum, Corpus Inscrip-*

tionum Judaicarum, Corpus Inscriptionum Latinarum, and *Corpus Inscriptionum Semiticarum.* In many, however, perhaps in most cases, these are not the most convenient sources for particular inscriptions.

The Philosophers and Poets (ch. 4)

The pre-Socratic philosophers are of doubtful importance for the student of early Christianity; the extant fragments of their works are translated in K. Freeman's *Ancilla to the Pre-Socratic Philosophers* (Blackwell, Oxford 1948).

The story of Socrates is presumably still common knowledge. The essential parts of it can be conveniently read in the Penguin volume, *The Last Days of Socrates.* For Plato himself it is, perhaps, best to begin with the *Republic*, which provides an introduction to both his philosophical and his political thought. In Aristotle's *Nicomachean Ethics* the reader will find valuable discussions of a number of ethical and religious terms which reappear—though by no means always with the same meanings—in the New Testament.

The surviving works of Epicurus are not many; they are translated by C. Bailey in his book *Epicurus* (Oxford 1926).

The earlier Stoics are difficult of access to the English reader. The fragments of their works are admirably collected in H. von Arnim, *Stoicorum Veterum Fragmenta* (four volumes, Leipzig 1903–24), but no one has yet done for this volume what Miss Freeman (see above) has done for H. Diels, *Fragmente der Vorsokratiker* (three volumes, Berlin 1951, 1952). There is, however, an excellent selection in E. Bevan's *Later Greek Religion* (London 1927), an admirable collection of documents. Epictetus and Marcus Aurelius are available in several translations, and are well worth serious study.

Those commonly called 'philosophers' were not the only Greek thinkers who pondered deeply the problems of human existence. The great tragic poets, Aeschylus, Sophocles, and Euripides, are among the most important representatives of the Greek power to observe and consider, and their work is a significant part of the New Testament background. Many of the plays are to be found in translation in the Penguin Classics.

Finally, the student may be recommended to read through Philostratus's *Life of Apollonius of Tyana*, which provides a striking picture not only of this itinerant philosopher but also of the life of the Graeco-Roman world; and is a very entertaining story too.

Gnosticism (ch. 5)

The best introduction to the difficult field of Gnosticism is provided by R. McL. Wilson's *Gnosis and the New Testament* (Blackwell, Oxford 1968), which may be followed by his *The Gnostic Problem* (Mowbray, London 1958). There is, however, nothing to equal reading the texts, and a beginner will find helpful *Gnosticism, an Anthology* (R. M. Grant, ed., Collins, London 1961). There is more material in the two volumes of *Gnosis* (W. Foerster, ed., ETr. R. McL. Wilson, ed., Oxford University Press, I 1972, II 1974).

Mystery Religions (ch. 6)

For the reasons given in this chapter, study of the Mystery Religions is very difficult, and there are few simple, straightforward texts that can be recommended for reading. The whole of Apuleius's *Metamorphoses* xi (part of which is quoted: **110**) may be read; and Euripides's *Bacchae*. Beyond these works, the reader may be referred to the exemplary treatment of one mystery religion by F. Cumont in *The Mysteries of Mithra* (ETr., London and Chicago 1910), or, better still, by the same author in *Textes et Monuments Figurés relatifs aux Mystères de Mithra* (two volumes, Brussels 1896, 1899). See also M. J. Vermaseren, *Corpus Inscriptionum Religionis Mithriacae* (The Hague 1956).

Jewish History (ch. 7)

The story of the Jews in the Maccabean period is told in 1 and 2 Maccabees. The history is taken further by Josephus; see the *War* and *Antiquities* xii–xx. These are the main, and indispensable, sources. Parallel narratives, Jewish and non-Jewish, exist here and there; most of them are referred to in the notes in the edition of Josephus in the Loeb Classical Library, and need not be specified here.

Rabbinic Literature and Rabbinic Judaism (ch. 8)

An admirable introduction to reading in the Rabbinic literature is provided in *A Rabbinic Anthology*, edited by C. G. Montefiore and H. Loewe (London 1938). It is of course true that, as the editors point out, their anthology *is* an anthology—that is, they were interested in collecting flowers, not weeds; and the weeds which undoubtedly exist in so wide a field are not found in the anthology. When this book of extracts has been used the reader should attempt a solid and continuous piece. There are two means to this end. One is the invaluable translation of the whole Mishnah by H. Danby (Oxford 1933). The other is the series of Rabbinical texts (mostly Mishnah tractates) published by the SPCK. Some of these contain text only, some text and translation, some translation only. The following Mishnah tractates are recommended for introductory study: Berakoth, Shabbath, Pesahim, Yoma, Sukkah, Megillah, Nedarim, Sanhedrin, Abodah Zarah, Aboth. Among the early midrashim, there is a very convenient edition of Mekilta (text and translation) by J. Z. Lauterbach (Philadelphia 1933–1935). Valuable English translations of later and longer Rabbinic texts have been published by the Soncino Press.

Qumran (ch. 9)

The best introduction to the Qumran texts is *The Dead Sea Scrolls*, by G. Vermes (Collins, London 1977), and the handiest text for the English reader is the same author's *The Dead Sea Scrolls in English* (Penguin Books, Harmondsworth 1962). It is unfortunate that there is no English equivalent to E. Lohse, *Die Texte aus Qumran* (Kösel-Verlag, Munich 1964), which gives the original texts of the most important non-biblical manuscripts with a German translation. Still useful are *The Dead Sea Scrolls* and *More Light on the Dead Sea Scrolls* by Millar Burrows (Secker & Warburg, London 1956 and 1958).

Philo (ch. 10)

For all but the philosopher, Philo is best approached by way of his historical writings, the book against Flaccus (*In Flaccum*), and the account of the Jewish mission from Alexandria to the Emperor Gaius (*Legatio ad Gaium*). These works show Philo as a loyal Jew, an aspect of his character which is of fundamental importance, though it is easy in his more philosophical writings to lose sight of it. From these straightforward narratives (which incidentally are historical documents of great importance) it is possible to work back to books like that *On Abraham*, where Philo retells the biblical story, and draws from it on the whole moral rather than metaphysical lessons. Finally (though Philo himself might have reckoned it first in importance) may be read the detailed allegorical exposition of the Pentateuch. Much of Philo's most characteristic speculative thought is to be found in *On the Creation of the World* and *Allegories of the Laws*, both of which deal with the first few verses of Genesis and accordingly allow Philo to develop his cosmology. There are separate editions of some of Philo's books, but of greatest use are the excellent twelve volumes of the Loeb edition.

Josephus (ch. 11)

Some of the works of Josephus were referred to above. There is much to be said for beginning the study of Josephus with the *Life* (in which he recapitulates a good deal of the story of the war with Rome) and the apologetic work *Against Apion*. The earlier books of the *Antiquities* may be left till last; for the most part Josephus rewrites in his own words the stories of the Old Testament, and rarely if ever improves them. Some of Josephus's work has appeared in the Penguin Classics, but the complete edition of the original with a translation and very useful notes in the Loeb series is of great value.

Septuagint and Targum (ch. 12)

The Septuagint may be studied from two points of view. In the first place, it is most instructive (not least for the student of the New Testament) to set side by side and compare the Hebrew and Greek texts of the Old Testament. Through the Greek, Hebraic thought and speech came into the New Testament, but at the same time the Hebraic contents of the Old Testament suffered a measure of transposition. This kind of study of course requires knowledge of Hebrew and Greek. In the second place, the Septuagint presents the reader with a number of books not contained in the Hebrew Bible. These may be read in the Apocrypha published with or as supplementary to the ordinary English Bible. The first edition of this book mentioned the translations and short commentaries contained in *The Apocrypha and Pseudepigrapha of the Old Testament*, edited by R. H. Charles (Oxford 1913; two volumes—the apocryphal books, with the exception of 4 Ezra (2 Esdras), are in the first). This edition is still useful though it has for many purposes been replaced by a new Oxford University Press volume, *The Apocryphal Old Testament* (H. F. D. Sparks, ed. 1984), which however does not contain the works generally known as the Apocrypha and has no rightful place under the heading of

Septuagint, and by two volumes edited by J. H. Charlesworth, *The Old Testament Pseudepigrapha* (Darton, Longman and Todd, London 1983 and 1985), which contains a few books belonging to the Septuagint. There are also very useful volumes in the SPCK series (see above).

Of the apocryphal books, 1 and 2 Maccabees were referred to above; the Wisdom of Solomon, and Ecclesiasticus, belong to the Wisdom literature; Tobit and Judith are religious and moral romances; 4 Ezra is an apocalypse.

The whole of the Epistle of Aristeas, with its long (and legendary) account of the making of the Septuagint, can be read in the second volume of Charles's *Apocrypha and Pseudepigrapha*.

On the Targums, the best introduction is J. Bowker, *The Targums and the Rabbinic Literature* (Cambridge University Press 1969), which translates and discusses a considerable number of passages.

Apocalyptic (ch. 13)

For the Apocalypses the works of Sparks and of Charlesworth are indispensable; Charles is still useful, and the appropriate volumes in the SPCK series are very valuable. The apocalyptic material contained in the Old Testament itself (notably Daniel) should not be neglected. Of material not contained in the Septuagint, the Similitudes of Enoch (i.e. 1 Enoch 37–71), 2 Baruch, and the Testaments of the Twelve Patriarchs (though here Christian influence—and even Christian authorship—may be suspected) may be recommended for study. Useful guides are D. S. Russell, *The Method and Message of Jewish Apocalyptic* (SCM Press, London 1964) and, with valuable new insights, C. Rowland, *The Open Heaven* (SPCK, London 1982).

1 The Roman Empire

Augustus and the Imperial Settlement

The roots of that Empire in which the Christian faith was born ran deep and in many directions, not only into the Roman Republic but also into the Macedonian Empire of Alexander, and the Greek city states. Eventually, the Empire was able to seek philosophical justification in the cosmopolitanism of developed Stoicism (see **73–81**); but at first it needed no justification beyond its own achievements. A world weary of civil war with its attendant social and economic disturbance and distress was prepared to welcome the victor of Actium as a saviour—after all, what more did the average man ask of his gods than the peace, security, and social welfare Augustus gave him? Of course, there were some malcontents. The senatorial families deplored changes which deprived them of the substance of power and placed it in the hands of one man, armed with an ultimate, if generally veiled, authority over life and property. But to the majority the Senate mattered little, and the provinces knew that they were far better governed than ever they had been under the Republic.

The character, motives, and intentions of Augustus; the political basis of the imperial constitution; the varying relations between the Emperors and the Senate—these all present historical problems of unusual depth and complexity. Here, at the risk of undue simplification, will be given only a few passages illustrating the work of Augustus and some of the succeeding Emperors.

I

Res Gestae Divi Augusti 12f., 24–7, 34f.

Towards the close of his life, Augustus deposited with the Vestal Virgins four documents. One was his will, disposing of his personal property. Of the remaining three, one contained directions for the celebration of his funeral, another an account of the things he had done (*rerum a se gestarum*; Suetonius, *Augustus* 101), and the third a military and financial account of the state of the Empire. The brass tablets on which, pursuant to Augustus's instructions, the *Res Gestae* were engraved have not been found; but the greater part of the document has been recovered from a bilingual (Greek-Latin) inscription in the temple of Rome and Augustus at Ancyra (the

Monumentum Ancyranum), now supplemented by a Greek text found at Apollonia (in Pisidia) and a Latin found at Pisidian Antioch. There can be little doubt that the *Res Gestae* were compiled partly for the purposes of propaganda; but the substantial accuracy of the facts contained in them seems to fail only through a few small lapses of memory.

At the same time, by decree of the Senate, a portion of the praetors and tribunes of the plebs, together with the consul, Q. Lucretius, and other men of note, were sent as far as Campania to meet my arrival, an honour which up to this day has been decreed to none other but
5 myself.

When in the consulship of Tiberius Nero and P. Quintilius I returned to Rome from Spain and Gaul after settling the affairs of those provinces with success, the Senate, to commemorate my return, ordered an altar to Pax Augusta to be consecrated in the Campus
10 Martius, at which it decreed that the magistrates, priests, and Vestal Virgins should celebrate an anniversary sacrifice.

Whereas our ancestors have willed that the gateway of Janus Quirinus should be shut, whenever victorious peace is secured by sea and by land throughout the empire of the Roman people, and
15 whereas before my birth twice only in all is it on record that the gateway has been shut, three times under my principate has the Senate decreed that it should be shut. . . .

After my victory I replaced in the temples of all the communities of the province of Asia the ornaments which my adversary in the
20 war had, after despoiling the temples, taken into his own possession.

Silver statues of myself, standing or on horseback or sitting in a chariot, were set up in the city to the number of about eighty, which I myself took down, and out of the money value I set up gifts of gold in the temple of Apollo in my own name and in the names of those
25 who had honoured me with the statues. I conquered the pirates and gave peace to the seas. In that war I handed over to their masters for punishment nearly 30,000 slaves who had run away from their owners, and taken up arms against the republic.

The whole of Italy of its own free will took the oath of fidelity to
30 me, and demanded me as its leader in the war of which Actium was the crowning victory. An oath was also taken to the same effect by the provinces of Gaul, Spain, Africa, Sicily, and Sardinia.

Among those who at that time served under my standards were more than seven hundred senators; out of that number, either before
35 that date or afterwards, up to the day on which these records were written, eighty-three attained the consulship, and about one hundred and seventy were elected to priesthoods.

I extended the frontiers of all the provinces of the Roman people, which had as neighbours races not obedient to our empire.

40 I restored peace to all the provinces of Gaul and Spain and to Germany, to all that region washed by the Ocean from Gades to the mouth of the Elbe.

Peace too I caused to be established in the Alps from the region nearest to the Hadriatic as far as the Tuscan sea, while no tribe was 45 wantonly attacked by war.

My fleet sailed along the Ocean from the mouth of the Rhine as far towards the east as the borders of the Cimbri, whither no Roman before that time had penetrated either by land or sea. The Cimbri and the Charydes and the Semnones and other German peoples of 50 the same region through their envoys petitioned for my friendship and that of the Roman people.

By my command and under my auspices two armies were led almost at the same time, one into Ethiopia, the other into that part of Arabia which is called Felix; and large forces of the enemy belonging 55 to both races were killed in battle, and many towns captured. In Ethiopia the army advanced as far as Napata, the nearest station to Meroe; in Arabia to the borders of the Sabaei to the town of Mariba.

Egypt I added to the empire of the Roman people.

Greater Armenia, on the murder of its king Artaxes, I could have 60 made into a province, but I preferred, following the precedent of our ancestors, and acting through Tiberius Nero, who was then my stepson, to hand it over as a kingdom to Tigranes, son of Artavasdes, and grandson of king Tigranes. Afterwards, when the same race revolted and rebelled, I subdued it by means of my son, Gaius, and 65 handed it over to the rule of king Ariobarzanes, the son of Artabazus, king of the Medes; and after his death, to his son, Artavasdes. On the latter being killed, I sent out to the kingdom Tigranes, a scion of the royal family of Armenia.

I regained possession of all the provinces on the farther side of the 70 Hadriatic towards the East and of all Cyrene, at a time when they were for the most part in the occupation of foreign kings, as I had already regained Sicily and Sardinia, when they were seized in the servile war. . . .

In my sixth and seventh consulships, after I had extinguished the 75 civil wars, having been put in supreme possession of the whole empire by the universal consent of all, I transferred the republic from my own power into the free control of the Senate and Roman people.

For the which service I received the appellation of Augustus by 80 decree of the Senate, and the door-posts of my house were publicly decked with laurel leaves; the civic crown was fixed up above my gate, and a golden shield set up in the Julian senate-house, which, as its inscription testifies, was granted to me by the Senate and Roman people to commemorate my virtue, clemency, justice, and piety.

85   After that time I stood before all others in dignity, but of actual
power I possessed no more than my colleagues in each several
magistracy.

While I was holding my thirteenth consulship, the Senate and
equestrian order and the whole Roman people gave me the title of
90   father of my country, and decreed that the title should be inscribed
in the vestibule of my house and in the senate-house and in the forum
of Augustus, under the chariot which was set up in my honour by
decree of the Senate.

At the time when I wrote these records, I was in my seventy-sixth
95   year.

l. 1   *At the same time.* On his return from Syria, October, 19 BC.

l. 6   *In the consulship of Tiberius Nero and P. Quintilius,* 13 BC. Tiberius Nero was
subsequently the emperor Tiberius, the successor of Augustus. The Altar of
the 'Augustan Peace' stood on the Flaminian Road. Fragments of it have been
preserved, and there are representations of it on the imperial coinage. Its
erection, like the closing of the temple of Janus (below), emphasizes the
blessing of peace and security bestowed on the world by Augustus.

l. 12   *The gateway of Janus Quirinus.* See the preceding note. According to Livy (i.
19) the gateway had been closed under king Numa and after the first Punic
War (235 BC). Under Augustus it was closed in 29 BC (after the battle of
Actium, in which Octavian (= Augustus) defeated Mark Antony and
brought the civil war to an end), in 25 BC (after the war with the Cantabri),
and again at a date that cannot be determined.

l. 18   *After my victory,* at Actium. 'My adversary' (*l.* 19) is of course Antony, in
contrast with whom Augustus shows his piety.

l. 25   *I conquered the pirates.* A reference to Octavian's victory over Sextus Pompeius
in 36 BC.

ll. 38, 40   *I extended the frontiers ... I restored peace.* Augustus's military and
administrative work in the provinces was far too extensive to be sketched
here; but it is important to note that greatly improved conditions in the
provinces were by no means the least achievement of the Augustan
settlement. The provinces were divided into two classes; some remained (as
under the Republic) under the direct control of the Senate, others (chiefly
those where the danger of armed invasion or revolt was greatest) being
reserved to the supervision of Augustus himself.

l. 58   *Egypt I added to the empire of the Roman people.* Egypt is not described as a
province. It was too rich and valuable a territory to entrust to a governor
who might become wealthy, strong, and rebellious, and was therefore kept
under the direct authority of the Emperor.

l. 74   *In my sixth and seventh consulships,* 28 and 27 BC.

l. 76   *I transferred the republic (rem publicam) ...* This sentence is of crucial
importance for the understanding of the position and authority of Augustus.
The Triumvirate (Octavian, Antony, and Lepidus) had taken absolute power
by law; when this association broke up, Octavian assumed (tacitly, it appears,
and without legal enactment; cf. however *ll.* 30ff.) universal authority, by

means of which he settled once for all (by operations of which some have been briefly indicated above) the military problems of the dying republic. When this had been done he (*a*) expunged illegal acts of the Triumvirate, and (*b*) handed back to the Senate and people the trust he had enjoyed. How much sincerity, and how much craft, there were in this act cannot here be discussed. It was clear to all that if Octavian had become again no more than a private citizen all the conditions that had led to civil war would automatically have returned. Accordingly means were found within the republican constitution for Octavian to retain the substance of power without dictatorial or monarchical titles. The appearance of a senatorial republic was retained together with the practical advantages of a principate.

l. 79 *I received the appellation of Augustus.* This honorific title expressed the 'unofficial' but sacred and dignified position of Octavian. *Rex*, and even *Romulus* (which Octavian would probably have liked), were titles too repugnant to Roman feeling. Octavian was *princeps senatus*.

l. 81 *Laurel leaves*, the sign of victory.
   The civic crown of oak leaves was an award for saving the lives of citizens.

l. 85 *Before all others in dignity.* Read, probably, *authority (auctoritate)*. *Auctoritas* is moral authority, almost '(power of) leadership'. The *auctoritas* of Augustus, backed by his tribunician and proconsular rights, in fact gave him all the *potestas*, or actual power, he needed.

l. 90 *Father of my country* was another title which, like Augustus, expressed the authority of Octavian, and also the real esteem and affection in which he was held by most Romans.

l. 94 *In my seventy-sixth year.* Augustus was seventy-five on 23 September AD 13. He died on 19 August AD 14.

2

Suetonius, *Augustus* 31

After the death of Lepidus he assumed the office of high priest, which he had never presumed to do while Lepidus was alive. He brought in from all quarters and burnt the books of prophecy, both Latin and Greek (in number more than two thousand), whose authors were
5 unknown or little known, retaining only the Sibylline books, and of these he made a selection. He placed them in two gilt bookcases under the base of the statue of Apollo Palatinus. He brought back to its original regularity the year which, set in order by the deified Julius, had subsequently through neglect fallen into disorder and
10 confusion. In this reordering he called by his own name the month Sextilis, choosing this rather than September, in which he was born, because in it he had won his first consulate and most notable victories. He increased the number, dignity, and emoluments of the priests, and especially of the Vestal Virgins. When it was necessary to choose
15 a new Vestal in place of one who had died, and many solicited not to be required to submit their daughters for election, he swore that if any of his granddaughters had been of the proper age he would have

offered her for the purpose. He restored several of the old ceremonies
which had gradually fallen into disuse, such as the augury of Salus,
20 the office of Flamen Dialis, the Lupercalian rite, the Secular and
Compitalitian Games. He forbad beardless boys to run in the
Lupercalia; and at the Secular Games he forbad young persons of
either sex to attend any of the shows at night unless accompanied by
some older relative. He ordered the Lares to be decorated twice a
25 year at the Compitalitia with spring flowers, and autumn flowers.
Next to the immortal gods he paid highest honour to the memory
of those generals who had extended the empire of the Roman people
from least to greatest. Accordingly he restored their public works,
retaining the original inscriptions, and erected statues of them all, in
30 triumphal dress, in both porches of his forum. He declared by
proclamation that his design was that the citizens should require of
him while he lived, and of princes in succeeding ages, that they
should copy their example. He also removed from the senate-house
where G. Caesar had been killed, and placed under a marble arch
35 over against the hall of his theatre, the statue of Pompey.

l. 1   *The office of high priest*, which Lepidus could vacate only by death. Augustus
was glad to take the opportunity of becoming religious head of the state and
proceeded to restore the Roman system of religion, partly as a return to what
was old and good, partly to provide a cement for the newly established
principate. Augustus is here represented as reformer of both religion and
morals.

l. 20   *The Secular . . . Games.* See below, **3**.

3

Horace, *Carmen Saeculare*

O Phoebus, and Diana, queen of forests, radiant glory of the heavens,
O ye ever cherished and ever to be cherished, grant the blessings that
we pray for at the holy season when the verses of the Sibyl have
commanded chosen maidens and spotless youths to sing the hymn in
5 honour of the gods who love the Seven Hills.
   O quickening Sun, that in thy shining car usherest in the day and
hidest it, and art reborn another and yet the same, ne'er mayst thou
be able to view aught greater than the city of Rome!
   O Ilithyia, that, according to thy office, art gracious to bring issues
10 in due season, protect our matrons, whether thou preferrest to be
invoked as 'Lucina' or as 'Genitalis'. Rear up our youth, O goddess,
and bless the Fathers' edicts concerning wedlock and the marriage-
law, destined, we pray, to be prolific in new offspring, that the sure
cycle of ten times eleven years may bring round again music and
15 games thronged on three bright days and as many gladsome nights!

And ye, O Fates, truthful in your oracles, as has once been ordained, and may the unyielding order of events confirm it, link happy destinies to those already past.

Bountiful in crops and cattle, may Mother Earth deck Ceres with
20 a crown of corn; and may Jove's wholesome rains and breezes give increase to the harvest!

Do thou, Apollo, gracious and benign, put aside thy weapon and give ear to thy suppliant sons! And do thou, O Luna, the constellations' crescent queen, to the maidens lend thine ear!
25 If Rome be your handiwork, and if from Ilium hailed the bands that gained the Tuscan shore (the remnant bidden to change their homes and city in auspicious course), they for whom righteous Aeneas, survivor of his country, unscathed 'mid blazing Troy, prepared a way for liberty, destined to bestow more than had been
30 left behind, then do ye, O gods, make teachable our youth and grant them virtuous ways; to the aged give tranquil peace; and to the race of Romulus, riches and offspring and every glory!

And what the glorious scion of Anchises and of Venus, with sacrifice of milk-white steers, entreats of you, that may he obtain,
35 triumphant o'er the warring foe, but generous to the fallen! Already the Parthian fears the hosts mighty on land and sea, and fears the Alban axes. Already the Indians and Scythians, but recently disdainful, are asking for our answer. Already Faith and Peace and Honour and ancient Modesty and neglected Virtue have courage to come back,
40 and blessed Plenty with her full horn is seen.

May Phoebus, the prophet, who goes adorned with the shining bow, who is dear to the Muses nine, and with his healing art relieves the body's wearied frame—may he, if he looks with favour on the altars of the Palatine, prolong the Roman power and Latium's
45 prosperity to cycles ever new and ages ever better! And may Diana, who holds Aventine and Algidus, heed the entreaty of the Fifteen Men and incline her gracious ears to the children's prayers! That such is the purpose of Jove and all the gods, we bear home the good and steadfast hope, we the chorus trained to hymn the praises of
50 Phoebus and Diana.

l. 3   *The verses of the Sibyl.* The Sibylline Books, carefully purged and preserved by Augustus (above, **2**), were the official prophetic literature of the Roman people. From them was derived the authority for holding the Secular Games (above, **2**), a celebration which took place only once in 110 years (or, according to other authorities, 100 years). The dates fell out conveniently for Augustus, who was able to celebrate his own achievements and the lasting vitality of Rome in a great festival in 17 BC. For this occasion the poet Horace was commissioned to write his *Carmen Saeculare*, which was sung by a choir of youths and maidens. It forms a poetic commentary on the work of Augustus, and represents many of his aims, and the general feeling of admiration for and gratitude to him.

l. 12   *The Fathers' edicts.* Childless marriages, and divorce, were at this period too common for the health of society. Augustus introduced into the Senate laws intended to deal with this situation.

l. 25   *From Ilium.* Horace shares with Virgil the legendary connection between Rome and Troy (Ilium) which is the foundation of the latter's *Aeneid.* See *l.* 33, below.

l. 33   *The glorious scion (sanguis) of Anchises and of Venus;* in the first instance Aeneas, the son of Anchises and Venus; but clearly Augustus is in mind.

l. 46   *The Fifteen Men,* the sacred body entrusted with the organization of the Games. Augustus (*Res Gestae* 22.2) tells us that he acted on their behalf.

4
Virgil, *Eclogue* IV

Muses of Sicily, essay we now
A somewhat loftier task! Not all men love
Coppice or lowly tamarisk: sing we woods,
Woods worthy of a Consul let them be.
5   Now the last age by Cumae's Sibyl sung
Has come and gone, and the majestic roll
Of circling centuries begins anew:
Justice returns, returns old Saturn's reign,
With a new breed of men sent down from heaven.
10 Only do thou, at the boy's birth in whom
The iron shall cease, the golden age arise,
Befriend him, chaste Lucina; 'tis thine own
Apollo reigns. And in thy consulate,
This glorious age, O Pollio, shall begin,
15 And the months enter on their mighty march.
Under thy guidance, whatso tracks remain
Of our old wickedness, once done away,
Shall free the earth from never-ceasing fear.
He shall receive the life of gods, and see
20 Heroes with gods commingling, and himself
Be seen of them, and with his father's worth
Reign o'er a world at peace. For thee, O boy,
First shall the earth, untilled, pour freely forth
Her childish gifts, the gadding ivy-spray
25 With foxglove and Egyptian bean-flower mixed,
And laughing-eyed acanthus. Of themselves,
Untended, will the she-goats then bring home
Their udders swollen with milk, while flocks afield
Shall of the monstrous lion have no fear . . .
30 . . . Nathless
Yet shall there lurk within of ancient wrong

Some traces, bidding tempt the deep with ships,
Gird towns with walls, with furrows cleave the earth.
Therewith a second Tiphys shall there be,
35 Her hero-freight a second Argo bear;
New wars too shall arise, and once again
Some great Achilles to some Troy be sent.
Then, when the mellowing years have made thee man,
No more shall mariner sail, nor pine-tree bark
40 Ply traffic on the sea, but every land
Shall all things bear alike: the glebe no more
Shall feel the harrow's grip, nor vine the hook;
The sturdy ploughman shall loose yoke from steer,
Nor wool with varying colours learn to lie;
45 But in the meadows shall the ram himself
Now with soft flush of purple, now with tint
Of yellow saffron, teach his fleece to shine.
While clothed in natural scarlet graze the lambs.
'Such still, such ages weave ye, as ye run,'
50 Sang to their spindles the consenting Fates
By Destiny's unalterable decree.
Assume thy greatness, for the time draws nigh,
Dear child of gods, great progeny of Jove!
See how it totters—the world's orbed might,
55 Earth, and wide ocean, and the vault profound,
All, see, enraptured of the coming time!
Ah! might such length of days to me be given,
And breath suffice me to rehearse thy deeds,
Nor Thracian Orpheus should out-sing me then,
60 Nor Linus, though his mother this, and that
His sire should aid—Orpheus Calliope,
And Linus fair Apollo. Nay, though Pan,
With Arcady for judge, my claim contest,
With Arcady for judge great Pan himself
65 Should own him foiled, and from the field retire.
    Begin to greet thy mother with a smile,
O baby-boy! ten months of weariness
For thee she bore: Oh baby-boy, begin!
For him, on whom his parents have not smiled,
70 Gods deem not worthy of their board or bed.

l. 10 *The boy's birth.* The identification of this 'boy', and in general the interpretation of this 'messianic eclogue', are endlessly debated. Probably the best view is that Virgil was celebrating the Peace of Brundisium in 40 BC, when the marriage of Antony and Octavia seemed to mean the end of civil war; and the son who might be hoped for from this marriage would see the hoped-for good time. If this is correct, Virgil's prophecy came too soon. The child was a girl, Antony forsook Octavia for Cleopatra, and war broke out afresh.

Tiberius

Tiberius succeeded his stepfather (and adoptive father) Augustus in AD 14. He was able, resolute, just, and (having regard to the fortunes of the Empire as a whole) successful; but he remained unpopular, and never stirred the public response that Augustus had won. A legend grew up about him which concealed his virtues and magnified his faults; the legend perverted the truth, but its very existence goes far to prove that all was not well. Yet for twenty-three years Tiberius maintained government (especially in the provinces) with undoubted efficiency.

5
Suetonius, *Tiberius* 36

> Foreign religions, the Egyptian and Jewish religious rites, he suppressed, and compelled those who were engaged in that superstition to burn their religious vestments with all their apparatus. The Jewish youth he dispersed, under pretence of military service,
> 5 into provinces of unhealthy climate; the rest of that race, and those who adopted similar opinions, he expelled from the city, on pain of perpetual slavery if they did not obey. He also banished the astrologers; but when they petitioned him, and promised that they would forsake their art, he pardoned them.

6
Tacitus, *Annals* ii. 85

> Another debate dealt with the proscription of the Egyptian and Jewish rites, and a senatorial edict directed that four thousand descendants of enfranchised slaves, tainted with that superstition and suitable in point of age, were to be shipped to Sardinia and there
> 5 employed in suppressing brigandage: 'if they succumbed to the pestilential climate, it was a cheap loss.' The rest had orders to leave Italy, unless they had renounced their impious ceremonial by a given date.

7
Tacitus, *Annals* vi. 51

> The son of Nero, on both sides he traced his origin to the Claudian house, though his mother, by successive acts of adoption, had passed

into the Livian and, later, the Julian families. From earliest infancy he experienced the hazards of fortune. At first the exiled attendant of
5 a proscribed father, he entered the house of Augustus in the quality of stepson; only to struggle against numerous rivals during the heyday of Marcellus and Agrippa and, later, of Gaius and Lucius Caesar; while even his brother Drusus was happier in the love of his countrymen. But his position was the most precarious after his
10 preferment to the hand of Julia, when he had to tolerate, or to elude, the infidelities of his wife. Then came the return from Rhodes; and he was master of the heirless imperial house for twelve years, and later arbiter of the Roman world for virtually twenty-three. His character, again, has its separate epochs. There was a noble season in
15 his life and fame while he lived a private citizen or a great official under Augustus: an inscrutable and disingenuous period of hypocritical virtues while Germanicus and Drusus remained: with his mother alive, he was still an amalgam of good and evil; so long as he loved, or feared, Sejanus, he was loathed for his cruelty, but his lust was
20 veiled; finally, when the restraints of shame and fear were gone, and nothing remained but to follow his own bent, he plunged impartially into crime and into ignominy.

l. 1   *Nero*. Not to be confused with the Emperor Nero.

l. 2   *His mother*. Livia, the wife of Augustus (her second husband, not the father of Tiberius).

l. 21   *He plunged impartially into crime and into ignominy*. Tacitus is the chief exponent of the legend of Tiberius. He represents the point of view of the senatorial class, whom Tiberius ruthlessly repressed.

Gaius (Caligula)

Emperor from AD 37 to 41. Again, it is not easy to penetrate to Gaius's true character through the cloud of hatred with which he came to be surrounded. He seems to have suffered from megalomania, if from no other form of madness. The following incident illustrates the character of Gaius and his thoughtless policy, and at the same time the self-sacrificing public spirit of a Roman provincial governor of the best kind, whose first thought was for the good of those entrusted to his care.

8

Josephus, *War* ii, 184–7, 192–203

The insolence with which the emperor Gaius defied fortune surpassed all bounds: he wished to be considered a god and to be hailed as such, he cut off the flower of the nobility of his country, and his impiety extended even to Judaea. In fact, he sent Petronius with an army to

5 Jerusalem to instal in the sanctuary statues of himself; in the event of the Jews refusing to admit them, his orders were to put the recalcitrants to death and to reduce the whole nation to slavery. But these orders, as the sequel showed, were under God's care. Petronius accordingly with three legions and a large contingent of Syrian
10 auxiliaries, left Antioch on the march for Judaea. Among the Jews, some put no belief in the rumours of war, others believed, but saw no means of defence: alarm, however, soon became universal, the army having already reached Ptolemais. . . .

The Jews assembled with their wives and children in the plain of
15 Ptolemais and implored Petronius to have regard first for the laws of their fathers, and next for themselves. Yielding so far to this vast multitude and their entreaties, he left the statues and his troops at Ptolemais and advanced into Galilee, where he summoned the people, with all persons of distinction, to Tiberias. There he dwelt upon the
20 power of the Romans and the emperor's menaces, and, moreover, pointed out the recklessness of their request; all the subject nations, he urged, had erected in each of their cities statues of Caesar, along with those of their other gods, and that they alone should oppose this practice amounted almost to rebellion, aggravated by insult.

25 When the Jews appealed to their law and the custom of their ancestors, and pleaded that they were forbidden to place an image of God, much more of a man, not only in their sanctuary but even in any unconsecrated spot throughout the country, Petronius replied, 'But I too must obey the law of my master; if I transgress it and spare
30 you, I shall be put to death, with justice. War will be made on you by him who sent me, not by me; for I too, like you, am under orders.' At this the multitude cried out that they were ready to endure everything for the law. Petronius, having checked their clamour, said, 'Will you then go to war with Caesar?' The Jews replied that
35 they offered sacrifice twice daily for Caesar and the Roman people, but that if he wished to set up these statues, he must first sacrifice the entire Jewish nation; and that they presented themselves, their wives and their children, ready for the slaughter. These words filled Petronius with astonishment and pity at the spectacle of the
40 incomparable devotion of this people to their religion and their unflinching resignation to death. So for the time he dismissed them, nothing being decided.

During the ensuing days he held crowded private conferences with the aristocracy, and public meetings with the people; at these
45 he had recourse alternately to entreaty, to advice, most often, however, to threats, holding over their heads the might of the Romans, the fury of Gaius, and the necessity which circumstances imposed upon himself. As, however, none of these efforts would induce them to yield, and as he saw that the country was in danger

50 of remaining unsown—for it was seed-time and the people had spent
fifty days idly waiting upon him—he finally called them together
and said: 'It is better that I should take the risk. Either, God aiding
me, I shall prevail with Caesar and have the satisfaction of saving
myself as well as you, or, if his indignation is roused, I am ready on
55 behalf of the lives of so many to surrender my own.' With that he
dismissed the multitude, who rained blessings on his head, and
collecting his troops left Ptolemais and returned to Antioch. From
that city he hastened to report to Caesar his expedition into Judaea
and the entreaties of the nation, adding that, unless he wished to
60 destroy the country as well as its inhabitants, he ought to respect
their law and revoke the order. To this dispatch Gaius replied in no
measured terms, threatening to put Petronius to death for his tardiness
in executing his orders. However, it so happened that the bearers of
this message were weather-bound for three months at sea, while
65 others, who brought the news of the death of Gaius, had a fortunate
passage. So Petronius received this last information twenty-seven
days earlier than the letter conveying his own death-warrant.

l. 4 *Petronius,* governor of the province of Syria.

l. 45 *Alternately.* I correct a small misprint in the translation used.

Claudius

Like Tiberius, Claudius (AD 41–54) has probably suffered from
misrepresentation. Probably he was often wiser than his critics, and by no
means the half-wit they depict. He instituted not a few constitutional and
administrative reforms. For his treatment of the difficult situation at
Alexandria see **48**. He touches the New Testament at several points, one
of which is treated in the first passage quoted. Whether or not the second
(on the violation of tombs) is directly relevant to the New Testament is
disputed. It is clear that those who did not accept the Christian faith in the
resurrection of Jesus might well accuse his disciples of breaking the seal on
his grave and stealing his body (cf. Matt. 27. 62–6; 28. 11–15). The name
Nazareth is also suggestive. But it must be remembered that Jesus was not
buried at Nazareth, that Nazareth did not, so far as we know, become a
major centre of the Church, that the disciples were not prosecuted for
violation, and that the date of the inscription is not certain—it may go
back to the time of Augustus.

9

Suetonius, *Claudius* 25

... He forbade men of foreign birth to use the Roman names so far
as those of the clans were concerned. Those who usurped the

privileges of Roman citizenship he executed in the Esquiline field.
He restored to the Senate the provinces of Achaea and Macedonia,
5 which Tiberius had taken into his own charge. He deprived the
Lycians of their independence because of deadly intestine feuds, and
restored theirs to the Rhodians, since they had given up their former
faults. He allowed the people of Ilium perpetual exemption from
tribute, on the ground that they were the founders of the Roman
10 race, reading an ancient letter of the Senate and people of Rome
written in Greek to king Seleucus, in which they promised him their
friendship and alliance only on condition that he should keep their
kinsfolk of Ilium free from every burden. Since the Jews constantly
made disturbances at the instigation of Chrestus, he expelled them
15 from Rome. He allowed the envoys of the Germans to sit in the
orchestra, led by their naïve self-confidence; for when they had been
taken to the seats occupied by the common people and saw the
Parthian and Armenian envoys sitting with the Senate, they moved
of their own accord to the same part of the theatre, protesting that
20 their merits and rank were no whit inferior. He utterly abolished the
cruel and inhuman religion of the Druids among the Gauls, which
under Augustus had merely been prohibited to Roman citizens; on
the other hand he even attempted to transfer the Eleusinian rites
from Attica to Rome, and had the temple of Venus Erycina in Sicily,
25 which had fallen to ruin through age, restored at the expense of the
treasury of the Roman people. He struck his treaties with foreign
princes in the Forum, sacrificing a pig and reciting the ancient
formula of the fetial priests. But these and other acts, and indeed
almost the whole conduct of his reign, were dictated not so much by
30 his own judgement as that of his wives and freedmen, since he nearly
always acted in accordance with their interests and desires.

l. 4   *He restored to the Senate . . .* See above **1** *ll.* 76-7 and notes for the arrangement
by which Augustus assumed responsibility for the government and defence
of certain provinces, leaving others to the Senate.

l. 14   *At the instigation of Chrestus.* This is a not uncommon name, but it is possible
that the disturbances were caused by Jewish-Christian controversy (*impulsore
Christo*). Cf. Acts 18.2. The context in which this expulsion is described by
Suetonius is illuminating.

l. 30   *His wives and freedmen.* Whether Claudius in fact lived in leading-strings is
doubtful. Some of the regulations mentioned in this passage were not inspired
by freedmen.

10

Claudius, *An Ordinance*

See *Journal of Roman Studies* xxii. (1932), 184–97 (F. de Zulueta); also
Documents illustrating the reigns of Claudius and Nero (compiled by M. P.

Charlesworth, 1939), 15. An inscription discovered in the neighbourhood of Nazareth. For further discussion see A. Momigliano, *Claudius the Emperor and his Achievement*, 1934, pp. 35–7, and more recently H. H. Scullard, *From the Gracchi to Nero*, 1979, p. 467.

> Ordinance of Caesar. It is my pleasure that graves and tombs remain undisturbed in perpetuity for those who have made them for the cult of their ancestors or children or members of their house. If however any man lay information that another has either demolished them,
> 5 or has in any other way extracted the buried, or has maliciously transferred them to other places in order to wrong them, or has displaced the sealing or other stones, against such a one I order that a trial be instituted, as in respect of the gods, so in regard to the cult of mortals. For it shall be much more obligatory to honour the buried.
> 10 Let it be absolutely forbidden for any one to disturb them. In case of contravention I desire that the offender be sentenced to capital punishment on charge of violation of sepulture.

l. 2   *For those*, reading τούτοις for τούτους.

l. 11   *Capital punishment*. This was unusually harsh. It has been explained as due to desire to put down the incipient Christian movement (for the belief that the disciples of Jesus had stolen his body from the tomb see Matt. 28. 13) or as a supplement made by the owner of the tomb, or possibly by a local Roman authority unfamiliar with the relevant laws.

Nero

After five years of good rule (the so-called *Quinquennium Neronis*), Nero (AD 54–68) lapsed into vicious ways and irresponsible government. His death led to a period of civil war in which Otho, Galba, Vitellius, and Vespasian (see below) successively seized power. The legal basis of Nero's persecution of Christians is obscure. The New Testament (Rev. 17. 12–17) as well as other sources attests the belief that Nero would after his death return to avenge himself upon his enemies.

11

Tacitus, *Annals* xv. 44

> But all human efforts, all the lavish gifts of the emperor, and the propitiations of the gods did not banish the sinister belief that the conflagration was the result of an order. Consequently, to get rid of the report, Nero fastened the guilt and inflicted the most exquisite
> 5 tortures on a class hated for their abominations, called Christians by the populace. Christus, from whom the name had its origin, suffered the extreme penalty during the reign of Tiberius at the hands of one

of our procurators, Pontius Pilatus, and a most mischievous superstition thus checked for the moment, again broke out not only
10 in Judaea, the first source of the evil, but even in Rome, where all things hideous and shameful from every part of the world find their centre and become popular. Accordingly, an arrest was first made of all who pleaded guilty; then, upon their information, an immense multitude was convicted, not so much of the crime of firing the city,
15 as of hatred against mankind. Mockery of every sort was added to their deaths. Covered with the skins of beasts, they were torn by dogs and perished, or were nailed to crosses, or were doomed to the flames and burnt, to serve as a nightly illumination when daylight had expired. Nero offered his gardens for the spectacle, and was exhibiting
20 a show in the circus, while he mingled with the people in the dress of a charioteer or stood aloft on a car. Hence, even for criminals who deserve extreme and exemplary punishment, there arose a feeling of compassion; for it was not, as it seemed, for the public good, but to glut one man's cruelty, that they were being destroyed.

l. 5   Hated for their abominations. According to Tacitus, Nero, to divert attention from himself, made scapegoats of an unpopular class. No legal machinery beyond the absolute power of the emperor was involved.

12

Suetonius, *Nero* 16

He devised a new form for the buildings of the city and in front of the houses and apartments he erected porches, from the flat roofs of which fires could be fought; and these he put up at his own cost. He had also planned to extend the walls as far as Ostia and to bring the
5 sea from there to Rome by a canal.

During his reign many abuses were severely punished and put down, and no fewer new laws were made: a limit was set to expenditures; the public banquets were confined to a distribution of food; the sale of any kind of cooked viands in the taverns was
10 forbidden, with the exception of pulse and vegetables, whereas before every sort of dainty was exposed for sale. Punishment was inflicted on the Christians, a class of men given to a new and mischievous superstition. He put an end to the diversions of the chariot drivers, who from immunity of long standing claimed the right of ranging
15 at large and amusing themselves by cheating and robbing the people. The pantomimic actors and their partisans were banished from the city.

l. 11   Punishment was inflicted on the Christians. This notice is included with a number of other police measures, apparently intended to secure the good order of the city. There is no reference to the great fire (though *l.* 3 probably indicates that it had at this time taken place).

13

Sulpicius Severus, *Chronicle* ii. 29

In the meantime, the number of the Christians being now very large, it happened that Rome was destroyed by fire, while Nero was stationed at Antium. But the opinion of all cast the odium of causing the fire upon the emperor, and he was believed in this way to have
5 sought for the glory of building a new city. And in fact Nero could not, by any means he tried, escape from the charge that the fire had been caused by his orders. He therefore turned the accusation against the Christians, and the most cruel tortures were accordingly inflicted upon the innocent. Nay, even new kinds of deaths were invented, so
10 that, being covered in the skins of wild beasts, they perished by being devoured by dogs, while many were crucified or slain by fire, and not a few were set apart for this purpose, that, when the day came to a close, they should be consumed to serve for light during the night. In this way, cruelty first began to be manifested against the Christians.
15 Afterwards, too, their religion was prohibited by laws which were enacted; and by edicts openly set forth it was proclaimed unlawful to be a Christian. At that time Paul and Peter were condemned to death, the former being beheaded with a sword, while Peter suffered crucifixion.

l. 15 *Afterwards.* Sulpicius indicates that Nero's was the first exhibition of cruelty to the Christians, and also that from this time the new religion was legally proscribed. For discussion of the historicity of this statement by Sulpicius see W. H. C. Frend, *Martyrdom and Persecution in the Early Church*, 1965, pp. 165–171.

14

Suetonius, *Nero* 57

He met his death in the thirty-second year of his age, on the anniversary of the murder of Octavia, and such was the public rejoicing that the people put on liberty-caps and ran about all over the city. Yet there were some who for a long time decorated his
5 tomb with spring and summer flowers, and now produced his statues on the rostra in the fringed toga, and now his edicts, as if he were still alive and would shortly return and deal destruction to his enemies. Nay more, Vologaesus, king of the Parthians, when he sent envoys to the Senate to renew his alliance, earnestly begged this too, that

10 honour be paid to the memory of Nero. In fact, twenty years later, when I was a young man, a person of obscure origin appeared, who gave out that he was Nero, and the name was still in such favour with the Parthians that they supported him vigorously and surrendered him with great reluctance.

l. 2 *Octavia*, Nero's wife, whom he had put to death.

Vespasian

The death of Nero and the ensuing disturbances took place while Vespasian was engaged in the subjugation of Judaea (see **141** and preceding note); in due course he came to the purple, leaving his son Titus to continue military operations against Jerusalem. He was a wise, strong, sober ruler (AD 69–79), and Titus who succeeded him reproduced his good qualities, but unfortunately reigned only two years before being succeeded by his brother Domitian, who may have murdered him.

15

Tacitus, *Histories* ii. 4f.

After inspecting the costly regal gifts and other objects which the Greek mind, with its love for antiquity, assigns to a dim and distant past, Titus inquired first about his own voyage. Assured of a prosperous course over a tranquil sea, he sacrificed a number of 5 victims, and then put some dark questions about himself. The priest, whose name was Sostratus, perceiving that the entrails were all alike favourable, and that the goddess looked approvingly upon some great enterprise, gave a brief and ordinary answer for the moment, and then, granting a private interview, disclosed the future. Titus 10 made his way back to his father in high spirits, bringing with him a great accession of confidence to the hesitating minds of the army and the provincials.

Vespasian had well nigh concluded the Judaean war. Nothing remained but the siege of Jerusalem, an undertaking formidable 15 rather from the mountainous character of the site, and the invincible superstition of the inhabitants, than because their forces were strong enough to endure the extremities of a siege. Vespasian himself, as above related, had three legions, inured to war, under his command; Mucianus had four. These last had seen no service; but they had been 20 saved from lethargy by an ambition to rival the glories of the neighbouring army, and they had gained as much in vigour from a period of unbroken rest, and by escaping the hardships of war, as the other army had acquired of hardihood by undergoing its toil and dangers. Each general had his auxiliaries of horse and foot, his fleets

25 and allied princes; each enjoyed an equal, though a different, reputation.

Vespasian was a keen soldier. He would march in front of his men, and choose the spots for encampment; he would work day and night over his plans, and himself take part in the fighting, if need were; 30 content with any food that came, scarce distinguishable in dress and bearing from any common soldier, had he only been free from avarice, he might have been ranked with the generals of olden days.

Mucianus, on the contrary, was a magnificent person. In wealth, and in everything else, he lived on a scale above that of private life: 35 more ready of speech than Vespasian, he had more skill and foresight in the conduct of civil affairs: the virtues of the two men without the faults of either would have formed an admirable temper for an emperor.

As governors of adjoining provinces—Syria and Judaea—they had 40 been at variance, and jealous of each other; but on the death of Nero they gave up their animosity and made common cause. In the first instance friends had intervened; but it was Titus who became the chief bond of concord between them, putting an end to unworthy rivalry in view of their common interests, being a man specially 45 fitted both by nature and by training to attract even such a person as Mucianus.

The tribunes, centurions, and common soldiers were brought over to the cause by their energy or their indolence, by the calls of virtue or of pleasure, according to their several natures.

l. 3 *Titus inquired first*, at the temple of Paphian Venus, on Cyprus. This was in AD 69.

l. 18 *As above related.* In *Histories* i. 10.

Domitian

With Domitian (AD 81–96) the rule of 'bad' emperors returned, and a second reign of terror, more serious than Tiberius's, began. The century closed hopefully, however, and the work of Domitian's successors, Nerva, Trajan, and Hadrian, saw the empire enter upon the happiest and most prosperous period in its history.

16

Suetonius, *Domitian* 13

When he became emperor, he did not hesitate to boast in the Senate that he had conferred their power on both his father and his brother, and that they had but returned him his own; nor on taking back his wife after their divorce, that he had 'recalled her to his divine couch'.

5 He delighted to hear the people in the amphitheatre shout on his feast
   day: 'Good Fortune attend our Lord and Mistress.' Even more, in the
   Capitoline competition, when all the people begged him with great
   unanimity to restore Palfurius Sura, who had been banished some
   time before from the Senate, and on that occasion received the prize
10 for oratory, he deigned no reply, but merely had a crier bid them be
   silent. With no less arrogance he began as follows in issuing a circular
   letter in the name of his procurators, 'Our Master and our God bids
   that this be done.' And so the custom arose of henceforth addressing
   him in no other way even in writing or in conversation. He suffered
15 no statues to be set up in his honour in the Capitol, except of gold
   and silver and of a fixed weight. He erected so many and such huge
   vaulted passage-ways and arches in the various regions of the city,
   adorned with chariots and triumphal emblems, that on one of them
   someone wrote in Greek: 'It is enough.' He held the consulship
20 seventeen times, more often than any of his predecessors. Of these the
   seven middle ones were in successive years, but all of them he filled
   in name only, continuing none beyond the first of May and few after
   the Ides of January. Having assumed the surname after his two
   triumphs, he renamed the months of September and October from
25 his own names, calling them 'Germanicus' and 'Domitianus', because
   in the former he had come to the throne and was born in the latter.

l. 12 *Our Master and our God.* Most of the earlier emperors had hesitated to claim
   divinity.

l. 19 *'It is enough'.* The Greek word ἀρκεῖ, which could also serve as a transliteration
   of *arci*, one form of the plural of *arcus*, an arch.

17

Suetonius, *Domitian* 12

   Reduced to financial straits by the cost of his buildings and shows, as
   well as by the additions he had made to the pay of the soldiers, he
   tried to lighten the military expenses by diminishing the number of
   his troops; but perceiving that in this way he exposed himself to the
5 attacks of the barbarians, and nevertheless had difficulty in easing his
   burdens, he had no hesitation in resorting to every sort of robbery.
   The property of the living and the dead was seized everywhere on
   any charge brought by any accuser. It was enough to allege any
   action or word derogatory to the majesty of the prince. Estates of
10 those in any way connected with him were confiscated, if but one
   man came forward to declare that he had heard from the deceased
   during his lifetime that Caesar was his heir. Besides other taxes, that
   on the Jews was levied with the utmost rigour, and those were
   prosecuted who without publicly acknowledging that faith yet lived
15 as Jews, as well as those who concealed their origin and did not pay

the tribute levied upon their people. I recall being present in my youth when the person of a man ninety years old was examined before the procurator and a very crowded court, to see whether he was circumcised. . . .

l. 13 *That on the Jews.* See **144**. After the fall of Jerusalem in AD 70 the tax formerly paid to the Temple was required by the Romans.

l. 14 *Without publicly acknowledging that faith.* See **148** and p. 174.

l. 15 *Who concealed their origin.* Christians, who were readily confounded with the Jews yet knew themselves to be distinct from them, may have been included here.

18

Tacitus, *Agricola* 2

It is recorded that when Rusticus Arulenus extolled Thrasea Paetus, when Herennius Senecio extolled Helvidius Priscus, their praise became a capital offence, so that persecution fell not merely on the authors themselves but on the very books: to the public hangman, in
5 fact, was given the task of burning in the courtyard of the forum the memorials of our noblest characters.

They imagined, no doubt, that in those flames disappeared the voice of the people, the liberty of the Senate, the conscience of mankind; especially as the votaries of philosophy also were expelled,
10 and all liberal culture exiled, in order that nowhere might anything of good report present itself to men's eyes.

19

Dio Cassius, *Epitome* 67.14.1-3

At this time the road leading from Sinuessa to Puteoli was paved with stone. And the same year Domitian slew, along with many others, Flavius Clemens the consul, although he was a cousin and had to wife Flavia Domitilla, who was also a relative of the emperor's.
5 The charge brought against them both was that of atheism, a charge on which many others who drifted into Jewish ways were condemned. Some of these were put to death, and the rest were at least deprived of their property. Domitilla was merely banished to Pandateria. But Glabrio, who had been Trajan's colleague in the
10 consulship, was put to death, having been accused of the same crimes as most of the others, and, in particular, of fighting as a gladiator with wild beasts. Indeed, his prowess in the arena was the chief cause of the emperor's anger against him, an anger prompted by jealousy. For in Glabrio's consulship Domitian had summoned him to his
15 Alban estate to attend the festival called the Juvenalia and had

imposed on him the task of killing a large lion; and Glabrio not only had escaped all injury but had despatched the lion with most accurate aim.

l. 2　*The same year.* AD 95.

l. 3　*Flavius Clemens.* Described by Suetonius (*Domitian* 15) as a man *contemptissimae inertiae*, of disgraceful idleness. This is sometimes taken to refer not to a natural characteristic but to a withdrawal from public life due to his adoption of Judaism (or perhaps Christianity). His 'atheism' means failure to carry out the practices of the state religion, which would lead to a charge of disloyalty.

l. 4　*Flavia Domitilla* was a niece of the emperor. Her name is connected with a catacomb on the Via Ardeatina at Rome, but this does not seem to be earlier than about AD 200.

l. 9　*Glabrio.* Acilius Glabrio, consul in AD 91; he had already been exiled (Suetonius, *Vespasian* 10). He was probably a Christian; he or at least his family is connected with the catacombs of Priscilla.

2   The Papyri

No single material substance has in recent years contributed to our knowledge of the world in which the New Testament was written, and indeed of the New Testament itself, more than papyrus. This writing material, the preparation and characteristics of which are described below, was in common use before, in, and after New Testament times. The oldest New Testament MSS. are papyri, and it is very probable that the autographs themselves of the New Testament books were written on papyrus. Even more important, however, than this, is the fact that during the last century or so thousands of papyrus documents—the vast majority of them fleeting notes never intended for perpetuity—have been recovered and edited. Not only do they throw a flood of light upon the social and religious customs of the country of their origin (almost all have been found in Egypt where alone the climatic conditions favour the preservation of papyrus); they also illustrate in a most striking way the language, and sometimes the thought, of the New Testament and the early Church.

The bearing of the papyri upon social and religious history will be briefly illustrated in the following pages. Here it must be emphasized that they are essentially non-literary. It is true that numbers of papyri have been found containing literary texts, and some have contributed fresh material to the known corpus of Greek literature; but the great bulk of papyrus material represents the writing of everyday life. We read countless private letters, bills, contracts, agreements, schoolboys' exercises, magical spells, charms, prayers, public announcements, petitions, and so on. We see the officials and common folk of Egypt (in many ways a unique, yet in others a not unrepresentative, district of the eastern part of the Roman Empire) going about their daily tasks with no suspicion that they are being observed, governing and being governed, buying and selling, teaching and learning, marrying and being given in marriage, begetting children and either exposing them or rearing and educating them. Here then is a quantity of source material such as the historian dreams of but (in ancient history) rarely sees. On the basis of it not the political history only but the daily life of a people can be reconstructed.

The grammatical and lexicographical importance of the papyri cannot be treated here. The student should consult first the Introduction to the *Vocabulary of the Greek Testament* by J. H. Moulton and G. Milligan, where are given excellent examples of the way in which linguistic problems in the New Testament have been solved by means of the new texts. There is much further material in G. A. Deissmann's *Bible Studies* and *Light from the Ancient East*, and in J. H. Moulton's *Grammar of New Testament Greek*. The contribution made by papyrology to the understanding of New Testament Greek must not be underestimated; but it seems right to add here that it is perhaps not quite so great as its most enthusiastic advocates have suggested. The language of the New Testament is not identical with that of the papyri. Simple words with a commercial or legal background, such as ἀρραβών (*earnest*) and βεβαιοῦν (*guarantee*), are admirably illuminated by the commercial and legal papyri, but the central words of the New Testament, such as ἀγάπη (*love*) and δικαιοσύνη (*righteousness*), cannot be adequately explained on this basis; the background must be extended to take into account not only the LXX (see Chapter 12) but also the unique creative impulse which produced the New Testament and laid its stamp upon the language in which the New Testament was written. In the third volume of Moulton's *Grammar*, written by N. Turner, the balance has perhaps swung the other way, and the ordinariness of New Testament Greek, its resemblance to the common Greek of the papyri, is to some extent undervalued.

Preparation and Use of Papyrus

The following account needs little explanation. It is given at some length not only because knowledge of the materials and make-up of papyrus is useful in palaeography but also because it affords interesting information about manufacturing processes and economic conditions in antiquity.

20

Pliny, *Natural History* xiii. 68–83

>   We have not yet touched on the marsh-plants nor the shrubs that
>   grow by rivers. But before we leave Egypt we shall also describe the
>   nature of papyrus, since our civilization or at all events our records
>   depend very largely on the employment of paper. According to
> 5 Marcus Varro we owe even the discovery of paper to the victory of
>   Alexander the Great, when he founded Alexandria in Egypt, before
>   which time paper was not used. First of all people used to write on
>   palm-leaves and then on the bark of certain trees, and afterwards
>   folding sheets of lead began to be employed for official muniments,
> 10 and then also sheets of linen or tablets of wax for private documents;
>   for we find in Homer [*Iliad* vi. 168] that the use of writing tablets
>   existed even before the Trojan period, but when he was writing even
>   the land itself which is now thought of as Egypt did not exist as such,

while now paper grows in the Sebennytic and Saitic nomes of Egypt,
15 the land having been subsequently heaped up by the Nile, inasmuch
as Homer wrote that the island of Pharos, which is now joined to
Alexandria by a bridge, was twenty-four hours' distance by sailing-
ship from the land. Subsequently, also according to Varro, when
owing to the rivalry between King Ptolemy and King Eumenes
20 about their libraries Ptolemy suppressed the export of paper,
parchment was invented at Pergamum; and afterwards the employment of the material on which the immortality of human beings
depends spread indiscriminately.

Papyrus then grows in the swamps of Egypt or else in the sluggish
25 waters of the Nile where they have overflowed and lie stagnant in
pools not more than about three feet in depth; it has a sloping root as
thick as a man's arm, and tapers gracefully up with triangular sides to
a length of not more than about fifteen feet, ending in a head like a
thyrsus; it has no seed, and is of no use except that the flowers are
30 made into wreaths for statues of the gods. The roots are employed by
the natives for timber, and not only to serve as firewood but also for
making various utensils and vessels; indeed the papyrus itself is
plaited to make boats, and the inner bark is woven into sail-cloth and
matting, and also cloth, as well as blankets and ropes. It is also used as
35 chewing-gum, both in the raw state and when boiled, though only
the juice is swallowed.

Papyrus also grows in Syria on the borders of the lake round
which grows the scented reed already mentioned [xii. 104], and
King Antiochus would only allow ropes made from this Syrian
40 papyrus to be used in his navy, the employment of esparto not yet
having become general. It has recently been realized that papyrus
growing in the Euphrates near Babylon can also be used in the same
way for paper; nevertheless up to the present the Parthians prefer to
embroider letters upon cloths.

45 The process of making paper from papyrus is to split it with a
needle into very thin strips made as broad as possible, the best quality
being in the centre of the plant, and so on in the order of its splitting
up. The first quality used to be called 'hieratic paper' and was in early
times devoted solely to books connected with religion, but in a spirit
50 of flattery it was given the name of Augustus, just as the second best
was called 'Livia paper' after his consort, and thus the name 'hieratic'
came down to the third class. The next quality had been given the
name of 'amphitheatre paper', from the place of its manufacture. This
paper was taken over by the clever workshop of Fannius at Rome,
55 and its texture was made finer by a careful process of insertion, so
that it was changed from common paper into one of first-class
quality, and received the name of the maker; but the paper of this
kind that did not have this additional treatment remained in its own

class as amphitheatre paper. Next to this is the Saitic paper named
60 from the town where it is produced in the greatest abundance, being
made from shavings of inferior quality, and the Taeneotic, from a
neighbouring place, made from material still nearer the outside skin,
in the case of which we reach a variety that is sold by mere weight
and not for its quality. As for what is called 'emporitic' paper, it is no
65 good for writing but serves to provide covers for documents and
wrappers for merchandise, and consequently takes its name from the
Greek word for a merchant. After this comes the actual papyrus, and
its outermost layer, which resembles a rush and is of no use even for
making ropes except those used in water.

70   Paper of all kinds is 'woven' on a board moistened with water
from the Nile, muddy liquid supplying the effect of glue. First an
upright layer is smeared on to the table, using the full length of
papyrus available after the trimmings have been cut off at both ends,
and afterwards cross strips complete the lattice-work. The next step
75 is to press it in presses, and the sheets are dried in the sun and then
joined together, the next strip used always diminishing in quality
down to the worst of all. There are never more than twenty sheets
to a roll.

There is a great difference in the breadth of the various kinds of
80 paper: the best is thirteen inches wide, the hieratic two inches less,
the Fannian measures ten inches and the amphitheatre paper one less,
while the Saitic is still fewer inches across and is not as wide as the
mallet used in making it, as the emporitic kind is so narrow that it
does not exceed six inches. Other points looked at in paper are
85 fineness, stoutness, whiteness and smoothness. The status of best
quality was altered by the Emperor Claudius. The reason was that
the thin paper of the period of Augustus was not strong enough to
stand the friction of the pen, and moreover as it let the writing show
through there was a fear of a smudge being caused by what was
90 written on the back, and the great transparency of the paper had an
unattractive look in other respects. Consequently the foundation was
made of leaves of second quality and the woof or cross layer of leaves
of the first quality. Claudius also increased the width of the sheet,
making it a foot across. There were also eighteen-inch sheets called
95 '*macrocola*', but examination detected a defect in them, as tearing off a
single strip damaged several pages. On this account Claudius paper
has come to be preferred to all other kinds, although the Augustus
kind still holds the field for correspondence; but Livia paper, having
no quality of a first-class kind, but being entirely second class, has
100 retained its position.

Roughness is smoothed out with a piece of ivory or a shell, but
this makes the lettering apt to fade, as owing to the polish so given
the paper does not take the ink so well, but has a shinier surface. The

damping process if carelessly applied often causes difficulty in writing
105 at first, and it can be detected by a blow with the mallet, or even by
the musty smell if the process has been rather carelessly carried out.
Spottiness also may be detected by the eye, but a bad porous strip
inserted in the middle of the pasted joins, owing to the sponginess of
the papyrus, sucks up the ink and so can scarcely be detected except
110 when the ink of a letter runs: so much opportunity is there for
cheating. The consquence is that another task is added to the process
of paper-weaving.

The common kind of paste for paper is made of fine flour of the
best quality mixed with boiling water, with a very small sprinkle of
115 vinegar; for carpenter's paste and gum make too brittle a compound.
But a more careful process is to strain the crumb of leavened bread
in boiling water; this method requires the smallest amount of paste
at the seams, and produces a paper softer than even linen. But all the
paste used ought to be exactly a day old—not more nor yet less.
120 Afterwards the paper is beaten thin with a mallet and run over with
a layer of paste, and then again has its creases removed by pressure
and is flattened out with the mallet. This process may enable records
to last a long time; at the house of the poet and most distinguished
citizen Pomponius Secundus I have seen documents in the hands of
125 Tiberius and Gaius Gracchus; while as for autographs of Cicero, of
his late Majesty Augustus, and of Virgil, we see them constantly.

l. 5 *Marcus Varro.* Varro of Reate (so called to distinguish him from Varro of
Atax); 116–27 BC.

l. 14 *Nomes*, the ancient provinces into which Egypt was divided; they were
retained in Ptolemaic and Roman administration.

l. 19 *King Eumenes*, presumably Eumenes II (197–158 BC) is meant. The tale finds
some support in the name περγαμηνή, *pergamena* (parchment).

l. 29 *Thyrsus:* 'A staff twined round with ivy and vine-shoots, borne by Bacchus
and the Bacchantes' (Lewis and Short, *s.v.*). *It has no seed.* This is not strictly
correct.

l. 71 *The effect of glue, vim glutinis.* The translation is perhaps not correct. *Glutinis*
is probably not the genitive of *gluten* but the dative plural of *glutinum*, the
form of the word used by Pliny (e.g. *l.* 115, below). Some kind of glue was
used with the muddy Nile water.

l. 80 *Thirteen inches.* 'Inch' here (and throughout this passage) renders the Latin
digitus, which is approximately threequarters of an English inch.

l. 95 *Macrocola.* '"Long-limbed", in long strips; Cicero, *ad Atticum* XVI. 3. 1 and
XIII. 25. 3, and some MSS. here also give *macrocollum*, "long-glued", made of
strips pasted together' (H. Rackham, Loeb Classical Library, ad loc.).

l. 122 *This process may enable records to last a long time.* The best papyrus remains
however much less durable than parchment. It follows that very early MSS.
of the New Testament will always be few; and those that are found will
almost all be of Egyptian origin. From the manufacturing process described

by Pliny it will readily be understood that papyrus was usually (because most conveniently) formed into rolls, not codices. The fact that New Testament papyrus codices did exist is therefore significant; no more than one Gospel could be written on a roll and the Christians evidently felt it necessary to keep their sacred books together since they formed a collection (or canon). This seems a probable conclusion, but a different view is taken by Dr C. H. Roberts (*JTS* l. (1949), 155–68); also idem, *Manuscript, Society and Belief in Early Christian Egypt*, Schweich Lectures 1977, London 1979.

Form and Style of Letter-writing in the Papyri

Of the twenty-seven books of the New Testament twenty-one are (or appear to be) letters. In addition, Revelation contains the seven letters to the seven churches, and Acts the letter sent by the Council of Jerusalem to the churches of Asia Minor (15.23–9) and that sent by the tribune Claudius Lysias to the procurator Felix (23.26–30). It has already been noted that many of the papyri are letters, and it is not surprising that there are frequent similarities between the New Testament letters and letters roughly contemporary with them. A few illustrations of this resemblance will suffice. References are inserted where possible to the admirable collection of papyri edited by A. S. Hunt and C. C. Edgar (Loeb Classical Library, two volumes, 1932 and 1934), as H&E.

21

P. Lond. 42 (H&E 97). *A letter from wife to husband.* 168 BC

Isias to her brother Hephaestion greeting. If you are well and other things are going right, it would accord with the prayer which I make continually to the gods. I myself and the child and all the household are in good health and think of you always. When I received your
5 letter from Horus, in which you announce that you are in detention in the Serapeum at Memphis, for the news that you are well I straightway thanked the gods, but about your not coming home, when all the others who had been secluded there have come, I am ill-pleased, because after having piloted myself and your child through
10 such bad times and been driven to every extremity owing to the price of corn I thought that now at least, with you at home, I should enjoy some respite, whereas you have not even thought of coming home nor given any regard to our circumstances, remembering how I was in want of everything while you were still here, not to mention
15 this long lapse of time and these critical days, during which you have sent us nothing. As, moreover, Horus who delivered the letter has brought news of your having been released from detention, I am thoroughly ill-pleased. Notwithstanding, as your mother also is annoyed, for her sake as well as for mine please return to the city, if

20 nothing more pressing holds you back. You will do me a favour by taking care of your bodily health. Goodbye. Year 2, Epeiph 30. [Addressed] To Hephaestion.

l. 1   *Brother.* It is clear from the letter that Hephaestion and Isias are man and wife. 'Brother' (ἀδελφός) may be a term of endearment, or may be intended literally. Marriage between brother and sister was not unusual in Egypt. *Greeting.* In this papyrus the word 'Greeting' (χαίρειν) is supplied by the editor in a small hiatus. The restoration is however certain, because the word is so common in the opening sentences of letters. As here, the form is usually 'A to B, greeting'. In the New Testament χαίρειν (as an epistolary formula) is used only at Acts 15.23; 23.26; James 1.1; in the Pauline epistles the similar but characteristically Christian word χάρις (*grace*) is used (together with εἰρήνη, which recalls the common Semitic greeting, שלום, *peace*).

l. 2   *The prayer which I make continually.* The Pauline epistles also regularly begin with thanksgiving and prayer.

l. 5   *In detention in the Serapeum.* Serapis, presumably, had, through his priests, ordered Hephaestion to remain in the temple.

l. 16   (cf. *l.* 5) *Horus.* In Paul's epistles we sometimes hear of a messenger who carries the letter and is also able to give supplementary information; e.g. Col. 4.7ff. (All my affairs shall Tychicus make known unto you . . . whom I have sent unto you for this very purpose. . . . They shall make known unto you all things that are done here).

l. 21   *Goodbye*, ἔρρωσο. This word occurs in Acts 15. 29 (in the plural) and 23. 30 (according to some texts). Paul regularly uses Christian formulas.

l. 22   *To Hephaestion.* The letter is addressed, as usual, on the verso.

22

P. Oxy. 292 (H&E 106). *A letter of commendation.* About AD 25

Theon to the most honoured Tyrannus very many greetings. Heraclides, the bearer of this letter, is my brother, wherefore I entreat you with all my power to take him under your protection. I have also asked your brother Hermias by letter to inform you about him.
5 You will do me the greatest favour if you let him win your approval. Before all else I pray that you may have health and the best of success, unharmed by the evil eye. Goodbye. [Addressed] To Tyrannus the dioecetes.

l. 2   *I entreat you . . . to take him under your protection.* Letters of commendation are naturally not rare among the papyri. In the New Testament cf. Rom. 16.1 (συνίστημι δὲ ὑμῖν Φοίβην τὴν ἀδελφὴν ἡμῶν, I commend unto you Phoebe our sister) and 2 Cor. 3. 1 (Are we beginning again to commend (συνιστάνειν) ourselves? or need we, as do some, epistles of commendation (συστατικῶν ἐπιστολῶν) to you or from you?) The word in this document translated 'under your protection' is συνεσταμένον.

l. 8   Dioecetes: in Ptolemaic times a very important financial officer of the crown; later a subordinate official.

23

BGU 27 (H&E 113). *A letter from a brother.* Second or third century AD

> Irenaeus to Apollinarius his dearest brother many greetings. I pray continually for your health, and I myself am well. I wish you to know that I reached land on the sixth of the month Epeiph and we unloaded our cargo on the eighteenth of the same month. I went up
> 5 to Rome, on the twenty-fifth of the same month and the place welcomed us as the god willed, and we are daily expecting our discharge, it so being that up till to-day nobody in the corn fleet has been released. Many salutations to your wife and to Serenus and to all who love you, each by name. Goodbye. Mesore 9. [Addressed]
> 10 To Apollinarius from his brother Irenaeus.

l. 7   The corn fleet, from Egypt to Rome.

l. 9   Each by name, κατ' ὄνομα. Cf. 3 John 15.

It will be convenient at this point to turn aside from the non-literary papyri in order to illustrate another kind of letter. Attention has been drawn (see especially H. D. Betz, *A Commentary on Paul's Letter to the Churches in Galatia,* 1979) to the importance of the apologetic epistle, which provides parallels with the epistles of Paul. These letters are not easy to represent since 'most of the pertinent literature did not survive' (Betz, p. 15), and those who would use them are obliged to augment epistolary evidence with apologetic speeches. The *Seventh Epistle of Plato,* though relevant, is too long to quote; shorter letters may serve to indicate the spirit of the literature but cannot parallel the structure of a letter such as Galatians. The extracts here are from 'The Epistles of Diogenes' translated by B. Fiore sj, in the recent collection by A. J. Malherbe, *The Cynic Epistles* (1977).

24

The Epistles of Diogenes (in Malherbe, op. cit.) 7. *To Hicetas*

> Diogenes to Hicetas. Do not be upset, Father, that I am called a dog and put on a double, coarse cloak, carry a wallet over my shoulders, and have a staff in my hand. It is not worth while getting distressed over such matters, but you should rather be glad that your son is
> 5 satisfied with little, while being free from popular opinion, to which

all, Greeks and barbarians alike, are subservient. Now the name, besides not being in accord with my deeds, is a sign that is notable as it is. For I am called heaven's dog, not earth's, since I liken myself to it, living as I do, not in conformity with popular opinion but
10 according to nature, free under Zeus, and crediting the good to him and not to my neighbour. (2) As for my clothing, even Homer writes that Odysseus, the wisest of the Greeks, so dressed while he was returning home from Ilium under Athena's direction. And the vesture is so fine that it is commonly acknowledged to be a discovery
15 not of men but of the gods.

First she gave him a cloak, tunic and mantle, seedy, dirty, stained by filthy smoke. She put around him a large, hairless hide of swift deer and gave him a staff and a poor leather pouch, riddled with holes, with a knapsack strap on it (Homer, *Odyssey* 13. 434–38)
20 Take heart, Father, at the name which they call me, and at my clothing, since the dog is under the protection of the gods and his clothing is god's invention.

l. 1   The letter is not an authentic work of Diogenes but comes probably from the second century BC. A. J. Malherbe, op. cit. 1977, pp. 98–9.
Dog. In Greek, κύων (*kyon*), whence the word *cynic* was derived. The philosopher's clothing and equipment recall Mark 6. 8, 9 and parallels.

25

The Epistles of Diogenes (in Malherbe, op. cit.) 45. *To Perdiccas*

Diogenes to Perdiccas, do well. Be ashamed at the threats you wrote me, since you haven't convinced me at all that I am worse than Eriphyle and that I have bartered myself venally for gold. You think this fit, and you probably won't put off assaulting me verbally. You
5 threaten to kill me—the threat of an insect! Nor are you aware that if you do this you in turn will suffer. For there is someone who cares about us, and he exacts equal satisfaction for such deeds from those who initiate unjust actions. From the living it's a single penalty, but from the dead ten-fold. I write this not out of fear of your threats,
10 but wishing that you do not do anything wrong on my account.

l. 10   The language is strikingly similar to that of 2 Cor. 13. 7.

Magical and Religious Papyri

Jewish and Christian papyri are not included here, nor are MSS. of literary texts. It is partly for this reason that the papyri quoted may give the impression that the religion of Egypt in the Hellenistic and Roman periods had little real religious feeling in it, but was on the one hand commercial and official, on the other magical. One would not expect the more personal and mystical aspects of religion to be treated in non-literary documents of the kind commonly preserved among the papyri.

26

P. Oxy. 1211 (H&E 403). *Articles for sacrifice.* Second century AD

This note lists the articles needed for a sacrifice at 'the festival which is still held about the summer solstice when the river begins to rise' (H&E ii. 525). Evidently the strategus was responsible for providing the sacrificial material, or at least for paying for it.

> To the strategus. Articles for the sacrifice to the most sacred Nile on Pauni 30: 1 calf, 2 jars of sweet-smelling wine, 16 wafers, 16 garlands, 16 pine-cones, 16 cakes, 16 green palm-branches, 16 reeds likewise, oil, honey, milk, every spice except frankincense.

l. 1   *Strategus* (στρατηγός): not, as usually in Greek, a military title, but that of the local civil administrative official.

27

P. Tebt. 294 (H&E 353). *Application for the office of prophet.* AD 146

The religion of Egypt was maintained by the state, and its servants held official paid positions for which application, accompanied by a fee, had to be made to the local authorities. It will be seen that the duties of the 'prophet' are very different from the activities of Old Testament and Christian prophets.

> Copy. To Tiberius Claudius Justus, administrator of the private account, from Pakebkis son of Marsisouchus, exempted priest of the famous temple of Soknebtunis also called Cronus and the most great associated gods, which is situated in the village of Tebtunis in the
> 5 division of Polemon in the Arsinoite nome. I wish to purchase the office of prophet in the aforesaid temple, which has been offered for sale for a long time, on the understanding that I shall . . . and carry the palm-branches and perform the other functions of the office of prophet and receive in accordance with the orders the fifth part of all
> 10 the revenue which falls to the temple, at the total price of 2,200 drachmae instead of the 640 drachmae offered long ago by Marsisouchus son of Pakebkis, which sum I will pay, if my appointment is ratified, into the local public bank at the customary dates; and I and my descendants and successors shall have the
> 15 permanent ownership and possession of this office for ever with all the same privileges and rights, on payment (by each one) of 200 drachmae for admission. If therefore it seem good to you, my lord,

you will ratify my appointment here in the city upon these terms
and write to the strategus of the nome about this matter, in order
20 that the due services of the gods who love you may be performed.
The fifth share of the proceeds of the revenues which falls to me, as
aforesaid, after deducting expenses is 50 artabae of wheat, 9⅝ artabae
of lentils, 60 drachmae of silver. Farewell. The 10th year of the
Emperor Caesar Titus Aelius Hadrianus Antoninus Augustus Pius,
25 Tubi 10.

l. 1   *The private account,* ἴδιος λόγος. The ancient kingdom of Egypt was regarded
as the private property of its kings, and its revenues were their own income.
This conception was continued by the Ptolemies and adopted by Augustus,
who in this as in many other ways treated Egypt differently from other
provinces.

l. 2   *Exempted,* that is, from the payment of certain taxes. This was one of the
advantages of holding an official religious position.

l. 6   *The office of prophet,* ἡ προφητεία.

l. 10   *The revenue which falls to the temple.* The temples possessed estates of 'sacred
land' which were administered for their financial benefit.

l. 18   *The city,* Alexandria.

28

P. Oxy. 1148 (H&E 193). *A question addressed to an oracle.* First
century AD

O Lord Sarapis Helios, beneficent one. [Say] whether it is fitting that
Phanias my son and his wife should not agree now with his father,
but oppose him and not make a contract. Tell me this truly. Goodbye.

l. 3   *Goodbye.* The form of the request suggests a letter to the god; see above, **21**
and notes.

29

P. Oxy. 1478 (H&E 198). *A charm for victory.* About AD 300

Charm for victory for Sarapammon son of Apollonius . . . [Here
follow ten or eleven magical symbols] . . . Give victory and safety in
the racecourse and the crowd to the aforesaid Sarapammon in the
name of Sulicusesus.

l. 4   *Sulicusesus:* a god, of whom nothing is known.

30

Paris Magical Papyrus (lines 3,007–3,085). *Charms and formulas.*
About AD 300

Published by C. Wessely, 'Griechische Zauberpapyri von Paris und
London', in *Denkschrift der kaiserlichen Akademie der Wissenschaften zu
Wien, Phil.-Hist. Klasse*, xxxvi. (1888). See also G. A. Deissmann, *Light
from the Ancient East*, 250–60. Outside the official cults maintained by the
state, religion in Egypt reflected the mixed population of the country, in
which native Egyptians, Greek settlers, merchants and administrators, and
Roman soldiers and officials were joined by various orientals, including
numerous Jews. Those in particular who practised magic were willing to
adopt from any source names and formulas which sounded impressive
and effective. Of the resulting amalgam the following passage is an
excellent example. Its Jewish affiliations are unmistakable; but it was
certainly not written by an orthodox Jew, and probably not by a Jew of
any kind. Yet there were Jewish exorcists (cf. e.g. Matt. 12. 27 = Luke 11.
19; Acts 19. 13), and it may be that some of them used methods akin to
those described in this papyrus. The reality of the demon world, constantly
assumed in the New Testament, is clearly presupposed.

> For those possessed by daemons, an approved charm by Pibechis.
> Take oil made from unripe olives, together with the plant
> mastigia and lotus pith, and boil it with marjoram
> (very colourless), saying: 'Joel, Ossarthiomi,
> 5 Emori, Theochipsoith, Sithemeoch, Sothe,
> Joe, Mimipsothiooph, Phersothi, Aeeioyo,
> Joe, Eochariphtha: come out of such an one (and the other usual
>   formulae).'
> But write this phylactery upon a little sheet of
> tin: 'Jaeo, Abraothioch, Phtha, Mesen-
> 10 tiniao, Pheoch, Jaeo, Charsoc', and hang it
> round the sufferer: it is of every demon a thing to be trembled at,
>   which
> he fears. Standing opposite, adjure him. The adjuration is
> this: 'I adjure thee by the god of the Hebrews
> Jesu, Jaba, Jae, Abraoth, Aia, Thoth, Ele,
> 15 Elo, Aeo, Eu, Jiibaech, Abarmas, Jaba-
> rau, Abelbel, Lona, Abra, Maroia, arm,
> thou that appearest in fire, thou that art in the midst of earth and
>   snow
> and vapour, Tannetis: let thy angel descend,
> the implacable one, and let him draw into captivity the
> 20 daemon as he flieth around this creature

which God formed in his holy paradise.
For I pray to the holy god, through the might of Ammon-
ipsentancho.' Sentence. 'I adjure thee with bold, rash words: Jacuth,
Ablanathanalba, Acramm.' Sentence. 'Aoth, Jatha-
25 bathra, Chachthabratha, Chamynchel, Abro-
oth. Thou art Abrasiloth, Allelu, Jelosai,
Jael: I adjure thee by him who appeared unto
Osrael in the pillar of light and in the cloud by
day, and who delivered his word from the taskwork
30 of Pharaoh and brought upon Pharaoh the
ten plagues because he heard not. I adjure
thee, every daemonic spirit, say whatsoever
thou art. For I adjure thee by the seal
which Solomon laid upon the tongue
35 of Jeremiah and he spake. And say thou
whatsoever thou art, in heaven, or of the air,
or on earth, or under the earth or below the ground,
or an Ebusaean, or a Chersaean, or a Pharisee. Say
whatsoever thou art, for I adjure thee by God the light-
40 bringer, invincible, who knoweth what is in the heart
of all life, who of the dust hath formed the race
of men, who hath brought out of uncertain [places]
and maketh thick the clouds and causeth it to rain upon the earth
and blesseth the fruits thereof; who is
45 blessed by every power in heaven of angels,
of archangels. I adjure thee by the great God Sabaoth,
through whom the river Jordan returned
backward,—the Red Sea also,
which Israel journeyed over and it stood impassable.
50 For I adjure thee by him who revealed the hundred
and forty tongues and divided them
by his command. I adjure thee by him who
with his lightnings the [race?] of stiff-necked giants consumed, to whom the heaven of heavens sings praises,
55 to whom Cherubin his wings sing praises.
I adjure thee by him who hath set mountains about the sea,
a wall of sand, and hath charged it not to pass
over, and the deep hearkened. And do thou
hearken, every daemonic spirit, for I adjure thee
60 by him that moveth the four winds since
the holy aeons, him the heaven-like, sea-
like, cloud-like, the light-bringer, invincible.
I adjure thee by him that is in Jerosolymum the pure, to whom the
unquenchable fire through every aeon is
65 offered, through his holy name Jaeo-

baphrenemum (Sentence), before whom trembleth the Genna of fire
and flames flame round about and iron
bursteth and every mountain feareth from its foundations.
I adjure thee, every daemonic spirit, by him that
70 looketh down on earth and maketh tremble the
foundations thereof and hath made all things
out of things which are not into Being.' But I adjure thee,
thou that usest this adjuration: the flesh of swine
eat not, and there shall be subject unto thee every spirit
75 and daemon, whatsoever he be. But when thou adjurest,
blow, sending the breath from above [to the feet] and
from the feet to the face, and he [the daemon] will
be drawn into captivity. Be pure and keep it. For the sentence
is Hebrew and kept by men
80 that are pure.

l. 1   *Those possessed by daemons,* δαιμονιαζομένους. Cf. the New Testament word
δαιμονίζεσθαι.
An approved charm, δόκιμον. For this word and its meaning cf. 1 Pet. 1. 7.
'Charm' is here, of course, supplied by the context.

l. 4   *Joel.* Some of the curious words in this and similar papyri have no
discoverable meaning, and are probably mere mumbo-jumbo which
doubtless sounded very impressive when uttered in the right way and in the
right circles. Others were borrowed from various sources, some in this
papyrus from the Old Testament.

l. 6   *Joe.* This may be a form of the Hebrew divine name יהוה (YHWH). Cf.
Jaeo, Jaba, Jae, below.
Aeeioyo; not a word, but the vowels of the Greek alphabet.

l. 7   *Come out of,* ἔξελθε ἀπό. The same command is used in the New Testament
(Luke 4. 35, cf. Mark 1. 25; 5. 8; 9. 25). It was probably a common formula
with exorcists.

l. 9   *Phtha,* the name of an Egyptian god.

l. 11   *A thing to be trembled at,* φρικτόν. Cf. James 2. 19.

l. 12   *Adjure,* ὁρκίζειν. Cf. e.g. Acts 19. 13. This too was probably a common word
with exorcists.

l. 14   *Jesu.* As Deissmann points out, neither a Jew nor a Christian would speak of
Jesus as the god of the Hebrews. But a non-Christian gentile (or perhaps even
a very unorthodox Jew) might well hear the name and, recognizing both its
effectiveness in exorcism and its connection with Judaism, think it appropriate
for his purpose. In the list of names which follows Jaba and Jae recall
YHWH; Thoth is the name of an Egyptian god, and Ele, Elo suggest the
Hebrew אל, אלהים ('el, 'elohim; God).

l. 17   *Thou that appearest in fire.* There may be an allusion to the appearance of God
to Moses in the burning bush (Exod. 3. 2); but fire is a common element in
theophanies.

l. 21 *Which God formed* (ἔπλασεν—cf. Gen. 2. 7) *in his holy paradise*; a reference to the biblical narrative of the creation of man, but not necessarily at first hand; cf. *Corpus Hermeticum* i. and the notes on **95–6**.

l. 22 *Through the might of* . . . This renders ἐπί . . . Cf. the New Testament formula ἐπὶ τῷ ὀνόματι.

l. 28 *Osrael* may be simply a slip for Israel. If it is a genuine mistake the writer of the papyrus certainly had no first-hand aquaintance with the Old Testament; but the correct form occurs in l. 49.
In the pillar of light and in the cloud by day. Another biblical allusion (Exod. 13. 21f.), but again an imperfect one. In the Old Testament we have 'pillar of fire' (πυρός), not 'pillar of light' (στῦλος φωτινός).

l. 29 *Word*—a slip; λόγον was written instead of λαόν, *people*.

ll. 32f. (and 38f.) *Say whatever thou art.* The New Testament also illustrates the importance attached to knowing the name of a demon; cf. Mark 5. 9.

l. 34 *Solomon* enjoyed great repute as an exorcist and his seal was well known; but the connection with Jeremiah does not seem to be attested elsewhere.

l. 38 *Pharisee.* This is evidently the name of a demon or class of demons; the writer was probably not familiar with the Jewish party bearing this name. Deissmann explains the proper names in this line as follows (p. 257). 'This remarkable trio of daemons obviously comes from the LXX, Gen. 15. 20; Exod. 3. 8, 17 etc., where we find Χετταῖοι (who have become Χερσαῖοι i.e. "land daemons"), Φερεζαῖοι (who have become the more intelligible "Pharisees"), and Ἰεβουσαῖοι.'

l. 39 (and 62) *Light-bringer*; possibly an allusion to Gen. 1. 3, and other Old Testament passages; there are many such allusions in the following lines.

l. 50 *The hundred and forty tongues.* Some Jews believed that on Sinai the Law was delivered in seventy languages, corresponding to the seventy nations of the earth. This does not account for the number 140; it is quite possible that the exorcist was simply trying to improve on the traditional and orthodox number by doubling it; or he may have conceived the notion of a heavenly corresponding to each earthly language; or he may have had a different tradition.

l. 55 *Cherubin his wings.* Deissmann apparently so translates in order to bring out the fact that Cherubin is in the papyrus wrongly taken as a singular (τοῦ χερουβίν). The same mistake is made in the LXX (2 Sam. 22. 11; 2 Chron. 3. 11), as well as in some later VSS. of the Old Testament.

l. 56 *Mountains,* ὄρη, is probably a corruption of 'bounds', ὅρια.

l. 63 *Jerosolymum, sic.*

l. 66 *Genna, sic.*

l. 68 *Bursteth.* Deissmann's translation is not certain, but probably correct.

l. 73 *The flesh of swine eat not.* This Jewish prohibition could easily be accommodated in Egyptian religion, and in the partly ascetical practice of gnostic magic. It is to be noted that the Jewish law in its entirety is not enjoined.

l. 79 *Hebrew.* Clearly not in language, but in origin. Foreign origin, like the use of unintelligible names, was probably thought to add to the efficacy of a charm.

31

P. Tebt. 276. *Astrology.* Late second or third century AD

A special feature of gnostic-magical religion was astrology, which fascinated the Hellenistic world, and held with a paralysing grip the Hellenistic mind. The following is a fragment from a 'technical' astrological work.

> ... If in addition Mercury is in conjunction, and Saturn is irregularly situated, ... from an unfavourable position; if at the same time Mars is in opposition to Saturn, the aforesaid position being maintained [he will destroy?] profits of transactions. Saturn in triangular relation
> 5 to Mars signifies [bad] fortune. Jupiter in triangular relation to Mars or in conjunction makes great kingdoms and empires. Venus in conjunction with Mars causes fornications and adulteries; if in addition Mercury is in conjunction with them, they in consequence make scandals and lusts. If Mercury is in conjunction with Jupiter or
> 10 appears in triangular relation, this causes favourable actions or commerce, or a man will gain his living by ... or by reason, and ... If Mars appear in triangular relation to Jupiter and Saturn, this causes great happiness, and he will make great acquisitions and ... If while Jupiter and Saturn are in this position Mars comes into conjunction
> 15 with either, ... after obtaining [wealth] and collecting a fortune he will spend and lose it. If Jupiter, Mercury, and Venus are in conjunction, they cause glories and empires and great prosperity; and if the conjunction takes place at the morning rising [of Venus], they cause prosperity from youth upwards.

Papyri illustrating Social and Economic Conditions

There is hardly one of the thousands of extant papyri which could not be quoted with some degree of relevance under this head. In the following pages an attempt is made to illustrate some of the conditions of private life—birth, employment, marriage, the family, death; to show how the papyri afford data for economic history—goods, prices, taxes, and the like; and to give some examples of legal documents. Finally one very important political document is quoted. For the most part these papyri (except when used by specialists for detailed study) require little comment, but the reader who will pursue them—and the many similar papyri— with attention and sympathetic imagination will be rewarded with an insight into the world of primitive Christianity which he could hardly obtain by any other means.

32

P. Tebt. 299. *Notice of birth.* About AD 50

This papyrus is mutilated in places, and the restorations are not certain; but all are probable.

> To Arius son of Lysimachus, comogrammateus of Tebtunis, from
> Psoiphis son of Harpocras son of Pakebkis, his mother being
> Thenmarsisuchus daughter of Psoithis and Kellauthis, inhabitants of
> the village, priest of the fifth tribe of the gods at the village, Cronos,
> 5 the most great god, and Isis and Sarapis, the great gods, and one of
> the fifty exempted persons. I register Pakebkis, the son born to me
> and Taasies daughter of . . . and Taopis in the 10th year of Tiberius
> Claudius Caesar Augustus Germanicus Imperator, and request that
> the name of my aforesaid son Pakebkis be entered on the list. . . .

l. 1   *Comogrammateus,* an official of the village (κώμη).

l. 6   *Exempted.* See above, **27**, and note.

l. 9   *Entered on the list.* It is probable that the boy was intended for the priesthood.

33

P. Oxy. 275 (H&E 13). *Agreement of apprenticeship.* AD 66

> Tryphon son of Dionysius son of Tryphon and of Thamounis
> daughter of Onnophris, and Ptolemaeus son of Pausirion son of
> Ptolemaeus and of Ophelous daughter of Theon, weaver, both being
> inhabitants of Oxyrhynchus, mutually acknowledge that Tryphon
> 5 has apprenticed to Ptolemaeus his son Thoonis, whose mother is
> Saraeus daughter of Apion, and who is not yet of age, for a period of
> one year from the present day, to serve and to follow all the
> instructions given to him by Ptolemaeus in the art of weaving as far
> as he himself knows it, the boy to be fed and clothed for the whole
> 10 period by his father Tryphon, who will also be responsible for all the
> taxes on him, on the condition that Ptolemaeus will pay to him
> monthly on account of food five drachmae and at the close of the
> whole period on account of clothing twelve drachmae, nor shall
> Tryphon have the right to remove the boy from Ptolemaeus until
> 15 the completion of the period, and for whatever days therein the boy
> plays truant, he shall send him to work for the like number at the
> end of it or else forfeit one drachma of silver for each day, and for
> removing him within the period he shall pay a penalty of 100
> drachmae and the like sum to the Treasury. If Ptolemaeus fails to
> 20 instruct the boy fully, he shall be liable to the same penalties. This
> contract of apprenticeship is valid. The 13th year of Nero Claudius
> Caesar Augustus Germanicus Imperator, the 21st of the month

Sebastus. [Signed—in a different hand] I, Ptolemaeus son of Pausirion son of Ptolemaeus and of Ophelous daughter of Theon, will do
25 everything in the one year. I, Zoilus son of Horus son of Zoilus and of Dieus daughter of Sokeus have written for him, as he is illiterate. The 13th year of Nero Claudius Caesar Augustus Germanicus Imperator, Sebastus 21.

34

BGU 1052 (H&E 3). *A contract of marriage.* 13 BC

To Protarchus from Thermion daughter of Apion, with her guardian Apollonius son of Chaereas, and from Apollonius son of Ptolemaeus. Thermion and Apollonius son of Ptolemaeus agree that they have come together to share a common life, and the said Apollonius son
5 of Ptolemaeus acknowledges that he has received from Thermion by hand from the house a dowry of a pair of gold earrings weighing three quarters and ... silver drachmae; and from now Apollonius son of Ptolemaeus shall furnish to Thermion as his wedded wife all necessaries and clothing in proportion to his means and shall not ill-
10 treat her nor cast her out nor bring in another wife, or he shall straightway forfeit the dowry increased by half, with right of execution upon both the person of Apollonius son of Ptolemaeus and all his property as if by legal decision, and Thermion shall fulfil her duties towards her husband and their common life and shall not
15 absent herself from the house for a night or a day without the consent of Apollonius son of Ptolemaeus nor dishonour nor injure their common home nor consort with another man, or she again if guilty of any of these actions shall, after trial, be deprived of the dowry, and in addition the transgressing party shall be liable to the prescribed
20 fine. The 17th year of Caesar, Pharmouthi 20.

l. 20 *Caesar.* The emperor Augustus is meant.

35

P. Oxy. 744 (H&E 105). *A letter from husband to wife.* 1 BC

Hilarion to his sister Alis very many greetings, likewise to my lady Berous and Apollonarion. Know that we are still in Alexandria. Do not be anxious; if they really go home, I will remain in Alexandria. I beg and entreat you, take care of the little one, and as soon as we
5 receive our pay I will send it up to you. If by chance you bear a child, if it is a boy, let it be, if it is a girl, cast it out. You have said to Aphrodisias 'Do not forget me.' How can I forget you? I beg you then not to be anxious. The 29th year of Caesar, Pauni 23. [Addressed, on the verso] Deliver to Alis from Hilarion.

l. 1 *Sister.* See **21**, note on *brother.*

l. 6 *Cast it out.* The exposure of children was apparently not uncommon; the author of the Epistle to Diognetus thinks it worth while to point out that though Christians marry and beget as do other men they do not cast out their children (5. 6).

l. 7 *Aphrodisias*, who brought the message to Hilarion, possibly with a letter.

l. 8 *Caesar.* See above, **34**.

36

Rev. Ég. 1919, p. 201 (H&E 133). *A letter from son to father.* Early third century AD

To my lord and father Arion from Thonis greeting. Before all else I make supplication for you every day, praying also before the ancestral gods of my present abode that I may find you and all our folk thriving. Look you, this is my fifth letter to you, and you have not
5 written to me except only once, not even a word about your welfare, nor come to see me; though you promised me saying 'I am coming,' you have not come to find out whether the teacher is looking after me or not. He himself is inquiring about you almost every day, saying, 'Is he not coming yet?' And I just say 'Yes.' Endeavour then
10 to come to me quickly in order that he may teach me as he is eager to do. If you had come up with me, I should have been taught long ago. And when you come, remember what I have often written to you about. Come to us quickly then before he goes up country. I send my salutations to all our folk, each by name, together with those
15 who love us. Salutations also to my teachers. Goodbye, my lord and father, and may you prosper, as I pray, for many years along with my brothers whom may the evil eye harm not. [Postscript] Remember our pigeons. [Addressed] To Arion my father from . . .

37

BGU 1103 (H&E 6). *Deed of divorce.* 13 BC

To Protarchus from Zois daughter of Heraclides, with her guardian her brother Irenaeus son of Heraclides, and from Antipater son of Zenon. Zois and Antipater agree that they have separated from each other, severing the union which they had formed on the basis of an
5 agreement made through the same tribunal in Hathur of the current 17th year of Caesar, and Zois acknowledges that she has received from Antipater by hand from his house the material which he received for dowry, clothes to the value of 120 drachmae and a pair of gold earrings. The agreement of marriage shall henceforth be null,
10 and neither Zois nor other person acting for her shall take proceedings

against Antipater for restitution of the dowry, nor shall either party take proceedings against the other about cohabitation or any other matter whatsoever up to the present day, and hereafter it shall be lawful both for Zois to marry another man and for Antipater to
15 marry another woman without either of them being answerable. In addition to this agreement being valid, the one who transgresses it shall moreover be liable both to damages and to the prescribed fine. The 17th year of Caesar, Pharmouthi 2.

38

P. Tebt. 381. *A will.* AD 123

The 8th year of the Emperor Caesar Trajanus Hadrianus Augustus, Choiak 22, at Tebtunis in the division of Polemon of the Arsinoite nome. Thaesis daughter of Orsenouphis son of Onnophris, her mother being Thenobastis, of the aforesaid village of Tebtunis, aged
5 about seventy-eight years, having a scar on the right forearm, acting with her guardian, her kinsman Cronion son of Ameis, aged about twenty-seven, having a scar between his eyebrows, acknowledges that she, the acknowledging party, Thaesis, has consented that after her death there shall belong to Thenpetesuchus, her daughter by her
10 late departed husband Pansais, and also to Sansneus son of Tephersos, the son of her other daughter Taorseus, now dead, to the two of them, property as follows: to Thenpetesuchus alone, the house, yard and all effects belonging to Thaesis in the said village of Tebtunis by right of purchase from Thenpetesuchus daughter of Petesuchus, and
15 the furniture, utensils, household stock and apparel left by Thaesis, and the sums due to her and other property of any kind whatsoever, while to Sansneus she has bequeathed eight drachmae of silver, which Sansneus shall receive from Thenpetesuchus after the death of Thaesis; on condition that the daughter Thenpetesuchus shall
20 properly perform the obsequies and laying out of her mother, and shall discharge such private debts as Thaesis shall prove to owe, but as long as her mother Thaesis lives she shall have power to . . .

l. 6   *Guardian.* As a woman, though an elderly one, Thaesis has a male guardian, though he is fifty years younger than she.

l. 17   *Eight drachmae of silver.* There is some evidence that this sum was a conventional amount bequeathed where only a courtesy legacy was intended.

l. 22   The will probably continued with the assertion that during her life Thaesis should have full right of disposal of her own property; this provision is fairly common in wills.

39

P. Oxy. 39. *Release on medical grounds from military service.* AD 52

Copy of a release dated and signed in the 12th year of Tiberius
Claudius Caesar Augustus Germanicus Imperator, Pharmouthi 29.
Release from service was granted by Gn. Vergilius Capito, praefect
of Upper and Lower Egypt, to Tryphon, son of Dionysius, weaver,
5 suffering from cataract and shortness of sight, of the metropolis of
Oxyrhynchus. Examination was made in Alexandria.

l. 4   *Of Upper and Lower Egypt:* literally, 'of both' (ἀμφοτέρων). It is clear that the
two districts are intended.

40

P. Tebt. 300. *Notice of death.* AD 151

To Melanas, comogrammateus of Tebtunis, from Paopis son of
Psoiphis son of Paopis, exempted priest of the famous temple at
Tebtunis. My father Psoiphis son of Paopis and Asis, of the said
village, exempted priest of the said temple, died in the month Tubi
5 of the present 14th year of Antoninus Caesar the lord. Wherefore I
present this notice, that this name may be struck off and may be
inscribed in the list of such persons, and I swear by the Fortune of
Antoninus Caesar the lord that the information above given is true.
I, Paopis son of Psoiphis, have presented the notice. The 14th year of
10 the Emperor Caesar Titus Aelius Hadrianus Antoninus Augustus
Pius, Mecheir 15.
[On the verso is written the title of the document (ὑπόμ(νημα)
τελευτ(ῆς) Ψῦφις Παῶπις), with the signature of Melanas.]

l. 5   *The lord,* τοῦ κυρίου.

l. 7   *The Fortune,* τὴν . . . τύχην.

l. 9   *I, Paopis . . . the notice.* This sentence is in different handwriting from the rest,
presumably that of Paopis himself. The rest was no doubt written by a
professional writer or official.

41

P. Cairo Zen. 59092 (H&E 182). *A list of clothes.* About 257 BC

Zenon's trunk in which are contained: 1 linen wrap, washed; 1 clay-
coloured cloak, for winter, washed, and 1 worn, 1 for summer, half-
worn, 1 natural-coloured, for winter, washed, and 1 worn, 1 vetch-
coloured, for summer, new; 1 white tunic for winter, with sleeves,
5 washed, 1 natural-coloured, for winter, with sleeves, worn, 1 natural-
coloured, for winter, worn, 2 white, for winter, washed, and 1 half-
worn, 3 for summer, white, new, 1 unbleached, 1 half-worn; 1 outer

garment, white, for winter, washed; 1 coarse mantle; 1 summer garment, white, washed, and 1 half-worn; 1 pair of Sardian pillow-
10 cases; 2 pairs of socks, clay-coloured, new, 2 pairs of white, new; 2 girdles, white, new. [On the verso] From Pisicles, a list of Zenon's clothes.

42

P. Tebt. 35 (H&E 223). *Official regulation of the price of myrrh (a government monopoly).* 111 BC

Apollonius to the epistatae in the division of Polemon and to the other officials greeting. For the myrrh distributed in the villages no one shall exact more than 40 drachmae of silver for a mina-weight or in copper 3 talents 2,000 drachmae with a charge of 200 drachmae
5 on the talent for carriage; which sum shall be paid not later than the 3rd of Pharmouthi to the collector sent for the purpose. Let the subjoined notice be posted up with the concurrence of the village secretary, who shall sign his name below the order along with you. Whoever contravenes these instructions will render himself liable to
10 accusation. We have therefore also sent the sword-bearers. Goodbye. Year 6, Pharmouthi 2.

l. 1   *Epistatae.* Village overseers.

l. 5   *For carriage*, because the quantities of copper involved would be so heavy.

l. 7   *Subjoined notice.* The notice is still subjoined. It is not printed here because it repeats the earlier notice addressed to the epistatae almost word for word.

l. 10   *Sword-bearers.* Apollonius's action in sending armed police suggests that he expected the proclamation to be unpopular.

43

P. Oxy. 1439 (H&E 381). *A toll receipt.* AD 75

Sarapion has paid the one per cent tax for toll dues of the Oasis upon one ass-load of barley and one ass-load of garlic. The 2nd year of Vespasianus the lord, seventh (7th) day of Mecheir.

44

P. Amh. 51 (H&E 28). *Deed of sale of a house.* 88 BC

[Column 1, summary] The 26th year, Mesore 28. Peteesis son of Pates has sold to Pelaeas son of Eunous the house belonging to him in the eastern part of Pathyris, built raftered and furnished with doors, the boundaries of which are given in the deed of sale. [Column 2,
5 text of deed] In the 26th year of the reign of Ptolemy surnamed

Alexander and of Cleopatra the sister, gods Philometores Soteres, the priests and priestesses and the canephorus being those now in office, the 28th of the month Mesore, at Pathyris, before Hermias, agoranomus of the upper toparchy of the Pathyrite nome. Peteesis

10 son of Pates, Persian, aged about forty years, of medium height, fair-skinned, smooth-haired, long-faced, straight-nosed, with a scar under the left eyebrow, has sold the house belonging to him, built and raftered and furnished with doors, at the so-called fountain in the eastern part of Pathyris, of which the boundaries are, to the south the

15 house of Pelaeas the purchaser, on the north the house of Taenoutis daughter of Psenpoeris, of which Totoes son of Panechates has possession, on the east and west a royal street, or whatever the boundaries may be all round. Pelaeas son of Eunous has bought it for one talent of copper. Negotiator and guarantor of all the terms of

20 this deed of sale: Peteesis the vendor, who has been accepted by Pelaeas the purchaser. [Subscribed] Registered by me, Hermias.

l. 7   *Canephorus.* A priestess at Alexandria.

l. 9   *Agoranomus.* A public official through whom contracts were drawn up.

45

P. Ryl. 175 (H&E 278). *A householder's complaint to the police that he has been robbed.* AD 28–9

To Serapion, chief of police, from Orsenouphis son of Harpaesis, notable of the village of Euhemeria in the division of Themistes. In the month Mesore of the past 14th year of Tiberius Caesar Augustus I was having some old walls on my premises demolished by the

5 mason Petesouchus son of Petesouchus, and while I was absent from home to gain my living, Petesouchus in the process of demolition discovered a hoard which had been secreted by my mother in a little box as long ago as the 16th year of Caesar, consisting of a pair of gold earrings weighing 4 quarters, a gold crescent weighing 3 quarters, a

10 pair of silver armlets of the weight of 12 drachmae of uncoined metal, a necklace with silver ornaments worth 80 drachmae, and 60 silver drachmae. Diverting the attention of his assistants and my people he had them conveyed to his own home by his maiden daughter, and after emptying out the aforesaid objects he threw away

15 the box empty in my house, and he even admitted finding the box, though he pretends that it was empty. Wherefore I request, if you approve, that the accused be brought before you for the consequent punishment. Farewell.

Orsenouphis, aged fifty, scar on left forearm.

46

P. Hamb. i. 4 (H&E 249) *Engagement to appear in court.* AD 87

Copy of bond. To Nemesion, royal scribe of the division of
Heraclides, from Lucius Vettius Epaphroditus. I swear by the
Emperor Caesar Domitianus Augustus Germanicus that I will present
myself in Alexandria not later than the 23rd of the month
5 Pharmouthi of the current 6th year of the Emperor Caesar
Domitianus Augustus Germanicus and will attend the most sacred
court of his excellency the praefect Gaius Septimius Vegetus until I
have contested the case which Marcus Antonius Tituleius, soldier, is
bringing against me, in conformity with the order delivered to
10 Claudius Chares, late strategus, otherwise may I incur the consequences of the oath. Isidorus, public scribe, has written for him, as he
professes to be illiterate. Epaphroditus, aged thirty-five years, with a
scar on the small finger of the right hand, described by Tebulus,
assistant. The 6th year of the Emperor Caesar Domitianus Augustus
15 Germanicus, Pharmouthi 3.

l. 13 *Tebulus,* who adds this sentence, was apparently instructed to note down a
description of Epaphroditus, for later use, if necessary, in identification.

47

P. Oxy. 37 (H&E 257). *Minutes of legal proceedings before a strategus.*
AD 49

From the minutes of Tiberius Claudius Pasion, strategus. The 9th
year of Tiberius Claudius Caesar Augustus Germanicus Imperator,
Pharmouthi 3, at the court. Pesouris *versus* Saraeus. Aristocles,
advocate for Pesouris, said: 'Pesouris, for whom I appear, in the 7th
5 year of Tiberius Claudius Caesar the lord picked up from a rubbish-
heap a male foundling called Heraclas. This he entrusted to the
defendant, and the nurse's contract which was made here referred to
it as a son of Pesouris. She received her wages for the first year. The
pay-day for the second year came round and again she received them.
10 To show that these statements are true, we have her receipts in which
she acknowledges payment. As the foundling was being starved,
Pesouris took it away. Subsequently, seizing an opportunity, she
burst into the house of my client and carried the foundling off; and
she seeks to obtain the foundling as being her free-born child. I have
15 here, first, the written contract for nursing, I have, secondly, the
receipt for the wages. I demand that these be recognized.' Saraeus: 'I
weaned my own child and the foundling of these persons was
entrusted to me. I have received from them the whole eight staters.
Subsequently the foundling died, [.] staters being still unearned.
20 Now they seek to take away my own child.' Theon: 'We have the

papers relating to the foundling.' The strategus: 'Since from its looks the child appears to be the son of Saraeus, if she and her husband will sign a sworn declaration that the foundling entrusted to her by Pesouris has died, I give judgement in accordance with the decision

25 of our lord the praefect that on paying back the money which she has received she shall have her own child.'

l. 5 ... *picked up from a rubbish-heap* ...—perhaps not a very uncommon occurrence; cf. Hilarion's letter above, **35**.

l. 19 [.] *staters being still unearned*—that paid in advance for the latter part of the second year, after the child's death.

l. 20 *Theon.* Perhaps the advocate of Saraeus.

l. 25 *The praefect.* The strategus could act only under the direction of the praefect. Apparently he has already received an instruction from his superior.

48

P. Lond. 1912 (H&E 212). *A letter of the Emperor Claudius to the Alexandrians.* AD 41

This letter is of great historical and constitutional importance. See p. 13 and **148–9**.

Proclamation by Lucius Aemilius Rectus. Seeing that all the populace, owing to its numbers, was unable to be present at the reading of the most sacred and most beneficent letter to the city, I have deemed it necessary to display the letter publicly in order that reading it one by

5 one you may admire the majesty of our god Caesar and feel gratitude for his goodwill towards the city. Year 2 of Tiberius Claudius Caesar Augustus Germanicus Imperator, the 14th of Neus Sebastus.

Tiberius Claudius Caesar Augustus Germanicus Imperator, Pontifex Maximus, holder of the tribunician power, consul designate, to

10 the city of Alexandria greeting. Tiberius Claudius Barbillus, Apollonius son of Artemidorus, Chaeremon son of Leonidas, Marcus Julius Asclepiades, Gaius Julius Dionysius, Tiberius Claudius Phanias, Pasion son of Potamon, Dionysius son of Sabbion, Tiberius Claudius Archibius, Apollonius son of Ariston, Gaius Julius Apollonius,

15 Hermaiscus son of Apollonius, your ambassadors, having delivered to me the decree, discoursed at length concerning the city, directing my attention to your goodwill towards us, which from long ago, you may be sure, had been stored up to your advantage in my memory; for you are by nature reverent towards the Augusti, as I

20 know from many proofs, and in particular have taken a warm interest in my house, warmly reciprocated, of which fact (to mention the last instance, passing over the others) the supreme witness is my brother Germanicus addressing you in words more clearly stamped

as his own. Wherefore I gladly accepted the honours given to me by
25 you, though I have no weakness for such things. And first I permit
you to keep my birthday as a *dies Augustus* as you have yourselves
proposed, and I agree to the erection in their several places of the
statues of myself and my family; for I see that you were anxious to
establish on every side memorials of your reverence for my house.
30 Of the two golden statues the one made to represent the Pax Augusta
Claudiana, as my most honoured Barbillus suggested and entreated
when I wished to refuse for fear of being thought too offensive, shall
be erected at Rome, and the other according to your request shall be
carried in procession on name-days in your city; and it shall be
35 accompanied by a throne, adorned with whatever trappings you
choose. It would perhaps be foolish, while accepting such great
honours, to refuse the institution of a Claudian tribe and the
establishment of groves after the manner of Egypt; wherefore I grant
you these requests as well, and if you wish you may also erect the
40 equestrian statues given by Vitrasius Pollio my procurator. As for
the erection of those in four-horse chariots which you wish to set up
to me at the entrances into the country, I consent to let one be placed
at Taposiris, the Libyan town of that name, another at Pharos in
Alexandria, and a third at Pelusium in Egypt. But I deprecate the
45 appointment of a high priest to me and the building of temples, for I
do not wish to be offensive to my contemporaries, and my opinion
is that temples and such forms of honour have by all ages been
granted as a prerogative to the gods alone.

Concerning the requests which you have been anxious to obtain
50 from me, I decide as follows. All those who have become *ephebi* up
to the time of my principate I confirm and maintain in possession of
the Alexandrian citizenship with all the privileges and indulgences
enjoyed by the city, excepting such as by beguiling you have
contrived to become *ephebi* though born of servile mothers; and it is
55 equally my will that all the other favours shall be confirmed which
were granted to you by former princes and kings and praefects, as
the deified Augustus also confirmed them. It is my will that the
neocori of the temple of the deified Augustus in Alexandria shall be
chosen by lot in the same way as those of the said deified Augustus in
60 Canopus are chosen by lot. With regard to the civic magistracies
being made triennial your proposal seems to me to be very good; for
through fear of being called to account for any abuse of power your
magistrates will behave with greater circumspection during their
term of office. Concerning the senate, what your custom may have
65 been under the ancient kings I have no means of saying, but that you
had no senate under the former Augusti you are well aware. As this
is the first broaching of a novel project, whose utility to the city and
to my government is not evident, I have written to Aemilius Rectus

to hold an inquiry and inform me whether in the first place it is right
70 that a senate should be constituted and, if it should be right to create
one, in what manner this is to be done.

As for the question which party was responsible for the riots and
feud (or rather, if the truth must be told, the war) with the Jews,
although in confrontation with their opponents your ambassadors,
75 and particularly Dionysius son of Theon, contended with great zeal,
nevertheless I was unwilling to make a strict inquiry, though
guarding within me a store of immutable indignation against
whichever party renews the conflict; and I tell you once for all that
unless you put a stop to this ruinous and obstinate enmity against
80 each other, I shall be driven to show what a benevolent prince can be
when turned to righteous indignation. Wherefore once again I
conjure you that on the one hand the Alexandrians show themselves
forbearing and kindly towards the Jews who for many years have
dwelt in the same city, and dishonour none of the rites observed by
85 them in the worship of their god, but allow them to observe their
customs as in the time of the deified Augustus, which customs I also,
after hearing both sides, have sanctioned; and on the other hand I
explicitly order the Jews not to agitate for more privileges than they
formerly possessed, and not in future to send out a separate embassy
90 as if they lived in a separate city, a thing unprecedented, and not to
force their way into gymnasiarchic or cosmetic games, while
enjoying their own privileges and sharing a great abundance of
advantages in a city not their own, and not to bring in or admit Jews
who come down the river from Syria or Egypt, a proceeding which
95 will compel me to conceive serious suspicions; otherwise I will by
all means take vengeance on them as fomenters of what is a general
plague infecting the whole world. If desisting from these courses you
consent to live with mutual forbearance and kindliness, I on my side
will exercise a solicitude of very long standing for the city, as one
100 which is bound to us by traditional friendship. I bear witness to my
friend Barbillus of the solicitude which he has always shown for you
in my presence and of the extreme zeal with which he has now
advocated your cause, and likewise to my friend Tiberius Claudius
Archibius. Farewell.

l. 1   *Lucius Aemilius Rectus*, the praefect.

l. 23   ... *in words more clearly stamped as his own*—because they were spoken in
Greek, not written in Latin.

l. 37   *A Claudian tribe*, in the city of Alexandria.

l. 50   *Ephebi*: youths born in families possessing the citizenship.

l. 58   *Neocori*: official temple guardians.

l. 73   For the large and turbulent Jewish population in Alexandria see **149**.

l. 91 *Gymnasiarchic:* organized by the gymnasiarch, or superintendent of athletic training in the city.

Cosmetic: probably games given or organized by the cosmetes, or magistrate in charge of the *ephebi* in the city (see *l.* 50). An alternative but less probable translation would see here a reference not to games but elections for the offices of gymnasiarch and cosmetes.

3   Inscriptions

An immense number of inscribed stones and metals, written in Latin, Greek, and Semitic languages, has been preserved, in various degrees of mutilation, from the world in which primitive Christianity arose. Taken together they furnish a very great deal of valuable material for the reconstruction of the military, political, social, and religious history of the ancient world. A complete account, or even an adequate sketch, of this material would clearly be out of place in this book, as would also be a description of the methods by which inscriptions may be, and have been, sought, excavated, deciphered, and interpreted. The following non-Christian inscriptions all bear directly, though in different ways, upon the history of early Christianity; it must be remembered that other inscriptions, which have no such direct reference, are nevertheless of great importance to the historian who would study the New Testament and other early Christian documents in their original setting. Other inscriptions will be found at **1, 10, 113, 114, 115**.

The Gallio inscription at Delphi

49

W. Dittenberger, *Sylloge Inscriptionum Graecarum*, 3rd edn. 801D

There is a full and convenient account in F. J. F. Jackson and K. Lake, *The Beginnings of Christianity*, V, pp. 460–4. Four fragments of a stone bearing a rescript of the emperor Claudius (see **9, 10**) were discovered in the present century at Delphi, in Greece (Achaea), which refer to Gallio as proconsul of the province; cf. Acts 18. 12. The stone is dated, and consequently makes possible greater precision in the dating of Paul's visit to Corinth. Parts of the inscription have perished, and conjectural supplements (most of which are very probable) are indicated by square brackets, so far as this is possible in translation.

> Tiberius [Claudius] Caesar Augustus Germanicus, [Pontifex maximus, in his tribunician] power
> [year 12, acclaimed Emperor for] the 26th time, father of the country, [consul for the 5th time, censor, sends greeting to the city of Delphi.]

> I have for long been zealous for the city of Delphi [and favourable to
>   it from the]
> beginning, and I have always observed the cult of the [Pythian]
>   Apollo, [but with regard to]
> 5 the present stories, and those quarrels of the citizens of which [a
>   report has been made by Lucius]
> Junius Gallio my friend, and [pro]consul [of Achaea] . . .

Several lines follow which can be read with only partial certainty, and are
not significant for the present purpose.

l. 1   *Claudius* . . . The extent of the supplements in this and other lines is less
striking than may appear at first sight. Most official inscriptions are
stereotyped in form, and a knowledge of the usual formulae and of the space
which must once have been filled often suffices for confident reconstruction.

l. 2   *Year* 12, *acclaimed Emperor for the 26th time.* The number 26 is extant in the
inscription; 12 is a supplement. The figures are of great importance, since it
is by means of them that the inscription is dated. It is to be noted that the
emperors assumed the tribunician power at their accession and retained it
continuously, the years being reckoned from the date of accession (for
Claudius, 25 January 41); the acclamations were irregular, and (often) more
frequent. The exact date of Claudius's 26th acclamation is not known. In his
11th year (of reign and tribunician power) he was acclaimed for the 22nd,
23rd and 24th times; in his 12th (and not later than 1 August) he was
acclaimed for the 27th time. (These facts are all drawn from other
inscriptions). The 26th acclamation must therefore have taken place at the
close of the 11th year (which would require five acclamations in that year),
or, as is perhaps more probable, in the first half of the 12th year (i.e. between
25 January and 1 August AD 52); consequently the inscription itself falls
within this period.

l. 4   *The Pythian Apollo.* The god who granted the famous oracles of Delphi.

l. 5   *The present stories.* We can only conjecture what disturbances had taken place
at Delphi.

l. 6   *Gallio . . . proconsul of Achaea.* Achaea was a senatorial province, governed by
a proconsul appointed by the Senate (see **1**, *ll.* 76–end and notes). It was
customary for such provincial governors to remain in office for one year, or,
less frequently, for two. They took up their duties in early summer, perhaps
June. It thus appears that the latest date for Gallio's entry upon his office is
June 52; this however is not likely, since it would mean that between June
and the end of July Claudius had dealt with the trouble at Delphi, his rescript
had been recorded and he had been acclaimed the 27th time. This is of course
not impossible, but it seems on the whole more likely that Gallio became
proconsul of Achaea in 51, or in 50, if he held office two years. This is an
important datum for New Testament chronology, though it is to be noted
that we do not know at what point in his proconsulship Paul was brought
before Gallio.

A Temple Inscription

50

W. Dittenberger, *Orientis Graeci Inscriptiones Selectae*, 598

The inscription translated below explains itself. Gentiles were allowed in the outer but not the inner areas of the temple at Jerusalem and Josephus (*War* v. 193f.; cf. *War* vi. 125; *Ant.* xv. 417; Philo, *Leg. ad Gaium* 212) says: 'Proceeding across this [the open court] towards the second court of the temple, one found it surrounded by a stone balustrade, three cubits high and of exquisite workmanship; in this at regular intervals stood slabs giving warning, some in Greek, others in Latin characters, of the law of purification, to wit that no foreigner was permitted to enter the holy place, for so the second enclosure of the temple was called.' One of these warning notices was discovered in 1871 by Clermont-Ganneau. It runs:

> No man of another nation to enter within the fence and enclosure round the temple. And whoever is caught will have himself to blame that his death ensues.

We may compare Acts 21. 26–30; Eph. 2. 14.

Synagogue Inscriptions

See A. Deissmann, *Light from the Ancient East* (1927), p. 16; E. Schürer, *The History of the Jewish People in the Age of Jesus Christ* (new ed.) III. i. 90f.; F. J. F. Jackson and K. Lake, *Beginnings of Christianity*, IV, p. 67; V. p. 64. Jewish communities, many of them equipped with synagogues, were to be found in many towns of the Roman Empire. The following inscriptions attest the existence of synagogues at Corinth, Rome, and Jerusalem.

51

Corpus Inscriptionum Judaicarum 718. A Synagogue at Corinth

See Deissmann, loc. cit.
> [Syn]agogue of the Hebr[ews].

52

CIJ 510 (= *CIG*, 9909). A Synagogue at Rome

> Here lies
> Salo[me]
> daughter of Ga-
> dia, father

 5 of the synagogue
   of the Hebrews. She
   lived forty-one years.
   In peace
   be her
10 sleep.

l. 5   Synagogue of the Hebrews. On the synagogue in general see **187–194** and introductory note. The exact meaning of the expressions in these inscriptions, and particularly in that found at Rome, turns upon the meaning of 'Hebrews'; does this mean Hebrews by race, or Hebrew- (or Aramaic-) speaking Jews? Perhaps the best suggestion is that this synagogue (and at Rome there were, as inscriptions attest, synagogues of the Augusteans, the Volumnians, the Herodians, the Campesians, the Syburesians, the Vernaculi, the Calcaremians, the Tripolitans, the Elaians, the Sekeni, and (?) the Calabrians) was that of the original small group of Jews resident in Rome (as early as the time of Pompey), and that when other synagogues were added fresh and more particular names were found for them. But it must be understood that this, like all other suggestions on the matter, is hypothetical.

53
A Synagogue at Jerusalem. *CIJ*, 1404

See Jackson and Lake, op. cit. IV, p. 67; also E. L. Sukenik, *Ancient Synagogues in Palestine and Greece*, 1934, pp. 69f.

   Theodotus, son of Vettenus, priest and
   archisynagogue, son of an archisynagogue, grandson of an archisynagogue, built
   the synagogue for the read-
 5 ing of the Law and the teaching of the commandments, and
   the guest-house and the rooms and the wa-
   ter supplies as an inn for those
   who have need when they come from abroad; which [synagogue]
   his fathers founded and the eld-
10 ers and Simonides.

l. 1   Theodotus, Son of Vettenus. It is very improbable that a Jewish inscription would be made in Jerusalem after AD 70 (see **142**), and the appearance of the inscribed letters confirms a date not far from the middle of the first century AD. The combination of the Greek name Theodotus with the Latin Vettenus (in a Greek inscription) suggests the possibility that Theodotus was a freedman, since freedmen often took the names of their former owners, and the inscription may therefore throw light upon Acts 6. 9 (the synagogue called that of the Libertines, or freedmen); but it must be remembered that the inscription does not say that either Theodotus or Vettenus was a freedman.

Priest and archisynagogue. For the office of archisynagogue cf. Mark 5. 22. Theodotus was also a priest; temple and synagogue were not in opposition to one another, even though the former was to some extent the stronghold of the Sadducees, the latter of the Pharisees.

ll. 4, 5   The reading of the Law and the teaching of the commandments. The purpose for which the synagogue existed is made clear by these words.

l. 6   The guest-house. Jews of the dispersion attended the Pilgrim Feasts as far as they were able (see **178–181** and notes), and did so in such numbers that it became extremely difficult to find accommodation in Jerusalem. The advantage of a synagogue building equipped as a hostel is evident.

l. 9   His fathers founded, i.e. probably, the father and grandfather referred to above. The probable meaning is that they founded the establishment, and that Theodotus rebuilt and perhaps increased it. Simonides is unknown.

Sacral Manumission

In the ancient world slavery was a common and hardly questioned institution. Consequently the states of freedom and bondage, and the transition between the two, were more familiar to the New Testament writers than to ourselves. As there were many ways by which a person might become a slave, so also there were several methods of emancipation. For example, a god and his priests might assist the process; this method suggests the possibility of parallels with various New Testament metaphors, and may be illustrated by the following inscriptions.

54

W. Dittenberger, *Sylloge Inscriptionum Graecarum*, 2nd edn 845.

An inscription of 200–199 BC, found (with others) on a wall of the temple of Apollo at Delphi.

> The Pythian Apollo
> bought from Sosibius
> of Amphissa for freedom
> a female slave, whose name
> 5 is Nicaea, by race a Roman, at a price
> of three silver minas and
> a half-mina. Former seller according to
> the law was Eumnastus
> of Amphissa. He has received
> 10 the price. The deed of sale
> Nicaea has entrusted to
> Apollo for freedom.

l. 1   The Pythian Apollo bought. On Apollo at Delphi see **49**. The god is said to have bought the slave from her former owner, but it is clear, from this and other inscriptions, that the slave had first paid the price into the temple treasury; as a slave she could not herself negotiate the sale.

l. 3   *For freedom* (cf. *l.* 12). The god has purchased the slave not with a view to her serving him as a slave, but with a view to her freedom; the contract is therefore a form of manumission.

l. 8   *Eumnastus*, who sold Nicaea to Sosibius, is named as guaranteeing Sosibius's right to sell.

l. 10   *The deed of sale* is in fact the inscription, given publicity and permanence in the temple. An alternative translation of the word (ὠνά—written for ὠνή) is 'price'; Nicaea entrusted the purchase money to Apollo who then effected the transaction.

55

CIJ 683 (= *CIG* 2114 *bb*)

This inscription was found at Panticapaeum, in the Crimea. It is plainly of Jewish origin, and shows both the wide extent of the Diaspora (see **148–152**), and that the Jews also practised manumission at their sacred places.

> In the reign of king Tibe-
> rius Julius Rhescuporis, friend of
> Caesar and friend of Rome, the pi-
> ous; in the year 377, in the month Peniti-
> 5 us, the 20th [or 23rd], I, Chreste, formerly wife
> of Nicias, son of Sotas, release at the house of
> prayer my slave Heraclas
> to be completely free according to my vow.
> He is not to be retained or dis-
> 10 turbed by any heir of mine,
> but to go wherever he wish-
> es, without let or hindrance according to
> my vow, except for the house of prayer
> which is for worship and meet-
> 15 ing. Assent is given to this
> also by my heirs, Peri-
> cleides and Heliconias.
> Joint oversight will be taken also by the
> synagogue of the Jews.

l. 4   *In the year* 377 . . . . The date is January AD 81.

l. 6   *The house of prayer.* This word (προσευχή, not συναγωγή) is frequently used of the building (or place) used for Jewish worship. It can also be quoted in heathen use (e.g. *CIG* 2079), but there is no question of the Jewish origin of the present inscription (see *l.* 19). It may be noted also that this inscription, unlike the last, makes no reference to a fictitious sale to a god.

l. 8   *My vow.* The owner had evidently vowed the freedom of Heraclas in circumstances of which we are not informed. It is the vow, not a sale, which is here operative in manumission.

l. 13   *Except for the house of prayer.* The meaning of the phrase is obscure. Probably Heraclas was to continue under certain obligations as far as the house of prayer was concerned. This recalls, though distantly, pagan forms of sacral manumission.

l. 19   *The synagogue of the Jews.* Synagogue here means not a place of meeting but the local Jewish community, which met in the house of prayer.

Two Ossuaries

In 1945 a large grave chamber was discovered at Talpioth, a suburb of Jerusalem. It seems to have been in use from about 50 BC to about AD 50, and contained fourteen ossuaries, on some of which inscriptions were still legible, some in Aramaic, some in Greek. The two Greek inscriptions are transliterated as follows; their interpretation is disputed.

56

Iesous iou

57

Iesous aloth

The name *Jesus* is clear and unquestioned. The letters that follow have been given different interpretations. Probably the best view is that *Iou* and *Aloth* are both personal names, indicating that the bones in question were those of Jesus son of Iou (or of Ias, taking ιου to be genitive of Ἰάς) and of Jesus son of Aloth. On this view the ossuaries have nothing to do with Christian origins—an interesting conclusion, since some also bear incised crosses, which must be interpreted as Jewish symbols (see E. Dinkler, *Signum Crucis* (Tübingen 1967), 3–15). Some however hold that the name Jesus refers to Jesus of Nazareth; E. L. Sukenik (*American Journal of Archaeology* 51 (1947) 351–365) thinks that *iou* and *aloth* are both cries of woe; in the presence of death the bereaved address their sorrow to Jesus. B. Gustafsson (*New Testament Studies* 3, (1956) 65–69) thinks this to be entirely correct for *iou*, which he takes as an appeal for help: Jesus, help! *Aloth* he connects with the Hebrew עלה, *'alah*, and understands the inscription to mean, Jesus, let (him who rests here) arise!

4 Philosophers and Poets

Philosophy, in the strict sense in which the term is now understood, plays only a small part in the background of the New Testament. In the early Christian period the age of the great philosophers was past. The 'failure of nerve' (to use Dr Gilbert Murray's vivid phrase) had long set in. The fearless freedom of thought which had marked Periclean Athens had disappeared; men had lost confidence in the power of their own intelligence to solve by abstract ratiocination the problems of mind and matter, man and the universe. Dogmatism, revelation, religion, and even superstition replaced independent thought; interest in metaphysics was replaced by interest in practical ethics—how was a virtuous man to live in evil surroundings? When the problems of cosmology were envisaged they were seen as divine secrets revealed only to the elect.

To write thus is to paint perhaps too dark a picture. A preoccupation with ethics is after all no discredit to any age, and Christianity (like the Judaism from which it emerged) entered the ancient world as a revelation. But even a slight sketch of Platonism and Aristotelianism as metaphysical systems would be out of place in this book. Plato's work as the virtual founder of idealism was even in the first century important enough; but what the first century made of it was Gnosticism, or something much like Gnosticism (see Chapter 5), and the 'philosophy' condemned in Col. 2. 8 was a worship of angels rather than a pursuit of truth and the Ideal Good. The first century was in philosophy an eclectic age, and no attempt will be made here to delineate the views of the several philosophical 'schools' (though certain venerable labels will be retained). The extracts given below may, however, help to suggest the atmosphere in which the Christian faith was propagated.

It is not only professional philosophers who think deeply and instructively about the meaning of life, nor do they always impress their contemporaries as being the wisest and most reputable of men. Poets, and not only tragic poets, took their place in an intellectual environment, and the criticism levelled by a comic writer such as Aristophanes was much more than a modern chaffing of the absent-minded professor. Men like him were shocked by the essential levity, and the profiteering rapacity, of the sophists, who were prepared to prove that black was white to make a living. Socrates deserved the criticism less than most, but his personal characteristics and his fame invited it. And Aristophanes had serious if cynically expressed things to say about, for example, war and peace, men and women. It is however to the great writers of tragedy that one turns for profound reflection on human duty and destiny. They took their plots from the common stock of Greek legend, and saw in them, and used them to express, the issues of life and death.

Heraclitus and the Logos

It is very improbable that those fragments of the philosopher Heraclitus (who flourished in Ephesus in the fifth century BC) that contain the word λόγος have anything to do with John's Logos-doctrine, or indeed with any New Testament doctrine. It has, however, been maintained that Heraclitus's extremely obscure remarks are important for the study of the New Testament, and they are included here for the convenience of the reader, who may consider the question for himself. The references given are to R. Walzer, *Eraclito: raccolta dei Frammenti* (Florence, 1939).

58

Heraclitus, Fragment (in Walzer, op. cit.) 1

> Though the word always exists men are without understanding, both before they hear it, and after they have heard it the first time. For though all things happen in accordance with this word men seem as if they had no acquaintance with them, making trial of both words
> 5 and deeds such as I set forth, distinguishing each thing according to its nature and showing how it is. But other men know not what they do even when they are awake, as they forget what they do when they are asleep.

l. 1 *Though the word always exists*; perhaps, though the word is always true. It seems clear that both here and in *l.* 3 λόγος means the speech, almost the prophetic oracle, of Heraclitus.

59

Heraclitus, Fragment (in Walzer, op. cit.) 2

> It is necessary therefore to follow the common. But though the word is common most men live as if they had a wisdom of their own.

l. 1 The word again seems to refer to Heraclitus's message.

60

Heraclitus, Fragment (in Walzer, op. cit.) 31

> Transformations of fire: first, sea, and half of sea is earth, and half is
> waterspout.... The sea liquefies and is measured by the same measure
> as before it became earth.

l. 2   Measure, λόγος. The word has no special sense here. There is a similar use in
Fragments 45, 115.

61

Heraclitus, Fragment (in Walzer, op. cit.) 50

> It is wise to listen not to me but to the word, and to confess that all
> things are one.

l. 1   It would be accurate to render, 'to my word'; Heraclitus means that his
message is true, whatever may be thought of the messenger.

Plato: the Philosopher's Mission and the Doctrine of Ideas

A discussion of the relation between Socrates and the Sophists would take
us far beyond the limits of this book. That Socrates himself was able to
distinguish sharply between his own work and that of the common run
of sophists is clear; but it is equally clear that there was no small superficial
resemblance between them. He sometimes appeared, like them, to make
'the worse appear the better reason'; this was because he questioned every
conventional, unexamined motive, bade men examine themselves and
their presuppositions, and dared to give a fresh opinion—or at least ask
fresh questions—on such matters as the religion and established order of
the state. He made powerful enemies by the devastating *elenchus* with
which he exposed the hollow shams especially of those who were reputed
to be wise and influential. The sophists were teachers of rhetoric; Socrates
taught men to know themselves, and in that knowledge to discover their
own ignorance. This was his mission to Athens, and in the faithful
execution of it he became the prototype of the philosophic missionary (see
below, **85–9** and introductory note), and indeed of the philosophic martyr.

62

Plato, *Apology of Socrates* 28D–30C

In this work (which cannot be regarded as conveying the words of
Socrates himself: Xenophon also wrote a somewhat similar, but different,
Apology) Socrates answers the charge, on which he was convicted and put

to death, that 'he had corrupted the young men of the city, and did not believe in the gods believed in by the city but had introduced other new divinities'. In reply Socrates describes the origin of his 'mission'. The Delphic oracle had pronounced him the wisest of men. This he found incredible, and to prove it false he proceeded to interrogate those who had a reputation for wisdom. He was amazed to find that, notwithstanding their reputation, they were ignorant men, and came to believe that he might after all be the wisest of men since, though he too was ignorant, he at least knew that he was ignorant (cf. *l.* 18 below). The theme of his mission is developed further.

Strange, indeed, would be my conduct, O men of Athens, if I who, when I was ordered by the generals whom you chose to command me at Potidaea and Amphipolis and Delium, remained where they placed me, like any other man, facing death—if now, when, as I
5 conceive and imagine, God orders me to fulfil the philosopher's mission of searching into myself and other men, I were to desert my post through fear of death, or any other fear; that would indeed be strange, and I might justly be arraigned in court for denying the existence of the gods, if I disobeyed the oracle because I was afraid of
10 death, fancying that I was wise when I was not wise. For the fear of death is indeed the pretence of wisdom, and not real wisdom, being a pretence of knowing the unknown; and no one knows whether death, which men in their fear apprehend to be the greatest evil, may not be the greatest good. Is not this ignorance of a disgraceful sort,
15 the ignorance which is the conceit that a man knows what he does not know? And in this respect only I believe myself to differ from men in general, and may perhaps claim to be wiser than they are:— that whereas I know but little of the world below, I do not suppose that I know: but I do know that injustice and disobedience to a
20 better, whether God or man, is evil and dishonourable, and I will never fear or avoid a possible good rather than a certain evil. And therefore if you let me go now, and are not convinced by Anytus, who said that since I had been prosecuted I must be put to death; (or if not that I ought never to have been prosecuted at all); and that if I
25 escape now, your sons will all be utterly ruined by listening to my words—if you say to me, Socrates, this time we will not mind Anytus, and you shall be let off, but upon one condition, that you are not to inquire and speculate in this way any more, and that if you are caught doing so again you shall die;—if this was the condition on
30 which you let me go, I should reply: Men of Athens, I honour and love you; but I shall obey God rather than you, and while I have life and strength I shall never cease from the practice and teaching of philosophy, exhorting any one whom I meet and saying to him after my manner: You, my friend,—a citizen of the great and mighty and

35   wise city of Athens,—are you not ashamed of heaping up the greatest
amount of money and honour and reputation, and caring so little
about wisdom and truth and the greatest improvement of the soul,
which you never regard or heed at all? And if the person with whom
I am arguing, says: Yes, but I do care; then I do not leave him or let
40   him go at once; but I proceed to interrogate and examine and cross-
examine him, and if I think that he has no virtue in him, but only
says that he has, I reproach him with undervaluing the greater, and
overvaluing the less. And I shall repeat the same words to every one
whom I meet, young and old, citizen and alien, but especially to the
45   citizens, inasmuch as they are my brethren. For know that this is the
command of God; and I believe that no greater good has ever
happened in the state than my service to the God. For I do nothing
but go about persuading you all, old and young alike, not to take
thought for your persons or your properties, but first and chiefly to
50   care about the greatest improvement of the soul. I tell you that virtue
is not given by money, but that from virtue comes money and every
other good of man, public as well as private. This is my teaching, and
if this is the doctrine which corrupts the youth, I am a mischievous
person. But if any one says that this is not my teaching, he is speaking
55   an untruth. Wherefore, O men of Athens, I say to you, do as Anytus
bids or not as Anytus bids, and either acquit me or not: but whichever
you do, understand that I shall never alter my ways, not even if I
have to die many times.

l. 1   *Strange, indeed, would be my conduct* . . . Socrates explains why he has not
abandoned the task of philosophizing and 'examination'.

l. 3   *At Potidaea and Amphipolis and Delium.* At the battles fought in these places,
in 432, 422 and 424 BC respectively. In at least two of these Socrates was
distinguished by his bravery.

l. 5   *God orders me*; by the Delphic oracle; perhaps there is a reference also to the
'daemon' or guiding spirit by which Socrates believed himself to be directed.
Cf. *l.* 46.

l. 58   See **24–5**, and **85–9** below on the philosophic missionary and martyr.

63

Plato, *Republic* vii. 514A–517A

This famous Allegory of the Cave sets forth in outline Plato's doctrine of
ideas. It is significant that the allegory is given a practical, moral, setting
and application.

And now, I said, let me show in a figure how far our nature is
enlightened or unenlightened:—Behold! human beings living in an
underground den, which has a mouth open towards the light and
reaching all along the den; here they have been from their childhood,

5 and have their legs and necks chained so that they cannot move, and can only see before them, being prevented by the chains from turning round their heads. Above and behind them a fire is blazing at a distance, and between the fire and the prisoners there is a raised way; and you will see, if you look, a low wall built along the way, like the
10 screen which marionette players have in front of them, over which they show the puppets.

I see.

And do you see, I said, men passing all along the wall carrying all sorts of vessels, and statues and figures of animals made of wood and
15 stone and various materials, which appear over the wall? Some of them are talking, others silent.

You have shown me a strange image, and they are strange prisoners.

Like ourselves, I replied; and they see only their own shadows, or
20 the shadows of one another, which the fire throws on the opposite wall of the cave?

True, he said; how could they see anything but the shadows if they were never allowed to move their heads?

And of the objects which are being carried in like manner they
25 would only see the shadows?

Yes, he said.

And if they were able to converse with one another, would they not suppose that they were naming what was actually before them?

Very true.

30 And suppose further that the prison had an echo which came from the other side, would they not be sure to fancy when one of the passers-by spoke that the voice which they heard came from the passing shadow?

No question, he replied.

35 To them, I said, the truth would be literally nothing but the shadows of the images.

That is certain.

And now look again, and see what will naturally follow if the prisoners are released and disabused of their error. At first, when any
40 of them is liberated and compelled suddenly to stand up and turn his neck round and walk and look towards the light, he will suffer sharp pains; the glare will distress him, and he will be unable to see the realities of which in his former state he had seen the shadows; and then conceive someone saying to him, that what he saw before was
45 an illusion, but that now, when he is approaching nearer to being and his eye is turned towards more real existence, he has a clearer vision,—what will be his reply? And you may further imagine that his instructor is pointing to the objects as they pass and requiring him to name them,—will he not be perplexed? Will he not fancy that

50 the shadows which he formerly saw are truer than the objects which
are now shown to him?

Far truer.

And if he is compelled to look straight at the light, will he not
have a pain in his eyes which will make him turn away to take refuge
55 in the objects of vision which he can see, and which he will conceive
to be in reality clearer than the things which are now being shown
to him?

True, he said.

And suppose once more, that he is reluctantly dragged up a steep
60 and rugged ascent, and held fast until he is forced into the presence of
the sun himself, is he not likely to be pained and irritated? When he
approaches the light his eyes will be dazzled, and he will not be able
to see anything at all of what are now called realities.

Not all in a moment, he said.

65 He will require to grow accustomed to the sight of the upper
world. And first he will see the shadows best, next the reflections of
men and other objects in the water, and then the objects themselves;
then he will gaze upon the light of the moon and the stars and the
spangled heaven; and he will see the sky and the stars by night better
70 than the sun or the light of the sun by day?

Certainly.

Last of all he will be able to see the sun, and not mere reflections of
him in the water, but he will see him in his own proper place, and
not in another; and he will contemplate him as he is.

75 Certainly.

He will then proceed to argue that this is he who gives the seasons
and the years, and is the guardian of all that is in the visible world,
and in a certain way the cause of all things which he and his fellows
have been accustomed to behold?

80 Clearly, he said, he would first see the sun and then reason about
him.

And when he remembered his old habitation, and the wisdom of
the den and his fellow-prisoners, do you not suppose that he would
felicitate himself on the change, and pity them?

85 Certainly, he would.

And if they were in the habit of conferring honours among
themselves on those who were quickest to observe the passing
shadows and to remark which of them went before, and which
followed after, and which were together; and who were therefore
90 best able to draw conclusions as to the future, do you think that he
would care for such honours and glories, or envy the possessors of
them? Would he not say with Homer,

'Better to be the poor servant of a poor master,'

and to endure anything, rather than think as they do and live after
95 their manner?

Yes, he said, I think that he would rather suffer anything than entertain these false notions and live in this miserable manner.

Imagine once more, I said, such an one coming suddenly out of the sun to be replaced in his old situation; would he not be certain to
100 have his eyes full of darkness?

To be sure, he said.

And if there were a contest, and he had to compete in measuring the shadows with the prisoners who had never moved out of the den, while his sight was still weak, and before his eyes had become steady
105 (and the time which would be needed to acquire this new habit of sight might be very considerable), would he not be ridiculous? Men would say of him that up he went and down he came without his eyes; and that it was better not even to think of ascending; and if any one tried to loose another and lead him up to the light, let them only
110 catch the offender, and they would put him to death.

No question, he said.

The Earlier Stoics

As a philosophical system, Stoicism was materialist; much more important than this, however, is the fact that in spirit it was deeply religious and thoroughly moral. The universe, the Stoics held, was not a meaningless place, nor was man's place in it fortuitous. Pervading the whole of the material order was Reason and Purpose, λόγος, itself divine and indeed the only god the Stoics recognized (see however **66** for their readiness to make some acknowledgement of the gods popularly believed in). It was this divine Reason that ordered the regular motions of the heavenly bodies, the rotation of the seasons and the exact performance by natural objects of their appointed functions. Man's duty was to live in accordance with this Reason or Natural Law (κατὰ λόγον); indeed a spark or seed of the universal Reason (a λόγος σπερματικός) resided within men, or at least within the best and wisest of them. Like Socrates, the Stoic must obey the divine spark at all costs, even at the cost of life itself. It might even in certain circumstances be the most appropriate course for the wise and dutiful man to take his own life—life that had lost its dignity and worth was not to be preferred to death. This sounds a cold and cheerless creed, and so perhaps it was; yet beyond question it nerved many a man to face the battle of life with a clear head and a brave heart, and it inculcated humanity and forbearance in a world in which these virtues were not common.

The works of none of the earlier Stoics have come down to us in their entirety, and the authors themselves are imperfectly known to us. The founder of the school was Zeno (*c.* 336–263 BC) who taught in the Painted

Porch (*Stoa*) at Athens—whence the name of the school. Almost contemporary with him was Cleanthes (*c.* 331–232 BC). In a later generation Chrysippus (*c.* 280–205 BC) was perhaps the most voluminous of all Stoic writers. Posidonius, who is also quoted in this section, belongs to a later period (*c.* 135–51 BC), and is particularly important because he did much to fuse Stoic and Platonic thought.

64

Zeno, *Fragments* in J. von Arnim, *Stoicorum Veterum Fragmenta*, I (1964), 175, 176

> Destiny is the concatenated causality of things, or the scheme according to which the kosmos is directed.
>
> Zeno defined Destiny as 'a power which moves Stuff'. 'Providence' and 'Nature' are other names which he gave to the same thing.

l. 1   *Destiny* (εἱμαρμένη) . . . *the scheme* (λόγος). Already in Zeno appears the characteristic Stoic doctrine that the universe is informed by Logos, which is at once the scheme according to which things move, and the power that makes them move. Through the notion of Destiny it is linked with the regular movements of the celestial bodies, which in their turn controlled the affairs of men.

65

Zeno, *Fragment* 98

> The element of all the things which exist is Fire, and the origins of this Fire are Stuff and God. Both of these are bodily substances: God the active substance, and Stuff the passive substance. At certain destined periods of time the whole universe is turned to fire; then
> 5 again it is once more constituted an ordered manifold world. But the primal fire subsists in it like a kind of seminal fluid, containing in itself the formulas and causes of all the things which have been and are and shall be; the concatenation and sequence of these things is Destiny or Understanding or Truth, an inevitable and ineluctable
> 10 Law of things. Thus the whole universe is governed excellently well, like a city-state in which Law reigns supreme.

l. 2   *The origins of this Fire are Stuff* (ὕλη) *and God.* This is a scarcely accurate representation (by Eusebius) of Stoic thought. God *was* fire; and when the cosmos was constituted some fire was turned into stuff.

l. 4   *The whole universe is turned to fire.* This, the Stoics believed, happened periodically. The process was called ἐκπύρωσις.

l. 5   *It is once more constituted.* This also was a recurring event. Fire became matter; see above.

l. 7   *Formulas* (λόγοι). The Logos, or reason of the whole universe, could be distinguished (though hardly separated) from the logoi which controlled every single being.

66

Zeno, *Fragments* 162, 152.

The General Law, which is Right Reason, pervading everything, is the same as Zeus, the Supreme Head of the government of the universe.
　　Zeno used to propound the following argument:
5　'It is reasonable to honour the gods:
but it is not reasonable to honour beings which do not exist: therefore gods exist.'

l. 1   *Right Reason* (ὀρθὸς λόγος) . . . *is the same as Zeus.* In this way Stoicism came to terms with theism; though, as appears from this passage, its theism was pantheism.

l. 5   *It is reasonable to honour the gods.* It is astonishing that Zeno failed to see the *petitio principii* involved in this premise.

67

Cleanthes, *Fragment* in von Arnim, op. cit., 537

　　Thou, O Zeus, art praised above all gods: many are thy names and thine is all power for ever.
　　The beginning of the world was from thee: and with law thou rulest over all things.
5　Unto thee may all flesh speak: for we are thy offspring.
　　Therefore will I raise a hymn unto thee: and will ever sing of thy power.
　　The whole order of the heavens obeyeth thy word: as it moveth around the earth.
10　With little and great lights mixed together: how great art thou, King above all for ever!
　　Nor is anything done upon earth apart from thee: nor in the firmament, nor in the seas:
　　Save that which the wicked do: by their own folly.
15　But thine is the skill to set even the crooked straight: what is without fashion is fashioned and the alien akin before thee.
　　Thus hast thou fitted together all things in one: the good with the evil:
　　That thy word should be one in all things: abiding for ever.
20　Let folly be dispersed from our souls: that we may repay thee the honour, wherewith thou has honoured us:
　　Singing praise of thy works for ever: as becometh the sons of men.

l. 1   *O Zeus.* For Stoic readiness to countenance the accepted gods, see above; but Zeus in this hymn (as it may rightly be called) differs much from the Zeus of popular belief.

l. 3   *Law* (νόμος), the right reason which governs the universe (above, **66**), here represented as the instrument of a personal god.

l. 5   *We are thy offspring*; perhaps rather, *They* are thy offspring (see von Arnim, ad loc.). A similar statement was made by Aratus of Soli (*Phaenomena* 5), and quoted by Paul at Athens (Acts 17. 28).

l. 14   *Save that which the wicked do.* Evil is the revolt of men against the divine Logos, or law; God cannot be held responsible for it.

68

Chrysippus, *Fragment* (in von Arnim, op. cit. II (1964)) 625

The Stoics say that when the planets return, at certain fixed periods of time, to the same relative positions, in length and breadth, which they had at the beginning, when the cosmos was first constituted, this produces the conflagration and destruction of everything which
5   exists. Then again the cosmos is restored anew in a precisely similar arrangement as before. The stars again move in their orbits, each performing its revolution in the former period, without any variation. Socrates and Plato and each individual man will live again, with the same friends and fellow-citizens. They will go through the
10   same experiences and the same activities. Every city and village and field will be restored, just as it was. And this restoration of the universe takes place, not once, but over and over again—indeed to all eternity without end. Those of the gods who are not subject to destruction, having observed the course of one period, know from
15   this everything which is going to happen in all subsequent periods. For there will never be any new thing other than that which has been before, but everything is repeated down to the minutest detail.

l. 1   *The planets.* The fatalistic belief in destiny (above, **64**) was closely bound up with astrology; there is no doubt that the regular unalterable movement of the stars was a most impressive and influential phenomenon.

l. 4   *The conflagration and destruction.* See above, **65**. History was a succession of cycles, each exactly the same as the last.

69

Chrysippus, *Fragment* 1169. On the problem of evil

There can be nothing more inept than the people who suppose that good could have existed without the existence of evil. Good and evil being antithetical, both must needs subsist in opposition, each serving, as it were, by its contrary pressure as a prop to the other. No contrary,

5 in fact can exist, without its correlative contrary. How could there
be any meaning in 'justice', unless there were such things as wrongs?
What *is* justice but the prevention of injustice? What could anyone
understand by 'courage', but for the antithesis of cowardice? Or by
'continence', but for that of self-indulgence? What room for
10 prudence, unless there was imprudence? Why do not such men in
their folly go on to ask that there should be such a thing as truth, and
not such a thing as falsehood? The same may be said of good and
evil, felicity and inconvenience, pleasure and pain. These things are
tied, as Plato puts it, each to the other, by their heads: if you take
15 away one, you take away the other.

70

Chrysippus, *Fragment* 1192

If there are gods and they do not declare to men beforehand future
events, either (1) they do not love men, or (2) they are themselves
ignorant of the future, or (3) they do not consider that it is to man's
interest to have knowledge of the future, or (4) they do not think
5 that it sorts with their dignity to foreshow the future to men, or (5)
the gods themselves have not the power to do it. But (1) it is not the
case that they do not love us, being beneficent and friends of
mankind; (2) they cannot be ignorant of things which they
themselves have instituted and ordained; (3) it *is* to our interest to
10 know what is going to happen, for we shall act more prudently, if
we know; (4) the gods cannot think such disclosure beneath their
dignity, for nothing is of higher worth than to do good; and lastly
(5) divination regarding the future cannot lie outside their power.
To suppose, then, that there are gods and that they do not give signs
15 of the future, is impossible. But there are gods. Therefore they must
give signs of the future. Further, if they give signs, it cannot be that
they give us no means of reading those signs; for in that case they
would give signs to no purpose. If they give us the means, we cannot
deny the existence of divination. Therefore divination is a reality.

l. 9 They themselves have instituted and ordained. That all things have been
predestined by the 'gods' is a popular way of saying that all things happen in
accordance with universal reason. The Stoics were thus able to defend the
popular belief in divination.

71

Posidonius, *apud Sextus Empiricus, adv. Math.* vii. 93

Just as light, Posidonius says, explaining Plato's *Timaeus*, is
apprehended by the vision, which is itself of luminous quality, just as
a voice is apprehended by the hearing, which is itself of airy quality,

so the Nature of the Universe ought to be apprehended by the
5 Reason, which is akin to it.

l. I   *Explaining Plato's Timaeus.* Platonism now (with Posidonius) began strongly
to influence Stoicism. The *Timaeus* in particular came to be looked on almost
as Holy Writ, an inspired revelation of the nature of things.

72

Posidonius [Cf. Galen, *De Hippocratis et Platonis Decretis* iv. 7]

The cause of the passions—the cause, that is, of disharmony and of
the unhappy life—is that men do not follow absolutely the daemon
that is in them, which is akin to, and has a like nature with, the
Power governing the whole cosmos, but turn aside after the lower
5 animal principle, and let it run away with them. Those who fail to
see this neither thereby set the cause of the passions in any better
light, nor hold the right belief regarding happiness and concord.
They do not perceive that the very first point in happiness is to be
led in nothing by the irrational, unhappy, godless element in the soul.

l. 2   *The daemon that is in them*, or seminal reason (λόγος σπερματικός; see above,
p. 65); but this force leading to right thought and conduct was now thought
of in more personal terms, and the view of human nature involved becomes
more dualistic. Cf. the 'daemon' of Socrates, by which he was guided.

l. 7   *Happiness and concord, sc.* 'with self and Nature' (Bevan).

Stoic Ethics

It has already been stated that Stoicism was from the beginning a moral
philosophy; but the earlier Stoics engaged in a speculative physics which,
though it was by no means abandoned by their successors in the Roman
period, retreated into the background, ethical interests becoming more
and more predominant as Stoicism became the prevailing philosophy of
the ever practical Romans. Epictetus was a lame slave belonging to
Epaphroditus, himself a freedman of Nero's. He was allowed to study
philosophy, and eventually emancipated. He was born in Asia Minor,
came to Rome, and later settled at Nicopolis in Epirus. The exact dates of
his life cannot be determined, but he was already active as a philosopher
in AD 89, and survived till towards the middle of the second century.
Marcus Aurelius Antoninus was emperor of Rome from AD 161 to 180.
From an early age he was marked for high distinction, and enjoyed all that
wealth and position could afford. These things, however, meant nothing
to him in comparison with the virtuous life of a moral philosopher, and
he was perhaps history's nearest approach to the ideal of the philosopher-

king. 'It is a striking testimony to the wide range of Stoic influence that it should have found its highest expression in a Roman Emperor and a Greek slave, both finding common ground in the Stoic doctrine and the language of the later Greek world' (P. E. Matheson, *Epictetus, The Discourses and Manual* (Oxford 1916) i. 13).

73

Epictetus, *Discourses* I, xvi. 1–8, 15–21. On Providence

Marvel not that the other creatures have their bodily needs supplied— not only meat and drink, but a bed to lie on—and that they want no shoes nor rugs nor clothes, while we want all these things. For it would not have been a good thing that these creatures, born not for
5 themselves but for service, should have been created liable to wants. Consider what it would be for us to have to take thought not only for ourselves but for sheep and asses, how they were to dress and what shoes they were to put on, and how they should find meat and drink. But just as soldiers when they appear before their general are
10 ready shod, and clothed and armed, and it would be a strange thing indeed if the tribune had to go round and shoe or clothe his regiment, so also nature has made the creatures that are born for service ready and prepared and able to dispense with any attention. So one small child can drive sheep with a rod.
15 Yet we forbear to give thanks that we have not to pay the same attention to them as to ourselves, and proceed to complain against God on our own account. I declare, by Zeus and all the gods, one single fact of nature would suffice to make him that is reverent and grateful realize the providence of God: no great matter, I mean; take
20 the mere fact that milk is produced from grass and cheese from milk and wool from skin. Who is it that has created or contrived these things?

'No one', he says.

Oh, the depth of man's stupidity and shamelessness! . . .
25 If we had sense we ought to do nothing else, in public and in private, than praise and bless God and pay him due thanks. Ought we not, as we dig and plough and eat, to sing the hymn to God? 'Great is God that he gave us these instruments wherewith we shall till the earth. Great is God that he has given us hands, and power to
30 swallow, and a belly, and the power to grow without knowing it, and to draw our breath in sleep.' At every moment we ought to sing these praises and above all the greatest and divinest praise, that God gave us the faculty to comprehend these gifts and to use the way of reason.
35 More than that: since most of you are walking in blindness, should

there not be some one to discharge this duty and sing praises to God for all? What else can a lame old man as I am do but chant the praise of God? If, indeed, I were a nightingale I should sing as a nightingale, if a swan, as a swan: but as I am a rational creature I must praise God.

40 This is my task, and I do it: and I will not abandon this duty, so long as it is given me; and I invite you all to join in this same song.

l. 39   A rational creature, λογικός, endowed with λόγος and therefore corresponding to the divine nature of things.

74

Epictetus, *Discourses* II, viii. 9–14

Will you not then seek the true nature of the good in that, the want of which makes you refuse to predicate good in other things?

'What do you mean? Are not they too God's works?'

They are, but not his principal works, nor parts of the Divine. But
5 you are a principal work, a fragment of God himself, you have in yourself a part of him. Why then are you ignorant of your high birth? Why do you not know whence you have come? Will you not remember, when you eat, who you are that eat, and whom you are feeding, and the same in your relations with women? When you
10 take part in society, or training, or conversation, do you not know that it is God you are nourishing and training? You bear God about with you, poor wretch, and know it not. Do you think I speak of some external god of silver or gold? No, you bear him about within you and are unaware that you are defiling him with unclean thoughts
15 and foul actions. If an image of God were present, you would not dare to do any of the things you do; yet when God himself is present within you and sees and hears all things, you are not ashamed of thinking and acting thus: O slow to understand your nature, and estranged from God!

l. 3   They too, secondary objects, which show God's providence in that they are equipped with properties that make them serviceable to us; see **73** above.

l. 5   A fragment of God himself, in that there is within you a spark or seed of that universal λόγος which is God.

75

Epictetus, *Discourses* IV, i. 1–23, 128–31

That man is free, who lives as he wishes, who is proof against compulsion and hindrance and violence, whose impulses are untrammelled, who gets what he wills to get and avoids what he wills to avoid.

5   Who then would live in error?

No one.

Who would live deceived, reckless, unjust, intemperate, querulous, abject?

No one.

10 No bad man then lives as he would, and so no bad man is free.

Who would live in a state of distress, fear, envy, pity, failing in the will to get and in the will to avoid?

No one.

Do we then find any bad man without distress or fear, above 15 circumstance, free from failure?

None. Then we find none free.

If a man who has been twice consul hear this, he will forgive you if you add, 'But *you* are wise, this does not concern you.' But if you tell him the truth, saying, 'You are just as much a slave yourself as 20 those who have been thrice sold', what can you expect but a flogging?

'How can I be a slave?' he says; 'my father is free, my mother is free, no one has bought me; nay, I am a senator, and a friend of Caesar, I have been consul and have many slaves.'

In the first place, most excellent senator, perhaps your father too 25 was a slave of the same kind as you, yes and your mother and your grandfather and the whole line of your ancestors. And if really they were ever so free, how does that affect you? What does it matter if they had a fine spirit, when you have none, if they were fearless and you are a coward, if they were self-controlled and you are 30 intemperate?

'Nay, what has this to do with being a slave?' he replies.

Does it seem to you slavery to act against your will, under compulsion and with groaning?

'I grant you that,' he says, 'but who can compel me except Caesar, 35 who is lord of all?'

Why, then, your own lips confess that you have one master: you must not comfort yourself with the thought that he is, as you say, the common master of all, but realize that you are a slave in a large household. You are just like the people of Nicopolis, who are wont 40 to cry aloud, 'By Caesar's fortune, we are free.'

However, let us leave Caesar for the moment if you please, but tell me this: Did you never fall in love with any one, with a girl, or a boy, or a slave, or a free man?

'What has that to do with slavery or freedom?'

45 Were you never commanded by her you loved to do anything you did not wish? Did you never flatter your precious slave-boy? Did you never kiss his feet? Yet if any one compel you to kiss Caesar's, you count it an outrage, the very extravagance of tyranny. What is this if not slavery? Did you never go out at night where you 50 did not wish, and spend more than you wished and utter words of

lamentation and groaning? Did you put up with being reviled and
shut out? If you are ashamed to confess your own story, see what
Thrasonides says and does: he had served in as many campaigns or
more perhaps than you and yet, first of all, he has gone out at night,
55   at an hour when Getas does not dare to go, nay, if he were forced by
his master to go, he would have made a loud outcry and have gone
with lamentations over his cruel slavery, and then, what does he say?

A worthless girl has made a slave of me,
Whom never foe subdued.

60   Poor wretch, to be a slave to a paltry girl and a worthless one too!
Why do you call yourself free then any more? Why do you boast of
your campaigns? Then he asks for a sword, and is angry with the
friend who refuses it out of goodwill, and sends gifts to the girl who
hates him, and falls to praying and weeping, and then again when he
65   has a little luck he is exultant. How can we call him free when he has
not learnt to give up desire and fear? ...

Come now and let us review the conclusions we have agreed to.
He is free, whom none can hinder, the man who can deal with things
as he wishes. But the man who can be hindered or compelled or
70   fettered or driven into anything against his will, is a slave. And who
is he whom none can hinder? The man who fixes his aim on nothing
that is not his own. And what does 'not his own' mean? All that it
does not lie in our power to have or not to have, or to have of a
particular quality or under particular conditions. The body then does
75   not belong to us, its parts do not belong to us, our property does not
belong to us. If then you set your heart on one of these as though it
were your own, you will pay the penalty deserved by him who
desires what does not belong to him. The road that leads to freedom,
the only release from slavery is this, to be able to say with your
80   whole soul:

Lead me, O Zeus, and lead me, Destiny,
Whither ordainéd is by your decree.

76

Marcus Aurelius, *To Himself* ii. 1

Say to thyself at daybreak: I shall come across the busybody, the
thankless, the bully, the treacherous, the envious, the unneighbourly.
All this has befallen them because they know not good from evil.
But I, in that I have comprehended the nature of the Good that it is
5   beautiful, and the nature of Evil that it is ugly, and the nature of the
wrong-doer himself that it is akin to me, not as partaker of the same
blood and seed but of intelligence and a morsel of the Divine, can
neither be injured by any of them—for no one can involve me in
what is debasing—nor can I be wroth with my kinsman and hate

10   him. For we have come into being for co-operation, as have the feet, the hands, the eyelids, the rows of upper and lower teeth. Therefore to thwart one another is against Nature; and we do thwart one another by shewing resentment and aversion.

l. 1   *Say to thyself at daybreak.* Marcus's meditations (addressed to himself) are characteristically full of counsels for the discipline and culture of the moral life.

l. 8   *No one can involve me in what is debasing*: that is, against my will. Others may injure my body, but I only can debase myself.

77
Marcus Aurelius, *To Himself* iii. 7

Prize not anything as being to thine interest that shall ever force thee to break thy troth, to surrender thine honour, to hate, suspect, or curse any one, to play the hypocrite, to lust after anything that needs walls and curtains. For he that has chosen before all else his own
5 intelligence and good 'genius', and to be a devotee of its supreme worth, does not strike a tragic attitude or whine, nor will he ask for either a wilderness or a concourse of men; above all he will live neither chasing anything nor shunning it. And he recks not at all whether he is to have his soul imprisoned in his body for a longer or
10 a shorter span of time, for even if he must take his departure at once, he will go as willingly as if he were to discharge any other function that can be discharged with decency and orderliness, making sure through life of this one thing, that his thoughts should not in any case assume a character out of keeping with a rational and civic
15 creature.

l. 14   *A rational and civic creature*, νοερὸν καὶ πολιτικὸν ζῷον. That man is, or should be, a creature of intelligence (νοῦς) is of course common to all the Stoics; that Marcus insists upon his social obligations is not indeed peculiar to but is characteristic of him. Cf. **79, 80** below.

78
Marcus Aurelius, *To Himself* iv. 7

Efface the opinion, *I am harmed*, and at once the feeling of being harmed disappears; efface the feeling, and the harm disappears at once.

79

Marcus Aurelius, *To Himself* vi. 54

That which is not in the interests of the hive cannot be in the interests of the bee.

80

Marcus Aurelius, *To Himself* viii. 34

Thou hast seen a hand cut off or a foot, or a head severed from the trunk, and lying at some distance from the rest of the body. Just so does the man treat himself, as far as he may, who wills not what befalls and severs himself from mankind or acts unsocially. Say thou
5 hast been torn away in some sort from the unity of Nature; for by the law of thy birth thou wast a part; but now thou hast cut thyself off. Yet here comes in that exquisite provision, that thou canst return again to thy unity. To no other part has God granted this, to come together again, when once separated and cleft asunder. Aye, behold
10 his goodness, wherewith he hath glorified man! For he hath let it rest with a man that he be never rent away from the Whole, and if he do rend himself away, to return again and grow onto the rest and take up his position again as part.

81

Marcus Aurelius, *To Himself* xii. 35f

Not even death can bring terror to him who regards that alone as good which comes in due season, and to whom it is all one whether his acts in obedience to right reason are few or many, and a matter of indifference whether he look upon the world for a longer or a shorter
5 time.
    Man, thou hast been a citizen in this World-City, what matters it to thee if for five years or a hundred? For under its laws equal treatment is meted out to all. What hardship then is there in being banished from the city, not by a tyrant or an unjust judge but by
10 Nature who settled thee in it? So might a praetor who commissions a comic actor, dismiss him from the stage. *But I have not played my five acts, but only three.* Very possibly, but in life three acts count as a full play. For he, that is responsible for thy composition originally and thy dissolution now, decides when it is complete. But thou art
15 responsible for neither. Depart then with a good grace, for he that dismisses thee is gracious.

l. 1   *Not even death* ... These are the last words of Marcus's book.

l. 6   *A citizen of this World-City.* Since all men were related by their common participation in logos it was more reasonable (according to the Stoics) to think of oneself as a citizen of the world than of any single state. The relationship especially between the wise and good cuts across all frontiers.

Aristotle

Of this great and influential philosopher all that will be given here is one passage which gives a small illustration of his logic and of his careful attention to the definition of words.

82

Nicomachean Ethics V, iv. 7–12

This is why when disputes occur men have recourse to a judge. To go to a judge is to go to justice, for the ideal judge is so to speak justice personified. Also, men require a judge to be a middle term or *medium*—indeed in some places judges are called mediators—, for
5 they think that if they get the mean they will get what is just. Thus the just is a sort of mean, inasmuch as the judge is a medium between the litigants.

Now the judge restores equality: if we represent the matter by a line divided into two unequal parts, he takes away from the greater
10 segment that portion by which it exceeds one-half of the whole line, and adds it to the lesser segment. When the whole has been divided into two halves, people then say that they 'have their own', having got what is equal. This is indeed the origin of the word *dikaion* (just): it means *dicha* (in half), as if one were to pronounce it *dichaion*; and a
15 *dikast* (judge) is a *dichast* (halver). The equal is a mean by way of arithmetical proportion between the greater and the less. For when of two equals a part is taken from the one and added to the other, the latter will exceed the former by twice that part, since if it had been taken from the one but not added to the other, the latter would
20 exceed the former by once the part in question only. Therefore the latter will exceed the mean by once the part, and the mean will exceed the former, from which the part was taken, by once that part. This process then will enable us to ascertain what we ought to take away from the party that has too much and what to add to the one
25 that has too little: we must add to the one that has too little the amount whereby the mean between them exceeds him, and take away from the greatest of the three the amount by which the mean is exceeded by him. Let the lines AA′, BB′, CC′ be equal to one another; let the segment AE be taken away from the line AA′, and
30 let the segment CD be added to be added to the line CC′, so that the whole line DCC′ exceeds the line EA′ by CD + CF; then DCC′ will exceed BB′ by CD.

```
         A       E                      A′

         B                              B′

    D    C       F                      C′
```

l. 1 *Judge*, δικαστής.

l. 2 *Justice*, τὸ δίκαιον.

l. 3 *Justice personified*, δίκαιον ἔμψυχον.

l. 4 *Medium*, μέσον.

Epicurus

Stoics and Epicureans resembled one another more closely than either party would allow. Both saw that in a chaotic world the only way to peace was the disciplining of desire. Epicurus (*c.* 342–270 BC), though often called an atheist, did not deny the existence of gods, but taught that as they are beings who themselves enjoy continual bliss they will never cause harm or suffering to men; there is nothing to fear from them, but neither can they be placated or cajoled—if they listened to all the prayers men offer the whole race would come to an end, so foolish and contradictory are the petitions they would hear. Suffering does come to men, but it can be endured, as Epicurus himself had proved, not merely with 'Stoicism' but with happiness. Severe pains are short; lasting pains are rarely severe. Moreover, pains can never hurt us if our minds are abstracted from them. Pleasure (Epicurus does not mean sensual or individualist pleasure) is the chief good; and it can be attained by those who seek it wisely. In Physics, Epicurus taught an atomic system. Lucretius, who is quoted here, was a Roman Epicurean (*c.* 99–55 BC) who found, as many did, in the teaching of Epicurus so great a relief from fear and distress that he could express it only in the language of religion; Epicurus was a Saviour—from religion.

83

Lucretius, *On the Nature of Things* i. 62–79

> When Man's life upon earth in base dismay,
> Crushed by the burthen of Religion, lay,
> Whose face, from all the regions of the sky,
> Hung, glaring hate upon mortality,
> 5 First one Greek man against her dared to raise
> His eyes, against her strive through all his days;
> Him noise of gods nor lightnings nor the roar

Of raging heaven subdued, but pricked the more
His spirit's valiance, till he longed the Gate
10   To burst of this low prison of man's fate.
And thus the living ardour of his mind
Conquered, and clove its way; he passed behind
The world's last flaming wall, and through the whole
Of space uncharted ranged his mind and soul.
15   Whence, conquering, he returned to make Man see
At last what can, what cannot, come to be;
By what law to each Thing its power hath been
Assigned, and what deep boundary set between;
Till underfoot is tamed religion trod,
20   And, by his victory, Man ascends to God.

l. 2   *The burthen of Religion.* Religion consisted in the multifarious rites, prayers, and sacrifices necessary to propitiate the gods and ensure their favour.

84

Epicurus, *Epistle to Menoeceus* 123ff., 127*b*–132

The things which I used unceasingly to commend to you, these do and practise, considering them to be the first principles of the good life. First of all believe that god is a being immortal and blessed, even as the common idea of a god is engraved on men's minds, and do not
5   assign to him anything alien to his immortality or ill-suited to his blessedness: but believe about him everything that can uphold his blessedness and immortality. For gods there are, since the knowledge of them is by clear vision. But they are not such as the many believe them to be: for indeed they do not consistently represent them as
10   they believe them to be. And the impious man is not he who denies the gods of the many, but he who attaches to the gods the beliefs of the many. For the statements of the many about the gods are not conceptions derived from sensation, but false suppositions, according to which the greatest misfortunes befall the wicked and the greatest
15   blessings [the good] by the gift of the gods. For men being accustomed always to their own virtues welcome those like themselves, but regard all that is not of their nature as alien.

Become accustomed to the belief that death is nothing to us. For all good and evil consists in sensation, but death is deprivation of
20   sensation. And therefore a right understanding that death is nothing to us makes the mortality of life enjoyable, not because it adds to it an infinite span of time, but because it takes away the craving for immortality. For there is nothing terrible in life for the man who has truly comprehended that there is nothing terrible in not living. So
25   that the man speaks but idly who says that he fears death not because

it will be painful when it comes, but because it is painful in anticipation. For that which gives no trouble when it comes, is but an empty pain in anticipation. So death, the most terrifying of ills, is nothing to us, since so long as we exist, death is not with us; but
30 when death comes, then we do not exist. It does not then concern either the living or the dead, since for the former it is not, and the latter are no more. . . .

   We must consider that of desires some are natural, others vain, and of the natural some are necessary and others merely natural; and of
35 the necessary some are necessary for happiness, others for the repose of the body, and others for very life. The right understanding of these facts enables us to refer all choice and avoidance to the health of the body and [the soul's] freedom from disturbance, since this is the aim of the life of blessedness. For it is to obtain this end that we
40 always act, namely, to avoid pain and fear. And when this is once secured for us, all the tempest of the soul is dispersed, since the living creature has not to wander as though in search of something that is missing, and to look for some other thing by which he can fulfil the good of the soul and the good of the body. For it is then that we have
45 need of pleasure, when we feel pain owing to the absence of pleasure; [but when we do not feel pain], we no longer need pleasure. And for this cause we call pleasure the beginning and end of the blessed life. For we recognize pleasure as the first good innate in us, and from pleasure we begin every act of choice and avoidance, and to pleasure
50 we return again, using the feeling as the standard by which we judge every good.

   And since pleasure is the first good and natural to us, for this reason we do not choose every pleasure, but sometimes we pass over many pleasures, when greater discomfort accrues to us as the result of them:
55 and similarly we think many pains better than pleasures, since a greater pleasure comes to us when we have endured pains for a long time. Every pleasure then because of its natural kinship to us is good, yet not every pleasure is to be chosen: even as every pain also is an evil, yet not all are always of a nature to be avoided. Yet by a scale of
60 comparison and by the consideration of advantages and disadvantages we must form our judgement on all these matters. For the good on certain occasions we treat as bad, and conversely the bad as good.

   And again independence of desire we think a great good—not that we may at all times enjoy but a few things, but that, if we do not
65 possess many, we may enjoy the few in the genuine persuasion that those have the sweetest pleasure in luxury who least need it, and that all that is natural is easy to be obtained, but that which is superfluous is hard. And so plain savours bring us a pleasure equal to a luxurious diet, when all the pain due to want is removed; and bread and water
70 produce the highest pleasure, when one who needs them puts them

to his lips. To grow accustomed therefore to simple and not luxurious diet gives us health to the full, and makes a man alert for the needful employments of life, and when after long intervals we approach luxuries disposes us better towards them, and fits us to be fearless of
75 fortune.

When, therefore, we maintain that pleasure is the end, we do not mean the pleasures of profligates and those that consist in sensuality, as is supposed by some who are either ignorant or disagree with us or do not understand, but freedom from pain in the body and from
80 trouble in the mind. For it is not continuous drinkings and revellings, nor the satisfaction of lusts, nor the enjoyment of fish and other luxuries of the wealthy table, which produce a pleasant life, but sober reasoning, searching out the motives for all choice and avoidance, and banishing mere opinions, to which are due the greatest disturbance
85 of the spirit.

l. 14 *The greatest misfortunes . . . the greatest blessings.* On the contrary, there is nothing either to hope or to fear from the gods. By recognizing what is necessary and what is not man is delivered from the chains of destiny (cf. **64**).

l. 38 *Freedom from disturbance,* ἀταραξία, the Epicurean goal.

l. 80 *For it is not . . .* The common modern use of the adjective 'Epicurean' is a slander upon Epicurus.

The Philosophic Missionary

In the age of the New Testament philosophy was not exclusively the affair of the study and university. It was essentially practical, and was intended to be practised. The teachers of philosophy saw their own beliefs as the needed cure for men's ills and proceeded to offer them to the public. The philosopher became a street-corner orator, and the Cynics in particular preached their 'gospel' to all who would listen (see above, **24, 25**), and it was often delivered—and received—less as a reasoned system of beliefs about the universe than as a divine revelation. The philosopher became a figure who may have contributed something to the New Testament picture of the apostles, especially as he took on the role of sufferer and martyr (see above, **62**), and at the same time that of one who was more than human, a divine man (θεῖος ἀνήρ).

85

Epictetus, *Discourses* III, xxii. 19–26

First then you must make your Governing Principle pure, and hold fast this rule of life, 'Henceforth my mind is the material I have to

work on, as the carpenter has his timber and the shoemaker his leather: my business is to deal with my impressions aright. My
5 wretched body is nothing to me, its parts are nothing to me. Death? Let it come when it will, whether to my whole body or to a part of it. Exile? Can one be sent into exile beyond the Universe? One cannot. Wherever I go, there is the sun, there is the moon, there are the stars, dreams, auguries, conversation with the gods.'
10   The true Cynic when he has ordered himself thus cannot be satisfied with this: he must know that he is sent as a messenger from God to men concerning things good and evil, to show them that they have gone astray and are seeking the true nature of good and evil where it is not to be found, and take no thought where it really
15 is: he must realize, in the words of Diogenes when brought before Philip after the battle of Chaeronea, that he is sent 'to reconnoitre'. For indeed the Cynic has to discover what things are friendly to men and what are hostile: and when he has accurately made his observations he must return and report the truth, not driven by fear
20 to point out enemies where there are none, nor in any other way disturbed or confounded by his impressions.

He must then be able, if chance so offer, to come forward on the tragic stage, and with a loud voice utter the words of Socrates: 'Oh race of men, whither are ye hurrying? What are you doing, miserable
25 creatures? You wander up and down like blind folk: you have left the true path and go away on a vain errand, you seek peace and happiness elsewhere, where it is not to be found, and believe not when another shows the way.'

l. 16 *To reconnoitre,* as a spy (κατάσκοπος). The philosopher discovers, for example, that there is nothing to fear in death, and he communicates his knowledge to the main army of men.

86

Philostratus, *Life of Apollonius* i. 17

When a certain quibbler asked him, why he asked no questions of him, he replied: 'Because I asked questions when I was a stripling; and it is not my business to ask questions now, but to teach people what I have discovered.' 'How then,' the other asked him afresh, 'O
5 Apollonius, should the sage converse?' 'Like a law-giver,' he replied, 'for it is the duty of the law-giver to deliver to the many the instructions of whose truth he has persuaded himself.' This was the line he pursued during his stay in Antioch, and he converted to himself the most unrefined people.

l. 1   *A certain quibbler asked him,* that is, Apollonius. Apollonius of Tyana lived
through most of the first Christian century. The *Life* by Philostratus
published some time after AD 2 1 7, contains legendary material but probably
conveys a not altogether false impression of this very impressive Pythagorean
philosopher, who travelled extensively, worked miracles, and taught
everywhere.

87

Philostratus, *Life of Apollonius* iv. 20

Now while he was discussing the question of libations, there chanced
to be present in his audience a young dandy who bore so evil a
reputation for licentiousness, that his conduct had once been the
subject of coarse street-corner songs. His home was Corcyra, and he
5 traced his pedigree to Alcinous the Phaeacian who entertained
Odysseus. Apollonius then was talking about libations, and was
urging them not to drink out of a particular cup, but to reserve it for
the gods, without ever touching it or drinking out of it. But when
he also urged them to have handles on the cup, and to pour the
10 libation over the handle, because that is the part of the cup at which
men are least likely to drink, the youth burst out into loud and coarse
laughter, and quite drowned his voice. Then Apollonius looked up
at him and said: 'It is not yourself that perpetrates this insult, but the
demon, who drives you on without your knowing it.' And in fact
15 the youth was, without knowing it, possessed by a devil; for he
would laugh at things that no one else laughed at, and then he would
fall to weeping for no reason at all, and he would talk and sing to
himself. Now most people thought that it was the boisterous humour
of youth which led him into such excesses; but he was really the
20 mouthpiece of a devil, though it only seemed a drunken frolic in
which on that occasion he was indulging. Now when Apollonius
gazed on him, the ghost in him began to utter cries of fear and rage,
such as one hears from people who are being branded or racked; and
the ghost swore that he would leave the young man alone and never
25 take possession of any man again. But Apollonius addressed him with
anger, as a master might a shifty, rascally, and shameless slave and so
on, and he ordered him to quit the young man and show by a visible
sign that he had done so. 'I will throw down yonder statue,' said the
devil, and pointed to one of the images which was in the king's
30 portico, for there it was that the scene took place. But when the statue
began by moving gently, and then fell down, it would defy anyone
to describe the hubbub which arose thereat and the way they clapped
their hands with wonder. But the young man rubbed his eyes as
though he had just woke up, and he looked towards the rays of the
35 sun, and won the consideration of all who now had turned their

attention to him; for he no longer showed himself licentious, nor did he stare madly about, but he had returned to his own self, as thoroughly as if he had been treated with drugs; and he gave up his dainty dress and summery garments and the rest of his sybaritic way
40 of life, and he fell in love with the austerity of philosophers, and donned their cloak, and stripping off his old self modelled his life in future upon that of Apollonius.

l. 40   *He fell in love with the austerity of philosophers.* The similarity between this narrative of exorcism and conversion and some of the New Testament stories appears in several places.

88

Philostratus, *Life of Apollonius* v. 24

Such were his experiences in Rhodes, and others ensued in Alexandria, as soon as his voyage ended there. Even before he arrived Alexandria was in love with him, and its inhabitants longed to see Apollonius as one friend longs for another; and as the people of Upper Egypt are
5 intensely religious they too prayed him to visit their several societies. For owing to the fact that so many come hither and mix with us from Egypt, while an equal number pass hence to visit Egypt, Apollonius was already celebrated among them and the ears of the Egyptians were literally pricked up to hear him. It is no exaggeration
10 to say that, as he advanced from the ship into the city, they gazed upon him as if he was a god, and made way for him in the alleys, as they would for priests carrying the sacraments. As he was being thus escorted with more pomp than if he had been a governor of the country, he met twelve men who were being led to execution on the
15 charge of being bandits; he looked at them and said: 'They are not all guilty, for this one,' and he gave his name, 'has been falsely accused or he would not be going with you.' And to the executioners by whom they were being led, he said: 'I order you to relax your pace and bring them to the ditch a little more leisurely, and to put this
20 one to death last of all, for he is guiltless of the charge; but you would anyhow act with more piety, if you spared them for a brief portion of the day, since it were better not to slay them at all.' And withal he dwelt upon this theme at what was for him unusual length. And the reason for his doing so was immediately shown; for when eight of
25 them had had their heads cut off, a man on horseback rode up to the ditch, and shouted: 'Spare Pharion; for', he added, 'he is no robber, but he gave false evidence against himself from fear of being racked, and others of them in their examination under torture have acknowledged that he is guiltless.' I need not describe the exultation
30 of Egypt, nor how the people, who were anyhow ready to admire him, applauded him for this action.

89

Apollonius of Tyana, *Epistle iii*

> You have visited the countries that lie between me and Italy,
> beginning from Syria, parading yourself in the so-called royal cities.
> And you had a philosopher's doublet all the time, and a long white
> beard, but besides that nothing. And now how comes it that you are
> 5 returning by sea with a full cargo of silver, of gold, of vases of all
> sorts, of embroidered raiment, of every other sort of ornament, not
> to mention overweening pride, and boasting and unhappiness? What
> cargo is this, and what the purport of these strange purchases? Zeno
> never purchased but dried fruits.

l. 1   *You*, one Euphrates, who for the sake of gain had acted as a travelling
philosopher.

Poetic Comment

For a note on the poets and their significance see above, pp. 58f.
Aristophanes (*c.* 448–*c.* 380 BC) drew satirical pictures of the great men of
his time; in the *Clouds*, of Socrates. The caricature seems bitter, but may
not have been taken too seriously. Plato thought of Aristophanes as a
pleasant and amusing companion who could lighten a conversation that
was getting too serious. Aeschylus (*c.* 525–*c.* 456 BC) fought in the Persian
Wars and wrote about ninety plays, of which seven survive. They show
innovation in stage technique and are plays of destiny, of inherited guilt,
and of the doom that overweening pride (ὕβρις) brings upon itself.
Sophocles (*c.* 496–406 BC) was perhaps the least critical of the great
tragedians; religion he takes for granted, but he is deeply concerned with
character and the clash of duties, as in the passage quoted below. Euripides
(*c.* 485–406 BC) on the other hand was always an independent thinker,
capable of shocking public opinion by criticizing its conventions.

90

Aristophanes, *Clouds* 222–274

> Strepsiades: Socrates! Socrates!
>   Sweet Socrates!
> Socrates: Mortal! Why callest thou me?
> Strepsiades: O, first of all, please tell me what you are doing.
> 5 Socrates: I walk on air, and contemplate the Sun.
> Strepsiades: O then from a basket you contemn the Gods,
>   And not from the earth, at any rate?

Socrates:	Most true.
	I could not have searched out celestial matters
10	Without suspending judgement, and infusing
	My subtle spirit with the kindred air.
	If from the ground I were to seek these things,
	I could not find: so surely doth the earth
	Draw to herself the essence of our thought.
15	The same too is the case with water-cress.
Strepsiades:	Hillo! What's that?
	Thought draws the essence into water-cress?
	Come down, sweet Socrates, more near my level,
	And teach the lessons which I came to learn.
20 Socrates:	And wherefore art thou come?
Strepsiades:	To learn to speak.
	For owing to my horrid debts and duns,
	My goods are seized, I'm robbed, and mobbed, and
	plundered.
Socrates:	How did you get involved with your eyes open?
25 Strepsiades:	A galloping consumption seized my money.
	Come now: do let me learn the unjust Logic
	That can shrink debts: now do just let me learn it.
	Name your own price, by all the Gods I'll pay it.
Socrates:	The Gods! why you must know the Gods with us
30	Don't pass for current coin.
Strepsiades:	Eh? what do you use then?
	Have you got iron, as the Byzantines have?
Socrates:	Come, would you like to learn celestial matters,
	How their truth stands?
35 Strepsiades:	Yes, if there's any truth.
Socrates:	And to hold intercourse with yon bright Clouds,
	Our virgin Goddesses?
Strepsiades:	Yes, that I should.
Socrates:	Then sit you down upon that sacred bed.
40 Strepsiades:	Well, I am sitting.
Socrates:	Here then, take this chaplet.
Strepsiades:	Chaplet? why? why? now, never, Socrates:
	Don't sacrifice poor me, like Athamas.
Socrates:	Fear not: our entrance-services require
45	All to do this.
Strepsiades:	But what am I to gain?
Socrates:	You'll be the flower of talkers, prattlers, gossips:
	Only keep quiet.

Strepsiades:	Zeus! your words come true!
50	I shall be flour indeed with all this peppering.
Socrates:	Old man sit you still, and attend to my will,
	and hearken in peace to my prayer.
	O Master and King, holding earth in your swing,
	O measureless infinite Air;
55	And thou glowing Ether, and Clouds who enwreathe her
	with thunder, and lightning, and storms,
	Arise ye and shine, bright Ladies Divine,
	to your student in bodily forms.
Strepsiades:	No, but stay, no, but stay, just one moment I pray,
60	while my cloak round my temples I wrap.
	To think that I've come, stupid fool, from my home,
	with never a waterproof cap!
Socrates:	Come forth, come forth, dread Clouds, and to earth
	your glorious majesty show;
65	Whether lightly ye rest on the time-honoured crest
	of Olympus environed in snow,
	Or tread the soft dance 'mid the stately expanse
	of Ocean the nymphs to beguile,
	Or stoop to enfold with your pitchers of gold,
70	the mystical waves of the Nile,
	Or around the white foam of Maeotis ye roam,
	or Mimas all wintry and bare,
	O hear while we pray, and turn not away
	from the rites which your servants prepare.

l. 5   Cf. Plato, *Apology.* 19 BC (*Socrates is speaking*): 'I will sum up their words in an affidavit: "Socrates is an evil-doer, and a curious person, who searches into things under the earth and in heaven, and he makes the worse appear the better cause; and he teaches the aforesaid doctrines to others." Such is the accusation, and is just what you have yourselves seen in the comedy of Aristophanes, who has introduced a man whom he calls Socrates, going about and saying that he can walk in the air, and talking a deal of nonsense concerning matters of which I do not pretend to know either much or little—not that I mean to speak disparagingly of any one who is a student of natural philosophy.'

l. 21   The art of speech was a primary subject in ancient education and was taught by the sophists, whom Socrates in some respects resembled, though he distinguished himself from them sharply.

l. 26   *Unjust Logic.* In the *Clouds* Right Logic (δίκαιος λόγος) and Wrong (or Unjust) Logic (ἄδικος λόγος) appear as characters. It is by the latter that, according to the allegation, Socrates proves the worse to be the better cause.

l. 32 Coins made of iron.

l. 41 *Chaplet*—such as might be placed on a sacrificial victim.

l. 57 The clouds approach and threaten rain.

91

Aeschylus, *Eumenides* 752–807

Athena: This man stands acquitted on the charge of murder. The numbers of the casts are equal. (*Apollo disappears.*)

Orestes: O Pallas, O Saviour of my house! I was bereft of fatherland, and it is thou who hast given me a home therein again. And it
5   shall be said in Hellas: 'The man is an Argive once more, and dwells in his father's heritage by grace of Pallas and of Loxias and of that third God, the all-ordaining one, the Saviour'— even he who hath had respect unto my father's death, and preserveth me, seeing that my mother's cause has advocates
10   such as these.

And now I depart unto my home, first unto this thy land and folk having pledged mine oath for the future, even to the fulness of all time to come, that verily no chieftain of my country shall come hither to bear against them the embattled
15   spear. For I myself, then in my grave, will bring it to pass by baffling ill-success, even by visiting their marches with discouragement and their ways with evil omens, that they who violate my present oath shall repent them of their enterprise. But while the straight course is preserved and they hold in
20   everlasting honour this city of Pallas with their confederate spears, I shall be the more graciously disposed unto them.

And so farewell—thou and thy people that guard thy city. May they struggle with thy foes, let none escape, and may it bring thee safety and victory in war. (*Exit.*)

Chorus: Shame! Ye younger gods, ye have ridden down the ancient laws and have wrested them from my grasp! And I, bereft of honour, unhappy that I am, in my grievous wrath, upon this land (and woe unto it!) discharge from my heart venom in requital for my grief, aye venom, in drops its soil shall not
30   endure. And from it a canker, blasting leaf, blasting child (ah! just return!), speeding over the land shall cast upon the ground infection ruinous to human kind. I groan aloud. What shall I do? I am mocked by the people. Intolerable are the wrongs I have suffered. Ah, cruel indeed the wrongs of the woeful
35   daughters of Night, bereft of honour and distressed!

Athena: Let me prevail with you not to bear it with sore lament. For ye have not been vanquished. Nay, the trial resulted fairly in ballots equally divided without disgrace to thee; but from Zeus

was offered testimony clear, and he that himself uttered the
40   oracle himself bore witness that Orestes should not suffer harm
for his deed. And be ye no longer indignant, launch not your
grievous wrath upon this land, nor visit it with unfruitfulness
by discharging drops whose wasting influence will devour the
seed. For I do promise you most sacredly that ye shall occupy a
45   cavernous seat in a righteous land, where by your hearths ye
shall sit on radiant thrones, worshipped with honour by my
burghers here.

l. 1   *This man*, Orestes, the son of Agamemnon and Clytemnestra. Before the
Trojan War Agamemnon sacrificed his daughter Iphigenia in order to secure
favourable conditions for the expedition. Clytemnestra never forgave him,
and when he returned from the war she, now accompanied by her lover
Aegisthus, murdered him. Orestes in revenge murdered his mother, urged
on to the deed by Apollo. Stirred by the ghost of Clytemnestra, the Furies
(Erinyes) seek the condemnation and death of Orestes, who is tried by the
Areopagus court in Athens, accused by the Erinyes, defended by Apollo. The
votes for condemnation and acquittal are equal; Athene (goddess of Athens)
gives her casting vote in favour of Orestes.

l. 11   *My home*, Argos.

l. 25   The Erinyes are incensed that the vote has gone against them and that blood
is not being avenged. Athene in the end succeeds in reconciling them, and
they become the Eumenides, the Kindly Ones. It is not the will of Zeus that
the chain of vengeance should persist for ever.

92

Sophocles, *Antigone* 441–70

	Creon:	Speak, girl, with head bent low and downcast eyes,
		Dost thou plead guilty or deny the deed?
	Antigone:	Guilty. I did it, I deny it not
	Creon:	(*to guard*)
5		Sirrah, begone whither thou wilt, and thank
		Thy luck that thou hast 'scaped a heavy charge.
		(*to Antigone*)
		Now answer this plain question, yes or no,
		Wast thou acquainted with the interdict?
10	Antigone:	I knew, all knew; how should I fail to know?
	Creon:	And yet wert bold enough to break the law?
	Antigone:	Yea, for these laws were not ordained of Zeus,
		And she who sits enthroned with gods below,
		Justice, enacted not these human laws.
15		Nor did I deem that thou, a mortal man,
		Could'st by a breath annul and override

The immutable unwritten laws of Heaven.
They were not born today nor yesterday;
They die not; and none knoweth whence they sprang.

20   I was not like, who feared no mortal's frown,
To disobey these laws and so provoke
The wrath of Heaven. I know that I must die,
E'en hadst thou not proclaimed it; and if death
Is thereby hastened, I shall count it gain.

25   For death is gain to him whose life, like mine,
Is full of misery. Thus my lot appears
Not sad, but blissful; for had I endured
To leave my mother's son unburied there,
I should have grieved with reason, but not now.

30   And if in this thou judgest me a fool,
Methinks the judge of folly's not acquit.

l. 2   *The deed.* Antigone had buried the body of her brother, Polynices, who had been killed in an attack on Thebes, now governed by Creon.

l. 4   The guard had caught Antigone in the act of burying her brother and brought her to Creon.

l. 9   Creon had issued an edict that the bodies of the enemy soldiers, and especially of Polynices, should not be buried. This was a grievous injury, affecting the afterlife.

l. 12   Antigone acts under the conviction that we must obey God rather than men.

l. 24   Antigone uses the word for *gain* (κέρδος) used by Paul in Phil. 1.21.

93

Euripides, *The Trojan Women* 634–683

Andromache: Mother, O mother, a fairer, truer word
Hear, that I may with solace touch thine heart:—
To have been unborn I count as one with death;
But better death than life in bitterness.

5   No pain feels death, which hath no sense of ills:
But who hath prospered, and hath fallen on woe,
Forlorn of soul strays far from olden bliss.
Thy child, as though she ne'er had looked on light,
Is dead, and nothing knoweth of her ills.

10   But I, who drew my bow at fair repute,
Won overmeasure, yet fair fortune missed.
All virtuous fame that women e'er have found,
This was my quest, my gain, 'neath Hector's roof.
First—be the woman smirched with other stain,

15   Or be she not—this very thing shall bring
Ill fame, if one abide not in the home:

So banished I such craving, kept the house:
Within my bowers I suffered not to come
The tinsel-talk of women, lived content
20   To be in virtue schooled by mine own heart;
With silent tongue, with quiet eye, still met
My lord: knew in what matters I should rule,
And where 'twas meet to yield him victory:
Whereof the fame to the Achaean host
25   Reached, for my ruin; for, when I was ta'en,
Achilles' son would have me for his wife—
His slave in mine own husband's murderers' halls!
If from mine heart I thrust my love, mine Hector,
And to this new lord ope the doors thereof,
30   I shall be traitress to the dead: but if
I loathe this prince, shall win my masters' hate.
And yet one night, say they, unknits the knot
Of woman's hate of any husband's couch!
I scorn the wife who flings her sometime lord
35   Away, and on a new couch loves another!
Not even the steed, from her stall-mate disyoked,
Will with a willing spirit draw the yoke;
Yet speech nor understanding in the brute
Is found, whose nature lags behind the man.
40   Thou, O mine Hector, wast my fitting mate
In birth and wisdom, mighty in wealth and valour.
Stainless from my sire's halls thou tookest me,
And first didst yoke with thine my maiden couch.
Now hast thou perished: sea-borne I shall be,
45   Spear-won to Hellas, unto thraldom's yoke.
Hath not the doom then of Polyxena,
Whom thou lamentest, lesser ills than mine?
With me not even is hope, which lingers last
With all: nor with far vision of good I cheat
50   Mine heart, though sweet thereof the day-dream were.

l. 1   *Andromache* had been the wife of Hector, son of Priam, king of Troy, and Hecuba, who is here addressed. Troy has now fallen to the Greeks. Hector is dead; the surviving women are being distributed among the conquerors. Hecuba herself will go to Odysseus, her daughter Cassandra to Agamemnon, Andromache to Neoptolemus, the son of Achilles. Hecuba's other daughter, Polyxena, has been sacrificed on the tomb of Achilles. Astyanax, the child of Andromache and Hector, is to be killed, and before the end of the play his body is brought in and placed in his grandmother's arms. The play surveys and discusses the tragic situation of the women concerned. It gains point— and was intended to gain—from the fact that it was produced in the year (415 BC) in which the Athenians captured the island of Melos, put to death all the men of military age, and sold the remaining inhabitants into slavery.

5   Gnosis and Gnosticism

Not only the origins but even the definition of Gnosticism are matters of dispute. Gnosticism is sometimes defined as the common trend and substance of a group of Christian heresies in the second century. Under this definition it is of course impossible to consider Gnosticism as part of the background of the New Testament; it did not come into existence until after the New Testament was complete. There is much to be said for this definition; it has the merit of objectivity, and the merit too of being related to documents, persons, and events which are capable of being dated. Yet it is not entirely satisfactory, for when this second-century Gnosticism is analysed it shows a number of characteristics to which some New Testament writers appear to be reacting, so that we must conclude that though the developed Christian heresies arose after and to some extent on the basis of the New Testament writings there must already have been in existence, before at least some parts of the New Testament were written, a body of religious thought manifesting at least some of the characteristics of the second-century gnostic movement. Some describe the pre-Christian movement as Gnosticism, others retain that title for the later movement and describe the earlier as Gnosis, others again as Proto-Gnosticism, or some similar term. It matters little what terminology is employed, though it is of fundamental importance that any writer should make absolutely clear how he is using the words in question, and a universally agreed terminology would be very desirable. Here Gnosticism will be used for the Christian deviations of the second and later centuries, Gnosis for the comparable movement of religious thought earlier than and contemporary with the New Testament. This distinction is useful, though its usefulness is diminished by the fact that both nouns must share the one adjective gnostic. And the definition once adopted leaves unanswered a group of questions of very great complexity. What was Gnosis? From what sources is it known? How is it related to Gnosticism?

It is not the purpose of this chapter to answer, or attempt to answer, these questions. In a volume of background documents, however, it must be plainly stated that, though it is as near certain as may be that Gnosis existed, there are no sources that prove that it existed, that tell us exactly what it was, or show its relation to Gnosticism. To a great extent it must be reconstructed from the New Testament, which names it (1 Tim. 6.20), refers to it under other terms (e.g. Col. 2.8), and refers to those who proudly made the claim, I know him (God) (1 John 2.4). It would not be proper to collect New Testament evidence in this book. Most of the passages that will be adduced are drawn inevitably from the later period; some are heretical Christian, others are simply non-Christian. In each case, however, they bear indirect witness to an earlier stage in which Christian, Jewish, Greek, and oriental streams were running together to form the still unco-ordinated and variable forms of Gnosis. In addition to material quoted here Philo is an important witness to the earliest stages of Gnosis; see Chapter 10, and especially **234–7**.

The following passages are arranged in relation to their origin rather than topically, but they should serve to bring out some of the main themes of Gnosis, and to give some indication of the way in which they developed into Gnosticism.

The Hermetic Literature

There have been transmitted from antiquity, mainly through Christian channels, a considerable number of tractates more or less closely connected with the divine person Hermes Trismegistus. Of these, many are simply astrological or magical, and may be discounted. The rest contain a body of teaching which might with equal justice be called religious or philosophical. This teaching, which here and there shows contact with the Greek Old Testament, is an important element in the background of the New Testament.

Hermes Trismegistus (Thrice-Greatest Hermes) is the Greek title of the Egyptian god Thoth. Trismegistus probably represents an Egyptian expression meaning 'very great', and served to distinguish the foreign god from the native Greek Hermes. In most of the tractates Hermes himself, or a similar divine figure, communicates secret knowledge (*gnosis*) about God, about creation, or about salvation, to a disciple, who is sometimes but not always named. The revelation is generally given in the form of a dialogue in which the disciple's share is limited to asking questions and expressing admiration. Prayers and praise addressed to God are also found.

The date of the Hermetic writings cannot be established with certainty, but it seems probable that most of them were composed between AD 100 and 200, though it is by no means impossible that some fall within the first century AD. What is more important is that these literary remains give the impression of being the deposit of many years of oral teaching, as well as of reflection and mystical meditation. It seems very probable, though the matter is not capable of proof, that ideas similar to those contained in the written *Hermetica* were entertained and discussed, in Egypt and perhaps elsewhere, at the time when the New Testament documents were written and when Christianity was spreading westwards from Palestine into the Greek world.

This westward movement of Christianity is to be noted here because the *Hermetica* also represent, in part, the transition of Jewish and Egyptian, that is of Oriental, thoughts into Greek shape and expression. In order to understand the *Hermetica* it is above all necessary to grasp that their authors were men who believed that there had been revealed to them a Gospel which it was their mission to preach to mankind.

The first Hermetic tractate, often called the *Poimandres*, makes this message particularly clear, and most of the passages quoted below are taken from it. 'It tells how the God revealed to his prophet in ecstasy the divine origin of the universe and of man, and commissioned him to preach the way of salvation to mankind in general. It makes use of various forms of religious appeal familiar to us from the literature of Judaism and Christianity—the inspired myth of the beginning of things, the doctrine of immortality, the divine promises and threats of judgement, eschatology, and the call to repentance, concluding with a hymn of praise and aspiration. Its actual teaching is of a type common to most of the *Hermetica*, but this teaching is presented in a more imaginative way than is usual, with more appeal to the emotions, and its address to all who will hear contrasts with the esotericism of some of the other Hermetic writings' (C. H. Dodd, *The Bible and the Greeks* (1935), p. 99). The tractate opens with the appearance of Poimandres, and the disciple's request for knowledge. Thereupon is manifested a vision which teaches the origin of the universe, and, in mythical form, the origin, and hence the nature, of man is revealed. His story is traced from original archetypal man to the present state of empirical fallen humanity. In this way both the cause and character of man's ills are indicated, and with them the way of escape. Leaving behind everything mortal and corruptible the soul must rise through the seven spheres until it enters into God himself and so becomes divine. That this may take place is the Gospel of Poimandres. Having received it the disciple becomes an apostle and preaches to mankind the way of salvation; some refuse it, others accept, and seek instruction. These last the prophet gathers about him and bids them give thanks to God. When they have departed he himself blesses God in a short psalm.

94

Corpus Hermeticum 1. *Poimandres* 1ff. Introduction

> It happened once that, when I had begun to reflect upon the things that are, and my thoughts had been caught up on high, and when my bodily senses had been put under restraint, like those who are

weighed down by sleep resulting from overeating or bodily fatigue,
5 I seemed to see an immense figure of boundless size who was calling
me by name and saying to me, 'What do you wish to hear and to
behold, and, by your thought, to learn and know?' 'Who are you?' I
said. 'I am Poimandres,' said he, 'the Mind of the Sovereignty. I know
what you wish, and I am with you everywhere.' 'I wish', I said, 'to
10 learn the things that are, and to understand their nature, and to know
God; how I wish to hear this!' He replied, 'Keep in your mind the
things you wish to learn, and I will teach you.'

l. 3 *When my bodily senses had been put under restraint.* It is a consequence of the
dualism which plays so large a part in the *Hermetica* (as in much mystical
literature) that spiritual vision is believed to become most acute when bodily
perception ceases. This thought is common (for example) in Philo; thus
Legum Allegoriae iii. 42: It is not possible that he whose abode is in the body
should attain to being with God; this is possible only for him whom God
rescues out of the prison Cf. *Corpus Hermeticum* xiii. 7.

l. 8 *Poimandres, the Mind* (νοῦς) *of the Sovereignty.* This designation is not very
different from what a Christian might have understood by the Word (λόγος)
or Spirit (πνεῦμα) of the supreme God. It is probably incorrect to derive the
name Poimandres from the Greek ποιμήν (shepherd), ἀνήρ (man). It is rather
a Greek form of the Coptic *p-eimi-n-re*, 'the knowledge of the [sun-] God'.
For such a name cf. Manda dḤaiyê, 'the knowledge of life' (or salvation), the
name given by the Mandaeans to the saviour and revealer.

l. 10 *To learn the things that are, and to understand their nature, and to know God.* It
would be difficult to sum up more comprehensively and clearly the goal at
which the Hermetists aimed and which they believed they had in some
measure attained. Knowledge of God was everything; 'this alone brings
salvation to man, the knowledge of God (ἡ γνῶσις τοῦ θεοῦ)' (*Corpus
Hermeticum* x. 15).

95

Corpus Hermeticum 1. *Poimandres* 4ff., 9. Cosmogony

When he had said this his aspect changed. Everything was opened to
me in a moment, and I beheld a boundless vision; all became light, a
calm and joyous light, and when I saw it I was captivated by it. And
after a little there came in its turn a downwardbearing darkness,
5 terrible and grim, twisted in crooked spirals, like (it seemed to me) a
snake. Then the darkness changed into a wet nature, unspeakably
agitated and giving forth smoke, as from a fire, and producing an
unutterable mournful sound. Then was sent out from it an inarticulate
cry, like (it seemed) the noise of a fire, and coming from the light . . .
10 a holy Word assailed the nature, and fire unmixed leapt up from the
wet nature towards the height. It was light and swift, and at the same
time active, and the air, being light, followed the [fiery] breath,
ascending from the earth and water as far as the fire, so that it seemed

to be suspended from it; but the earth and water remained in their
15 place mingled together, so that the earth could not be distinguished
from the water. Earth and water were kept in motion by the breath-
like word which was rushing audibly over them.

Then said Poimandres to me, 'Have you understood what this
vision means?' 'I shall know it,' I said. 'That light', said he, 'am I,
20 Mind, thy God, who was before the wet nature which appeared out
of darkness; the luminous Word which came forth from Mind is son
of God,' 'What then?' 'You must understand it thus. That which sees
and hears in you is the word of the Lord, and your mind is God the
Father. These are not separated one from another, for the union of
25 them is life.' 'Thank you,' I said. 'But now', he went on, 'consider the
light and understand that.' . . .

Then Mind (or God), being bisexual, existing as life and light,
generated by a word another Mind, as Demiurge. The latter, being
god of fire and breath, created seven administrators, who in their
30 orbits envelop the world of sense perception. Their administration is
called Destiny.

ll. 2, 4   All became light . . . a downward-bearing darkness. Dualism is naturally
expressed in terms of light and darkness. The myth of Gen. 1 is recalled, but
here light, not darkness, is mentioned first, because, as will be stated below,
the light *is* God. Darkness and light are in the beginning distinct. The origin
of the empirical universe, and of empirical humanity, lies in the mingling of
the two.

l. 10   A holy word assailed the nature. It is, as in the biblical narrative, the divine
word that produces coherent activity in the wet nature (or chaos).

*l. 16   Earth and water were kept in motion by the breath-like word which was rushing
audibly over them.* Here the dependence of the Hermetist upon Genesis (1. 2)
is particularly clear, both in language and in the substance of the thought. In
Genesis the Spirit of God (πνεῦμα θεοῦ) is said to have been rushing over
(ἐπεφέρετο) the water. In the *Hermetica* πνεῦμα has not the same meaning as
in the Bible; it is warm gas or breath. Accordingly, to make the matter clear,
we have the breath-like word (πνευματικὸς λόγος) rushing over (ἐπιφερόμε-
νον) and keeping in motion earth and water, which are not yet distinguished.
Here, as in Genesis, it is the all-powerful Word of God that creates; but, as
will appear, the Word is not simply the biblical word of command ('Let
there be . . .'). Jewish thinkers, however, conceived of the activity of Wisdom
or Torah in the process of creation.

l. 19   That light am I, Mind (νοῦς), *thy God.* There is some confusion here; earlier
it seemed that Poimandres was the Mind of the supreme God; now Mind *is*
the supreme God.

l. 21   The luminous word which came forth from Mind is son of God. The meaning is
made clear by analogy. In man the mind corresponds to God the Father, the
process of seeing and hearing to the Word (λόγος). In the divine, as in
human, life, the one is prior to the other, but the two are inseparable.

l. 27   *Then.* In *Poimandres* 7f., which are not printed here, it is said that the Light, being the divine mind and archetypal world, resolved itself into innumerable divine powers. The lower world, animated by the divine Word, imitated the archetypal world, and thus came into being the infinite number of souls. *Bisexual . . . life and light.* The idea of the bisexuality of God, and the use of the terms life and light, are both very widespread in the literature of the gnostic piety of which the *Hermetica* are an example. Life and light are also biblical terms (e.g. John 1. 3f.), and in some Jewish speculation the first man was said (in dependence on Gen. 1. 27) to be bisexual.

l. 28   *Another Mind as Demiurge.* The primal God, being above all contact with matter and time, must produce a second Mind to set in motion the process of creation.

l. 29   *Seven administrators . . . destiny.* The seven administrators closely correspond to the seven planets ruling in their seven spheres, which lie between man and God. Genesis also (1. 14–18) records the creation of heavenly bodies designed both to give light and to rule. Destiny (εἱμαρμένη) is a Stoic word and concept; it is here (as often) bound up with astrological ideas. In 10f. the emergence of animal life is described.

96

Corpus Hermeticum 1. *Poimandres* 12–15. Archetypal Man and his Fall

Mind, the Father of all, being life and light, generated a Man equal to himself, whom he loved as being his own offspring, for he was very beautiful since he bore the image of his father. Truly therefore did God love his own form, and delivered over to him all his own
5 creations. And when the Man had considered the creation which the Demiurge had made in the fire, he himself also wished to create, and was permitted to do so by his father. He came into the sphere of the Demiurge, where he was to have all authority, and considered the creations of his brother. They loved him, and each one gave him a
10 share in his own rank. Having perceived their essence and partaken of their nature, he wished to break out of the bounding circle of the orbits and to know the might of him who is set over the fire.
    And he that had all authority over the world of mortal beings and the irrational creatures looked down through the framework of the
15 orbits, having broken through the vault of heaven, and he showed the fair form of God to the downward-bearing Nature. When Nature saw him who had in himself the unfailing beauty and all the power of the administrators, and the form of God, she smiled in love because she saw the image of the Man's most beautiful form reflected
20 in the water and his shadow upon the earth. When he saw this form like himself in her, reflected, that is, in the water, he loved it, and desired to dwell there. With the will came the act, and he inhabited the irrational form; but Nature, when she had received him whom

she loved, enfolded him altogether and they were united; for they
25 were in love.

And for this reason, alone among all the living creatures upon
earth, man is twofold. He is mortal by reason of the body, immortal
by reason of the essential Man. For although he is immortal and has
authority over all things, yet he endures mortal conditions since he is
30 subjected to Destiny. Although therefore he is above the framework
of the orbits he has yet become a slave to it; and although he is
bisexual, since he came from a bisexual father, and not subject to
sleep since he came from one not subject to sleep, yet is he held
fast. . . .

l. 1   *A Man equal to himself.* We have not yet reached the creation of empirical
man. The supreme God can make only perfect creatures, Mind and archetypal
Man. The latter was (cf. Gen. 1. 26f.) the image of God and so might properly
be loved by the gnostic God, since in loving him God loved his own
perfection.

l. 9   *The creations of his brother,* that is, the things made by the second Mind, the
first creation of the supreme God as the Man was his second.

l. 13   *He that had all authority;* that is, the archetypal Man. We now reach the
climax of the Poimandres myth. The crux of every gnostic system was the
explanation of the appearance in the world of evil; since a perfect God could
create only good, how comes the evil which is manifest in creation? Some
unfortunate accident must have occurred. So it is here.

l. 24   *They were united.* A mythical marriage between Nature and the archetypal
Man, the perfect creation of the supreme God, accounts for the mixed nature
of man. It is to be observed that whereas Nature fell in love with Man, who
showed her the fair image of God, Man fell in love with the image of himself
reflected in the primeval water; like God, he could love only himself.

l. 27   *Man is twofold,* for the reason already given. He is mortal because he is
composed partly of corruptible nature; he is subject to Destiny, because Man
descended through the seven spheres of the administrators. Yet, equally with
Nature, the essential, real, Man was a partner in the union, and man does not
altogether lose his immortality.

l. 34   *He is held fast . . .* Something is wanting in the text; perhaps 'by love and
sleep'. In the following paragraphs (16f.), which are not printed here, we
learn that the issue of the marriage is seven men, bisexual, and similar to the
seven administrators.

97

Corpus Hermeticum 1. *Poimandres* 27ff. The Prophet's Mission

When he had said these things Poimandres before my eyes mingled
with the Powers. And I, having given thanks and blessed the Father
of all things, was dismissed by him[Poimandres], filled with power
and instructed regarding the nature of the universe and the supreme
5 vision. And I began to preach to men the beauty of piety and

knowledge: 'O peoples, earth-born men, who have given yourselves up to drunkenness and sleep and to ignorance of God, be sober, cease your orgies, bewitched as you are by irrational sleep.'

When they heard, they joined me with one accord. I said, 'Why,
10 O earth-born men, have you given yourselves up to death, when you have the right to partake of immortality? Repent, you who have journeyed with error and kept company with ignorance. Rid yourselves of the light which is darkness. Abandon corruption, partake of immortality.'

15 And some of them mocked me and went away, having given themselves up to the way of death; others begged me to teach them, throwing themselves at my feet. I raised them up and became the guide of the human race, teaching them the doctrine which showed how and in what way they should be saved. I sowed in them the
20 words of wisdom, and they were nourished upon the water of immortality. And when evening was come and the sun's light had begun to disappear completely, I bade them give thanks to God, and when they had completed the thanksgiving each one turned to his own bed.

l. 5 *I began to preach to men the beauty of piety and knowledge.* The tractate is not indulging in fiction; we need not doubt that Hermetic philosophers did preach their Gospel, and found both converts and opponents. Ammonius Saccas, for example, must have taught a doctrine very similar to that of the *Hermetica*, and in his teaching Plotinus, after a long search, found that which satisfied his longings.

l. 11 *The right to partake of immortality.* Cf. John 1. 12.
Repent. Cf. Mark 1. 15; and the New Testament *passim*.

l. 15 *Some of them ... others.* The same mixed reception was accorded to the Christian preachers; cf. e.g. 1 Cor. 1. 18.

l. 19 *I sowed in them.* For the metaphor cf. Mark 4. 14; 1 John 3. 9. It is not uncommon elsewhere.

l. 20 *The water of immortality.* Cf. John 4. 10.

98

Corpus Hermeticum 1. *Poimandres* 30ff. The Sacrifice of Praise and Thanksgiving

But for my part I wrote down for myself (*or*, inscribed in memory) the benefaction of Poimandres, and, being filled with those things I had desired, I rejoiced greatly. For the sleep of my body had become watchfulness of soul, and the closing of my eyes true vision, and my
5 silence pregnant with good, and the utterance of my speech a brood of good things. This befell me because I received them from my mind, that is, from Poimandres, the word of the Sovereignty. So I came, inspired with the spirit of truth.

Wherefore with all my soul and with all my strength I offer
10 blessing to God the Father.
Holy is God, the Father of all things.
Holy is God, whose will is accomplished by his own Powers.
Holy is God, who wills to be known and who is known to his
own.
15 Holy art thou, who by the Word hast constituted all things that
are.
Holy art thou, of whom all Nature is the image.
Holy art thou, whom Nature did not form.
Holy art thou, who art stronger than every Power.
20 Holy art thou, who art greater than all excellence.
Holy art thou, who art above praises.
Accept pure rational sacrifices from a soul and a heart stretched
upward toward thee, O thou ineffable, unspeakable, named in silence.
Grant me my prayer that I may not fall from the knowledge which
25 befits our essence, and empower me. Then will I enlighten with this
grace those of the human race who are in ignorance, my brothers,
thy sons. Wherefore I believe and I bear witness; I move into life and
light. Blessed art thou, O Father. Thy man wishes to share in thy
holiness, as thou hast delivered to him all authority.

l. 13 *Who wills to be known and who is known to his own* (τοῖς ἰδίοις; cf. John 1.
11). It is the nature of the supreme God to communicate knowledge of
himself; he takes the initiative in salvation. But not all men receive
knowledge.

l. 15 *Who by the Word hast constituted all things that are.* For Word should perhaps
be substituted speech. God spoke and it was done. Gen. 1 is in the writer's
mind.

l. 17 *Of whom all Nature is the image,* since Nature received the man who bears the
image of God.

l. 22 *Pure rational sacrifices.* In the New Testament cf. Rom. 12. 1; 1 Peter 2.2,5;
Heb. 13. 15. Like other philosophers, and like some Jewish and Christian
propagandists, the Hermetists would have nothing to do with material
sacrifices; and logically enough, for a God who must not be defiled by matter
cannot be honoured by the offering of animals.

l. 27 *I believe and I bear witness; I move into life and light.* The Christian (and, more
specifically, Johannine) words are striking; but there is no ground for
suspecting Christian influence. God is life and light; the mystic moves into
God, and therefore moves into life and light. The insistence upon his witness-
bearing is important.

l. 28 *Thy man wishes to share in thy holiness.* The translation is difficult (συναγιάζειν
σοι βούλεται); perhaps, 'wishes to share with thee in the work of sanctification.'

l. 29 *As thou hast delivered to him all authority* (τὴν πᾶσαν ἐξουσίαν). Cf. Matt. 11.
27 (=Luke 10. 22); Matt. 28. 18; John 5. 20, 27, *et passim.* The supreme
God earlier gave authority to the archetypal Man (13), together with power

over all creatures, and leave to create. Apparently the mystic has reached the
position of the archetypal Man, made in the image of God.

99

Corpus Hermeticum 4. The Bowl 3–7

Reason, O Tat, God has distributed among all men, but he has not
done this with mind. It is not that he grudged it to any; for grudging
envy does not come from above but is found below in the souls of
men who do not possess mind.

5   Why then, my father, did God not distribute mind to all?
He willed, my son, to set it before souls as a prize that they might
win.
And where did he set it?
He filled a great bowl with it and set it down. He provided a
10   herald and ordered him to proclaim to the hearts of men the
following message. Dip yourself, you who can, into this bowl, you
who believe that you will ascend to him who sent the bowl down,
you who know for what purpose you have come into being.
Those therefore who have understood the proclamation and
15   dipped themselves in mind partook of *gnosis* and became perfect
men, since they had received mind. But those who ignored the
proclamation, these are the *logikoi*, who have not received mind in
addition (to reason) and do not know for what purpose they have
come into being, or from what source. The perceptions of these men
20   are akin to those of irrational animals. Their temperament is one of
anger and wrath, they do not admire the things that are worthy of
contemplation, they attend to the pleasures and desires of their bodies,
and believe that it is for the sake of these things that man has come
into being. But those who have partaken of the gift that comes from
25   God, these, O Tat, by a comparison of their works are no longer
mortal but immortal, for they have embraced all things in their own
mind, the things on earth, the things in heaven, and anything there
may be beyond heaven. Having thus raised themselves to such a
height they have seen the Good, and having seen it considered their
30   stay on earth an unhappy chance. They have despised all things, both
corporeal and incorporeal, and press on towards the One and Only.
This, O Tat, is the knowledge of mind: an abundance of divine
things and the understanding of God, since the bowl is divine.
I too wish to be dipped, my father.
35   Unless first, my child, you hate your body, you cannot love
yourself. But if you love yourself you shall have mind, and having
mind you will partake of knowledge.
What do you mean by this, father?

It is impossible, my child, to attach yourself to both things mortal
40 and things divine. For since there are two kinds of being, the
corporeal and the incorporeal, and these include the mortal and the
divine, the choice between them is left to him who wishes to choose.
For where choice remains it is impossible to have both, and the defeat
of the one manifests the active power of the other.

45   The choice of the better not only proves to be the finest thing for
him who has made the choice, since it leads to man's divinization,
but also demonstrates piety towards God. But the choice of the worse
means man's destruction, and offends against God only in this, that as
processions go through the midst of a city, unable to achieve anything
50 themselves and getting in the way of others, in the same way these
also go on procession in the world, drawn along by corporeal
pleasures.

ll. 1, 2   This tractate distinguishes between reason (λόγος), which seems to be
little more than the power of speech, and mind (νοῦς), the higher faculty
bestowed by God on the few.

l. 9   *A great bowl,* from which the tractate derives its title.

l. 15   *Dipped themselves* (ἐβαπτίσαντο). The middle voice indicates their own choice
in the matter. The word itself may owe something to Christian precedent.

l. 17   *Logikoi,* the adjective corresponding to the word *reason* (λόγος) in *l.* 1 and
elsewhere. There is no good English equivalent, though *rational* might serve.
In the next line the words 'to reason' are added to make the sense clear.

l. 26   *Their own mind.* νοῦς given to them by God becomes in a sense their own.

l. 49   *Of a city.* These words are added to clarify the text. Another possible
supplement would be 'of a crowd'.

100

Corpus Hermeticum 13. *Concerning Rebirth* 1,2

In the *General Discourses,* my father, you spoke in riddles and without
making things clear, when you discoursed on divinity. You revealed
nothing, when you said that no one could be saved before rebirth.
When I became your suppliant, on the descent from the mountain,
5 after you had discoursed with me, when I asked that I might learn
the doctrine of rebirth, since of all things this is the only one of which
I am ignorant, you said that you would commit it to me 'when you
are ready to distance yourself from the world'. I am ready, and I have
strengthened my mind to withstand the world's deceit. Now do you
10 supply my deficiencies by the things you have said you would deliver
to me regarding rebirth, making them known by speech or secretly.
O Trismegistus, I do not know from what kind of womb a man is
(re)born, of what kind of seed.

My child, it is intellectual Wisdom in Silence, and the seed is the
15 true Good.

Who provides the seed, father? I am altogether at a loss.

The will of God, my child.

And what sort of being is he that is begotten, father? for he has no share of the substance that is in me.

20 He who is begotten will be another person, God the child of God, the All in All, composed of all the Powers.

You are telling me a riddle, father, and not speaking as a father to his son.

This kind of thing, my child, is not taught, but when it is his will

25 God brings it to remembrance.

l. 1   A fuller title of this tractate is 'Hermes Trismegistus to his son Tat, a secret discourse on the mountain, concerning rebirth and the rule of silence'. The *General Discourses*, also addressed to Tat, are referred to in *Corpus Hermeticum* 10. 1.

l. 3   New Testament parallels are evident.

l. 14   Here and in some later lines capitals are used where divine powers are more or less personalized.

l. 25   Knowledge is a kind of remembering, for it is already implanted in man.

Coptic Gnostic Texts from Nag Hammadi

In 1945 a library of gnostic texts, written in Coptic, was discovered at Nag Hammadi in Egypt. They must have belonged to a gnostic Christian sect: most have a Christian element, some a very strong Christian element, but at the same time they bear witness to a gnostic movement that was not exclusively, and perhaps was not at all, of Christian origin. They have provided a much better understanding than was previously possible of the Christian gnostic heresies, which may now be known at first hand and not simply through the words of their opponents, and also indirectly shed light on the origins of the gnostic movement as a whole.

101

Nag Hammadi Codex III. 70–90. *Eugnostos the Blessed*

This appears to have been a document untouched by Christian influence. There is a parallel text, *The Sophia of Jesus Christ*, which is a Christianized version.

Eugnostos the Blessed, to those who are his.

Greetings! I wish you to know that all men born from the foundation of the world until now are dust. Inquiring about God, who he is, and what he is like, they have not found him. The wisest among them

5 have speculated about the truth from the ordering of the world. But

the speculation has not reached the truth. For the ordering is spoken
of in three (different) opinions by all the philosophers, (and) hence
they do not agree. For some of them say about the world that it was
directed by itself. Some, that it is providence (that directs it). Some,
10 that it is fate. Now, it is none of these. Again, (of) the three opinions
that I have just described, none is true. For whatever is from itself is
empty life, since it only makes itself. Providence is foolish. And the
inevitable is undiscerning.

Whoever, then, is able to get free of these three opinions that I
15 have just described and come by means of another view to confess
the God of truth, and be in harmony with everyone because of him,
he is an immortal who is in the midst of mortal men.

The one who is is ineffable. No sovereignty knew him, no
authority, no subjection, nor did any creature from the foundation
20 of the world, except himself. For he is immortal. He is eternal, having
no birth; for everyone who has birth will perish. He is unbegotten,
having no beginning; for everyone who has a beginning has an end.
No one rules over him, since he has no name; for whoever has a
name is the creation of another. He is unnameable. He has no human
25 form; for whoever has human form is the creation of another. He
has his own semblance—not like the semblance that we have received
or seen, but a strange semblance that surpasses all things and is better
than the totalities. It looks to every side and sees itself from itself. He
is without end; he is incomprehensible. He is ever imperishable, and
30 has no likeness to anything. He is unchanging good. He is faultless.
He is everlasting. He is blessed. He is unknowable, while he
nonetheless knows himself. He is immeasurable. He is untraceable.
He is perfect, having no defect. He is imperishably blessed. He is
called 'the Father of the Universe'.

35 Before anything was revealed of those that appear, the greatness
and the authorities that are in him, he embraced the totalities of the
totalities, and nothing embraced him. For he is all mind, thought and
reflecting, thinking, rationality, and power. They all are equal
powers. They are the sources of the totalities. And their whole race,
40 until the end, is in the foreknowledge of the Unbegotten. For that
which appears has not yet been arrived at.

Now a difference existed between the imperishable aeons and the
perishable ones. Let us, then, consider it in this way. Everything that
came from the perishable will perish, since they came from the
45 perishable. Whatever came from imperishableness will not perish
but will become imperishable, since it came from imperishableness.
Thus a multitude of men went astray; since they did not know this
difference, which has been stated, they died.

But let this suffice for now, since it is impossible for anyone to
50 dispute the nature of the words that I have just spoken in regard to

the blessed, imperishable, true God. Now, if anyone desires to believe the words that are set down here, let him investigate from what (sing.) is hidden to the completion of what (sing.) is revealed, and this thought will instruct him how the belief in those things that are
55 not revealed was found in what (sing.) is revealed. This thought is a source of knowledge.

The Lord of the Universe is not rightly called 'Father', but 'First Father'. For the Father is the source of what is revealed. For he is the beginningless First Father and beholds himself within himself as with
60 a mirror. He was revealed in his likeness as Self-Father, that is, Self-Begetter, and as Confronter, since he confronted the Unbegotten First-Existing One. Indeed he is of equal age with the one who is before his countenance, but he is not equal to him in power.

Afterward he revealed a multitude of confronting, self-begotten
65 ones, equal in age and power, being in glory, and without number. They are called 'the generation over whom there is no kingdom among the kingdoms that exist'. And the whole multitude there over which there is no kingdom is called 'the Sons of the Unbegotten Father'. Now he is the unknowable, who is ever full of imperishable-
70 ness and ineffable joy. They all are at rest in him, ever rejoicing in ineffable joy because of the unchanging glory and the measureless jubilation that was never heard or known among all the aeons and their worlds. But enough for now, lest we go on endlessly.

Another subject of knowledge is this, under the heading of the
75 begotten. Before the universe, the First was revealed. In the boundlessness he is a self-grown, self-constructed father who is full of shining, ineffable light. In the beginning he decided to have his form come to be as a great power. Immediately the beginning of that light was revealed as an immortal, androgynous man. His male name is
80 'the Begetting of the Perfect One'. And his female name is 'All-wise Begettress Sophia'. It is also said that she resembles her brother and her consort. It is a truth that is uncontested; for here below error, which exists with it, contests the truth.

Through Immortal Man was revealed a first designation (fem.),
85 namely divinity and kingdom; for the Father, who is called 'Self-Father Man', revealed this (masc.). He created for himself a great aeon corresponding to his greatness. He gave it great authority, and it ruled over all creations. He created for himself gods and archangels and angels, myriads without number for retinue. Now from that
90 man originated divinity and kingdom. Therefore he was called 'God of gods', 'King of kings'.

Now First Man is 'Faith (Pistis)' for those who will come to be after these. He was within a unique mind, thought, which is like it, reflecting and thinking, rationality and power. All the parts that exist
95 are perfect and immortal. In respect to imperishableness, they are

equal. However in respect to power, there is a difference, like the
difference between a father and a son, and a son and a thought, and
the thought and the remainder . . .

Now Immortal Man is full of every imperishable glory and
100 ineffable joy. His whole kingdom rejoices in everlasting rejoicing,
those who never have been heard or known in any aeon that came
after them, and its worlds. Afterward First Source came from
Immortal Man, the one who is called 'the Perfect Begetter'.

Man took his consort and revealed that first-begotten androgyny
105 whose name is 'First-begotten Son of the Father'. His female aspect is
called 'First-begotten Sophia, Mother of the Universe', whom some
call 'Love'. Now the First-begotten, since he has his authority from
his father, created a great aeon corresponding to his greatness, creating
for himself myriads of angels without number for retinue. The
110 whole multitude of those angels is called 'the Assembly of the Holy
Ones, the shadowless lights'. Now when these greet each other, their
embraces are for angels who are like them.

First-Begetter Father is called 'Adam of the Light'. And the
kingdom of Son of Man is full of ineffable joy and unchanging
115 jubilation because they rejoice continually in ineffable joy over their
imperishable glory, which has never been heard of, nor has it been
revealed to all the aeons that came to be and their worlds.

Now Son of Man harmonized with Sophia, his consort, and
revealed a great androgynous light. Some call his masculine name
120 'Saviour, Begetter of All Things'. His feminine name is called 'Sophia,
All-Begettress'. Some call her 'Pistis'.

Then the Saviour harmonized with his consort, Pistis Sophia. He
revealed six androgynous spiritual beings whose type is that of those
who preceded them . . .

125 Now the first aeon is that of Immortal Man. The second aeon is
that of Son of Man, the one who is called 'First Begetter'. The third
is that of the son of Son of Man, the one who is called 'Saviour'. The
one who embraces these is the aeon over whom there is no kingdom
in the divine, boundless eternity, the aeon of the aeons, with the
130 immortals who are in him, the one above the Eighth that was
revealed in chaos . . .

From his good pleasure and his thought the powers were revealed,
who were called 'gods'. And the gods by their thinkings revealed
divine gods. And the gods by their thinkings revealed lords. And the
135 lords of the lords by their words revealed lords. And the lords by
their powers revealed archangels. The archangels revealed angels. By
this (fem.), the semblance was revealed, with structure and form, to
name all the aeons and their worlds.

All the immortals, which I have just described, have authority—
140 all of them—by the power of Immortal Man and Sophia, his consort,

who was called 'Silence', and was named 'Silence' because in reflecting without a word she perfected her greatness. The imperishables, since they have the authority, each provided for themselves great kingdoms in all the immortal heavens and their firmaments, thrones, and
145 temples corresponding to their greatness. Some, indeed, who are in dwelling places and in chariots, being in ineffable glory, and not being able to be sent into any nature, provided for themselves hosts of angels, myriads without number for retinue and glory, even ineffable virgin spirits of light. They have no sickness nor weakness,
150 but it is only will, so it comes to be in an instant. The aeons and their heavens and the firmaments were complete for the glory of Immortal Man and Sophia, his consort.

This is where every aeon was and their worlds, and those that came after them, to provide there the types, their likenesses, in the
155 heavens of chaos and their worlds. And all natures, from the Immortal One from the time of the Unbegotten One to the revelation of (or: to) chaos, in the shining, shadowless light, and in ineffable joy, and unutterable jubilation, ever delight themselves on account of their unchanging glory and the immeasurable rest that is
160 impossible to speak of or even to conceive of among all the aeons that came to be and their powers.

But enough for now. Now all these things that I have just said to you (sing.) I have said in the way that you can accept, until the one who does not need to be taught is revealed among you, and he will
165 say all these things to you joyously and in pure knowledge.

Eugnostos the Blessed.

l. 3 *Inquiring about God.* It is to this inquiry that Gnosis addresses itself. What is otherwise unknown the gnostic revealer is able to communicate.

l. 31 *He is unknowable.* Most of the propositions about God given here, including this one, are negative, but some positive statements will appear.

l. 37 God is mind and rationality but he is not reached by rational processes.

l. 79 The chief problem in Gnosis is not to evolve a doctrine of salvation but to explain how creation can have taken place. If spirit (deity, immortality) and matter are absolute opposites, unable to have any contact with each other, how could the latter be produced by the former? In particular, how could the process of sexual generation be initiated? Several gnostic systems adopt the theory set forth in this tractate: originally bisexual beings evolved from themselves ('revealed') others, which in the end resulted in the sexually differentiated humanity that we know.

l. 114 It is surprising to find the term Son of man in a work independent of Christianity. It is possible that the expression was derived from Judaism but perhaps more probable that it constitutes an exception to the generally non-Christian character of Eugnostos.

102

Nag Hammadi Codex I. *The Gospel of Truth* 34–41

A book bearing this title is referred to by Irenaeus (*Adv. Haer.* 3.11.9); it seems to have been of Valentinian origin; some think that it was written by Valentinus himself. It is a Christian gnostic work, and probably a very early one; it bears witness to that Gnosis which helped to produce Christian Gnosticism.

This is the word of the gospel of the discovery of the pleroma, for those who await the salvation which is coming from on high. While their hope which they are waiting for is waiting—they whose image is light with no shadow in it—then at that time the pleroma is about
5 to come. The deficiency of matter has not arisen through the limitlessness of the Father, who is about to bring the time of the deficiency, although no one could say that the incorruptible one will come in this way. But the depth of the Father was multiplied and the thought of error did not exist with him. It is a thing that falls, it is a
10 thing that easily stands upright again in the discovery of him who has come to him whom he shall bring back. For the bringing back is called repentance.

For this reason incorruptibility breathed forth; it pursued the one who had sinned in order that he might rest. For forgiveness is what
15 remains for the light in the deficiency, the word of the pleroma. For the physician runs to the place where a sickness is because that is his will that is in him. He who has a deficiency, then, does not hide it, because one has what the other lacks. So with the pleroma, which has no deficiency; it fills up his deficiency—it is that which he provided
20 for filling up what he lacks, in order that therefore he might receive the grace. When he was deficient he did not have the grace. That is why there was diminution existing in the place where there is no grace. When that which was diminished was received, he revealed what he lacked, as a pleroma; that is the discovery of the light of
25 truth which rose upon him because it is immutable.

That is why Christ was spoken of in their midst, so that those who were disturbed might receive a bringing back, and he might anoint them with the ointment. The ointment is the mercy of the Father who will have mercy on them. But those whom he has anointed are
30 the ones who have become perfect. For full jars are the ones that are usually anointed. But when the anointing of one jar is dissolved, it is emptied, and the reason for there being a deficiency is the thing through which its ointment goes. For at that time a breath draws it, one by the power of the one with it. But from him who has no
35 deficiency no seal is removed, nor is anything emptied. But what he lacks the perfect Father fills again. He is good. He knows his plantings because it is he who planted them in his paradise. Now his paradise is his place of rest.

This is the perfection in the thought of the Father, and these are
40 the words of his meditation. Each one of his words is the work of his
one will in the revelation of his Word. While they were still in the
depth of his thought, the Word which was first to come forth
revealed them along with a mind that speaks the one Word in silent
grace. It (masc.) was called thought since they were in it (fem.) before
45 being revealed. It came about, then, that it was first to come forth at
the time that was pleasing to the will of him who willed. And the
will is what the Father rests in and is pleased with. Nothing happens
without him, nor does anything happen without the will of the
Father, but his will is incomprehensible. His trace is the will, and no
50 one will know it, nor is it possible for one to scrutinize it in order to
grasp it. But when he wills, what he wills is this—even if the sight
does not please them in any way—before God it is the will, the
Father. For he knows the beginning of all of them and their end. For
at their end he will question them directly (?). Now the end is
55 receiving knowledge about the one who is hidden, and this is the
Father, from whom the beginning came forth, to whom all will
return who have come forth from him. And they have appeared for
the glory and the joy of his name.

Now the name of the Father is the Son. It is he who first gave a
60 name to the one who came forth from him, who was himself, and he
begot him as a son. He gave him his name which belonged to him;
he is the one to whom belongs all that exists around him, the Father,
His is the name; his is the Son. It is possible for him to be seen. But
the name is invisible because it alone is the mystery of the invisible
65 which comes to ears that are completely filled with it. For indeed the
Father's name is not spoken, but it is apparent through a son.

In this way, then, the name is a great thing. Who therefore will be
able to utter a name for him, the great name, except him alone to
whom the name belongs and the sons of the name in whom rested
70 the name of the Father, who in turn themselves rested in his name?
Since the Father is unengendered, he alone is the one who begot a
name for himself before he brought forth the aeons in order that the
name of the Father should be over their head as lord, that is, the name
in truth, which is firm in his command through perfect power. For
75 the name is not from mere words, nor does his name consist of
appellations, but it is invisible. He gave a name to himself since he
sees himself, he alone having the power to give himself a name. For
he who does not exist has no name. For what name is given to him
who does not exist? But the one who exists exists also with his name,
80 and he knows himself. And to give himself a name is the prerogative
of the Father. The Son is his name. He did not therefore hide it in the
work, but the Son existed; he alone was given the name. The name
therefore is that of the Father, as the name of the Father is the Son.
Where indeed would mercy find a name except with the Father?

85   But no doubt one will say to his neighbour, 'Who is it who will
give a name to him who existed before himself, as if offspring did
not receive a name from those who begot them?' First, then, it is
fitting for us to reflect on this matter: what is the name? It is the
name in truth; it is not therefore the name from the father, for it is
90   the one which is the proper name. Therefore he did not receive the
name on loan as do others, according to the form in which each one
is to be produced. But this is the proper name. There is no one else
who gave it to him. But he is unnameable, indescribable, until the
time when he who is perfect spoke of himself. And it is he who has
95   the power to speak his name and to see it.

When therefore it pleased him that his name which is uttered
should be his Son, and he gave the name to him, that is, him who
came forth from the depth, he spoke about his secret things, knowing
that the Father is a being without evil. For that very reason he
100 brought him forth in order to speak about the place and his resting-
place from which he had come forth, and to glorify the pleroma, the
greatness of his name and the gentleness of the Father. About the
place each one came from he will speak, and to the region where he
received his essential being he will hasten to return again, and to be
105 taken from that place—the place where he stood—receiving a taste
from that place and receiving nourishment, receiving growth. And
his own resting-place is his pleroma.

Therefore all the emanations of the Father are pleromas, and the
root of all his emanations is in the one who made them all grow up
110 in himself. He assigned them their destinies. Each one of them is
apparent in order that through their own thought . . . For the place
to which they send their thought, that place is their root, which takes
them up in all the heights to the Father. They possess his head which
is rest for them and they hold on close to him, as though to say that
115 they have participated in his face by means of kisses. But they do not
appear in this way, for they did not surpass themselves nor lack the
glory of the Father nor think of him as small nor that he is harsh nor
that he is wrathful, but a being without evil, imperturbable, gentle,
knowing all spaces before they have come into existence, and having
120 no need to be instructed.

This is the manner of those who possess something from above of
the immeasurable greatness, as they stretch out after the one alone
and the perfect one, the one who is there for them. And they do not
go down to Hades nor have they envy nor groaning nor death
125 within them, but they rest in him who is at rest, not striving nor
being involved in the search for truth. But they themselves are the
truth; and the Father is within them and they are in the Father, being
perfect, being undivided in the truly good one, being in no way
deficient in anything, but they are set at rest, refreshed in the Spirit.

130 And they will heed their root. They will be concerned with those things in which he will find his root and not suffer loss to his soul. This is the place of the blessed; this is their place.

For the rest, then, may they know, in their places, that it is not fitting for me, having come to be in the resting place, to speak of
135 anything else. But it is in it that I shall come to be, to be concerned at all times with the Father of the all and the true brothers, those upon whom the love of the Father is poured out and in whose midst there is no lack of him. They are the ones who appear in truth since they exist in true and eternal life and speak of the light which is perfect
140 and filled with the seed of the Father, and which is in his heart and in the pleroma, while his Spirit rejoices in it and glorifies the one in whom it existed because he is good. And his children are perfect and worthy of his name, for he is the Father: it is children of this kind that he loves.

l. 1 *Pleroma.* The word occurs in the New Testament (see especially Col. 1. 19; 2. 9) and is very common in gnostic literature. It means fullness: the full content of any spiritual being, especially of the supreme God thought of as including the various emanations responsible for creation and salvation.

l. 12 *Repentance*; also *forgiveness* (*l.* 14). In the *Gospel of Truth* salvation is not simply the communication of truth; moral values also are involved.

l. 16 *The physician.* The *Gospel of Truth* contains no direct quotation from the New Testament, but there are probable allusions; here apparently to Mark 2.17 (or a parallel).

l. 26 *Christ.* Here the *Gospel* is using unmistakably Christian terminology. Notwithstanding a good deal of gnostic terminology it may be regarded as a fundamentally Christian work.

l. 36 *Plantings.* Cf. Matt. 15. 13.

l. 54 *The end is receiving knowledge about the one who is hidden.* The goal of man's existence as understood within Gnosis could not be more plainly expressed.

l. 59 *The name of the Father is the Son.* Cf. John 17. 26; 'I have made known to them thy name, and will make it known.' In the use of *Name* there is noteworthy kinship between the *Gospel* and Johannine thought.

l. 92 With this passage cf. Matt. 11.27; Luke 10. 22.

l. 136 *True brothers.* It is sometimes claimed that John narrows the thought of love, confining it to the Christian brotherhood rather than stressing that it must be given freely to enemies. The *Gospel* is perhaps even more exposed to this charge.

103

Nag Hammadi Codex II. *The Gospel of Thomas* 1–7, 24–27, 112–114

Unlike the *Gospel of Truth, Thomas* bears a close resemblance to the New Testament Gospels, though it consists entirely of sayings. Some think it to be a Gospel of equal age and historical value with those of the New Testament. A more probable view is that it was based upon those Gospels, or their sources, or on other earlier Gospels, and edited in the light of gnostic beliefs.

These are the secret sayings which the living Jesus spoke and which Didymos Judas Thomas wrote down.

And he said, 'Whoever finds the interpretation of these sayings will not experience death.'

5 Jesus said, 'Let him who seeks continue seeking until he finds. When he finds, he will become troubled. When he becomes troubled, he will be astonished, and he will rule over the All.'

Jesus said, 'If those who lead you say to you, "See, the Kingdom is in the sky," then the birds of the sky will precede you. If they say to 10 you, "It is in the sea," then the fish will precede you. Rather, the Kingdom is inside of you, and it is outside of you. When you come to know yourselves, then you will become known, and you will realize that it is you who are sons of the living Father. But if you will not know yourselves, you will dwell in poverty and it is you who 15 are that poverty.'

Jesus said, 'The man old in days will not hesitate to ask a small child seven days old about the place of life, and he will live. For many who are first will become last, and they will become one and the same.'

20 Jesus said, 'Recognize what is in your sight, and that which is hidden from you will become plain to you. For there is nothing hidden which will not become manifest.'

His disciples questioned Him and said to Him, 'Do You want us to fast? How shall we pray? Shall we give alms? What diet shall we 25 observe?'

Jesus said, 'Do not tell lies, and do not do what you hate, for all things are plain in the sight of Heaven. For nothing hidden will not become manifest, and nothing covered will remain without being uncovered.'

30 Jesus said, 'Blessed is the lion which becomes man when consumed by man; and cursed is the man whom the lion consumes, and the lion becomes man . . .'

His disciples said to Him, 'Show us the place where You are, since it is necessary for us to seek it.'

35 He said to them, 'Whoever has ears, let him hear. There is light within a man of light, and he (or: it) lights up the whole world. If he (or: it) does not shine, he (or: it) is darkness.'

Jesus said, 'Love your brother like your soul, guard him like the pupil of your eye.'

40 Jesus said, 'You see the mote in your brother's eye, but you do not

see the beam in your own eye. When you cast the beam out of your own eye, then you will see clearly to cast the mote from your brother's eye.'

Jesus said,'If you do not fast as regards the world, you will not find
45 the Kingdom. If you do not observe the Sabbath as a Sabbath, you will not see the Father . . .'

Jesus said, 'Woe to the flesh that depends on the soul; woe to the soul that depends on the flesh.'

His disciples said to Him, 'When will the Kingdom come?'
50 Jesus said, 'It will not come by waiting for it. It will not be a matter of saying, "Here it is" or "There it is." Rather, the Kingdom of the Father is spread out upon the earth, and men do not see it.'

Simon Peter said to them, 'Let Mary leave us, for women are not worthy of Life.'
55 Jesus said,'I myself shall lead her in order to make her male, so that she too may become a living spirit resembling you males. For every woman who will make herself male will enter the Kingdom of Heaven.'

The Gospel According to Thomas.

l. 1 *The living Jesus* is the risen Jesus. It was a common gnostic notion (contained also in the New Testament) that after the resurrection Jesus communicated special truths to chosen disciples.

l. 3 *He* may refer to Jesus himself, or to Thomas as his authorized interpreter. For the promise cf. John 8. 52.

l. 5 Cf. Matt. 7. 7; Luke 11. 9, 10; Matt. 6. 33. For the promise of ruling or reigning, cf. Matt. 19. 28; Luke 22. 29, 30.

l. 7 *The All* presumably is the universe, or perhaps more probably the totality of spiritual beings. See Saying 77, where it is said to proceed from Jesus and to extend unto him. Thus he himself is the All.

l. 11 It is ridiculous to locate the Kingdom in a place (such as the sky or the sea). It is within; cf. Luke 17. 21. It is a characteristically gnostic paradox to add that it is at the same time without; gnostic (and Greek) also to insist on the importance of self-knowledge.

l. 17 Children have an important place in the New Testament Gospels; and the saying about the first and the last appears in Matt. 19. 30; 20. 16; Mark 10. 31; Luke 13. 30. Distinctions of age and sex vanish for the gnostic (but see *l.* 55).

l. 22 Cf. Matt. 10. 26; Mark 4. 22; Luke 8. 17; 12.2.

l. 23 *Do You want us to fast?* It is implied that the Christian will not fast or follow other observances. There is only very incomplete parallelism here with the Sermon on the Mount (Matt. 6).

l. 30 *Blessed is the lion.* Perhaps the best explanation of this very obscure saying is that the lion is the (hostile) world. If the (gnostic) man consumes it the world becomes gnostic, and blessed; but if the (gnostic) man allows the world to consume him he is cursed.

l. 33 *Show us the place.* Cf. John 14.5.

l. 35 *Whoever has ears.* Cf. Mark 4. 9, and parallels. For the saying about eyes, cf. Matt. 6. 22, 23; Luke 11. 34–36. For disciples as the light of the world, cf. Matt. 5. 14.

l. 40 Cf. Matt. 7. 3–5; Luke 6. 41, 42.

l. 47 *Woe to the flesh . . .* There must be an absolute separation between the spiritual and the material.

l. 49 *When will the Kingdom come?* It does not belong to the future, and does not therefore have to be waited for; it is already spread out on the earth. Cf. Luke 17. 20, 21, for the wording, but not for the sense.

l. 55 *. . . in order to make her male.* It is a striking fact that the Gospel ends with a proposal attributed to Peter and dismissed as erroneous, at least in its conclusion. It may be correct that women as such are not worthy of life, but some women at least Jesus will make male. The gnostic sees the abolition of sexual distinction as the desirable end of the divine process, but in a very different way from Paul's 'neither male nor female'.

Mandaean Literature

The literature of the Mandaeans, who still exist in Iraq and Iran, is contained in manuscripts that are by no means ancient, and assessment of the original dates of composition is difficult, so that completely agreed results have not been reached. The relevance of these texts to the study of the New Testament also is disputed and cannot be discussed here; the following opinion however may be quoted. 'In Mandaic literature we have before us an important witness to the religion of "Gnosis" or gnosticism from late Antiquity, which probably reaches back to the pre-Christian era. Thus the Mandeans are the last surviving witnesses of this form of religion . . . Daring suppositions have associated them in their origins with the history of the beginnings of Christianity and explained them as descendants of an old group of John the Baptist's disciples. Although these hypotheses, which were especially advocated by Reitzenstein, cannot all be substantiated, yet it can today be claimed with confidence that the oldest elements of Mandaic literature have preserved for us a witness from the Oriental milieu of early Christianity which can be utilized in the interpretation of certain New Testament texts (in particular the Johannine corpus).' (K. Rudolph, in *Gnosis, a Selection of Gnostic Texts,* II Coptic and Mandean Sources, W. Foerster, ed., ETr. R. McL. Wilson, ed., pp. 125f.)

104

Right Ginza II. 3

In the name of the Great Life!
When I came, I, the messenger of light,
the king, who came here from the light,
then I came, laufa and radiance in my hand,
5   light and praise (or: radiance) upon me,
splendour and illumination upon me.
Voice and proclamation upon me,
the sign upon me and the baptism,
and I illuminate darkened hearts.
10 With my voice and my proclamation
I uttered a cry to the world.
A cry I uttered to the world,
from one end of the world to the other.
I uttered a cry to the world:
15 let everyone take care of himself.
Everyone who takes care of himself
shall be saved from the consuming fire.
Hail to the servants of Kušṭa,
the perfect and faithful.
20 Hail to the perfect,
who turn away from all evil.
I am the messenger of light,
whom the Great One sent into the world.
The true messenger am I,
25 in whom there is no falsehood,
The true one, in whom there is no falsehood,
in whom there is no imperfection or deficiency.
I am the messenger of light:
whoever smells at his scent is quickened to life.
30 Whoever receives his word (or: doctrine),
his eyes are filled with light.
With light his eyes are filled,
and his mouth is filled with praise.
With praise his mouth is filled,
35 and his heart is filled with wisdom.
The adulterers smelt at it
and they abandoned their adultery.
They abandoned their adultery and came,
and surrounded themselves with my scent.
40 They spoke:
'When we were ignorant, we practised adultery,
now, since we have knowledge, we do not commit adultery any
        more.'

I am the true messenger,
in whom there is no falsehood . . .

45 The liars smelt at it,
and they abandoned their lies.
They abandoned their lies,
came, and surrounded themselves with my scent.
They spoke:
50 'Our lord! When we were ignorant, we spoke lies,
now, since we have knowledge, we do not speak lies any longer.'
The messenger of the Life am I,
the true one, in whom there is no falsehood,
the true one, in whom there is no falsehood,
55 in whom there is no imperfection or deficiency.
The tree of praise,
from which everyone who smells it becomes alive.
Whoever smells at it,
his eyes are filled with light . . .

60 The murderers smelt at it,
and they abandoned their murders.
Their murders they abandoned,
they came, and surrounded themselves with my scent.
They spoke:
65 'Our lord! When we were ignorant, we committed murder,
now, since we have knowledge, we do not murder any more.'
The sorcerers smelt at it,
and they abandoned their sorcery.
Their sorcery they abandoned,
70 they came, and surrounded themselves with my scent.
They spoke:
'Our lord! When we were ignorant, we practised sorcery,
now, since we have knowledge, we practise sorcery no more.'
A vine am I, a vine of life,
75 a tree, in which there is no falsehood.
The tree of praise,
from which everyone who smells at it becomes alive.
Whoever hears his word (or: doctrine),
his eyes are filled with light.
80 With light his eyes are filled,
his mouth is filled with praise.
With praise his mouth is filled
and his heart is filled with kušṭa.
The winkers smelt at it,
85 and they abandoned their winking.
Their winking they abandoned,
they came, and surrounded themselves with my scent.

They spoke:
'When we were without knowledge, we winked (immodestly),
90   now, since we have knowledge, we do not wink any more.'
'From the day we saw you,
from the day we heard your words.
From the day we saw you,   ☉
our heart was filled with peace.
95   We believed in you, Good One,
we saw your light and will not forget you.
All our days we will not forget you
and will not let you out of our heart for one hour,
because our heart shall not become blind
100   and these souls shall not be obstructed in their ascent.'
I spoke to them:
'Whoever repents,
his soul shall not be cut off from the light,
and the lord will not cut him off (or: damn him).'
105   But the wicked ones, the liars,
cut themselves off from the light,
for it was manifest to them, and they would not see,
and they were called, and they would not listen or believe.
The wicked fall through their own will
110   into the great Ocean of Suf.
They will be housed in the darkness,
and the mountain of darkness will receive them,
until the day, the day of judgement,
until the hour, the hour, of salvation.
115   As for us, who praise you, our lord,
you will forgive our sins and guilt.
Praise be to you, King of Light,
who have sent us, your friends, the truth.
You are victorous, Manda dḤaiyê,
120   and you lead all your friends to victory.
And the Life triumphs over all evil works.

l. 4   *Laufa.* '"Union, communion", especially with the World of Light; realized cultically through baptism, performing Kušṭa, etc.; at funeral feasts the deceased and the living are joined in the "communion"' (Rudolph).

l. 8   *Baptism.* This plays an important part in the Mandaean texts; hence, in part, the suggestion that the Mandaeans may be traced back to disciples of John the Baptist.

l. 18   *Kušṭa.* See the note on *ll.* 24, 26.

ll. 24, 26   *The true (one).* The original is kuštana, related to the word Kušṭa, used in the note on *l.* 18. This word means '"truth, uprightness"; personified saving truth' (Rudolph).

l. 36   The adulterers. The ethical concern of the Mandaeans (unlike some Gnostics) is clear.

l. 41   When we were ignorant. For Gnostics, the root of evil is ignorance; the removal of ignorance by *Gnosis* is salvation.

l. 110   The great Ocean of Suf. 'Originally the "Sea of Reeds", reinterpreted as the "Sea of the End", specifying the place into which unbelievers and wicked souls fall (like the Egyptians in the biblical narrative: the departure of the Israelites from Egypt was evidently interpreted allegorically as the departure of the soul from the body)' (Rudolph).

l. 119   Manda dḤaiyê. '"Knowledge (Gnosis) of Life". Name of the most important messenger of light and redeemer' (Rudolph).

105

Left Ginza III. 19

> They (the uthras) spoke to it (the soul):
> 'What are your works, soul,
> so that we may be your escort on the way?'
> It spoke to them:
> 5 'My father distributed bread
> and my mother dispensed alms.
> My brothers recited hymns,
> and my sisters administered kušṭa.'
> They spoke to it:
> 10 'Your father, who distributed bread,
> distributed it for himself.
> Your mother who dispensed alms,
> dispensed them for her own soul.
> Your brothers who recited hymns,
> 15 will ascend on the path of kušṭa.
> Your sisters, who administered kušṭa,
> will Manda dḤaiyê support.
> But what are your works which you have done for yourself,
> so that we may be your escort?'
> 20 It spoke to them:
> 'I have loved the Life,
> and allowed Manda dḤaiyê to settle in my inner thoughts.
> At the close of Saturday in the evening
> and at the coming in of Sunday for the good (?)
> 25 I put alms in my pocket,
> and took a loaf of bread in my hand.
> I put alms in my pocket
> and went to the gate of the temple.
> I added the alms to the other alms
> 30 and the loaf of bread to the community meal.
> I found an orphan and sustained it,

I replenished the widow's pocket.
I found a naked person.
and clothed him in a garment for his nakedness.
35 I found a prisoner,
and I released him and sent him back to his village.'

l. 1   *The uthras.* '"Wealth"; designation of (good) beings of light of every kind, who inhabit the realm of light as angels and are also known as "kings" (*malkê*)' (Rudolph).

l. 8   *Kušṭa. See the note on* **104**, *ll.* 24, 26. But *administering*, or *performing*, kušṭa seems to be a cult act.

l. 17   *Manda dHaiyê.* See **104**, note on *l.* 119.

6 Mystery Religions

The evidence upon which our knowledge of the so-called mystery religions rests is for the most part fragmentary and by no means easy to interpret. Very much of it consists of single lines and passing allusions in ancient authors (many of whom were either bound to secrecy or inspired with loathing with regard to the subject of which they were treating), inscriptions (many of them incomplete), and artistic and other objects discovered by archaeologists. If a small selection of such evidence were given it would be meaningless, or perhaps misleading; if it were given in bulk it would swell this chapter into several volumes. It is impossible therefore to present here a serious account of even one mystery cult; instead, some of the longest and clearest passages available have been selected and arranged so as to illustrate features which were (in various forms and degrees) common to most of the cults.

The object of the mystery cults was to secure salvation for men who were subject to moral and physical evil, dominated by Destiny, and unable by themselves to escape from the corruption that beset the material side of their nature (cf. p. 94 and **96**). Salvation accordingly meant escape from Destiny, release from corruption and a renewed moral life. It was effected by what may broadly be called sacramental means. By taking part in prescribed rites the worshipper became united with God, was enabled in this life to enjoy mystical communion with him, and further was assured of immortality beyond death. This process rested upon the experiences (generally including the death and resurrection) of a Saviour-God, the Lord (κύριος) of his devotees. The myth, which seems often to have been cultically represented, rested in many of these religions upon the fundamental annual cycle of agricultural fertility; but rites which probably were in earlier days intended to secure productiveness in field and flock were now given an individual application and effect.

The following are among the most important features of the mystery religions.

The Myth

The saving cycle of events in the experience of the god were recounted in a tale conveniently described as a myth. Examples taken from two of the cults, that of Isis, which originated in the religion of ancient Egypt but became hellenized and came to have points of resemblance to the religion of Dionysus; and that of Cybele, the Great Mother, which was brought from Pessinus and installed in Rome in 205 BC during the second Punic War (Livy xxix. 10), are given here.

106

Plutarch, *Isis and Osiris* 12–19

They say that the Sun, when he became aware of Rhea's intercourse with Cronus, invoked a curse upon her that she should not give birth to a child in any month or any year; but Hermes, being enamoured of the goddess, consorted with her. Later, playing at draughts with
5 the moon, he won from her the seventieth part of each of her periods of illumination, and from all the winnings he composed five days, and intercalated them as an addition to the three hundred and sixty days. The Egyptians even now call these five days intercalated and celebrate them as the birthdays of the gods. They relate that on the
10 first of these days Osiris was born, and at the hour of his birth a voice issued forth saying, 'The Lord of All advances to the light.' . . . On the second of these days Arueris was born whom they call Apollo, and some call him also the elder Horus. On the third day Typhon was born, but not in due season or manner, but with a blow he broke
15 through his mother's side and leapt forth. On the fourth day Isis was born in the regions that are ever moist; and on the fifth Nephthys, to whom they give the name of Finality and the name of Aphrodite, and some also the name of Victory. There is also a tradition that Osiris and Arueris were sprung from the Sun, Isis from Hermes, and
20 Typhon and Nephthys from Cronus. . . . They relate, moreover, that Nephthys became the wife of Typhon; but Isis and Osiris were enamoured of each other and consorted together in the darkness of the womb before their birth. Some say that Arueris came from this union and was called the elder Horus by the Egyptians, but Apollo
25 by the Greeks.

One of the first acts related of Osiris in his reign was to deliver the Egyptians from their destitute and brutish manner of living. This he did by showing them the fruits of cultivation, by giving them laws, and by teaching them to honour the gods. Later he travelled over the
30 whole earth civilizing it without the slightest need of arms, but most of the peoples he won over to his way by the charm of his persuasive discourse combined with song and all manner of music. Hence the Greeks came to identify him with Dionysus.

During his absence the tradition is that Typhon attempted nothing
35 revolutionary because Isis, who was in control, was vigilant and alert; but when he returned home Typhon contrived a treacherous plot against him and formed a group of conspirators seventy-two in

number. He had also the co-operation of a queen from Ethiopia who
was there at the time and whose name they report as Aso. Typhon,
40 having secretly measured Osiris's body and having made ready a
beautiful chest of corresponding size artistically ornamented, caused
it to be brought into the room where the festivity was in progress.
The company was much pleased at the sight of it and admired it
greatly, whereupon Typhon jestingly promised to present it to the
45 man who should find the chest to be exactly his length when he lay
down in it. They all tried it in turn, but no one fitted it; then Osiris
got into it and lay down, and those who were in the plot ran to it
and slammed down the lid, which they fastened by nails from the
outside and also by using molten lead. Then they carried the chest to
50 the river and sent it on its way to the sea through the Tanitic Mouth.
...

... Isis, when the tidings reached her, at once cut off one of her
tresses and put on a garment of mourning in a place where the city
still bears the name of Kopto. Others think that the name means
55 deprivation, for they also express 'deprive' by means of 'koptein'. But
Isis wandered everywhere at her wits' end; no one whom she
approached did she fail to address, and even when she met some little
children she asked them about the chest. As it happened, they had
seen it, and they told her the mouth of the river through which the
60 friends of Typhon had launched the coffin into the sea ...

Thereafter Isis, as they relate, learned that the chest had been cast
up by the sea near the land of Byblus and that the waves had gently
set it down in the midst of a clump of heather. The heather in a short
time ran up into a very beautiful and massive stock and enfolded and
65 embraced the chest with its growth and concealed it within its trunk.
The king of the country admired the great size of the plant, and cut
off the portion that enfolded the chest (which was now hidden from
sight), and used it as a pillar to support the roof of his house. These
facts, they say, Isis ascertained by the divine inspiration of Rumour,
70 and came to Byblus and sat down by a spring, all dejection and tears;
she exchanged no word with anybody, save only that she welcomed
the queen's maidservants and treated them with great amiability ...

... Then the goddess disclosed herself and asked for the pillar
which served to support the roof. She removed it with the greatest
75 ease and cut away the wood of the heather which surrounded the
chest; then, when she had wrapped up the wood in a linen cloth and
had poured perfume upon it, she entrusted it to the care of the kings;
and even to this day the people of Byblus venerate this wood which
is preserved in the shrine of Isis. Then the goddess threw herself
80 down upon the coffin with such a dreadful wailing that the younger
of the king's sons expired on the spot. The elder son she kept with
her, and, having placed the coffin on board a boat, she put out from
land ...

In the first place where she found seclusion, when she was quite by
85 herself, they relate that she opened the chest and laid her face upon
the face within and caressed it and wept. The child came quietly up
behind her and saw what was there, and when the goddess became
aware of his presence, she turned about and gave him one awful look
of anger. The child could not endure the fright, and died . . .
90 As they relate, Isis proceeded to her son Horus, who was being
reared in Buto, and bestowed the chest in a place well out of the way;
but Typhon, who was hunting by night in the light of the moon,
happened upon it. Recognizing the body he divided it into fourteen
parts and scattered them, each in a different place. Isis learned of this
95 and sought for them again, sailing through the swamps in a boat of
papyrus . . .
The traditional result of Osiris's dismemberment is that there are
many so-called tombs of Osiris in Egypt; for Isis held a funeral for
each part when she had found it. . . .
100 Later, as they relate, Osiris came to Horus from the other world
and exercised and trained him for the battle. After a time Osiris asked
Horus what he held to be the most noble of all things. When Horus
replied, 'To avenge one's father and mother for evil done to them',
Osiris then asked him what animal he considered the most useful for
105 them who go forth to battle; and when Horus said, 'A horse', Osiris
was surprised and raised the question why it was that he had not
rather said a lion than a horse. Horus answered that a lion was a
useful thing for a man in need of assistance, but that a horse served
best for cutting off the flight of an enemy and annihilating him.
110 When Osiris heard this he was much pleased, since he felt that Horus
had now an adequate preparation. It is said that, as many were
continually transferring their allegiance to Horus, Typhon's concu-
bine, Thueris, also came over to him; and a serpent which pursued
her was cut to pieces by Horus's men, and now, in memory of this,
115 the people throw down a rope in their midst and chop it up.
Now the battle, as they relate, lasted many days and Horus
prevailed. Isis, however, to whom Typhon was delivered in chains,
did not cause him to be put to death, but released him and let him
go. Horus could not endure this with equanimity, but laid hands
120 upon his mother and wrested the royal diadem from her head; but
Hermes put upon her a helmet like unto the head of a cow.
Typhon formally accused Horus of being an illegitimate child,
but with the help of Hermes to plead his cause it was decided by the
gods that he also was legitimate. Typhon was then overcome in two
125 other battles. Osiris consorted with Isis after death, and she became
the mother of Harpocrates, untimely born and weak in his lower
limbs.

l. 16 *Ever moist.* Isis was goddess of the Nile, and of the sea; but it is not certain
that this is the allusion.

l. 33   *Dionysus.* This mythological connection corresponds to a practical connection between the cult of Isis and Osiris, and that of Dionysus.

l. 50   *The river*—the river Nile.

l. 55   *Koptein.* The Greek verb κόπτειν means in the active 'to smite', 'to smite with a cutting edge', hence 'to cut off'; and in the middle 'to smite oneself', hence 'to smite one's head or breast', 'to lament'.

l. 100   *Osiris came to Horus from the other world.* In Osiris's return to life lay the hope of his worshippers.

107

Plutarch, *Isis and Osiris* 27

This later passage begins to show the relation between myth and cult. See further **108**.

> Stories akin to these and to others like them they say are related about Typhon; how that, prompted by jealousy and hostility, he wrought terrible deeds and, by bringing utter confusion upon all things, filled the whole Earth, and the ocean as well, with ills, and later paid the
> 5 penalty therefor. But the avenger, the sister and wife of Osiris, after she had quenched and suppressed the madness and fury of Typhon, was not indifferent to the contests and struggles which she had endured, nor to her own wanderings nor to her manifold deeds of wisdom and many feats of bravery, nor would she accept oblivion
> 10 and silence for them, but she intermingled in the most holy rites portrayals and suggestions and representations of her experiences at that time, and sanctified them, both as a lesson in godliness and an encouragement for men and women who find themselves in the clutch of like calamities. She herself and Osiris, translated for their
> 15 virtues from good demigods into gods, as were Heracles and Dionysus later, not incongruously enjoy double honours, both those of gods and those of demigods, and their powers extend everywhere, but are greatest in the regions above the earth and beneath the earth. In fact, men assert that Pluto is none other than Serapis and that Persephone
> 20 is Isis, even as Archemachus of Euboea has said, and also Heracleides Ponticus who holds the oracle in Canopus to be an oracle of Pluto.

l. 1   Plutarch has been showing by examples that the use of the word δαίμων here translated *demigod*, is not universally good; it may be used of beings good and bad.

l. 2   *Typhon*, a monster who resisted Zeus but was finally overcome and buried beneath Aetna.

l. 14   *For their virtues*, δι' ἀρετήν; there is a variant, δι' ἀρετῆς, through virtue. *Heracles and Dionysus.* See Plutarch, *On the Malice of Herodotus* 13.

108

Eusebius, *Preparatio Evangelica* II, ii. 22ff

> The Phrygians say that Maeon was king of Phrygia and begat a
> daughter named Cybele, who first invented a pipe, and was called
> the Mountain Mother. And Marsyas the Phrygian, who was friendly
> with her, was the first to join flutes together, and he lived in chastity
> 5 to the end of his life.
>
> But Cybele became pregnant by intercourse with Attis, and when
> this was known, her father killed Attis and the nurses; and Cybele
> became mad and rushed out into the country, and there continued
> howling and beating a drum.
> 10 She was accompanied by Marsyas, who entered into a musical
> contest with Apollo, and was defeated, and flayed alive by Apollo.
>
> And Apollo became enamoured of Cybele and accompanied her
> in her wanderings as far as the Hyperboreans, and ordered the body
> of Attis to be buried, and Cybele to be honoured as a goddess.
> 15 Wherefore the Phrygians keep this custom even to the present
> day, lamenting the death of the youth, and erecting altars, and
> honouring Attis and Cybele with sacrifices.
>
> And afterwards, at Pessinus in Phrygia, they built a costly temple,
> and instituted most magnificent worship and sacrificial rites.

l. 9   Howling and beating a drum. This behaviour was recalled in the rites of the
Great Mother. The myth and the ritual alike could be, and were, understood
in the most diverse ways, as magical aids to fertility or as an allegory of the
soul's search for God.

l. 18   Pessinus. See above, p. 121.

Initiation

Rites of initiation opened the way into membership of the cults, and
generally seem to have consisted primarily of some ceremonial by means
of which the initiand was incorporated into the divine action of the myth,
and so achieved life by virtue of the resurrection of the god. Of the
following passages the former describes the rite of the *taurobolium*, in
which the worshipper was drenched with the blood of a bull. It will be
noted that the *taurobolium* described by Prudentius was carried out not as
a means of initiation but for the purpose of consecrating a priest (of the
Great Mother). It was to this cult that the rite originally belonged, but it
may also have become an institution of Mithraism. The latter passage
recounts Apuleius's initiation into the religion of Isis; it is less explicit in
details, but it is impossible to doubt the reality and sincerity of Apuleius's
conversion. See also **115**.

109

Prudentius, *Peristephanon* x. 1011–50

The high priest who is to be consecrated is brought down under
ground in a pit dug deep, marvellously adorned with a fillet, binding
his festive temples with chaplets, his hair combed back under a
golden crown, and wearing a silken toga caught up with Gabine
5 girding.

Over this they make a wooden floor with wide spaces, woven of
planks with an open mesh; they then divide or bore the area and
repeatedly pierce the wood with a pointed tool that it may appear
full of small holes.

10   Hither a huge bull, fierce and shaggy in appearance, is led, bound
with flowery garlands about its flanks, and with its horns sheathed;
yea, the forehead of the victim sparkles with gold, and the flash of
metal plates colours its hair.

Here, as is ordained, the beast is to be slain, and they pierce its
15 breast with a sacred spear; the gaping wound emits a wave of hot
blood, and the smoking river flows into the woven structure beneath
it and surges wide.

Then by the many paths of the thousand openings in the lattice
the falling shower rains down a foul dew, which the priest buried
20 within catches, putting his shameful head under all the drops, defiled
both in his clothing and in all his body.

Yea, he throws back his face, he puts his cheeks in the way of the
blood, he puts under it his ears and lips, he interposes his nostrils, he
washes his very eyes with the fluid, nor does he even spare his throat
25 but moistens his tongue, until he actually drinks the dark gore.

Afterwards, the flamens draw the corpse, stiffening now that the
blood has gone forth, off the lattice, and the pontiff, horrible in
appearance, comes forth, and shows his wet head, his beard heavy
with blood, his dripping fillets and sodden garments.

30   This man, defiled with such contagions and foul with the gore of
the recent sacrifice, all hail and worship at a distance, because profane
blood and a dead ox have washed him while concealed in a filthy
cave.

l. 4   *With Gabine girding*, 'a manner of girding, in which the toga was tucked up;
its corner being thrown over the left shoulder, was brought under the right
arm round to the breast (this manner was customarily employed in religious
festivals)' (Lewis and Short, *s.v. cinctus*).

l. 11   *Sheathed*, restrained from doing damage (*impeditis*).

l. 31   *All hail and worship.* The consecrated priest, emerging from the blood bath
with the gift of divine life (drawn from the sacred bull) himself becomes
divine and is therefore worshipped. Those who received the *taurobolium*
could be described as 'born again for eternity' (*renatus in aeternum, CIL*, vi.

510; many other inscriptions refer to the *taurobolium* and prove the rite to have been in use early in the second century AD).

Profane blood. It must be remembered that Prudentius was a Christian and that to him the blood was profane (*vilis*) and the whole rite not only repulsive but blasphemous.

110

Apuleius, *The Golden Ass (Metamorphoses)* xi. 22–6

In a dark night she appeared to me in a vision, declaring in words not dark that the day was come which I had wished for so long; she told me what provision and charges I should be at for the supplications, and how that she had appointed her principal priest
5 Mithras, that was joined unto my destiny (as she said) by the ordering of the planets, to be a minister with me in my sacrifices. When I had heard these and the other divine commandments of the high goddess, I greatly rejoiced, and arose before day to speak with the great priest, whom I fortuned to espy coming out of his chamber. Then I saluted
10 him, and thought with myself to ask and demand with a bold courage that I should be initiate, as a thing now due; but as soon as he perceived me, he began first to say: 'O Lucius, now know I well that thou art most happy and blessed, whom the divine goddess doth so greatly accept with mercy. Why dost thou stand idle and delay?
15 Behold the day which thou didst desire with prayer, when as thou shalt receive at my hands the order of most secret and holy religion, according to the divine commandment of this goddess of many names.' Thereupon the old man took me by the hand, and led me courteously to the gate of the great temple, where, after that it was
20 religiously opened, he made a solemn celebration, and after the morning sacrifice was ended, he brought out of the secret place of the temple certain books written with unknown characters ... thence he interpreted to me such things as were necessary to the use and preparation of mine order. This done, I diligently gave in charge
25 to certain of my companions to buy liberally whatsoever was needful and convenient; but part thereof I bought myself. Then he brought me, when he found that the time was at hand, to the next baths, accompanied with all the religious sort, and demanding pardon of the gods, washed me and purified my body according to the custom:
30 after this, when two parts of the day was gone, he brought me back again to the temple and presented me before the feet of the goddess, giving me a charge of certain secret things unlawful to be uttered, and commanding me generally before all the rest to fast by the space of ten continual days, without eating of any beast or drinking of any
35 wine: which things I observed with a marvellous continency. Then behold the day approached when as the sacrifice of dedication should be done; and when the sun declined and evening came, there arrived

on every coast a great multitude of priests, who according to their
ancient order offered me many presents and gifts. Then was all the
40 laity and profane people commanded to depart, and when they had
put on my back a new linen robe, the priest took my hand and
brought me to the most secret and sacred place of the temple. Thou
wouldest peradventure demand, thou studious reader, what was said
and done there: verily I would tell thee if it were lawful for me to
45 tell, thou wouldest know if it were convenient for thee to hear; but
both thy ears and my tongue should incur the like pain of rash
curiosity. Howbeit I will not long torment thy mind, which
peradventure is somewhat religious and given to some devotion;
listen therefore, and believe it to be true. Thou shalt understand that
50 I approached near unto hell, even to the gates of Proserpine, and after
that I was ravished throughout all the elements, I returned to my
proper place: about midnight I saw the sun brightly shine, I saw
likewise the gods celestial and the gods infernal, before whom I
presented myself and worshipped them. Behold now have I told
55 thee, which although thou hast heard, yet it is necessary that thou
conceal it; wherefore this only will I tell, which may be declared
without offence for the understanding of the profane.

When morning came and that the solemnities were finished, I
came forth sanctified with twelve stoles and in a religious habit,
60 whereof I am not forbidden to speak, considering that many persons
saw me at that time ... In my right hand I carried a lighted torch,
and a garland of flowers was upon my head, with white palm-leaves
sprouting out on every side like rays; thus I was adorned like unto
the sun, and made in fashion of an image, when the curtains were
65 drawn aside and all the people compassed about to behold me. Then
they began to solemnize the feast, the nativity of my holy order ... I
began to say in this sort: 'O holy and blessed dame, the perpetual
comfort of human kind, who by thy bounty and grace nourishest all
the world, and bearest a great affection to the adversities of the
70 miserable as a loving mother, thou takest no rest night or day, neither
art thou idle at any time in giving benefits and succouring all men as
well on land as sea; thou art she that puttest away all storms and
dangers from men's life by stretching forth thy right hand, whereby
likewise thou dost unweave even the inextricable and tangled web
75 of fate, and appeasest the great tempests of fortune, and keepest back
the harmful course of the stars. The gods supernal do honour thee;
the gods infernal have thee in reverence; thou dost make all the earth
to turn, thou givest light to the sun, thou governest the world, thou
treadest down the power of hell. By thy mean the stars give answer,
80 the seasons return, the gods rejoice, the elements serve: at thy
commandment the winds do blow, the clouds nourish the earth, the
seeds prosper, and the fruits do grow. The birds of the air, the beasts

of the hill, the serpents of the den, and the fishes of the sea do tremble
at thy majesty: but my spirit is not able to give thee sufficient praise,
85 my patrimony is unable to satisfy thy sacrifices; my voice hath no
power to utter that which I think of thy majesty, no, not if I had a
thousand mouths and so many tongues and were able to continue for
ever. Howbeit as a good religious person, and according to my poor
estate, I will do what I may: I will always keep thy divine appearance
90 in remembrance, and close the imagination of thy most holy god-
head within my breast.'

When I ended my oration to the great goddess, I went to embrace
the great priest Mithras, now my spiritual father, clinging upon his
neck and kissing him oft, and demanding his pardon, considering I
95 was unable to recompense the good which he had done me: and after
much talk and great greetings and thanks I departed from him
straight to visit my parents and friends, after that I had been so long
absent. And so within a short while after, by the exhortation of the
goddess I made up my packet and took shipping towards the city of
100 Rome, and I voyaged very safely and swiftly with a prosperous wind
to the port of Augustus, and thence travelling by chariot, I arrived at
that holy city about the twelfth day of December in the evening.
And the greatest desire which I had there was daily to make my
prayers to the sovereign goddess Isis, who, by reason of the place
105 where her temple was builded, was called Campensis, and continually
is adored of the people of Rome: her minister and worshipper was I,
a stranger to her church, but not unknown to her religion.

l. 1   *She*, Isis. Apuleius had for some time been seeking initiation.

l. 17   *Of many names.* See below on *l.* 68.

l. 35   *A marvellous continency.* It cannot be said that Apuleius had shown this in the
early part of his story. It seems clear that his conversion to the religion of Isis
was not without moral accompaniments and consequences.

l. 42   *Thou wouldest peradventure demand.* Apuleius was of course under bond of
secrecy not to divulge the mystery of the cult.

l. 50   *The gates of Proserpine.* Prosperpine (in Greek, Persephone) was the daughter
of Demeter, who sought her when Pluto had carried her off to Hades. The
two goddesses were celebrated in the Eleusinian mysteries. Apuleius means
that he was brought down to (and up again from) the threshold of the
underworld.

l. 67   *The perpetual comfort . . .* Such aretalogies, listing the names (cf. *l.* 18), virtues,
and powers of the goddess, are characteristic of the worship of Isis.

l. 93   *My spiritual father.* For this relation of the initiating minister to the neophyte,
cf. in the New Testament 1 Cor. 4. 15; Gal. 4. 19.

l. 101   *The port of Augustus*, Ostia.

l. 102   *That holy city.* To more religions than one Rome was the Holy City. Cf.
W. L. Knox, *JTS* old series xlvii. 180–4.

l. 105   *Campensis.* The temple was in the Campus Martius.

l. 107   *A stranger to her church, fani quidem advena.* The translation quoted must not lead the reader to suppose that the word *ecclesia* is used.

Worship

Some rites of the mystery cults have already been described. They were almost infinitely various, ranging from the licentious to the truly spiritual.

III

Josephus, *Antiquities* xviii. 66–80

There was at Rome a woman whose name was Paulina: one who on account of the dignity of her ancestors, and by the regular conduct of a virtuous life, had a great reputation. She was also very rich. And although she were of a beautiful countenance, and in that flower of
5 age wherein women are the most gay, yet did she lead a life of great modesty. She was married to Saturninus; one that was every way answerable to her in an excellent character. Decius Mundus, a man very high in the equestrian order, fell in love with this woman: and as she was of too great dignity to be seduced by presents, and had
10 always rejected them, though they had been sent in great abundance, he was still more inflamed with love to her: insomuch that he promised to give her two hundred thousand Attic drachmae for one night's lodging. And when this would not prevail upon her, and he was not able to bear this misfortune in his amours, he resolved to
15 famish himself to death, for want of food, on account of Paulina's refusal: and he went on with his purpose accordingly. Now Mundus had a freedwoman, who had been made free by his father, whose name was Ide; one skilful in all sorts of mischief. This woman was much grieved at the young man's resolution to kill himself (for he
20 did not conceal his intentions to destroy himself from others); and came to him, and encouraged him by her discourse, and made him to hope, by some promises she gave him, that he might obtain a night's lodging with Paulina. And when he joyfully hearkened to her, she said, she wanted no more than fifty thousand drachmae for
25 entrapping of the woman. So when she had encouraged the young man, and gotten as much money as she required, she did not take the same methods as had been taken before; because she perceived that the woman was by no means to be tempted by money. But as she knew that she was much devoted to the worship of the goddess Isis,
30 she devised the following stratagem: She went to some of Isis's priests, and upon the strongest assurances of concealment, she persuaded them by words, but chiefly by the offer of twenty-five thousand drachmae in hand, and as much more when the thing had taken

effect; and told them the passion of the young man; and persuaded
35 them to use all possible means to beguile the woman. So they were
drawn in to promise so to do, by the large sum of gold they were to
have. Accordingly the oldest of them went immediately to Paulina;
and upon his admittance, he desired to speak with her by herself.
When that was granted him, he told her, that he was sent by the god
40 Anubis, who was fallen in love with her, and enjoined her to come
to him. Upon this she took the message very kindly: and valued
herself greatly upon this condescension of the deity: and told her
husband, that she had a message sent her, and was to sup and to lie
with Anubis. So he agreed to her acceptance of the offer, as fully
45 satisfied with the chastity of his wife. Accordingly she went to the
temple: and after she had supped there, and it was the hour to go to
sleep, the priest shut the doors of the temple; when in the holy part
of it the lights were also put out. Then did Mundus leap out; and she
was at his service all the night, as supposing he was the god. And
50 when he was gone away, which was before those priests who knew
nothing of this stratagem were stirring, Paulina came early to her
husband, and told him how Anubis had appeared to her. Among her
friends also she declared how great a value she put upon this favour.
They partly disbelieved the thing, when they reflected on its nature;
55 and partly were amazed at it, as having no pretence for not believing
it, when they considered the modesty, and the dignity of the person.
But on the third day after what had been done, Mundus met Paulina,
and said, 'Nay, Paulina, thou hast saved me two hundred thousand
drachmae; which sum thou mightest have added to thine own
60 family. Yet hast thou not failed to be at my service in the manner I
invited thee. As for the reproaches thou hast laid upon Mundus, I
value not the business of names; but I rejoice in the pleasure I reaped
by what I did, while I assumed the name of Anubis.' When he had
said this, he went his way. But now she began to come to the sense of
65 the grossness of what she had done; and rent her garments, and told
her husband of the horrid nature of this contrivance, and prayed him
not to neglect to assist her in this case. So he discovered the fact to the
emperor. Whereupon Tiberius inquired into the matter thoroughly,
by examining the priests about it; and ordered them to be crucified;
70 as well as Ide, who was the occasion of their perdition, and who had
contrived the whole matter, which was so injurious to the woman.
He also demolished the temple of Isis; and gave order that her statue
should be thrown into the river Tiber. But he only banished Mundus;
because he supposed that what crime he had committed was done
75 out of the passion of love.

l. 40 *Anubis* was the son of Osiris and Nephthys (the sister of Isis). It should be
noted that the whole sordid story narrated by Josephus presupposes the fact

that intelligent and respectable people like Paulina and Saturninus believed in the gods, and that a 'divine marriage' could take place.

112

Paris Papyrus 574. *A Mithras Liturgy*

See A. Dieterich, *Eine Mithrasliturgie* (3rd edition, Leipzig and Berlin, 1923), 2–15. It is now very widely agreed that this work, though still frequently referred to under the title given, has in fact nothing to do with the religion of Mithras. Whether it is properly described as a liturgy is a further question. It remains however an interesting example of the interpenetration of magic and religion.

Be gracious unto me, Providence and Fate, as I write down these first traditional mysteries, [granting] immortality to my only child, a worthy initiate into this our power, which the great god Helios Mithras commanded to be imparted to me by his archangel, in order
5　that I alone, an eagle, might tread heaven and behold all things.
　　This is the invocation of the prayer:
　　'First origin of my origin, first beginning of my beginning, spirit of spirit, firstfruit of the spirit within me, fire which art god-given to my mixing, the mixing of the mixings within me, firstfruit of the
10　fire within me, water of water, firstfruit of the water within me, earthy substance, firstfruit of the earthy substance within me, whole body of me, A, son of my mother B, framed by the honourable arm and incorruptible right hand in a world unilluminated yet bright, with no living soul, yet with a living soul: if it seem good to you to
15　give me, held as I am by my underlying nature, to immortal birth, in order that, after the present need which presses sore upon me, I may behold by deathless spirit the deathless Beginning, by deathless water, by solid earth and air, that I may be born anew by Thought, that I may be initiated and that the sacred spirit may breathe in me,
20　that I may marvel at the holy fire, that I may behold the terrible great deep of the Dayspring, that the life-giving and surrounding Aether may hear me; for to-day I am to gaze with deathless eyes, I who was born mortal from a mortal womb, but transformed by mighty power and an incorruptible right hand . . .'
25　. . . But you shall see how the gods gaze upon you, and influence you. Lay at once your right [fore-]finger upon your mouth and say, 'Silence! Silence! Silence!' (a symbol of the living, incorruptible god). 'Guard me, Silence!' Then whistle long, then sneeze, and say . . . and then you will see the gods looking graciously upon you, and no
30　longer influencing you but going upon their own course of business.
　　. . .
　　'O Lord, hail, great in power, king great in sovereignty, greatest of gods, Helios, Lord of heaven and earth, god of gods, mighty is thy

breath, mighty is thy power. Lord, if it please thee, announce me to
35 the greatest god, who hath begotten and made thee; for I am a man,
A, the son of my mother B, born of the mortal womb of B and of
lifegiving seed, and this day by thee who hast been regenerated, who
out of so many thousands have been brought into immortality in
this hour by the counsel of god, who is good beyond measure—a
40 man who wills and prays to worship thee according to his human
power.' When you have said this, he will come into the vault of
heaven and you will see him walking as on a road.

. . . Gaze on the god, groan long, and greet him thus: 'O Lord, hail,
ruler of water, hail, founder of earth, hail, sovereign of spirit. Lord,
45 having been born again I depart; increasing and having been
increased I die; born of a life-giving birth I am set free for death and
go on my way, as thou didst ordain, as thou didst enact and didst
make the mystery.'

l. 1   *I write down.* The writer of the papyrus provides instructions for his 'child',
who is to be born again as a disciple of the god.

l. 7   *First origin of my origin* . . .The prayers in this liturgy are marked by 'vain
repetition' and there are places where the original, and with it the translation,
does not make sense. It also contains many meaningless, magical, words,
which are not represented in the translation. The many parallels with New
Testament language are very striking, and will be apparent to the English
reader; they are even more evident in Greek.

l. 25   *Influence you*, in a harmful way; cf. *l. 30*.

l. 48   *Make the mystery.* Dieterich translates *'geschaffen hast das Sakrament'*, with
direct reference to the cult act in which regeneration takes place.

113

M. J. Vermaseren, *Corpus Inscriptionum et Monumentorum Religionis
Mithricae* I. 423. The dedication of a Mithraic chapel, in Rome.

This is a favoured place, holy, dear to the gods, and kindly, which
Mithras pointed out, and suggested to Proficientius, father of the
sacred rites, that he should make and dedicate for him a cave. And
pressing on with swift work he (now) completes the welcome duty,
5 which, under good auspices, he undertook with careful thought, that
the Syndexi might be able to perform their rites joyfully for ever.

These few lines were composed by Proficientius, most worthy
father of Mithra.

l. 2   *Father* (also line 8). A technical term denoting a leading officer in the religion.

l. 3   *Cave.* The Mithraic rites were performed in natural or artificial underground
chambers.

114

Vermaseren, *op. cit.* I, 473. A dedication in Rome.

> As a gift to Zeus, great Sun, unconquered Mithras, and the gods who
> share his shrine, Castus (father) and Castus (son), sacred Raven, set up
> two six-wicked bronze lampstands, and sanctified them, L. Satyrius
> Sporus and Pactumeius Lausus, fathers, and Modestus, Paralius,
> 5 Agathemerus, Felix, Apamenius, and Keloed, lions, assisting.

l. 2   *Raven.* The title of an order in the Mithraic cult.

l. 4   *Fathers.* Another Mithraic order.

l. 5   *Lions.* Another Mithraic order.

115

Vermaseren, *op. cit.* I, 523. Record of a taurobolium, in Rome.

> Under the third consulship of our lords Constantine and Maximin,
> Augusti, I, Gaius Magius Donatus Severianus, senator, father of the
> sacred rites of unconquered Mithras, hierophant of Father Liber and
> of the Hecates, made the taurobolium, on April 15.

l. 1   *The third consulship* . . . AD 313.

l. 2   *Senator, vir clarissimus,* the usual title of a senator, though it could mean
simply 'a very famous man'.
Father of the sacred rites. See **113**, *l.* 2.

l. 4   *April* 15. 17 Kal. Maias.

7   Jewish History

The history of the Jews in the New Testament period is a long story of which fortunately many details are known. To provide it here with even half complete documentation is neither possible nor necessary; instead, a few salient points receive brief illustration.

The Maccabean Period

In the first half of the second century BC the Jewish nation emerged from a period of relative obscurity, on which however, as on most of the ground covered in this chapter, Martin Hengel, *Judaism and Hellenism* (London 1974), should now be consulted. Alexander the Great's decade of vigorous campaigning had changed the shape of the Near East more radically than many preceding centuries; Alexandria and Antioch (to go no farther) became the centres of powerful Hellenistic monarchies, and Palestine suffered as a buffer state between the Ptolemies in the one and the Seleucids in the other. The Jews found themselves in a potent and persuasive atmosphere of Hellenistic life and culture, which undoubtedly began to influence their own civilization, and might well have long continued to do so had not Antiochus IV Epiphanes (of Syria; 176–164 BC), by seeking to accelerate the process, aroused the Jewish conscience, thereby provoking a fierce and resolute resistance which gave direction and impetus to the history of the next 300 years. Of the period dominated by the Maccabean family, 1 Maccabees is a more or less contemporary, sober, and on the whole trustworthy record; but not all its sources are of equal value.

116

1 *Maccabees* 1. 5–15

> And after these things he took to his bed, and perceived that he was about to die. Then he called his chief ministers, men who had been brought up with him from his youth, and divided his kingdom among them while he was yet alive. And Alexander had reigned
> 5 twelve years when he died. And his ministers ruled, each in his particular domain. And after he was dead they all assumed the diadem, and their sons after them did likewise; and this continued for many years. And these wrought much evil on the earth.

And a sinful shoot came forth from them, Antiochus Epiphanes,
10 the son of Antiochus the king, who had been a hostage in Rome, and
had become king in the one hundred and thirty-seventh year of the
Greek kingdom. In those days there came forth out of Israel lawless
men, and persuaded many, saying: 'Let us go and make a covenant
with the nations that are round about us; for since we separated
15 ourselves from them many evils have come upon us.' And the saying
appeared good in their eyes; and as certain of the people were eager
to carry this out, they went to the king, and he gave them authority
to introduce the customs of the gentiles. And they built a gymnasium
in Jerusalem according to the manner of the Gentiles. They also
20 submitted themselves to uncircumcision, and repudiated the holy
covenant; yea, they joined themselves to the Gentiles, and sold
themselves to do evil.

l. 1   *He took to his bed*—Alexander the Great, who was taken ill in the night of 31
May 323 BC, and died eleven days later. The author of 1 Maccabees is here
less accurate than usual—not unnaturally, since he is describing events which
took place long before his own time. Not all of Alexander's generals became
kings, nor is it probable that he divided his kingdom among them.

l. 9   *Antiochus Epiphanes.* His father, Antiochus III, was defeated by the Romans
at Magnesia in 190 BC, and the son lived twelve years in Rome as a hostage.
No doubt these experiences gave him a clear sense of the growing power of
Rome, and this probably lay behind the provocative actions which the
author of 1 Maccabees sees rather as the fruit of unbridled wickedness and
folly. For the payment of tribute to Rome, and for the accumulation of
treasure, Antiochus found it necessary to rob temples; that at Jerusalem was
not the only one that suffered. Further, he may well have come to believe
that the eastern states could only stand against Rome on the basis of a 'united
Hellenistic front', to which Jews no less than others were required to
conform.

l. 11   *The one hundred and thirty-seventh year of the Greek kingdom,* that is, of the
Seleucid kingdom, which was founded in 312 BC.

l. 12   *There came forth out of Israel lawless men.* The spontaneous movement towards
Hellenization (above, p. 135) received a new impulse. There are more details
in 2 Maccabees 4, where Jason the high priest is mentioned as one of the
Hellenizers.

117

1 *Maccabees* 1. 20–4

And Antiochus, after he had smitten Egypt, returned in the one
hundred and fifty-third year, and went up against Israel and Jerusalem
with a great army. And in his arrogance he entered into the sanctuary,
and took the golden altar, and the candlestick for the light, and all its
5 accessories, and the table of the shew-bread, and the cups, and the

bowls, and the golden censers, and the veil, and the crowns, and the golden adornment on the façade of the Temple, and he scaled it all off. Moreover, he took the silver, and the gold, and the choice vessels; he also took the hidden treasures which he found. And having taken
10 everything, he returned to his own land.

l. 1 *After he had smitten Egypt.* Antiochus's depradations began after his first Egyptian campaign. They were continued after his second (1 Macc. 1. 29f.). Certainly on the latter occasion, probably on the former (see Josephus, *Antiquities* xii. 244, 246), Antiochus had been repelled from Egypt not by local resistance but by Roman threats; these would doubtless intensify the fears mentioned above.

118

1 *Maccabees* 1. 54–64

And on the fifteenth day of Chislev in the one hundred and forty-fifth year they set up upon the altar an 'abomination of desolation', and in the cities of Judah on every side they established high-places; and they offered sacrifices at the doors of the houses and in the streets.
5 And the books of the Law which they found they rent in pieces, and burned them in the fire. And with whomsoever was found a book of the covenant, and if he was found consenting unto the Law, such an one was, according to the king's sentence, condemned to death. Thus did they in their might to the Israelites who were found month
10 by month in their cities. And on the twenty-fifth day of the month they sacrificed upon the altar which was upon the altar of burnt-offering. And, according to the decree, they put to death the women who had circumcised their children, hanging their babes round their mothers' necks, and they put to death their entire families, together
15 with those who had circumcised them. Nevertheless many in Israel stood firm and determined in their hearts that they would not eat unclean things, and chose rather to die so that they might not be defiled with meats, thereby profaning the holy covenant; and they did die. And exceeding great wrath came upon Israel.

l. 2 '*Abomination of desolation*'. Cf. Dan. 11. 31; 12. 11. This phrase refers to the heathen altar set up on the great altar of the Temple (see *l.* 11).

l. 10 *On the twenty-fifth day of the month.* On this day, three years later, the Temple was reconsecrated. See **121**.

l. 18 *And they did die,* perhaps the first martyrs for religion. See **256** and its preceding note.

119

I *Maccabees* 2. 15–28

And the king's officers who were enforcing the apostasy came to the city of Modin to make them sacrifice. And many from Israel went unto them; but Mattathias and his sons gathered themselves together. Then the king's officers answered and spake to Mattathias, saying: 'A
5   ruler art thou, and illustrious and great in this city, and upheld by sons and brothers. Do thou, therefore, come first, and carry out the king's command, as all the nations have done, and all the people of Judah, and they that have remained in Jerusalem; then shalt thou and thy house be numbered among the friends of the king, and thou and
10   thy sons shall be honoured with silver and gold, and with many gifts.' Thereupon Mattathias answered and said with a loud voice: 'If all the nations that are within the king's dominions obey him by forsaking, every one of them, the worship of their fathers, and have chosen for themselves to follow his commands, yet will I and my
15   sons and my brethren walk in the covenant of our fathers. Heaven forbid that we should forsake the Law and the ordinances; but the law of the king we will not obey by departing from our worship either to the right hand or to the left.' And as he ceased speaking these words, a Jew came forward in the sight of all to sacrifice upon the
20   altar in Modin in accordance with the king's command. And when Mattathias saw it, his zeal was kindled, and his heart quivered with wrath; and his indignation burst forth for judgement, so that he ran and slew him on the altar; and at the same time he also killed the king's officer who had come to enforce the sacrificing, pulled down
25   the altar, and thus showed forth his zeal for the Law, just as Phinehas had done in the case of Zimri the son of Salom. And Mattathias cried out with a loud voice in the city, saying, 'Let every one that is zealous for the Law and that would maintain the covenant come forth after me!' And he and his sons fled into the mountains, and left all that
30   they possessed in the city.

l. 3   *Mattathias and his sons.* Mattathias was a priest living at Modin; his sons were John, Simon, Judas (called Maccabaeus), Eleazar, and Jonathan.

l. 7   *As all the nations have done.* Antiochus's desire for conformity was probably due not so much to anti-Semitism as to his plan to unite the Hellenistic states (above, **116**, note on *l.* 9).

l. 9   *The friends of the king,* apparently an official title.

120

I *Maccabees* 3. 10–26

And Apollonius gathered the Gentiles together, and a great host from Samaria, to fight against Israel. And Judas perceived it, and went

forth to meet him, and smote him, and slew him; and many fell
wounded to death, and the rest fled. And they took their spoils; and
5 Judas took the sword of Apollonius, and therewith fought he all his
days.

And Seron, the commander of the host of Syria, heard that Judas
had gathered a gathering and a congregation of faithful men with
him, and of such as went out to war; and he said: 'I will make a name
10 for myself, and get me glory in the kingdom; and I will fight against
Judas and them that are with him, that set at nought the word of the
king.' And he went up again; and there went up with him a mighty
army of the ungodly to help him, to take vengeance on the children
of Israel. And he came near to the ascent of Bethhoron; and Judas
15 went forth to meet him with a small company. But when they saw
the army coming to meet them, they said unto Judas: 'What? shall
we be able, being a small company, to fight against so great and
strong a multitude? And we, for our part, are faint, having tasted no
food this day.' And Judas said: 'It is an easy thing for many to be shut
20 up in the hands of a few, and there is no difference in the sight of
Heaven to save by many or by few; for victory in battle standeth
not in the multitude of an host, but strength is from Heaven. They
come unto us in fullness of insolence and lawlessness, to destroy us
and our wives and our children, for to spoil us; but we fight for our
25 lives and our laws. And he himself will discomfit them before our
face; but as for you, be ye not afraid of them.' Now when he had left
off speaking he leapt suddenly upon them, and Seron and his army
were discomfited before him. And they pursued them at the descent
of Bethhoron unto the plain; and there fell of them about eight
30 hundred men; and the rest fled into the land of the Philistines.

Then began the fear of Judas and of his brethren, and the dread of
them fell upon the nations round about them. And his name came
near even unto the king; and every nation told of the battles of Judas.

l. 1 *Apollonius.* The name is introduced without explanation. Comparison of 1
Macc. 1. 29 with 2 Macc. 5. 24 suggests that Apollonius had previously been
entrusted with the spoliation of Jerusalem.

l. 2 *Judas.* His father Mattathias was now dead (1 Macc. 2. 70). He had
recommended Judas among his sons as fittest for military leadership.

l. 14 *The ascent of Bethhoron*; cf. *l.* 28, *descent of Bethhoron.* This place evidently
commanded the road down from Jerusalem to the coastal plain and was
more than once the scene of bitter fighting.

121

1 *Maccabees* 4. 36–61

But Judas and his brethren said: 'Behold, our enemies are discomfited:
let us go up to cleanse the Holy Place, and re-dedicate it.' And all the

army was gathered together, and they went unto mount Sion, and
they saw our sanctuary laid desolate, and the altar profaned, and the
5 gates burned up, and shrubs growing in the courts as in a forest or
upon one of the mountains, and the chambers of the priests pulled
down; and they rent their garments, and made great lamentation,
and put ashes on their heads; and they fell on their faces to the
ground, and they blew the solemn blasts upon the trumpets, and
10 cried unto heaven. Then Judas appointed a certain number of men to
fight against those that were in the citadel, until he should have
cleansed the Holy Place. And he chose blameless priests, such as had
delight in the Law; and they cleansed the Holy Place, and bare out
the stones of defilement into an unclean place. And they took counsel
15 concerning the altar of burnt-offerings, which had been profaned,
what they should do with it. And a good idea occurred to them
namely to pull it down, lest it should be a reproach unto them,
because the Gentiles had defiled it; so they pulled down the altar, and
laid down the stones in the mountain of the House, in a convenient
20 place, until a prophet should come and decide as to what should be
done concerning them. And they took whole stones according to the
Law, and built a new altar after the fashion of the former one; and
they built the Holy Place, and the inner parts of the house, and
hallowed the courts. And they made the holy vessels new, and they
25 brought the candlestick, and the altar of burnt-offerings and of
incense, and the table, into the Temple. And they burned incense
upon the altar, and they lighted the lamps that were upon the
candlestick in order to give light in the Temple. And they set loaves
upon the table, and hung up the veils, and finished all the works
30 which they had undertaken. And they rose up early in the morning
on the twenty-fifth day of the ninth month, which is the month
Chislev, in the one hundred and forty-eighth year, and offered
sacrifice, according to the Law, upon the new altar of burnt-offerings
which they had made. At the corresponding time of the month and
35 on the corresponding day on which the Gentiles had profaned it, on
that day was it dedicated afresh, with songs and harps and lutes, and
with cymbals. And all the people fell upon their faces, and
worshipped, and gave praise, looking up unto heaven, to him who
had prospered them. And they celebrated the dedication of the altar
40 for eight days, and offered burnt-offerings with gladness, and
sacrificed a sacrifice of deliverance and praise. And they decked the
forefront of the Temple with crowns of gold and small shields, and
dedicated afresh the gates and the chambers of the priests, and
furnished them with doors. And there was exceeding great gladness
45 among the people, and the reproach of the Gentiles was turned away.
And Judas and his brethren and the whole congregation of Israel
ordained, that the days of the dedication of the altar should be kept

in their seasons year by year for eight days, from the twenty-fifth
day of the month Chislev, with gladness and joy. And at that season
50 they built high walls and strong towers around mount Sion, lest
haply the Gentiles should come and tread them down, as they had
done aforetime. And he set there a force to keep it, and they fortified
Bethsura to keep it, that the people might have a stronghold over
against Idumaea.

l. 1 *Our enemies are discomfited.* Since the rout of Seron (above, **120**) the Jews had
defeated Gorgias and Lysias.

l. 11 *In the citadel.* Very early in his proceedings against the Jews Antiochus had
fortified 'the city of David', that is the southern, and lower, part of the
Temple mount. This 'became a sore menace, for it was a place to lie in wait
in against the sanctuary, and an evil adversary to Israel continually' (1 Macc.
1. 36). It remained in the possession of the Syrians until the time of Simon (1
Macc. 13. 50).

l. 14 *The stones of defilement,* the stones of which the heathen altar (the 'abomination
of desolation', see **118**) had been made.

l. 15 *The altar of burnt-offerings,* the Jewish altar which had been profaned by the
heathen altar erected upon it.

l. 46 *Judas and his brethren . . . ordained.* This was the origin of the feast of *Hanukkah*
(חנכה; in Greek, ἐγκαίνια, John 10. 22), also called the feast of Lights. (For
a different theory of its origin and meaning see O. S. Rankin, *The Origins of
the Festival of Hanukkah* (Edinburgh, 1930).) It was celebrated in a way
similar to the feast of Tabernacles or 'Booths' (see **181**), and was sometimes
called 'the feast of Tabernacles in the month Chislev'.

122

1 *Maccabees* 8. 17–32

And Judas chose Eupolemus, the son of John, the son of Accos, and
Jason, the son of Eleazar, and sent them to Rome, to make a league of
amity and confederacy with them, and that they should take the
yoke from them, when they saw that the kingdom of the Greeks did
5 keep Israel in bondage. And they went to Rome, and the way was
exceeding long; and they entered into the senate house, and answered
and said: 'Judas, who is also called Maccabaeus, and his brethren and
the whole people of the Jews, have sent us unto you, to make a
confederacy and peace with you, and that we might be registered as
10 your confederates and friends.' And the thing was well-pleasing in
their sight. And this is the copy of the writing which they wrote
back again on tablets of brass, and sent to Jerusalem, that it might be
with them there for a memorial of peace and confederacy:
'Good success be to the Romans, and to the nation of the Jews, by
15 sea and by land for ever; the sword also and the enemy be far from

them. But if war arise for Rome first, or for any of their confederates
in all their dominion, the nation of the Jews shall help them as
confederates as the occasion shall prescribe to them, with all their
heart; and unto them that make war they [i.e. the Jews] shall not
20 give, neither supply, food, arms, money, or ships, as it hath seemed
good unto Rome; and they [i.e. the Jews] shall observe their
obligations, receiving nothing [in the way of a bribe]. In the same
manner, moreover, if war come first upon the nation of the Jews, the
Romans shall help them as confederates with all their soul, as the
25 occasion shall prescribe to them; and to them that are confederates
there shall not be given corn, arms, money, or ships, as it hath seemed
good unto Rome; and they shall observe these obligations, and that
without deceit. According to these words have the Romans made a
treaty with the people of the Jews. But if hereafter the one party or
30 the other shall determine to add or diminish anything, they shall do
it at their pleasure, and whatsoever they shall add or take away shall
be established. And as touching the evils which king Demetrius
doeth unto you, we have written to him saying: "Wherefore hast
thou made thy yoke heavy upon our friends and confederates the
35 Jews? If, therefore, they plead any more against thee, we will do
them justice, and fight thee by sea and by land.'"

l. 1   *Judas . . . sent them to Rome.* Here may be noted on the one hand the astuteness
of the Jewish rulers throughout this period in picking the winning side in
foreign quarrels, and on the other the Roman principle of *divide et impera*—
the Jews might first be used against the Syrian kingdom, and then themselves
subjugated at leisure.

l. 20   *As it hath seemed good unto Rome*; cf. *l.* 26. The advantage given by the treaty
to Rome is manifest.

l. 32   *Demetrius.* Demetrius I, now king in Antioch.

123

1 *Maccabees* 11. 54–62

Now after this Tryphon returned, and with him the young child
Antiochus; and he reigned, and put on a diadem. And there were
gathered unto him all the forces which Demetrius had sent away in
disgrace; and they fought against him, and he fled, and was put to
5 rout. And Tryphon took the elephants, and became master of
Antioch. And the young Antiochus wrote unto Jonathan, saying: 'I
confirm unto thee the high-priesthood, and appoint thee over the
four governments, and to be one of the king's friends.' And he sent
unto him golden vessels and furniture for the table, and gave him
10 leave to drink in golden vessels, and to be clothed in purple, and to
have a golden buckle. And his brother Simon he made governor
over the district from the Ladder of Tyre unto the borders of Egypt.

And Jonathan went forth, and took his journey beyond the river, and through the cities; and all the forces of Syria gathered themselves
15 unto him for to be his confederates. And he came to Askalon, and they of the city met him honourably. And he departed thence to Gaza, and they of Gaza shut him out; and he laid siege unto it, and burned the suburbs thereof with fire, and spoiled them. And they of Gaza made request unto Jonathan, and he gave them his right hand,
20 and took the sons of their princes for hostages, and sent them away to Jerusalem. And he passed through the country as far as Damascus.

l. 1   *Tryphon* played a powerful part in the complicated politics of this period. He opposed king Demetrius II, and was responsible for putting forward Antiochus VI in his place.
The young child Antiochus, the son of Alexander Balas, who had been living in the care of Imalcue the Arabian. Tryphon doubtless hoped to be able to use the youthful king as a puppet while he himself retained the substance of power.

l. 3   *Demetrius.* Demetrius II, son of the Demetrius mentioned above (**122**).

l. 7   *I confirm unto thee the high-priesthood.* Jonathan (his brother Judas being now dead) had been appointed high priest by Alexander Balas (1 Macc. 10. 20). The family of Mattathias was a priestly family and therefore eligible for the office, which was regularly held by the later rulers of the Jews (see **124–6**).

l. 8   *The four governments,* the prefectures of Aphaerema, Lydda and Ramathaim; together with Judaea (which however is probably to be taken for granted, the other four governments being additional), or Ptolemais or Ekron.

l. 10 *Golden vessels, etc.* These are marks of royal dignity. This passage marks one of the peaks of Jewish good fortune in this period.

The High Priests

The rule of Jonathan may serve as a transition to the period in which a succession of high priests exercised both religious and civil power in Jerusalem. At first they continued to be of the Maccabean, or Hasmonean, family. The political history of the period is very complicated, and over-simplified conclusions must not be drawn from the few documents quoted here.

124

1 *Maccabees* 14. 25–49

But when the people heard these things, they said: 'What thanks shall we give to Simon and his sons? For he, and his brethren, and his father's house have made themselves strong, and have chased away in fight the enemies of Israel from them, and established liberty for it.'
5 And they wrote on tablets of brass, and set them upon a pillar in

mount Sion. And this is the copy of the writing: 'On the eighteenth day of Elul, in the one hundred and seventy-second year—that is the third year of Simon the high priest, and the prince of the people of God—in a great congregation of priests and people and princes of
10   the nation, and of the elders of the country, the following was promulgated by us: Forasmuch as oftentimes there have been wars in the country, Simon the son of Mattathias, the son of the children of Joarib, and his brethren, put themselves in jeopardy, and withstood the enemies of their nation, that their sanctuary and the Law might
15   be upheld; and they glorified their nation with great glory. And Jonathan assembled their nation together, and became high priest to them; and he was gathered to his people. Then their enemies determined to invade their country, that they might destroy their country utterly, and stretch forth their hands against their sanctuary.
20   Then rose up Simon and fought for his nation; and he spent much of his own substance, and armed the valiant men of his nation, and gave them wages. And he fortified the cities of Judaea, and Bethsura that lieth upon the borders of Judaea, where the arms of the enemies were aforetime, and set there a garrison of Jews. And he fortified Joppa
25   which is by the sea, and Gazara which is upon the borders of Azotus, wherein the enemies dwelt aforetime; and he placed Jews there, and whatsoever things were needful for the sustenance of these he put in them. And when the people saw the faith of Simon, and the glory which he sought to bring unto his nation, they made him their leader
30   and high priest, because he had done all these things, and because of the justice and the faith which he kept to his nation, and because he sought by all means to exalt his people. And in his days things prospered in his hands, so that the Gentiles were taken away out of their [the Jews'] country; and they also that were in the city of David,
35   they that were in Jerusalem, who had made themselves a citadel, out of which they issued, and polluted all things round about the sanctuary, and did great hurt unto its purity, these did he expel; and he made Jews to dwell therein, and fortified it for the safety of the country and of the city; and he made high the walls of Jerusalem.
40   And king Demetrius confirmed him in the high-priesthood in consequence of these things, and made him one of his friends, and honoured him with great honour. For he had heard that the Jews had been proclaimed by the Romans friends, and confederates, and brethren, and that they had met the ambassadors of Simon
45   honourably. And the Jews and the priests were well pleased that Simon should be their leader and high priest for ever, until a faithful prophet should arise; and that he should be a captain over them, to set them over their works, and over the country, and over the arms, and over the strongholds, and that he should take charge of the
50   sanctuary, and that he should be obeyed by all, and that all instruments

in the country should be written in his name, and that he should be
clothed in purple and wear gold; and that it should not be lawful for
anyone among the people or among the priests to set at nought any
of these things, or to gainsay the things spoken by him, or to gather
55 an assembly in the country without him, or that any other should be
clothed in purple, or wear a buckle of gold; but that whosoever
should do otherwise, or set at nought any of these things, should be
liable to punishment. And all the people consented to ordain for
Simon that it should be done according to these words. And Simon
60 accepted hereof and consented to fill the office of high priest, and to
be captain and governor of the Jews and of the priests, and to preside
over all matters.'

And they commanded to put this writing on tablets of brass, and
to set them up within the precincts of the sanctuary in a conspicuous
65 place; and copies of this they caused to be placed in the treasury, to
the end that Simon and his sons might have them.

l. 1   *What thanks shall we give to Simon?* Tryphon, no longer content to be the
power behind Antiochus's throne, resolved upon seizing the monarchy for
himself; fearing that Jonathan would prove faithful to Antiochus he had him
captured and killed by treachery. Simon succeeded his brother, defeated
Tryphon, made a treaty with Demetrius II, captured Gazara and the citadel
of Jerusalem (above, **121**), and renewed the treaty with Rome. His son John
became his general.

l. 8   *The high priest, and prince of the people of God.* The Greek reads 'the high priest
in Asaramel' (or Saramel). This is probably due to corruption of an original
Hebrew שַׂר עַם אֵל (*sar 'am 'el*) 'prince of the people of God', or perhaps of שַׂר יִשְׂרָאֵל (*sar yisra'el*) 'prince of Israel'. In any case it is clear
(*ll.* 59ff.) that Simon was the military and political head of his people as well
as high priest.

l. 46   *For ever*; that is, the office was to be hereditary in his family. The Hasmoneans
were in effect both kings and high priests.

125

Josephus, *Antiquities* xiii. 372–6

As for Alexander, his own people revolted against him—for the
nation was aroused against him—at the celebration of the festival,
and as he stood beside the altar and was about to sacrifice, they pelted
him with citrons, it being a custom among the Jews that at the
5 festival of Tabernacles everyone holds wands made of palm branches
and citrons—these we have described elsewhere; and they added
insult to injury by saying that he was descended from captives and
was unfit to hold office and to sacrifice; and being enraged at this, he
killed some six thousand of them, and also placed a wooden barrier
10 about the altar and the Temple as far as the coping [of the court]

which the priests alone were permitted to enter, and by this means blocked the people's way to him. He also maintained foreign troops of Pisidians and Cilicians, for he could not use Syrians, being at war with them. And after subduing the Arabs of Moab and Galaaditis,

15 whom he forced to pay tribute, he demolished Amathūs, as Theodorus did not venture to meet him in the field. Then he engaged in battle with Obedas, the king of the Arabs, and falling into an ambush in a rough and difficult region, he was pushed by a multitude of camels into a deep ravine near Garada, a village of Gaulanis, and

20 barely escaped with his own life, and fleeing from there, came to Jerusalem. But when the nation attacked him upon this misfortune, he made war on it and within six years slew no fewer than fifty thousand Jews. And so when he urged them to make an end of their hostility toward him, they only hated him the more on account of

25 what had happened. And when he asked what he ought to do and what they wanted of him, they all cried out, 'To die'; and they sent to Demetrius Akairos, asking him to come to their assistance.

l. 1   *Alexander,* Alexander Jannaeus, who ruled from 104 to 78 BC. His coins, bearing the bilingual inscription יהונתן המלך (King Jonathan), ΒΑΣΙΛ-ΕΩΣ ΑΛΕΞΑΝΔΡΟΥ (King Alexander), show that he claimed the royal title. He was unpopular with the people, among whom the Pharisees (see **135**, *ll.* 52–67) were gaining favour, but a vigorous and not unsuccessful soldier.

l. 7   *He was descended from captives.* This slander was brought against John Hyrcanus, father of Alexander (*Ant.* xiii. 292; cf. Lev. 21. 14).

l. 16   *Theodorus.* Amathūs was in Arab territory (east of Jordan), and Theodorus therefore probably an Arab chief. He had massacred 10,000 Jews and plundered Alexander's baggage (*Ant.* xiii. 356).

l. 19   *Gaulanis.* Read, against the MSS., on the ground of the parallel in *War* i. 90.

l. 27   *Demetrius Akairos*, Demetrius III, king of Syria. He defeated Alexander, but this reversal of fortune brought round many Jews to Alexander's side and he was able to recover his position.

126

Josephus, *Antiquities* xiv. 69–79

Now when the siege-engine was brought up, the largest of the towers was shaken and fell, making a breach through which the enemy poured in . . . And there was slaughter everywhere. For some of the Jews were slain by the Romans, and others by their fellows; and

5 there were some who hurled themselves down the precipices, and setting fire to their houses, burned themselves within them, for they could not bear to accept their fate. And so of the Jews there fell some twelve thousand, but of the Romans only a very few. One of those taken captive was Absalom, the uncle and at the same time father-in-

10 law of Aristobulus. And not light was the sin committed against the
sanctuary, which before that time had never been entered or seen.
For Pompey and not a few of his men went into it and saw what it
was unlawful for any but the high priests to see. But though the
golden table was there and the sacred lampstand and the libation
15 vessels and a great quantity of spices, and beside these, in the treasury,
the sacred moneys amounting to two thousand talents, he touched
none of these because of piety, and in this respect also he acted in a
manner worthy of his virtuous character. And on the morrow he
instructed the Temple servants to cleanse the Temple and to offer the
20 customary sacrifice to God, and he restored the high-priesthood to
Hyrcanus because in various ways he had been useful to him and
particularly because he had prevented the Jews throughout the
country from fighting on Aristobulus's side; and those responsible
for the war he executed by beheading ... And he made Jerusalem
25 tributary to the Romans, and took from its inhabitants the cities of
Coele-Syria which they had formerly subdued, and placed them
under his own governor; and the entire nation, which before had
raised itself so high, he confined within its own borders. He also
rebuilt Gadara, which had been demolished a little while before, to
30 please Demetrius the Gadarene, his freedman; and the other cities,
Hippus, Scythopolis, Pella, Dium, Samaria, as well as Marisa, Azotus,
Jamneia, and Arethusa, he restored to their own inhabitants. And not
only these cities in the interior, in addition to those that had been
demolished, but also the coast cities of Gaza, Joppa, Dora, and
35 Straton's Tower—this last city, which Herod refounded magnificently and adorned with harbours and temples, was later renamed
Caesarea—all these Pompey set free and annexed them to the
province.

For this misfortune which befell Jerusalem Hyrcanus and
40 Aristobulus were responsible, because of their dissension. For we lost
our freedom and became subject to the Romans, and the territory
which we had gained by our arms and taken from the Syrians we
were compelled to give back to them, and in addition the Romans
exacted of us in a short space of time more than ten thousand talents;
45 and the royal power which had formerly been bestowed on those
who were high priests by birth became the privilege of commoners.
But of this we shall speak in the proper place. Now Pompey gave
over to Scaurus Coele-Syria and the rest of Syria as far as the
Euphrates river and Egypt, and two Roman legions, and then went
50 off to Cilicia, making haste to reach Rome. And with him he took
Aristobulus in chains, together with his family; for he had two
daughters and as many sons; but one of them, Alexander, got away,
while the younger son, Antigonus, was carried off to Rome together
with his sisters.

l. 1   *Now,* in 63 BC. As at later times (see **138–44**), faction proved the downfall of the Jewish State. Alexander Jannaeus was succeeded by his widow Alexandra, who made her eldest son Hyrcanus high priest, and would have had him for her successor; but on her death his brother Aristobulus seized power. Civil war ensued. Pompey the Great was now active in the East and both parties solicited his aid. After complicated political manœuvres he found himself besieging the adherents of Aristobulus in Jerusalem.

l. 4   *By their fellows.* Within Jerusalem there were also adherents of Hyrcanus, who wished to open the gates to Pompey.

l. 11   *Had never been entered or seen,* except by the high priests.

l. 27   *His own governor,* the legate of the province of Syria, Scaurus; see *l.* 48.

l. 32   *He restored to their own inhabitants.* The cities had earlier been taken by the Jews from Gentile inhabitants. Josephus's list is incomplete; other cities in the same area reckoned their dates from their liberation by Pompey.

l. 38   *To the province,* of Syria.

l. 47   *In the proper place; in the next book, *Ant.* xv.

l. 50   *Making haste.* Nevertheless, he wintered in Asia Minor.

Herod the Great

We are brought to the threshold of the New Testament period by one of the most curious epochs in Jewish history. The Idumaean adventurer Antipater, and his son Herod the Great, both of them audacious, cunning, capable, and fortunate, became rulers of a Jewish kingdom, and founded a dynasty which lasted a century and a half—a long time in such turbulent days. Antipater had already been active before Pompey's intervention, as our first passage shows.

127

Josephus, *War* i. 123–6

The unexpected triumph of Aristobulus alarmed his adversaries, and, in particular, Antipater, an old and bitterly hated foe. An Idumaean by race, his ancestry, wealth, and other advantages put him in the front rank of his nation. It was he who now persuaded Hyrcanus to
5   seek refuge with Aretas, king of Arabia, with a view to recovering his kingdom, and at the same time urged Aretas to receive him and to reinstate him on the throne. Heaping aspersions on the character of Aristobulus and encomiums on Hyrcanus, he represented how becoming it would be in the sovereign of so brilliant a realm to
10   extend a protecting hand to the oppressed; and such, he said, was Hyrcanus, robbed of the throne which by right of primogeniture belonged to him.

Having thus prepared both parties for action, Antipater one night fled with Hyrcanus from the city, and, pushing on at full speed, safely

15 reached the capital of the Arabian kingdom, called Petra. There he
committed Hyrcanus into the hands of Aretas, and, by dint of
conciliatory speeches and cajoling presents, induced the king to
furnish an army, fifty thousand strong, both cavalry and infantry, to
reinstate his ward. This force Aristobulus was unable to resist.
20 Defeated in the first encounter he was driven into Jerusalem.

ll. 1, 4   *Aristobulus . . . Hyrcanus*. See above, **126** and notes.

l. 13   *Having thus prepared both parties for action*. The methods here described are
characteristic of Antipater and his son.

128

Josephus, *War* i. 199–207

After hearing both speakers, Caesar pronounced Hyrcanus to be the
more deserving claimant to the high-priesthood, and left Antipater
free choice of office. The latter, replying that it rested with him who
conferred the honour to fix the measure of the honour, was then
5 appointed viceroy of all Judaea. He was further authorized to rebuild
the ruined walls of the metropolis. Orders were sent by Caesar to
Rome for these honours to be graven in the Capitol, as a memorial
of his own justice and of Antipater's valour.

After escorting Caesar across Syria, Antipater returned to Judaea.
10 There his first act was to rebuild the wall of the capital which had
been overthrown by Pompey. He then proceeded to traverse the
country, quelling the local disturbances, and everywhere combining
menaces with advice. Their support of Hyrcanus, he told them,
would ensure them a prosperous and tranquil existence, in the
15 enjoyment of their own possessions and of the peace of the realm. If,
on the contrary, they put faith in the vain expectations raised by
persons who for personal profit desired revolution, they would find
in himself a master instead of a protector, in Hyrcanus a tyrant
instead of a king, in the Romans and Caesar enemies instead of rulers
20 and friends; for they would never suffer their own nominee to be
ousted from his office. But, while he spoke in this strain, he took the
organization of the country into his own hands, finding Hyrcanus
indolent and without the energy necessary to a king. He further
appointed his eldest son, Phasael, governor of Jerusalem and the
25 environs; the second, Herod, he sent with equal authority to Galilee,
though a mere lad.

Herod, energetic by nature, at once found material to test his
metal. Discovering that Ezekias, a brigand-chief, at the head of a large
horde, was ravaging the district on the Syrian frontier, he caught
30 him and put him and many of the brigands to death. This welcome
achievement was immensely admired by the Syrians. Up and down
the villages and in the towns the praises of Herod were sung, as the

restorer of their peace and possessions. This exploit, moreover, brought him to the notice of Sextus Caesar, a kinsman of the great
35 Caesar and governor of Syria. Phasael, on his side, with a generous emulation, vied with his brother's reputation; he increased his popularity with the inhabitants of Jerusalem, and kept the city under control without any tactless abuse of authority. Antipater, in consequence, was courted by the nation as if he were king and
40 universally honoured as lord of the realm. Notwithstanding this, his affection for Hyrcanus and his loyalty to him underwent no change.

l. 1   *Both speakers.* Antigonus, son of Aristobulus, and Antipater, who had accused each other.
Caesar, Julius Caesar. Pompey was now dead, and Antipater had promptly transferred his allegiance to the new master of the Roman world.

l. 5   *Viceroy,* or procurator.

l. 26   *A mere lad.* According to *Ant.* xiv. 158, Herod was fifteen years old.

129

Josephus, *War* i. 386f., 392*b*, 393*a*, 394, 396, 400

But, this peril surmounted, Herod was instantly plunged into anxiety about the security of his position. He was Antony's friend, and Antony had been defeated by Caesar at Actium. (In reality, he inspired more fear than he felt himself; for Caesar considered his
5 victory to be incomplete so long as Herod remained Antony's ally.) The king, nevertheless, resolved to confront the danger and, having sailed to Rhodes, where Caesar was sojourning, presented himself before him without a diadem, a commoner in dress and demeanour, but with the proud spirit of a king. His speech was direct; he told the
10 truth without reserve ...
   '... I therefore now confirm your kingdom to you by decree; and hereafter I shall endeavour to confer upon you some further benefit, that you may not feel the loss of Antony.'
   Having thus graciously addressed the king, he placed the diadem
15 on his head, and publicly notified this award by a decree, in which he expressed his commendation of the honoured man in ample and generous terms ...
   Subsequently, when Caesar passed through Syria on his way to Egypt, Herod entertained him for the first time with all the resources
20 of his realm; he accompanied the emperor on horseback when he reviewed his troops at Ptolemais; he entertained him and all his friends at a banquet; and he followed this up by making ample provision for the good cheer of the rest of the army....
   Accordingly, when Caesar reached Egypt, after the death of
25 Cleopatra and Antony, he not only conferred new honours upon

him, but also annexed to his kingdom the territory which Cleopatra
had appropriated, with the addition of Gadara, Hippos, and Samaria
and the maritime towns of Gaza, Anthedon, Joppa, and Strato's
Tower. . . .

30   Finally, on the death of Zenodorus, he further assigned to him all
the territory between Trachonitis and Galilee. But what Herod
valued more than all these privileges was that in Caesar's affection he
stood next after Agrippa, in Agrippa's next after Caesar. Thenceforth
he advanced to the utmost prosperity; his noble spirit rose to greater

35   heights, and his lofty ambition was mainly directed to works of
piety.

l. 1   *This peril surmounted*, an attack by the Arabs.

l. 3   *Caesar*, Octavius (subsequently Augustus).

l. 9   *His speech was direct.* In i. 388–90 Herod argues that his service to Antony
proves him a faithful friend to those who are his friends; Antony's downfall
was caused by his infatuation for Cleopatra. Caesar praises him for his
fidelity.

l. 28   *Strato's Tower.* See below, **130**.

l. 30   *Zenodorus*, who had ruled in the region of Trachonitis.

l. 33   *Agrippa* was Augustus's chief helper and confidant until his death in 12 BC.

130

Josephus, *War* i. 401ff., 408, 417, 422

Thus, in the fifteenth year of his reign, he restored the Temple and,
by erecting new foundation-walls, enlarged the surrounding area to
double its former extent. The expenditure devoted to this work was
incalculable, its magnificence never surpassed; as evidence one would

5   have pointed to the great colonnades around the Temple courts and
to the fortress which dominated it on the north. The colonnades
Herod reconstructed from the foundations; the fortress he restored
at a lavish cost in a style no way inferior to that of a palace, and called
it Antonia in honour of Antony. His own palace, which he erected

10   in the upper city, comprised two most spacious and beautiful
buildings, with which the Temple itself bore no comparison; these
he named after his friends, the one Caesareum, the other Agrippeum.

He was not content, however, to commemorate his patrons' names
by palaces only; his munificence extended to the creation of whole

15   cities. In the district of Samaria he built a town enclosed within
magnificent walls twenty furlongs in length, introduced into it six
thousand colonists, and gave them allotments of highly productive
land. In the centre of this settlement he erected a massive temple,
enclosed in ground, a furlong and a half in length, consecrated to

20   Caesar; while he named the town itself Sebaste. The inhabitants were

given a privileged constitution . . .

His notice was attracted by a town on the coast, called Strato's Tower, which, though then dilapidated, was, from its advantageous situation, suited for the exercise of his liberality. This he entirely
25 rebuilt with white stone, and adorned with the most magnificent palaces, displaying here, as nowhere else, the innate grandeur of his character . . .

No man ever showed greater filial affection. As a memorial to his father he founded a city in the fairest plain of his realm rich in rivers
30 and trees, and named it Antipatris. Above Jericho he built the walls of a fortress, remarkable alike for solidity and beauty, which he dedicated to his mother under the name of Cypros. . . .

After founding all these places, he proceeded to display his generosity to numerous cities outside his realm. Thus, he provided
35 gymnasia for Tripolis, Damascus, and Ptolemais, a wall for Byblus, halls, porticoes, temples, and market-places for Berytus and Tyre, theatres for Sidon and Damascus, an aqueduct for Laodicea-on-sea, baths, sumptuous fountains and colonnades, admirable alike for their architecture and proportions, for Ascalon; to other communities he
40 dedicated groves and meadow-land.

l. 20 *Sebaste* is Greek for Augusta.

l. 22 *Strato's Tower.* The new town was called Caesarea.

l. 34 *Numerous cities.* Notably, in addition to those mentioned in this paragraph, Athens and Antioch.

131

Josephus, *War* i. 429–33

Herod's genius was matched by his physical constitution. Always foremost in the chase, in which he distinguished himself above all by his skill in horsemanship, he on one occasion brought down forty wild beasts in a single day; for the country breeds boars and, in
5 greater abundance, stags and wild asses. As a fighter he was irresistible; and at practice spectators were often struck with astonishment at the precision with which he threw the javelin, the unerring aim with which he bent the bow. But besides these pre-eminent gifts of soul and body, he was blessed by good fortune; he rarely met with a
10 reverse in war, and, when he did, this was due not to his own fault, but either to treachery or to the recklessness of his troops.

But, in revenge for his public prosperity, fortune visited Herod with troubles at home; his ill-fated career originated with a woman to whom he was passionately attached. For, on ascending the throne,
15 he had dismissed the wife whom he had taken when he was still a

commoner, a native of Jerusalem named Doris, and married Mariamme, daughter of Alexander, the son of Aristobulus. It was she who brought into his house the discord, which, beginning at an early date, was greatly aggravated after his return from Rome. For, 20 in the first place, in the interests of his children by Mariamme, he banished from the capital the son whom he had had by Doris, namely Antipater, allowing him to visit it on the festivals only. Next he put to death, on suspicion of conspiracy, Hyrcanus, Mariamme's grandfather, who had come back from Parthia to Herod's court.

l. 17 *Alexander . . . Aristobulus.* See above, **127**.

l. 22 *He put to death . . . Hyrcanus.* Other executions and murders followed in a melancholy succession. His wives and his sons were not spared, so that it was said that it was safer to be Herod's pig (in view of his conformity to Jewish law) than Herod's son.

132

Tacitus, *Histories* V, 4, 5, 8, 9. Impressions of a Gentile

To establish his influence over this people for all time, Moses introduced new religious practices, quite opposed to those of all other religions. The Jews regard as profane all that we hold sacred; on the other hand, they permit all that we abhor. They dedicated, in a 5 shrine, a statue of that creature whose guidance enabled them to put an end to their wandering and thirst, sacrificing a ram, apparently in derision of Ammon. They likewise offer the ox, because the Egyptians worship Apis. They abstain from pork, in recollection of a plague, for the scab to which this animal is subject once afflicted them. By 10 frequent fasts even now they bear witness to the long hunger with which they were once distressed, and the unleavened Jewish bread is still employed in memory of the haste with which they seized the grain. They say that they first chose to rest on the seventh day because that day ended their toils; but after a time they were led by the 15 charms of indolence to give over the seventh year as well to inactivity. Others say that this is done in honour of Saturn, whether it be that the primitive elements of their religion were given by the Idaeans, who, according to tradition, were expelled with Saturn and became the founders of the Jewish race, or is due to the fact that, of the seven 20 planets that rule the fortunes of mankind, Saturn moves in the highest orbit and has the greatest potency; and that many of the heavenly bodies traverse their paths and courses in multiples of seven.

Whatever their origin, these rites are maintained by their antiquity: the other customs of the Jews are base and abominable, 25 and owe their persistence to their depravity. For the worst rascals among other peoples, renouncing their ancestral religions, always kept sending tribute and contributions to Jerusalem, thereby

increasing the wealth of the Jews; again, the Jews are extremely loyal toward one another, and always ready to show compassion, but
30   toward every other people they feel only hate and enmity. They sit apart at meals, and they sleep apart, and although as a race, they are prone to lust, they abstain from intercourse with foreign women; yet among themselves nothing is unlawful. They adopted circumcision to distinguish themselves from other peoples by this difference.
35   Those who are converted to their ways follow the same practice, and the earliest lesson they receive is to despise the gods, to disown their country, and to regard their parents, children, and brothers as of little account. However, they take thought to increase their numbers; for they regard it as a crime to kill any late-born child, and they believe
40   that the souls of those who are killed in battle or by the executioner are immortal: hence comes their passion for begetting children, and their scorn of death. They bury the body rather than burn it, thus following the Egyptians' custom; they likewise bestow the same care on the dead, and hold the same belief about the world below; but
45   their ideas of heavenly things are quite the opposite. The Egyptians worship many animals and monstrous images; the Jews conceive of one god only, and that with the mind alone: they regard as impious those who make from perishable materials representations of gods in man's image; that supreme and eternal being is to them incapable of
50   representation and without end. Therefore they set up no statues in their cities, still less in their temples; this flattery is not paid their kings, nor this honour given to the Caesars. But since their priests used to chant to the accompaniment of pipes and cymbals and to wear garlands of ivy, and because a golden vine was found in their
55   temple, some have thought that they were devotees of Father Liber, the conqueror of the East, in spite of the incongruity of their customs. For Liber established festive rites of a joyous nature, while the ways of the Jews are preposterous and mean . . .

A great part of Judea is covered with scattered villages, but there
60   are some towns also; Jerusalem is the capital of the Jews. In it was a temple possessing enormous riches. The first line of fortifications protected the ‸city, the next the palace, and the innermost wall the temple. Only a Jew might approach its doors, and all save the priests were forbidden to cross the threshold. While the East was under the
65   dominion of the Assyrians, Medes, and Persians, the Jews were regarded as the meanest of their subjects: but after the Macedonians gained supremacy, King Antiochus endeavoured to abolish Jewish superstition and to introduce Greek civilization; the war with the Parthians, however, prevented his improving this basest of peoples:
70   for it was exactly at that time that Arsaces had revolted. Later on, since the power of Macedon had waned, the Parthians had not yet come to their strength, and the Romans were far away, the Jews

selected their own kings. These in turn were expelled by the fickle mob; but recovering their throne by force of arms, they banished
75 citizens, destroyed towns, killed brothers, wives, and parents, and dared essay every other kind of royal crime without hesitation; but they fostered the national superstition, for they had assumed the priesthood to support their civil authority.

The first Roman to subdue the Jews and set foot in their temple
80 by right of conquest was Gnaeus Pompey: thereafter it was a matter of common knowledge that there were no representations of the gods within, but that the place was empty and the secret shrine contained nothing. The walls of Jerusalem were razed, but the temple remained standing. Later, in the time of our civil wars, when these
85 eastern provinces had fallen into the hands of Mark Antony, the Parthian prince, Pacorus, seized Judea, but he was slain by Publius Ventidius, and the Parthians were thrown back across the Euphrates: the Jews were subdued by Gaius Sosius. Antony gave the throne to Herod, and Augustus, after his victory, increased his power.

l. 5   *That creature.* An ass. The mixture in this account of some truth with a great deal of wild error is interesting and illuminating.

l. 15 *Indolence* was commonly believed among Gentiles to be the reason why the Jews observed the Sabbath.

l. 23 *Are maintained, 'defenduntur'.* The Romans were normally prepared to respect and permit rites that could claim ancient origin; innovations they distrusted.

l. 25 *The worst rascals,* that is, proselytes; neither liked nor encouraged by Romans.

l. 55 *Father Liber.* See **115**.

l. 63 *Only a Jew.* See **50**; Tacitus is not quite correct in his statement.

l. 67 *King Antiochus.* See **117**.

l. 80 *Gnaeus Pompey.* See **126**.

l. 89 *Herod.* See **128–31**.

Judaea under direct Roman Rule

After the death of Herod the Great (4 BC) his kingdom was divided among his surviving sons, but the arrangement did not last long. Judaea, after a short period of unsatisfactory rule by Archelaus, a son of Herod the Great, became a subordinate province. Its administrators (among them Pontius Pilate, Felix, and Festus) are often referred to as procurators; this title, however, though used from the time of Claudius, replaced the earlier (and more military) term *prefect*, as is proved by an inscription, discovered at Caesarea, which runs

> TIBERIEUM
> PON]TIUS PILATUS
> PRAEF]ECTUS IUDA[EA]E

For source and bibliography see E. Schürer, *The History of the Jewish People in the Age of Jesus Christ*, new edition by G. Vermes, F. Millar, M. Black, I (Edinburgh 1973), 358.

Later, parts of Herod the Great's dominions were ruled over by his grandson, Herod Agrippa I, and by his son, Herod Agrippa II. See Acts 12. 1 and 25. 23.

133

Josephus, *War* ii. 111ff., 117

Archelaus, on taking possession of his ethnarchy, did not forget old feuds, but treated not only the Jews but even the Samaritans with great brutality. Both parties sent deputies to Caesar to denounce him, and in the ninth year of his rule he was banished to Vienna, a town
5   in Gaul, and his property confiscated to the imperial treasury. It is said that, before he received his summons from Caesar, he had this dream: he thought he saw nine tall and full-grown ears of corn on which oxen were browsing. He sent for the soothsayers and some Chaldeans and asked them their opinion of its meaning. Various
10   interpretations being given, a certain Simon, of the sect of the Essenes, said that in his view the ears of corn denoted years and the oxen a revolution, because in ploughing they turn over the soil; he would therefore reign for as many years as there were ears of corn and would die after a chequered experience of revolutionary changes.
15   Five days later Archelaus was summoned to his trial. . . .

The territory of Archelaus was now reduced to a province, and Coponius, a Roman of the equestrian order, was sent out as procurator entrusted by Augustus with full powers, including the infliction of capital punishment.

l. 4   *The ninth year of his rule.* According to *Ant.* xvii. 342, the tenth. The year was AD 6.

l. 10   *The Essenes.* See **135**.

134

Josephus, *War* ii. 169–77

Pilate, being sent by Tiberius as procurator to Judaea, introduced into Jerusalem by night and under cover the effigies of Caesar which are called standards. This proceeding, when day broke, aroused immense excitement among the Jews; those on the spot were in
5   consternation, considering their laws to have been trampled under

foot, as those laws permit no image to be erected in the city; while the indignation of the townspeople stirred the countryfolk, who flocked together in crowds. Hastening after Pilate to Caesarea, the Jews implored him to remove the standards from Jerusalem and to
10 uphold the laws of their ancestors. When Pilate refused, they fell prostrate around his house and for five whole days and nights remained motionless in that position.

On the ensuing day Pilate took his seat on his tribunal in the great stadium and summoning the multitude, with the apparent intention
15 of answering them, gave the arranged signal to his armed soldiers to surround the Jews. Finding themselves in a ring of troops, three deep, the Jews were struck dumb at this unexpected sight. Pilate, after threatening to cut them down if they refused to admit Caesar's images, signalled to the soldiers to draw their swords. Thereupon the
20 Jews, as by concerted action, flung themselves in a body on the ground, extended their necks, and exclaimed that they were ready rather to die than to transgress the Law. Overcome with astonishment at such religious zeal, Pilate gave orders for the immediate removal of the standards from Jerusalem.

25 On a later occasion he provoked a fresh uproar by expending upon the construction of an aqueduct the sacred treasure known as *Corbonas*: the water was brought from a distance of 400 furlongs. Indignant at this proceeding, the populace formed a ring round the tribunal of Pilate, then on a visit to Jerusalem, and besieged him with
30 angry clamour. He, foreseeing the tumult, had interspersed among the crowd a troop of his soldiers, armed but disguised in civilian dress, with orders not to use their swords, but to beat any rioters with cudgels. He now from his tribunal gave the agreed signal. Large numbers of the Jews perished, some from the blows which they
35 received, others trodden to death by their companions in the ensuing flight. Cowed by the fate of the victims, the multitude was reduced to silence.

l. 1   *Pilate.* Pontius Pilate, procurator (Josephus uses the word current in his own time; see p. 155) from AD 26 to 36, was not the worst of the governors of Judaea. When he saw how seriously the Jews took the affair of the standards he withdrew; his aqueduct he probably regarded as a benefit conferred on Jerusalem. Certainly he had successors whose little finger was thicker than his loins. See **138–40**.

l. 3   *Standards.* Josephus writes more accurately in *Ant.* xviii. 55 when he speaks of the effigies (busts) attached to the standards.

Pharisees, Sadducees, and Essenes

Two of these Jewish parties occupy prominent places in the New Testament. The Sadducees were too closely bound up with the political

life of their nation to survive the disaster of AD 70, and the Rabbinic
literature, which was written down after that date, presents a consistently
Pharisaic point of view. Sadducees are nevertheless sometimes referred to;
see **159** in the chapter on Rabbinic Literature and Rabbinic Judaism. The
Essenes, though not mentioned in the New Testament, were certainly a
not unimportant sect. In addition to the paragraphs from Josephus and
Philo quoted below see the chapter on Qumran. Whether the Qumran
sect is to be identified with those who are elsewhere described as Essenes
(the name does not appear in the Qumran manuscripts) is a difficult and
disputed question, not to be discussed here.

135

Josephus, *War* ii. 119f., 122, 137–42, 152f., 162–6

Jewish philosophy, in fact, takes three forms. The followers of the
first school are called Pharisees, of the second Sadducees, of the third
Essenes.

5 The Essenes have a reputation for cultivating peculiar sanctity. Of
Jewish birth, they show a greater attachment to each other than do
the other sects. They shun pleasures as a vice and regard temperance
and the control of the passions as a special virtue. Marriage they
disdain, but they adopt other men's children, while yet pliable and
docile, and regard them as their kin and mould them in accordance
10 with their own principles . . .

Riches they despise, and their community of goods is truly
admirable; you will not find one among them distinguished by
greater opulence than another. They have a law that new members
on admission to the sect shall confiscate their property to the order,
15 with the result that you will nowhere see either abject poverty or
inordinate wealth; the individual's possessions join the common stock
and all, like brothers, enjoy a single patrimony . . .

A candidate anxious to join their sect is not immediately admitted.
For one year, during which he remains outside the fraternity, they
20 prescribe for him their own rule of life, presenting him with a small
hatchet, the loin-cloth already mentioned, and white raiment. Having
given proof of his temperance during this probationary period, he is
brought into closer touch with the rule and is allowed to share the
purer kind of holy water, but is not yet received into the meetings of
25 the community. For after this exhibition of endurance, his character
is tested for two years more, and only then, if found worthy, is he
enrolled in the society. But, before he may touch the common food,
he is made to swear tremendous oaths: first that he will practise piety
towards the Deity, next that he will observe justice towards men:
30 that he will wrong none whether of his own mind or under another's

orders; that he will for ever hate the unjust and fight the battle of the just; that he will for ever keep faith with all men, especially with the powers that be, since no ruler attains his office save by the will of God; that, should he himself bear rule, he will never abuse his
35 authority nor, either in dress or by other outward marks of superiority, outshine his subjects; to be for ever a lover of truth and to expose liars; to keep his hands from stealing and his soul pure from unholy gain; to conceal nothing from the members of the sect and to report none of their secrets to others, even though tortured to
40 death. He swears, moreover, to transmit their rules exactly as he himself received them; to abstain from robbery; and in like manner carefully to preserve the books of the sect and the names of the angels. Such are the oaths by which they secure their proselytes . . .

The war with the Romans tried their souls through and through
45 by every variety of test. Racked and twisted, burnt and broken, and made to pass through every instrument of torture, in order to induce them to blaspheme their lawgiver or to eat some forbidden thing, they refused to yield to either demand, nor ever once did they cringe to their persecutors or shed a tear. Smiling in their agonies and mildly
50 deriding their tormentors, they cheerfully resigned their souls, confident that they would receive them back again . . .

Of the two first-named schools, the Pharisees, who are considered the most accurate interpreters of the laws, and hold the position of the leading sect, attribute everything to Fate and to God; they hold
55 that to act rightly or otherwise rests, indeed, for the most part with men, but that in each action Fate co-operates. Every soul, they maintain, is imperishable, but the soul of the good alone passes into another body, while the souls of the wicked suffer eternal punishment.

The Sadducees, the second of the orders, do away with Fate
60 altogether, and remove God beyond, not merely the commission, but the very sight, of evil. They maintain that man has the free choice of good or evil, and that it rests with each man's will whether he follows the one or the other. As for the persistence of the soul after death, penalties in the underworld, and rewards, they will have none
65 of them.

The Pharisees are affectionate to each other and cultivate harmonious relations with the community. The Sadducees, on the contrary, are, even among themselves, rather boorish in their behaviour, and in their intercourse with their peers are as rude as to
70 aliens. Such is what I have to say on the Jewish philosophical schools.

l. 1 *Jewish philosophy* is a most inappropriate term for what Josephus proceeds to describe. He is trying to make his account easy for his Hellenistic readers.

l. 4 *The Essenes.* The origin of this name is unknown. No suggested explanation is entirely convincing.

l. 7   *Marriage they disdain.* In 160f. Josephus describes a group of Essenes who accepted marriage.

l. 21   *A small hatchet.* For the burial of excrement. Cf. Deut. 23. 12ff.
The loin-cloth already mentioned, in ii. 129. It was worn while bathing to avoid complete nakedness.

l. 24   *Holy water,* for lustrations. Frequent ceremonial baths were an important feature of Essene ritual.

l. 27   *Common food.* The Essenes took their two daily meals in silence in a refectory.

l. 42   *The books of the sect.* What books the Essenes used in addition to those of the Old Testament is not known. They held Moses in special veneration, but Josephus says (ii. 136): 'They display an extraordinary interest in the writings of the ancients ... with the help of these ... they make investigations into medicinal roots and the properties of stones.' Apparently holy books were also used in predicting the future (ii. 159). It is possible that the MSS. found in Palestine in and since 1947 were in some way connected with Essene (or similar) communities. See Chapter 9.
The names of the angels. Here again we can only conjecture what is meant.

l. 51   *Receive them back again.* Josephus goes on to explain the Essene belief that the body is corruptible but the soul immortal and imperishable. They shared, he says, in the 'belief of the sons of Greece' that there is for virtuous souls an 'abode beyond the ocean'.

l. 54   *Attribute everything to Fate and to God.* Cf. **157**. Josephus 'hellenizes'.

136

Philo, *Quod Omnis Probus Liber sit* 75–80.

Palestinian Syria, too, has not failed to produce high moral excellence. In this country live a considerable part of the very populous nation of the Jews, including as it is said, certain persons, more than four thousand in number, called Essenes. Their name which is, I think, a
5   variation, though the form of the Greek is inexact, of ὁσιότης (holiness), is given them, because they have shown themselves especially devout in the service of God, not by offering sacrifices of animals, but by resolving to sanctify their minds. The first thing about these people is that they live in villages and avoid the cities
10   because of the iniquities which have become inveterate among city dwellers, for they know that their company would have a deadly effect upon their own souls, like a disease brought by a pestilential atmosphere. Some of them labour on the land and others pursue such crafts as co-operate with peace and so benefit themselves and their
15   neighbours. They do not hoard gold and silver or acquire great slices of land because they desire the revenues therefrom, but provide what is needed for the necessary requirements of life. For while they stand almost alone in the whole of mankind in that they have become moneyless and landless by deliberate action rather than by lack of
20   good fortune, they are esteemed exceedingly rich, because they judge

frugality with contentment to be, as indeed it is, an abundance of wealth. As for darts, javelins, daggers, or the helmet, breastplate or shield, you could not find a single manufacturer of them, nor, in general, any person making weapons or plying any industry
25 concerned with war, nor, indeed, any of the peaceful kind, which easily lapse into vice, for they have not the vaguest idea of commerce either wholesale or retail or marine, but pack the inducements to covetousness off in disgrace. Not a single slave is to be found among them, but all are free, exchanging services with each other, and they
30 denounce the owners of slaves, not merely for their injustice in outraging the law of equality, but also for their impiety in annulling the statute of Nature, who mother-like has born and reared all men alike, and created them genuine brothers, not in mere name, but in very reality, though this kinship has been put to confusion by the
35 triumph of malignant covetousness, which has wrought estrangement instead of affinity and enmity instead of friendship. As for philosophy they abandon the logical part to quibbling verbalists as unnecessary for the acquisition of virtue, and the physical to visionary praters as beyond the grasp of human nature, only retaining that part which
40 treats philosophically of the existence of God and the creation of the universe. But the ethical part they study very industriously, taking for their trainers the laws of their fathers, which could not possibly have been conceived by the human soul without divine inspiration.

l. 6   Holiness. Philo's etymologies are as a rule edifying rather than scientifically convincing. See **231**.

137
Philo, *De Vita Contemplativa* 1–3

I have discussed the Essenes, who persistently pursued the active life and excelled in all or, to put it more moderately, in most of its departments. I will now proceed at once in accordance with the sequence required by the subject to say what is needed about those
5 who embraced the life of contemplation. In doing so I will not add anything of my own procuring to improve upon the facts as is constantly done by poets and historians through lack of excellence in the lives and practices which they record, but shall adhere absolutely to the actual truth. Though I know that in this case it is such as to
10 unnerve the greatest master of oratory, still we must persevere and not decline the conflict, for the magnitude of virtue shown by these men must not be allowed to tie the tongues of those who hold that nothing excellent should be passed over in silence.
    The vocation of these philosophers is at once made clear from
15 their title of Therapeutae and Therapeutrides, a name derived from

θεραπεύω, either in the sense of 'cure' because they profess an art of healing better than that current in the cities which cures only the bodies, while theirs treats also souls oppressed with grievous and well-nigh incurable diseases, inflicted by pleasures and desires and
20 griefs and fears, by acts of covetousness, folly and injustice and the countless host of the other passions and vices: or else in the sense of 'worship', because nature and the sacred laws have schooled them to worship the Self-existent who is better than the good, purer than the One and more primordial than the Monad. Who among those who
25 profess piety deserve to be compared with these?

l. 15 *Therapeutae.* This time Philo's etymology is better, no doubt because it involves only the Greek language. Over against the Palestinian Essenes the Therapeutae (who unlike the Essenes as described by Philo included women among their members) formed a community living in Egypt. They were purely contemplative—again in distinction from the Essenes.

The Jewish War of AD 66–70

The rigour and corruption of the procurators, together with the folly and excesses of the revolutionary minority of Jews, drove the country with ever-increasing swiftness to war. The story cannot be told here, but a few salient points will be mentioned. For some other events in the early course of the war see **239–40**.

138

Josephus, *War* ii. 254–6a, 258ff

But while the country was thus cleared of these pests, a new species of banditti was springing up in Jerusalem, the so-called *sicarii*, who committed murders in broad daylight in the heart of the city. The festivals were their special seasons, when they would mingle with
5 the crowd, carrying short daggers concealed under their clothing, with which they stabbed their enemies. Then, when they fell, the murderers joined in the cries of indignation and, through this plausible behaviour, were never discovered. The first to be assassinated by them was Jonathan the high priest; after his death there were
10 numerous daily murders . . .

Besides these there arose another body of villains, with purer hands but more impious intentions, who no less than the assassins ruined the peace of the city. Deceivers and impostors, under the pretence of divine inspiration fostering revolutionary changes, they persuaded
15 the multitude to act like madmen, and led them out into the desert in the belief that God would there give them tokens of deliverance. Against them Felix, regarding this as but the preliminary to

insurrection, sent a body of cavalry and heavy-armed infantry, and put a large number to the sword.

l. 1   *These pests*, brigands put down by the procurator Felix.

l. 5   *Daggers.* The *sicarii* probably drew their name from the Latin *sica*, a dagger.

139
Josephus, *War* ii. 271–8*a*

Festus, who succeeded Felix as procurator, proceeded to attack the principal plague of the country; he captured large numbers of the brigands and put not a few to death.

The administration of Albinus, who followed Festus, was of
5 another order; there was no form of villainy which he omitted to practise. Not only did he, in his official capacity, steal and plunder private property and burden the whole nation with extraordinary taxes, but he accepted ransoms from their relatives on behalf of those who had been imprisoned for robbery by the local councils or by
10 former procurators; and the only persons left in gaol as malefactors were those who failed to pay the price. Now, too, the audacity of the revolutionary party in Jerusalem was stimulated; the influential men among their number secured from Albinus, by means of bribes, immunity for their seditious practices; while of the populace all who
15 were dissatisfied with peace joined hands with the governor's accomplices. Each ruffian, with his own band of followers grouped around him, towered above his company like a brigand chief or tyrant, employing his bodyguard to plunder peaceable citizens. The result was that the victims of robbery kept their grievances, of which
20 they had every reason to complain, to themselves, while those who escaped injury cringed to wretches deserving of punishment, through fear of suffering the same fate. In short, none could now speak his mind, with tyrants on every side; and from this date were sown in the city the seeds of its impending fall.
25   Such was the character of Albinus, but his successor, Gessius Florus, made him appear by comparison a paragon of virtue. The crimes of Albinus were, for the most part, perpetrated in secret and with dissimulation; Gessius, on the contrary, ostentatiously paraded his outrages upon the nation, and, as though he had been sent as a
30 hangman of condemned criminals, abstained from no form of robbery or violence. Was there a call for compassion, he was the most cruel of men; for shame, none more shameless than he. No man ever poured greater contempt on truth; none invented more crafty methods of crime.

l. 1   *Procurator.* After the reign of Herod Agrippa I the government of Judaea reverted to Roman procurators. Felix governed AD 52–55, Festus 55(6)–62, Albinus 62–4, Gessius Florus 64–6.

140

Josephus, *War* ii. 285–96

The ostensible pretext for war was out of proportion to the magnitude of the disasters to which it led. The Jews in Caesarea had a synagogue adjoining a plot of ground owned by a Greek of that city; this site they had frequently endeavoured to purchase, offering
5 a price far exceeding its true value. The proprietor, disdaining their solicitations, by way of insult further proceeded to build upon the site and erect workshops, leaving the Jews only a narrow and extremely awkward passage. Thereupon, some of the hot-headed youths proceeded to set upon the builders and attempted to interrupt
10 operations. Florus having put a stop to their violence, the Jewish notables, with John the tax-collector, having no other expedient, offered Florus eight talents of silver to procure the cessation of the work. Florus, with his eye only on the money, promised them every assistance, but, having secured his pay, at once quitted Caesarea for
15 Sebaste, leaving a free field to sedition, as though he had sold the Jews a licence to fight the matter out.
    On the following day, which was a Sabbath, when the Jews assembled at the synagogue, they found that one of the Caesarean mischief-makers had placed beside the entrance a pot, turned bottom
20 upwards, upon which he was sacrificing birds. This spectacle of what they considered an outrage upon their laws and a desecration of the spot enraged the Jews beyond endurance. The steady-going and peaceable members of the congregation were in favour of immediate recourse to the authorities; but the factious folk and the passionate
25 youth were burning for a fight. The Caesarean party, on their side, stood prepared for action, for they had, by a concerted plan, sent the man on to the mock sacrifice; and so they soon came to blows. Jucundus, the cavalry commander commissioned to intervene, came up, removed the pot and endeavoured to quell the riot, but was
30 unable to cope with the violence of the Caesareans. The Jews, thereupon, snatched up their copy of the Law and withdrew to Narbata, a Jewish district sixty furlongs distant from Caesarea. Their leading men, twelve in number, with John at their head, waited upon Florus at Sebaste, bitterly complained of these proceedings and
35 besought his assistance, delicately reminding him of the matter of the eight talents. Florus actually had them arrested and put in irons on the charge of having carried off the copy of the Law from Caesarea.
    This news roused indignation at Jerusalem, though the citizens still restrained their feelings. But Florus, as if he had contracted to fan

40 the flames of war, sent to the temple treasury and extracted seventeen
talents, making the requirements of the imperial service his pretext.
Instantly fired by this outrage, the people rushed in a body to the
Temple and with piercing cries invoked the name of Caesar,
imploring him to liberate them from the tyranny of Florus. Some of
45 the malcontents railed on the procurator in the most opprobrious
terms and carrying round a basket begged coppers for him as for an
unfortunate destitute. These proceedings, however, far from checking
his avarice, only provoked him to further peculation. Accordingly,
instead of betaking himself, as he should have done, to Caesarea, to
50 extinguish the flames of war, there already breaking out, and to root
out the cause of those disorders—a task for which he had been paid—
he marched with an army of cavalry and infantry upon Jerusalem, in
order to attain his object with the aid of Roman arms, and by means
of intimidation and menaces to fleece the city.

The war thus provoked opened favourably for the Jews, and dragged on
indecisively. At length, Vespasian, entrusted (with his son Titus; on both
see **15**) with the conduct of the campaign, slowly but methodically penned
the Jewish forces in Jerusalem, where they were eventually destroyed as
much by starvation and internecine conflict as by the Roman arms.
Josephus was taken prisoner (see **240**), but not even his eloquence could
move his compatriots to surrender.

141
Josephus, *War* v. 362–74

Josephus, accordingly, went round the wall, and, endeavouring to
keep out of range of missiles and yet within earshot, repeatedly
implored them to save themselves and the people, to spare their
country and their Temple, and not to display towards them greater
5 indifference than was shown by aliens. The Romans, he urged,
though without a share in them, yet reverenced the holy places of
their enemies, and had thus far restrained their hands from them;
whereas men who had been brought up in them and, were they
preserved, would alone enjoy them, were bent on their destruction.
10 Indeed, they beheld their stoutest walls prostrate and but one
remaining, weaker than those which had fallen; they knew that the
might of the Romans was irresistible and that to serve them was no
new experience for themselves. Be it granted that it was noble to
fight for freedom, they should have done so at first; but, after having
15 once succumbed and submitted for so long, to seek then to shake off
the yoke was the part of men madly courting death, not of lovers of
liberty. To scorn meaner masters might, indeed, be legitimate, but
not those to whom the universe was subject. For what was there that

had escaped the Romans, save maybe some spot useless through heat
20 or cold? Fortune, indeed, had from all quarters passed over them,
and God who went the round of the nations, bringing to each in turn
the rod of empire, now rested over Italy. There was, in fact, an
established law, as supreme among brutes as among men, 'Yield to
the stronger' and 'The mastery is for those pre-eminent in arms'. That
25 was why their forefathers, men who in soul and body, aye and in
resources to boot, were by far their superiors, had yielded to the
Romans—a thing intolerable to them, had they not known that God
was on the Roman side. As for them, on what did they rely in thus
holding out, when the main part of the city was already captured,
30 and when those within it, though their walls still stood, were in a
plight even worse than capture? Assuredly, the Romans were not
ignorant of the famine raging in the city, which was now consuming
the populace, and would ere long consume the combatants as well.
For, even were the Romans to desist from the siege and not fall upon
35 the city with drawn swords, yet they had at their doors a war with
which none could contend, gaining strength every hour, unless
indeed they could take arms and fight against famine itself and, alone
of all men, master even its pangs. They would do well, he added, to
repent ere irretrievable disaster befell them and to incline to salutary
40 counsels while they had the opportunity; for the Romans would bear
them no malice for the past, unless they persisted in their contumacy
to the end: they were naturally lenient in victory, and would put
above vindictiveness considerations of expediency, which did not
consist in having on their hands either a depopulated city or a
45 devastated country. That was why, even at this late hour, Caesar
desired to grant them terms; whereas, if he took the city by storm,
he would not spare a man of them, especially after the rejection of
offers made to them when in extremities. That the third wall would
be quickly carried was vouched for by the fall of those already
50 captured; and even were that defence impregnable, the famine would
fight for the Romans against them.

l. 6   *Reverenced the holy places.* According to Josephus, Titus even in the end tried
unsuccessfully to save the Temple.

l. 42   *Lenient in victory.* Cf. Horace, *Carmen Saeculare* 51f. (**3**), and Virgil, *Aeneid*
vi. 851ff.:
> ... Remember, Roman, thou,
> To rule the nations as their master: these
> Thine arts shall be, to engraft the law of peace,
> Forbear the conquered, and war down the proud.

l. 45   *Caesar.* The Emperor Vespasian.

At length, in September AD 70, the city fell amid appalling scenes of
famine and bloodshed.

142

Josephus, *War* vi. 392ff., 399–403*a*, 404–8

The earthworks having now been completed after eighteen days' labour, on the seventh of the month Gorpiaeus the Romans brought up the engines. Of the rebels, some already despairing of the city retired from the ramparts to the Acra, others slunk down into the
5 mines; many, however, posting themselves along the wall, attempted to repel those who were bringing up the siege-engines. But these too the Romans overpowered by numbers and force, but, above all, by the high spirits in which they faced men already dispirited and unnerved. And when a portion of the wall broke down and some of
10 the towers succumbed to the battering of the rams, the defenders at once took flight, and even the tyrants were seized with a needlessly serious alarm . . . Here may we signally discern at once the power of God over unholy men and the fortune of the Romans. For the tyrants stripped themselves of their security and descended of their own
15 accord from those towers, whereon they could never have been overcome by force, and famine alone could have subdued them; while the Romans, after all the toil expended over weaker walls, mastered by the gift of fortune those that were impregnable to their artillery. For the three towers, which we have described above,
20 would have defied every engine of war.

Having then abandoned these, or rather been driven down from them by God, they found immediate refuge in the ravine below Siloam; but afterwards, having recovered a little from their panic, they rushed upon the adjoining section of the barrier. Their courage,
25 however, proving unequal to the occasion (for their strength was now broken alike by terror and misfortune), they were repulsed by the guards and dispersing hither and thither slunk down into the mines.

The Romans, now masters of the walls, planted their standards on the towers, and with clapping of hands and jubilation raised a paean
30 in honour of their victory. . . . Pouring into the alleys, sword in hand, they massacred indiscriminately all whom they met, and burnt the houses with all who had taken refuge within. Often in the course of their raids, on entering the houses for loot, they would find whole families dead and the rooms filled with the victims of the famine,
35 and then, shuddering at the sight, retire empty-handed. Yet, while they pitied those who had thus perished, they had no similar feelings for the living, but, running everyone through who fell in their way, they choked the alleys with corpses and deluged the whole city with blood, insomuch that many of the fires were extinguished by the
40 gory stream. Towards evening they ceased slaughtering, but when night fell the fire gained the mastery, and the dawn of the eighth day of the month Gorpiaeus broke upon Jerusalem in flames—a city

which had suffered such calamities during the siege, that, had she
from her foundation enjoyed an equal share of blessings she would
45 have been thought unquestionably enviable; a city undeserving,
moreover, of these great misfortunes on any other ground, save
that she produced a generation such as that which caused her
overthrow.

l. 2   *The seventh of the month Gorpiaeus.* About 25 September AD 70.

The final scenes in the military conflict were enacted at the fortress of
Masada, where the garrison's resistance, literally unto death, has in recent
years been confirmed by archaeology and is an inspiring record of courage
and of patriotic and religious devotion.

143

Josephus, War vii. 280–5, 295–6, 299, 315–16, 320–21, 333–6,
391–4, 400–01

A rock of no slight circumference and lofty from end to end is
abruptly terminated on every side by deep ravines, the precipices
rising sheer from an invisible base and being inaccessible to the foot
of any living creature, save in two places where the rock permits of
5 no easy ascent. Of these tracks one leads from the Lake Asphaltitis on
the east, the other, by which the approach is easier, from the west.
The former they call the snake, seeing a resemblance to that reptile
in its narrowness and continual windings; for its course is broken in
skirting the jutting crags and, returning frequently upon itself and
10 gradually lengthening out again, it makes painful headway. One
traversing this route must firmly plant each foot alternately.
Destruction faces him; for on either side yawn chasms so terrific as
to daunt the hardiest. After following this perilous track for thirty
furlongs, one reaches the summit, which, instead of tapering to a
15 sharp peak, expands into a plain. On this plateau the high priest
Jonathan first erected a fortress and called it Masada; the subsequent
planning of the place engaged the serious attention of King Herod
. . .
        But the stores laid up within would have excited still more
20 amazement, alike for their lavish splendour and their durability. For
here had been stored a mass of corn, amply sufficient to last for years,
abundance of wine and oil, besides every variety of pulse and piles of
dates . . . There was also found a mass of arms of every description,
hoarded up by the king and sufficient for ten thousand men, besides
25 unwrought iron, brass, and lead; these preparations having, in fact,
been made for grave reasons . . .
        Observing this, Silva, thinking it easier to destroy this wall by fire,
ordered his soldiers to hurl at it showers of burning torches. Being

mainly made of wood, it quickly caught fire, and, from its hollow
30 nature becoming ignited right through it blazed up in a volume of
flame . . .

However, neither did Eleazar himself contemplate flight, nor did
he intend to permit any other to do so. Seeing the wall consuming in
the flames, unable to devise any further means of deliverance or
35 gallant endeavour, and setting before his eyes what the Romans, if
victorious, would inflict on them, their children and their wives, he
deliberated on the death of all . . .

'. . . The penalty for those crimes let us pay not to our bitterest
foes, the Romans, but to God through the act of our own hands. It
40 will be more tolerable than the other. Let our wives thus die
undishonoured, our children unacquainted with slavery; and, when
they are gone, let us render a generous service to each other,
preserving our liberty as a noble winding-sheet. But first let us
destroy our chattels and the fortress by fire; for the Romans, well I
45 know, will be grieved to lose at once our persons and the lucre. Our
provisions only let us spare; for they will testify, when we are dead,
that it was not want which subdued us, but that, in keeping with our
initial resolve, we preferred death to slavery . . .'

. . . For, while they caressed and embraced their wives and took
50 their children in their arms, clinging in tears to those parting kisses,
at that same instant, as though served by hands other than their own,
they accomplished their purpose, having the thought of the ills they
would endure under their enemy's hands to console them for their
constraint in killing them. And in the end not one was found a truant
55 in so daring a deed: all carried through their task with their dearest
ones. Wretched victims of necessity, to whom to slay with their own
hands their own wives and children seemed the lightest of evils!
Unable, indeed, any longer to endure their anguish at what they had
done, and feeling that they wronged the slain by surviving them if it
60 were but for a moment, they quickly piled together all the stores and
set them on fire . . .

The victims numbered nine hundred and sixty, including women
and children; and the tragedy occurred on the fifteenth of the month
Xanthicus.

l. 16 *Jonathan.* Brother and successor of Judas Maccabaeus; see **119–23**.

l. 27 *Silva.* The Roman commander.

l. 32 *Eleazar.* The Jewish commander. The destruction of the wall had made the
site no longer defensible.

l. 48 Eleazar's first oration did not succeed in convincing his men that total suicide
was the only course; a second speech persuaded them.

l. 61 The next step was the selection by lot of ten men; these killed the rest. Of
the ten, one was selected by lot; he killed the nine, and finally killed himself.

l. 63 *The fifteenth of the month Xanthicus.* April 74.

144

Josephus, *War* vii. 216ff.

> About the same time Caesar sent instructions to Bassus and Laberius
> Maximus, the procurator, to farm out all Jewish territory. For he
> founded no city there, reserving the country as his private property,
> except that he did assign to eight hundred veterans discharged from
> 5 the army a place for habitation called Emmaus, distant thirty furlongs
> from Jerusalem. On all Jews, wheresoever resident, he imposed a
> poll-tax of two drachmae, to be paid annually into the Capitol as
> formerly contributed by them to the Temple at Jerusalem. Such was
> the position of Jewish affairs at this date.

l. 1   *Bassus,* legate in Judaea.

l. 5   *Emmaus.* Perhaps the Emmaus of Luke 24. 13, though the distances given by
Josephus and Luke do not agree.

l. 7   *Two drachmae.* Cf. Matt. 17. 24, where the temple tax is referred to as the
'didrachma'.

The Revolt of AD 132–5

After the terrible events of AD 70 Palestine remained on the whole quiet,
though there were Jewish and anti-Jewish disturbances in other parts of
the Empire. Further revolt in Palestine itself seems to have been provoked
by a law forbidding circumcision and by Hadrian's decision to build a
heathen temple on the site of the former Jewish Temple in Jerusalem (for
the former see Spartian, *Hadrian* 4; for the latter, Dio Cassius, quoted
below, **145**). Our knowledge of the course of the rebellion and the ensuing
war is unfortunately far from complete. The Jewish leader, hailed by R.
Akiba (see **157** and note on *l.* 1) as Messiah, was one Bar Cocheba (also
called, as is suggested by the coins, Simon). There can be no doubt that the
war was serious and protracted, and that Palestinian Christians (as well as
others) suffered considerably as a result of it.

145

Dio Cassius, *Roman History* lxix. 12ff

> At Jerusalem he [Hadrian] founded a city in place of the one which
> had been razed to the ground, naming it Aelia Capitolina, and on the
> site of the temple of the god he raised a new temple to Jupiter. This
> brought on a war of no slight importance nor of brief duration, for
> 5 the Jews deemed it intolerable that foreign races should be settled in
> their city and foreign religious rites planted there. So long, indeed, as
> Hadrian was close by in Egypt and again in Syria, they remained

quiet, save in so far as they purposely made of poor quality such
weapons as they were called upon to furnish, in order that the
10 Romans might reject them and they themselves might thus have the
use of them; but when he went farther away, they openly revolted.
To be sure, they did not dare try conclusions with the Romans in the
open field, but they occupied the advantageous positions in the
country and strengthened them with mines and walls, in order that
15 they might have places of refuge whenever they should be hard
pressed, and might meet together unobserved underground; and
they pierced these subterranean passages from above at intervals to
let in air and light.

At first the Romans took no account of them. Soon, however, all
20 Judaea had been stirred up, and the Jews everywhere were showing
signs of disturbance, were gathering together, and were giving
evidence of great hostility to the Romans, partly by secret and partly
by overt acts; many outside nations, too, were joining them through
eagerness for gain, and the whole earth, one might almost say, was
25 being stirred up over the matter. Then, indeed, Hadrian sent against
them his best generals. First of these was Julius Severus, who was
dispatched from Britain, where he was governor, against the Jews.
Severus did not venture to attack his opponents in the open at any
one point, in view of their numbers and their desperation, but by
30 intercepting small groups, thanks to the number of his soldiers and
his under-officers, and by depriving them of food and shutting them
up, he was able, rather slowly, to be sure, but with comparatively
little danger, to crush, exhaust and exterminate them. Very few of
them in fact survived. Fifty of their most important outposts and 985
35 of their most famous villages were razed to the ground. 580,000 men
were slain in the various raids and battles, and the number of those
that perished by famine, disease and fire was past finding out. Thus
nearly the whole of Judaea was made desolate, a result of which the
people had had forewarning before the war. For the tomb of
40 Solomon, which the Jews regard as an object of veneration, fell to
pieces of itself and collapsed, and many wolves and hyenas rushed
howling into their cities. Many Romans, moreover, perished in this
war. Therefore Hadrian in writing to the Senate did not employ the
opening phrase commonly affected by the emperors, 'If you and your
45 children are in health, it is well; I and the legions are in health.'

146

Eusebius, *Historia Ecclesiastica* IV, vi. 1–4

As the rebellion of the Jews at this time grew much more serious,
Rufus, governor of Judaea, after an auxiliary force had been sent him
by the emperor, using their madness as a pretext, proceeded against
them without mercy, and destroyed indiscriminately thousands of

5   men and women and children, and in accordance with the laws of
war reduced their country to a state of complete subjection. The
leader of the Jews at this time was a man by the name of Bar Cocheba
(which signifies a star), who possessed the character of a robber and a
murderer, but nevertheless, relying upon his name, boasted to them,
10 as if they were slaves, that he possessed wonderful powers; and he
pretended that he was a star that had come down to them out of
heaven to bring them light in the midst of their misfortunes. The
war raged most fiercely in the eighteenth year of Hadrian, at the city
of Bithara, which was a very secure fortress, situated not far from
15 Jerusalem. When the siege had lasted a long time, and the rebels had
been driven to the last extremity by hunger and thirst, and the
instigator of the rebellion had suffered his just punishment, the whole
nation was prohibited from this time on by a decree, and by the
commands of Hadrian, from ever going up to the country about
20 Jerusalem. For the emperor gave orders that they should not even see
from a distance the land of their fathers. Such is the account of Aristo
of Pella. And thus, when the city had been emptied of the Jewish
nation and had suffered the total destruction of its ancient inhabitants,
it was colonized by a different race, and the Roman city which
25 subsequently arose changed its name and was called Aelia, in honour
of the emperor Aelius Hadrian.

l. 9   Relying upon his name. Its significance was probably (or was probably taken
to be) messianic. Cf. Num. 24. 17, and R. Akiba's recognition of Bar Cocheba
as Messiah.

l. 21   Aristo of Pella. We know practically nothing of this author, nor how much
of Eusebius's narrative of the revolt is drawn from him.

147

Eusebius, *HE* IV, viii. 4

The same writer, speaking of the Jewish war which took place at that
time, adds the following: 'For in the late Jewish war Bar Cocheba,
the leader of the Jewish rebellion, commanded that Christians alone
should be visited with terrible punishments unless they would deny
5   and blaspheme Jesus Christ.'

l. 1   The same writer. Justin Martyr, who died in Rome *c.* AD 165.

l. 3   Christians. It is clear that even Jewish Christians could not recognize Bar
Cocheba as Messiah; in consequence they would be unable to join in the
rebellion and must have seemed traitors to their race.

The Dispersion

From an early date Jews began to find their way to various parts of the Mediterranean world, and to the lands east of it. Their presence in many places can be proved not only by literary references but also by inscriptions and (in Egypt) by papyri (see **30, 48**). They founded synagogues (for synagogues at Corinth, Rome, and Panticapaeum see **51–3**), and there are many traces of their community life, and of their relations with Jerusalem. The dispersed Jews did not always find it easy to live on good terms with their neighbours.

We are particularly well informed about the Jews in Alexandria, and their disputes with the Alexandrians. The letter of Claudius (**48**) regulated these disputes; previously embassies had been sent from both Jews and Alexandrian citizens to Claudius and to Gaius before him. Parts of the proceedings are described in great detail by Philo in the *Flaccus* and *Embassy to Gaius*.

148

Josephus, *Antiquities* xiv. 110–18

But no one need wonder that there was so much wealth in our Temple, for all the Jews throughout the habitable world, and those who worshipped God, even those from Asia and Europe, had been contributing to it for a very long time. And there is no lack of
5 witnesses to the great amount of the sums mentioned, nor have they been raised to so great a figure through boastfulness or exaggeration on our part, but there are many historians who bear us out, in particular Strabo of Cappadocia, who writes as follows. 'Mithridates sent to Cos and took the money which Queen Cleopatra had
10 deposited there, and eight hundred talents of the Jews.' Now there is no public money among us except that which is God's, and it is therefore evident that this money was transferred to Cos by the Jews of Asia because of their fear of Mithridates. For it is not likely that those in Judaea, who possessed a fortified city and the Temple, would
15 have sent money to Cos, nor is it probable that the Jews living in Alexandria would have done this either, since they had no fear of Mithridates. And this same Strabo in another passage testifies that at the time when Sulla crossed over to Greece to make war on Mithridates, and sent Lucullus to put down the revolt of our nation
20 in Cyrene, the habitable world was filled with Jews, for he writes as follows. 'There were four classes in the state of Cyrene; the first consisted of citizens, the second of farmers, the third of resident aliens (metics), and the fourth of Jews. This people has already made its way into every city, and it is not easy to find any place in the

25 habitable world which has not received this nation and in which it
has not made its power felt. And it has come about that Cyrene,
which had the same rulers as Egypt, has imitated it in many respects,
particularly in notably encouraging and aiding the expansion of the
organized groups of Jews, which observe the national Jewish laws. In
30 Egypt, for example, territory has been set apart for a Jewish
settlement, and in Alexandria a great part of the city has been
allocated to this nation. And an ethnarch of their own has been
installed, who governs the people and adjudicates suits and supervises
contracts and ordinances, just as if he were the head of a sovereign
35 state. And so this nation has flourished in Egypt because the Jews
were originally Egyptians and because those who left that country
made their homes near by; and they migrated to Cyrene because this
country bordered on the kingdom of Egypt, as did Judaea—or rather,
it formerly belonged to that kingdom.' These are Strabo's own
40 words.

l. 2   *Those who worshipped God*, οἱ σεβόμενοι τὸν θεόν. The same expression occurs
in the New Testament. It does not now seem as clear as it once did that it
denotes a group of Gentiles, distinct from proselytes, who were attracted to
the Synagogue and observed some parts of the Law.

l. 8   *Strabo of Cappadocia*; known to us primarily as a geographer who wrote in
the time of Augustus, but he also wrote a large history.
Mithridates, king of Pontus, who defeated the Romans in 88 BC.

l. 23   *Metics*, μέτοικοι, a technical term for this class, frequent in the papyri and
elsewhere.

l. 32   *An ethnarch.* Cf. Philo, *In Flaccum* 74 (below, **149**); Augustus apparently
replaced the ethnarch by a senate.

l. 35   *The Jews were originally Egyptians.* A common opinion, rebutted elsewhere
by Josephus himself.

149

Philo, *In Flaccum* 73ff.

Having broken into everything like a burglar and left no side of
Jewish life untouched by a hostility carried to the highest pitch,
Flaccus devised another monstrous and unparalleled line of attack
worthy of this perpetrator of enormities and inventor of novel
5 iniquities. Our Senate had been appointed to take charge of Jewish
affairs by our saviour and benefactor Augustus, after the death of the
ethnarch, orders to that effect having been given to Magius Maximus
when he was about to take office for the second time as Governor of
Alexandria and the country. Of this Senate the members who were
10 found in their houses, thirty-eight in number, were arrested by
Flaccus, who having ordered them to be straightway put in bonds
marshalled a fine procession through the middle of the market of

these elderly men trussed and pinioned, some with thongs and others
with iron chains, and then taken into the theatre, a spectacle most
15 pitiable and incongruous with the occasion. Then as they stood with
their enemies seated in front to signalize their disgrace he ordered
them all to be stripped and lacerated with scourges which are
commonly used for the degradation of the vilest malefactor, so that
in consequence of the flogging some had to be carried out on
20 stretchers and died at once, while others lay sick for a long time
despairing of recovery.

l. 3 *Flaccus*, governor of the province of Egypt. After years of good government
under the emperor Tiberius, he began to persecute the Jews, apparently in
order to gain favour with Gaius, when he became emperor. The incident
narrated here is by no means the most horrible in the record narrated by
Philo.

Finally it may be of interest to note how Jews appeared to an observant
Gentile.

150

Juvenal, *Satire* II. 10–16

But while all his goods and chattels were being packed upon a single
waggon, my friend halted at the dripping archway of the old Porta
Capena. Here Numa held his nightly assignations with his mistress;
but now the holy fount and grove and shrine are let out to Jews, who
5 possess a basket and a truss of hay for all their furnishings. For as
every tree nowadays has to pay toll to the people, the Muses have
been ejected, and the wood has to go a-begging.

l. 2 *Porta Capena.* 'The Porta Capena was on the Appian Way, the great S. road
from Rome. Over the gate passed an aqueduct, carrying the waters of the
Aqua Marcia. Hence "the dripping archway"' (G. G. Ramsay, ad loc.). *Numa*,
the legendary second king of Rome, was believed to consort with the goddess
Egeria.

151

Juvenal, *Satire* VI. 153–60, 542–7

Then in the winter time, when the merchant Jason is shut out from
view, and his armed sailors are blocked out by the white booths, she
will carry off huge crystal vases, vases bigger still of agate, and finally
a diamond of great renown, made famous by the finger of Berenice.
5 It was given as a present long ago by the barbarian Agrippa to his
incestuous sister, in that country where kings celebrate festal sabbaths
with bare feet, and where a long-established clemency suffers pigs to
attain old age . . .

No sooner has that fellow departed then a palsied Jewess, leaving
10 her basket and her truss of hay, comes begging to her secret ear; she
is an interpreter of the laws of Jerusalem, a high priestess of the tree,
a trusty go-between of highest heaven. She, too, fills her palm, but
more sparingly, for a Jew will tell you dreams of any kind you please
for the minutest of coins.

l. 4   *Berenice.* Cf. Acts 25. 23.

l. 9   *That fellow.* The priest impersonating Anubis.

152

Juvenal, Satire XIV. 96–106

Some who have had a father who reveres the Sabbath, worship
nothing but the clouds, and the divinity of the heavens, and see no
difference between eating swine's flesh, from which their father
abstained, and that of man; and in time they take to circumcision.
5 Having been wont to flout the laws of Rome, they learn and practise
and revere the Jewish law, and all that Moses committed to his secret
tome, forbidding to point out the way to any not worshipping the
same rites, and conducting none but the circumcised to the desired
fountain. For all which the father was to blame, who gave up every
10 seventh day to idleness, keeping it apart from all the concerns of life.

l. 2   *The divinity of the heavens.* 'The phrase *caeli numen* is hard to translate. What
Juvenal means is that the Jews worshipped no concrete deity, such as could
be portrayed, but only some impalpable mysterious spirit. They did not
worship the sky or the heavens, but only the *numen* of the heavens. This is
what Tacitus means when he says (*Hist.* V. 5) "The Jews worship with the
mind alone." So Lucan ii. 592–3: *dedita sacris Incerti Judaea dei'* (G. G. Ramsay,
ad loc.).

l. 4   Juvenal was no doubt right in seeing conversion to Judaism as a process that
often stretched over several generations.

l. 6   *All that Moses committed to his secret tome,* 'tradidit arcano quodcumque volumine
Moyses', perhaps 'handed down in his secret tome'.

l. 10   *Idleness.* Cf. Tacitus, *Histories* V. 4 (**132** above).

8 Rabbinic Literature and Rabbinic Judaism

The Rabbis

Rabbinic Judaism, though it claimed to have sprung directly from Moses, may be said to have begun with Ezra and his contemporaries, and to have been handed down from them as the staple form of religion in Palestine in the time of our Lord. The following passages are intended (*a*) to bring out the strongly traditional character of Rabbinic Judaism, and (*b*) to introduce the names of a number of important Rabbis.

153

Aboth 1. 1ff.

> Moses received the Law from Sinai and committed it to Joshua, and Joshua to the elders, and the elders to the Prophets; and the Prophets committed it to the men of the Great Synagogue. They said three things: Be deliberate in judgement, raise up many disciples, and make
> 5 a fence around the Law.
> Simeon the Just was of the remnants of the Great Synagogue. He used to say: By three things is the world sustained; by the Law, by the Temple-service, and by deeds of loving-kindness.
> Antigonus of Soko received the Law from Simeon the Just. He
> 10 used to say: Be not like slaves that minister to the master for the sake of receiving a bounty, but be like slaves that minister to the master not for the sake of receiving a bounty; and let the fear of Heaven be upon you.

l. 1   *The Law* (תורה, *Torah*). Here the oral Law is meant. This was a body of material which in fact grew up as explanation and expansion of the written Law of the Old Testament, The Rabbis however regarded it as equally ancient and equally important with the written Law. Both were received by Moses from (God on) Sinai, but the latter was committed to writing at once.

l. 2   *The elders.* Cf. Josh. 24. 31.

l. 3   *The Great Synagogue.* This was popularly interpreted as a body, 120 strong, of prophets and teachers in the time of Ezra; but the reference to Simeon suggests that the Mishnah referred to a succession of teachers of whom he was one of the latest. That this account of what did not happen should be vague is of course not surprising.

l. 5   *Make a fence around the Law.* Make additional commandments in order to safeguard the original commandments; for example, certain acts should be avoided towards the approach of evening on Friday lest one should forget and inadvertently continue to do them on the Sabbath.

l. 6   *Simeon the Just.* See Josephus, *Antiquities* xii. 43, 157, 224. It is impossible to determine with certainty whether this Simeon, who was high priest, lived at the beginning or at the end of the third century BC. The saying attributed to him is characteristic of Rabbinic religion, The three pillars on which the world rests are God's revelation of himself and his will in the Law, written and unwritten, and man's study of and obedience to this revelation (for this is included in the word *torah*); the cultic worship carried out in the Temple (*ʿabodah*), and the doing of acts of kindness (*gᵉmilluth hᵃsadim*)—acts not specifically commanded in the Law but performed out of compassion and goodness. Truth, worship, and love sustain the universe.

l. 9   *Antigonus of Soko.* There is no reliable evidence about Antigonus. His Greek name should be noted; tradition made him one of the founders of the Sadducees. The saying attributed to him is important; the attitude of Judaism to rewards is not as simple as is all too often assumed.

154

Aboth 1. 12–15

Hillel and Shammai received the Law from them. Hillel said: Be of the disciples of Aaron, loving peace and pursuing peace, loving mankind and bringing them nigh to the Law.

He used to say: A name made great is a name destroyed, and he 5 that increases not decreases, and he that learns not is worthy of death, and he that makes worldly use of the crown shall perish.

He used to say: If I am not for myself who is for me? and being for mine own self what am I? and if not now, when?

Shammai said: Make thy study of the Law a fixed habit; say little 10 and do much, and receive all men with a cheerful countenance.

l. 1   *Hillel and Shammai* stand here in a series of 'pairs' (*zugoth*) of names which were sometimes supposed to be those of Presidents and Vice-Presidents of the Sanhedrin. This however they cannot have been since (before the destruction of the Temple) the President was always the high priest. Hillel and Shammai would moreover have been very uneasy colleagues in the presidency, since many divergent and even contradictory interpretations and rulings were traced back to them, and they became the heads of two rival schools or factions (Beth Hillel, Beth Shammai). Both were active about the beginning of the Christian era; in general the former took the gentler and more lenient, the latter the stricter, view of any subject under debate. This general rule is 'proved' in *Eduyoth* 4f. by a number of exceptions, in which 'the School of Shammai adopted the more lenient, and the School of Hillel the more stringent ruling'; for example, 'If an egg was laid on a Festival-day the School of Shammai say, It may be eaten. The School of Hillel say: It may not be eaten' (*Eduyoth* 4. 1); and is itself illustrated in *Gittin* 9. 10 ('The School of Shammai say: A man may not divorce his wife unless he has found unchastity in her. . . . And the School of Hillel say: He may divorce her even if she spoiled a dish for him. . . .')

l. 1   *From them, sc.* from Shemaiah and Abtalion.

l. 3   *Mankind,* literally, 'the creatures', is used here, as the next sentence shows, of the Gentiles. Hillel advocates the making of proselytes (see below, **197–8**).

l. 4   *A name made great* . . . He that exalts himself shall be abased.

l. 5   *He that increases not decreases.* This saying is probably to be interpreted in the light of the next. He who does not add to the common store of knowledge and learning is as if he diminished it.

l. 6   *The crown* is the crown of the Law, the privilege of knowing, teaching, and practising it. The saying is explained in *Aboth* 4. 5 ('Thus thou mayest learn that he that makes profit out of the words of the Law removes his life from the world'), and there are parallel sayings (e.g. *Nedarim* 62a, 'He who makes use of the crown of the Law is rooted out of the world. Do the words of the Law for the doing's sake, and speak of them for their own sake. Make them not a crown with which to exalt thyself, or a spud with which to weed').

l. 7   *If I am not for myself* . . . Of this very obscure saying there are three possible interpretations. (*a*) Hillel speaks of a representative man. If a man does not shoulder his own responsibilities and do his own duty, who will do it for him? Yet if he does so by himself alone (without the help of God) what can he effect? And if he does not give obedience and service to God *now* in this life, when will he have another opportunity for doing so? (*b*) Instead of this individualist interpretation we may suppose that 'I' is used for 'Israel'. (*c*) The 'I' (אֲנִי, *'ani*) may be taken as a cryptic reference to God (אֲדֹנָי, *'adonai*), who is alone and eternal. This last interpretation seems far-fetched, but cf. *Sukkah* 53a; *Lev. R.* 35. 1.

155

Aboth 2. 1

Rabbi said: Which is the straight way that a man should choose? That which is an honour to him and gets him honour from men. And be heedful of a light precept as of a weighty one, for thou knowest not the recompense of reward of each precept; and reckon the loss through the fulfilling of a precept against its reward, and the reward that comes from transgression against its loss. Consider three things and thou wilt not fall into the hands of transgression: know what is above thee—a seeing eye and a hearing ear and all thy deeds written in a book.

l. 1   *Rabbi* refers to R. Judah the Prince (or Patriarch; נָשִׂיא *nasi'*) who on the basis of earlier collections compiled the Mishnah (see below, p. 184). He was born AD 135, and probably lived till after the end of the century. It is worth noting that in addition to the customary Rabbinic studies he learned and liked Greek; and was said (though this must be regarded as quite uncertain) to have been a friend of a Roman emperor.

l. 3   *Be heedful of a light precept* ... This is a characteristic injunction. It was
regarded as dangerous, and therefore undesirable, to arrange precepts in
order of importance; to do so might lead to the neglect of those deemed to
be less important.

156

Aboth 2 8f.

> Rabban Johanan b. Zakkai received the Law from Hillel and from
> Shammai. He used to say: If thou hast wrought much in the Law
> claim not merit for thyself, for to this end wast thou created. Five
> disciples had Rabban Johanan b. Zakkai, and these are they: R. Eliezer
> 5 b. Hyrcanus, and R. Joshua b. Hananiah, and R. Jose the Priest, and
> R. Simeon b. Nathaniel, and R. Eleazar b. Arak. Thus used he to
> recount their praise: Eliezer b. Hyrcanus is a plastered cistern which
> loses not a drop; Joshua b. Hananiah—happy is she that bare him;
> Jose the Priest is a saintly man; Simeon b. Nathaniel is fearful of sin;
> 10 Eleazar b. Arak is an ever-flowing spring. He used to say: If all the
> Sages of Israel were in the one scale of the balance and Eliezer b.
> Hyrcanus in the other, he would outweigh them all. Abba Saul said
> in his name: If all the Sages of Israel were in the one scale of the
> balance and with them Eliezer b. Hyrcanus, and Eleazar b. Arak was
> 15 in the other, he would outweigh them all.
> He said to them: Go forth and see which is the good way to which
> a man should cleave. R. Eliezer said, A good eye. R. Joshua said, A
> good companion. R. Jose said, A good neighbour. R. Simeon said,
> One that sees what will be. R. Eleazar said, A good heart. He said to
> 20 them: I approve the words of Eleazar b. Arak more than your words,
> for in his words are your words included. He said to them: Go forth
> and see which is the evil way which a man should shun. R. Eliezer
> said, An evil eye. R. Joshua said, An evil companion. R. Jose said, an
> evil neighbour. R. Simeon said, He that borrows and does not repay.
> 25 He that borrows from man is as one that borrows from God, for it is
> written, *The wicked borroweth and payeth not again but the righteous
> dealeth graciously and giveth* (Ps. 37. 21). R. Eleazar said, An evil heart.
> He said to them: I approve the words of Eleazar b. Arak more than
> your words for in his words are your words included.

l. 1   *Rabban Johanan b. Zakkai* was one of the most important of all the Rabbis.
After the destruction of the Temple in AD 70 he reconstituted the Sanhedrin
at Jabneh, and thereby helped to preserve Judaism for the future. He died
about AD 80, having made a number of important modifications necessitated
by the removal of the Temple; e.g. *Sukkah* 3. 12 'Beforetime the *Lulab* (see
below, **181**) was carried seven days in the Temple, but in the provinces one
day only. After the Temple was destroyed, Rabban Johanan b. Zakkai
ordained that in the provinces it should be carried seven days in memory of
the Temple'.

157
Aboth 3. 14–17

R. Akiba said: Jesting and levity accustom a man to lewdness. The tradition is a fence around the Law; Tithes are a fence around riches; vows are a fence around abstinence; a fence around wisdom is silence.

He used to say: Beloved is man for he was created in the image [of
5 God]; still greater was the love in that it was made known to him that he was created in the image of God, as it is written, *For in the image of God made he man* (Gen. 9. 6). Beloved are Israel for they were called children of God; still greater was the love in that it was made known to them that they were called children of God, as it is
10 written, *Ye are the children of the Lord your God* (Deut. 14. 1). Beloved are Israel, for to them was given the precious instrument; still greater was the love, in that it was made known to them that to them was given the precious instrument by which the world was created, as it is written, *For I give you good doctrine; forsake ye not my law* (Prov.
15 4. 2).

All is foreseen, but freedom of choice is given; and the world is judged by grace, yet all is according to the excess of works [that be good or evil].

He used to say: All is given against a pledge, and the net is cast
20 over all living; the shop stands open and the shopkeeper gives credit and the account-book lies open and the hand writes and every one that wishes to borrow let him come and borrow; but the collectors go their round continually every day and exact payment of men with their consent or without their consent, for they have that on
25 which they can rely; and the judgement is a judgement of truth; and all is made ready for the banquet.

l. 1   *R. Akiba* b. Joseph was born *c.* AD 50 and died a martyr in the revolt of Bar Cocheba (see p. 170 and **145–7**) in AD 135. He did not enter Rabbinic circles naturally but was born an *ʿam ha-ʾaretz* (**195**), and became a Rabbi in later life (see *Pesahim* 49*b*: Akiba recalled his days as an *ʿam ha-ʾaretz* and declared that then he would wish to bite a scholar 'like an ass'. 'Like a dog', his disciples corrected him. But he replied, 'An ass's bite breaks the bone; a dog's does not'). He taught in Bᶜne Baraq; also in Lydda and Jabneh. When the revolt made head he proved himself a man of affairs as well as a scholar, and recognized Bar Cocheba as the Messiah. His great literary achievement was the first redaction of the oral Law in systematic written form. His 'Mishnah' was developed by R. Meir, and finally used by R. Judah himself (see above, **155**).

l. 2   *A fence.* See above, **153**, on *Aboth* 1. 1.

l. 5   *Still greater . . .* Some texts omit this sentence. It (like later similar sentences) stresses the supreme value of the revelation granted to Israel, and the graciousness of God in giving it.

l. 11   *The precious instrument.* The Law is meant. In Prov. 8 Wisdom (חכמה, *ḥokmah*) is represented as having been active in co-operation with God in the work of creation. Wisdom was equated with Law, and so to the Law also cosmological functions were assigned.

l. 16   *All is foreseen, but freedom of choice is given.* According to Josephus (*War* ii. 162f.) 'the Pharisees ... attribute everything to Fate (εἱμαρμένη) and to God; they hold that to act rightly or otherwise rests, indeed, for the most part with man, but that in each action Fate co-operates.' This resolute assertion of the paradox of determinism and free will, with no attempt to explain it, is characteristic of the unphilosophical style of Rabbinic thought.

l. 19   *All is given against a pledge.* This long and apparently complicated metaphor is in fact straightforward. God is a creditor, to whom men are indebted; they owe him obedience and good works.

l. 24   *That on which they can rely*; the record of men's debts kept in heaven.

l. 26   *The banquet*—the feast of the Age to Come, or kingdom of God.

158

Aboth 4. 1

Ben Zoma said: Who is wise? He that learns from all men, as it is written, *From all my teachers have I got understanding* (Ps. 119. 99). Who is mighty? He that subdues his [evil] nature, as it is written, *He that is slow to anger is better than the mighty, and he that ruleth his spirit*
5   *than he that taketh a city* (Prov. 16. 32). Who is rich? He that rejoiceth in his portion, as it is written, *When thou eatest the labour of thy hands happy shalt thou be, and it shall be well with thee* (Ps. 128. 2). *Happy shalt thou be*—in this world; *and it shall be well with thee*—in the world to come. Who is honoured? He that honours mankind, as it is
10   written, *For them that honour me I will honour, and they that despise me shall be lightly esteemed* (1 Sam. 2. 30).

l. 1   *Ben Zoma*, a younger contemporary of R. Akiba, was in high repute as an expositor: 'When Ben Zoma died there were no more expounders' (*Sotah* 9. 15). But he 'entered into Paradise' (engaged in mystical exegesis and theosophical speculation) and incurred suspicion. It should be noted that he is not styled 'Rabbi'.

l. 2   *From all my teachers*, a common Rabbinic rendering of this verse; cf. RV, 'I have more understanding than all my teachers.'

l. 3   *His evil nature*, his *yetzer* (יצר). This word (cf. in the Bible Gen. 6. 5; 8. 21; Deut. 31. 21; Isa. 26. 3; 1 Chron. 28. 9; 29. 18) is used to describe the *inclination* within man which gives him a tendency to sin, an innate source of temptation. It was not in itself altogether bad since it was created by God and could be used for good purposes (e.g. it is very frequently linked by the Rabbis with sexual passion and temptation; but they also point out that without it 'no man would build a house, marry a wife, beget children, or engage in trade' (*Gen. R.* 9. 7)). The inclination may be restrained by repentance and the study of the Law. The earlier sources seem to have spoken of only one (bad) inclination, the later of two, good and bad, acting in conflict; see e.g. *Berakoth* 9. 5, where 'with *all* thy heart' (Deut. 6. 5) is said to mean 'with both thine impulses, thy good impulse and thine evil impulse'.

ll. 8f. *In this world . . . in the world to come.* For this contrast see **267–8**.

159

Yadaim 4. 6, 7

The Sadducees say, We cry out against you, O ye Pharisees, for ye say, 'The Holy Scriptures render the hands unclean', [and] 'The writings of Hamiram do not render the hands unclean'. Rabban Johanan ben Zakkai said, Have we naught against the Pharisees save
5 this!—for lo, they say, 'The bones of an ass are clean, and the bones of Johanan the High Priest are unclean'. They said to him, As is our love for them so is their uncleanness—that no man make spoons of the bones of his father or mother. He said to them, Even so the Holy Scriptures: as is our love for them so is their uncleanness; [whereas]
10 the writings of Hamiram which are held in no account do not render the hands unclean.
   The Sadducees say, We cry out against you, O ye Pharisees, for ye declare clean an unbroken stream of liquid. The Pharisees say, we cry out against you, O ye Sadducees, for ye declare clean a channel of
15 water that flows from a burial ground. The Sadducees say, We cry out against you, O ye Pharisees, for ye say, 'If my ox or my ass have done an injury they are culpable, but if my bondman or my bondwoman have done an injury they are not culpable'—if, in the case of my ox or my ass (about which no commandments are laid
20 upon me) I am responsible for the injury that they do, how much more in the case of my bondman or my bondwoman (about whom certain commandments are laid upon me) must I be responsible for the injury that they do! They said to them, No!—as ye argue concerning my ox or my ass (which have no understanding) would
25 ye likewise argue concerning my bondman or my bondwoman which have understanding?—for if I provoke him to anger he may go and set fire to another's stack of corn, and it is I that must make restitution!

l. 1   *The Sadducees . . . Pharisees.* For Josephus's account of these two groups see **135**. Their disagreements are mentioned from time to time in the Mishnah.

l. 3   *Hamiram.* There are several variants. The reference may be to the books of the heretics (*Minim*) or to the books of Homer.
         Rabban Johanan ben Zakkai. See **156**.

l. 13   *An unbroken stream of liquid,* poured from a clean vessel into an unclean one does not transfer uncleanness from the latter to the former.

The Literature

The foundation of orthodox Judaism was the biblical Law. This was however supplemented by a tradition (in the New Testament, and Josephus, παράδοσις), at first oral but later written down. This oral Law (תורה שבעל פה) was believed equally with the written to have originated with Moses (see on *Aboth* I. I (**153**) above), and was consequently of equal authority. The process of writing down the oral Law, at first frowned upon, passed through several stages in the second century AD, until at the end of the century the Mishnah as we know it was compiled, on the basis of earlier documents (notably the Mishnah of R. Meir), by R. Judah (see above note on **155** *l*. I). The Mishnah is on the whole a systematization and application of the Old Testament regulations for ceremonial and civil procedure (the tractate *Aboth* quoted in the preceding section and consisting mainly of religious and ethical maxims is exceptional), and is divided into six Orders, or Books, containing in all sixty-three tractates. The whole body of oral legal tradition was not used in R. Judah's Mishnah; a quantity that was left over forms the *Tosephta*, a body of material parallel in form and content to the Mishnah itself but lacking its authority. In turn the Mishnah was expounded and expanded, and in due course the whole body of Mishnah and comment was edited as the *Talmud*. The comment was known as *Gemara* and exists in two forms, which (with the Mishnah, which is common to both) make up the two Talmuds, the Babylonian and the Jerusalem, edited in the two main centres of Rabbinic activity, Babylonia and Palestine, *c*. AD 500. Most of the Talmudic material is *Halakah*; that is, it contains specific and authoritative direction for the life of Jewish obedience. (In addition to authorized *halakoth* it contains also many juridical opinions which were finally rejected by the majority of scholars.) Though the final date of recension is, as has been said, fairly late, the Talmuds contain a good deal that is early enough to be relevant to New Testament studies; in particular, the Gemara contains sayings described by the word *Baraita*; these are sayings of *Tannaim* (Rabbis of the pre-mishnaic period) which were not included in the Mishnah.

Halakah represents only one kind of Rabbinic literary activity. The other main direction of Rabbinic work was *Haggadah*—practical, homiletic, and often imaginative and even fanciful interpretation of Scripture. This kind of exposition is to be found principally in the *Midrashim*, among which may be noted *Mekilta* (a commentary on Exodus), *Siphra* (on Leviticus), *Siphre* (on Numbers), *Siphre* (on Deuteronomy), and the *Midrash Rabbah* (or *Large Midrash*, on the Pentateuch and the five *Megilloth*). One other kind of literature may be noted—the liturgical. Here the most important sources for our purpose are the Book of Daily Prayers, still in use in various forms in the synagogue today, and the *Passover Haggadah*, or service for use in the home on Passover night. Parts of the Prayer Book are medieval and parts are modern; but others are very ancient (see for example **187–94**). Comparison of the Passover service with the Mishnaic instructions regarding the feast proves that much of it also is primitive.

An exhaustive analysis of the literature cannot be attempted here, but the following passages exemplify forms which are of interest to the student of the New Testament.

EXEGESIS

Much of the Rabbinic literature consists of the exegesis of Scripture. Though this may often appear to the modern reader arbitrary it was in fact generally conducted in accordance with certain established principles (*Middoth*). Several sets of such principles exist: the seven *middoth* of Hillel (quoted below); the thirteen *middoth* of R. Ishmael (died *c.* AD 135); the thirty-two *middoth* of R. Eliezer ben R. Jose the Galilean (end of the second century AD).

160

Tosephta Sanhedrin 7. 11 (p. 427)

Hillel the Elder expounded seven principles (*middoth*) before the elders of Petherah: *a minori ad maius*, analogy, a standard conclusion based on one passage (of scripture), a standard conclusion based on two passages, general and particular—particular and general, analogy
5 with another passage, proof from the context. These seven things did Hillel the Elder expound before the men of Petherah.

l. 2 *A minori ad maius*, literally, 'light and heavy', covering arguments from the less to the greater and from the greater to the less. This is a very common argument in Rabbinic usage.
Analogy; an argument from one passage of Scripture to another, similar one. The validity of the analogy might be disputed, as for example in *Betzah* 1. 6: The School of Shammai say: They may not take Dough-offering or [Priests'] Dues to the priest on a Festival-day whether they were set apart on the day before or on the same day. And the School of Hillel permit it. The School of Shammai replied with an analogy (*g⁽ᵉ⁾zerah shawah*—the second *middah*): Dough-offering and [Priests'] Dues are a gift to the priest, and the Heave-Offering is a gift to the priest; as they may not bring Heave-offering, neither may they bring [Priests'] Dues. The School of Hillel replied: No! as ye argue of Heave-offering (which a man has not the right to set apart [on a Festival-

day]) would ye also argue of [Priests'] Dues (which a man has the right to set apart [on a Festival-day])?

l. 4   General and particular—particular and general. This rule was expanded by R. Ishmael (see above) into eight.

161

Siphre Numbers 82, 83 (on Numbers 10. 33, 34)

And they set forward from the mount of the Lord three days journey, and the ark of the covenant of the Lord went before them three days journey to seek out a resting-place for them (Num. 10. 33). This suggests that the Shekinah went in advance of them thirty-six miles on that day, in
5   order that they should enter the land. They (the sages) told it in a parable. What can it be likened unto? It is like unto men who go out to war. On the way to the battlefield they rejoice, but as soon as they get exhausted, their hands hang down. But it was not so with Israel; for when they got tired, they encouraged each other and said: 'Come,
10 let us take the land of Israel in possession!' Another interpretation. They said: 'Our fathers have sinned, and it was decreed by God that "their bodies should fall in the wilderness" Num. 14. 29. Let us not sin [like them], lest we should die, but let us go and take the land of Israel in possession!'
15   *And the ark of the covenant of the Lord went before them.* This ark which went with them into the camp contained the broken tablets [of the law]. R. Shimeon ben Joḥai says: 'It is a parable. It is like to a Viceroy (ante-Caesar) who went before his armies to prepare for them a place where they should camp; so the Shekina went before
20 Israel and prepared for them a place where they should dwell.'
        To seek out a resting-place for them. ('Seek out'—*la-thur*.) What is the meaning of these words? It is an allusion to the words, *And the Canaanite, the King of Arad, heard* (Num. 21. 1), (namely) as soon as the Canaanites heard that the *spies* were dead, they said: 'Their *spies*
25 who went to investigate the land are dead, let us go and fight against them.' R. Shimeon ben Joḥai says: 'It says: "*for Israel passed the way of* ITHARIM", which means: *I-tharim, i.e.* no guides. For as soon as Aaron died, the Canaanites said: "Their high priest is dead, their *great guide* (*tayyar*) and the pillar of cloud, which fought for them, have
30 gone. Lo! the best time to fight them!"' R. Shimeon ben Joḥai says: 'Israel was much to be blamed, for at the time when they said, "*Let us send men to investigate the land*" (Deut. 1. 22), God said to them: "If when ye have been in the wilderness, I have fed you and supported you, how much more will it be the case when ye enter into a good
35 and wide land, a land flowing with milk and honey."'
        And the cloud of the Lord was over them by day (Num. 10. 34). Hence they (the sages) said that there were seven clouds (cf. Exod. 40. 28;

Num. 9. 19; 14. 14). Four on their four sides, one above, and one
below, and one in front. Every hilly place it (the cloud) levelled, and
40 every depression it raised, and it killed the serpents and the scorpions.
R. Judah says: 'There were *thirteen* clouds: two on every side, two
above, two below, and one in front.' R. Josiah says: 'There were four.'
Rabbi says: 'There were two.'

And the cloud of the Lord was over them by day. Over the lame, over
45 the blind, over those with an issue, and over the lepers.

And the cloud, etc. Whence do we know (sayest thou) that if one of
the Israelites dropped out from under the wings of the cloud, the
pillar of cloud gathered him from behind until he joined the main
body? Because it says: '*And the cloud of the Lord was over them.*' Should
50 we think that, as it shielded the Israelites, so it also shielded the peoples
of the world? It says: 'Over *them*'; only Israel it shielded, not the
nations of the World. Should we think that as it shielded them by
day, it shielded them also by night? It says: '*By day.*' R. Shimeon ben
El'azar said: 'Whence do we know that all the forty years that the
55 Israelites spent in the desert they had no need for a lamp, but even if
a person went into the innermost part of a house, a lantern, as it were,
entered with him and stayed until he returned? Because it goes on to
say: "*For the eyes of the whole house of Israel in all their journeys.*" Lo,
even if a man went into the innermost part of a house, the pillar of
60 fire lighted before him!'

l. 4   *Shekinah*, the glorious presence of God.

l. 18   *Ante-Caesar* (*sic*). The word is אנטיקסר which presumably represented
ἀντικαίσαρος; this word however does not appear to exist in Greek (or in
Latin, though in Latin we may compare *proconsul*).

l. 27   *I-tharim.* Cf. Ichabod, No glory.

l. 43   *Rabbi.* That is, R. Judah ha-Nasi.

MAXIMS

Much of the moral teaching of the Rabbis resembles that of the older
Wisdom literature in that it is delivered in the form of maxims: brief,
sententious utterances, often epigrammatic in form. Some examples have
already been given (see **153–8**); hundreds more could be quoted.

162

Aboth 2. 7

Moreover he saw a skull floating on the face of the water and he said
unto it, Because thou drownedst they drowned thee and at the last
they that drowned thee shall be drowned. He used to say: The more
flesh the more worms; the more possessions the more care; the more

5 women the more witchcrafts; the more bondwomen the more
lewdness; the more bondmen the more thieving; the more study of
the Law the more life; the more schooling the more wisdom; the
more counsel the more understanding; the more righteousness the
more peace. If a man has gained a good name he has gained somewhat
10 for himself; if he has gained for himself words of the Law he has
gained for himself life in the world to come.

l. 1   *He.* Hillel.

l. 7   *The more life.* The Law is the means of (eternal) life—a very characteristic
affirmation; cf. *l.* 11.

163

Aboth 3. 5

R. Nehunya b. Ha-Kanah [*c.* AD 70–130] said: He that takes upon
himself the yoke of the Law, from him shall be taken away the yoke
of the kingdom and the yoke of worldly care; but he that throws off
the yoke of the Law, upon him shall be laid the yoke of the kingdom
5 and the yoke of worldly care.

l. 3   *The kingdom.* When 'the kingdom' is used absolutely in Rabbinic writings its
meaning is usually 'the earthly kingdom', the present authorities; often of
course the Roman Empire. R. Nehunya means that the pious student of the
Law will be delivered from trouble with the authorities.

Naturally, legal as well as moral pronouncements were cast in the form of
maxims, for example the pronouncement of R. Meir in a question of what
might or might not be permitted on the Sabbath.

164

Shabbath 15. 1

These are knots for which they [that tie them on the Sabbath] are
accounted culpable: camel-drivers' knots and sailors' knots; and as a
man is culpable through the tying of them so is he culpable through
the untying of them. R. Meir says: None is accounted culpable
5 because of any knot which can be untied with one hand.

PARABLES

Parables constitute another very common rabbinic form. There is rarely
any difficulty in their interpretation. Their most common logical basis is
that of the 'light and heavy' argument (see above, **160** and note), but
details are sometimes allegorized.

165

Aboth 3. 18

R. Eleazar b. Azariah [*c.* AD 50–120] said: If there is no study of the Law there is no seemly behaviour, if there is no seemly behaviour there is no study of the Law; if there is no wisdom there is no fear [of God], if there is no fear [of God] there is no wisdom; if there is no
5 knowledge there is no discernment, if there is no discernment there is no knowledge; if there is no meal there is no study of the Law, if there is no study of the Law there is no meal. He used to say: He whose wisdom is more abundant than his works, to what is he like? To a tree whose branches are abundant but whose roots are few; and
10 the wind comes and uproots it and overturns it, as it is written, *He shall be like a tamarisk in the desert and shall not see when good cometh; but shall inhabit the parched places in the wilderness* (Jer. 17. 6). But he whose works are more abundant than his wisdom, to what is he like? To a tree whose branches are few but whose roots are many; so that
15 even if all the winds in the world come and blow against it, it cannot be stirred from its place, as it is written, *He shall be as a tree planted by the waters, and that spreadeth out his roots by the river, and shall not fear when heat cometh, and his leaf shall be green; and shall not be careful in the year of drought, neither shall cease from yielding fruit* (Jer. 17. 8).

166

Sukkah 2. 9

Throughout the seven [days of the Feast] a man must make his *Sukkah* a regular abode and his house a chance abode. If rain fell, when may he empty out [*the Sukkah*]? When the porridge would spoil. They propounded a parable: To what can it be compared?—
5 to a slave who came to fill the cup for his master and he poured the pitcher over his face.

l. 2   *Sukkah*, the booth in which he was required to dwell during the Feast of Booths (below, **181**).

l. 6   *His face.* 'The slave's. At the Feast of Tabernacles rain is a sign of God's anger (*Taanith* 1. 1). The slave (Israel) would perform his duties (the observance of the divinely ordained Feasts and living in booths), but his master (God) only shows his displeasure' (Danby, ad loc.).

167

Shabbath 153*a*

R. Eliezer said: Repent one day before your death. His disciples asked R. Eliezer: But does a man know on what day he will die? He said: So much the more must he repent today; perhaps he will die

tomorrow. It follows that a man should repent every day. Even so
5 said Solomon in his wisdom, *Let thy garments be always white; and let
not thy head lack ointment* (Eccles. 9. 8). R. Johanan b. Zakkai spoke a
parable: [It is like] a king who invited his servants to a feast and did
not appoint them a time. The wise among them adorned themselves
and sat down by the door of the palace, for they said: Is anything
10 lacking in a palace? The foolish among them went to their work, for
they said: Is a feast ever given without preparation? Suddenly the
king summoned his servants. The wise among them went in before
him adorned as they were, and the foolish went in before him in
their working clothes. The king rejoiced to see the wise and was
15 angry to see the foolish, and said: These who adorned themselves for
the feast shall sit down and eat and drink; but those who did not
adorn themselves for the feast shall stand and look on. The son-in-
law of R. Meir said in the name of R. Meir: If so, the latter would
look on as waiters; but rather both shall sit down; the former shall
20 eat but the latter be hungry, the former shall drink but the latter be
thirsty, as it is said, *Behold, my servants shall eat, but ye shall be hungry*
... (Isa. 65. 13, 14).

NARRATIVE

The Rabbinic books often use narrative as a means of expressing or
suggesting truth. Sometimes the narratives are straightforward stories of
ordinary events leading to a legal question and decision; sometimes they
are used for other purposes, for example, to reflect credit upon Israel or
upon individual Jews. Miracles also are found, some of which form
interesting parallels to the New Testament miracles.

168

Nedarim 9. 5

This narrative raises a question, and leads to a decision, about the validity
and alterability of a vow.

They may open the way for a man by reason of his wife's *Ketubah*. It
once happened that a man vowed to have no benefit from his wife,
whose *Ketubah* was 400 *denars*. She came before R. Akiba and he
declared him liable to pay her her *Ketubah*. He said, 'Rabbi, my father
5 left about 800 *denars*, and my brother took 400 *denars* and I took
400; is it not enough that she should take 200 *denars* and I 200?' R.
Akiba said to him, 'Even if thou must sell the hair of thy head thou
shalt pay her her *Ketubah*'. The husband answered, 'Had I known
that this was so, I had not made my vow', and R. Akiba released him
10 from his vow.

l. 1   *Ketubah.* 'Literally, "a written document"; a wife's "jointure". The word is used (*a*) for the document (cf *Ketuboth* 4. 7–12) in which the bridegroom pledges himself to assign a certain sum of money to the bride in the event of his death or of his divorcing her; and (*b*) for the sum of money so assigned (cf. *Ketuboth* 5. 1)' (Danby, p 794).

l. 7   *Even if thou must sell . . .* The obligation of the *ketubah* is absolutely binding; the divorced woman may have no other resource at all.

l. 9   *Released him from his vow,* 'opened the way for him' (*l.* 1). This example of the annulment of a vow occurs among others in which it is held that a man may be released because when he made his vow he failed to understand its implications.

169

Y. Baba Metzia ii. 5. 8c

Simeon b. Shetah [*fl. c.* 80 BC] was occupied with preparing flax. His disciples said to him, 'Rabbi, desist; we will buy you an ass, and you will not have to work so hard.' They went and bought an ass from an Arab, and a pearl was found on it. They came to him and said,

5 'From now on you need not work any more.' He said, 'Why?' They said, 'We bought you an ass from an Arab, and a pearl was found on it.' He said to them, 'Does its owner know of it?' They said, 'No.' He said to them, 'Go and give it back to him.' They said, 'But did not R. Huna, in the name of Rab, report that, even according to him who

10 said that no profit may be made [by a third party] from that which is *stolen* from a heathen, yet all the world agrees that, if you *find* something which belonged to a heathen, you may keep it?' He said, 'Do you think that Simeon b. Shetah is a barbarian? No, he would prefer to hear the Arab say, "Blessed be the God of the Jews", than to

15 possess all the riches of the world.'
     It is also proved, from the story of R. Hanina, that lost property should be restored for the sake of the sanctification of the Name. For once, some aged Rabbis bought a heap of corn from some soldiers, and they found in it a bundle of *denarii*, and they returned it to the

20 soldiers, who said, 'Blessed be the God of the Jews.'

170

Taanith 3. 8

Once they said to Onias the Circle-maker, 'Pray that rain may fall.' He answered, 'Go out and bring in the Passover ovens that they be not softened.' He prayed, but the rain did not fall. What did he do? He drew a circle and stood within it and said before God, 'O Lord of

5 the world, thy children have turned their faces to me, for that I am like a son of the house before thee. I swear by thy great name that I will not stir hence until thou have pity on thy children.' Rain began

falling drop by drop. He said, 'Not for such rain have I prayed, but for rain that will fill the cisterns, pits, and caverns.' It began to rain
10 with violence. He said, 'Not for such rain have I prayed, but for rain of goodwill, blessing, and graciousness.' Then it rained in moderation [and continued] until the Israelites went up from Jerusalem to the Temple Mount because of the rain. They went to him and said, 'Like as thou didst pray for the rain to come, so pray that it may go away!'
15 He replied, 'Go and see if the Stone of the Strayers has disappeared!' Simeon b. Shetah sent to him saying, 'Hadst thou not been Onias I had pronounced a ban against thee! But what shall I do to thee?—thou importunest God and he performeth thy will, like a son that importuneth his father and he performeth his will; and of thee
20 Scripture saith, *Let thy father and thy mother be glad, and let her that bare thee rejoice* (Prov. 23. 25)'.

l. 1   *Onias the Circle-maker* lived early in the first century BC. It is difficult not to think (especially in view of Simeon's complaint (*l.* 16)) that his circle-drawing was related to magic. In the Midrash on Ps. 77. 1, with reference to Hab. 2. 1 (I will stand upon my watch), circle-drawing is a mark of impatience: Habakkuk will not move from his circle until God answers his question. But this may be a reinterpretation of an action whose origins lie further back. See an important account of Onias (Honi) in G. Vermes, *Jesus the Jew* (London, 1973), pp 69–72.

l. 2   *Passover ovens*, specially made for roasting the paschal sacrifices. They were made of clay.

l. 6   *A son of the house*, and thus specially intimate with God, able to make importunate petitions and obtain what he asked.

l. 15   *The Stone of the Strayers*, 'Explained as a high stone from which lost articles were proclaimed (cf. *Baba Metzia* 2. 1–6), the "Strayers" being those in search of their missing property' (Danby, ad loc.).

l. 16   *Simeon b. Shetah*. See above, **169**. Evidently he felt the proceedings to be unorthodox, but Onias's evident power with God placed him above punishment.

The Law

The Law was not only the basis of Rabbinic scholarship and writing (above, pp. 184f.) but the foundation of both religious and social life. It came from God, it afforded a divine revelation of all needful truth, and provided a practical way of salvation.

171

Exodus Rabbah 33. 1

A parable. It is like a king who had one only daughter. There came a certain king and took her to wife; and he sought to go to his own

land and take his wife with him. The king said: My daughter, whom
I have given you, is my only daughter; I cannot be parted from her,
5 but neither can I say to you, Do not take her, for she is your wife.
But do me this kindness. Where you go, make a bedroom for me
that I may dwell with you, for I cannot let my daughter go. In the
same way said the Holy One (blessed be he) to Israel: I have given
you the Law, but I cannot be separated from it; nor can I say to you
10 Do not take it. But wherever you go make me a house in which I
may dwell, as it is said, *Let them make me a sanctuary that I may dwell
among them* (Exod. 25. 8).

l. 8   *I have given you the Law*. It must not be thought that the father–daughter
relationship in the parable assigns any metaphysical status to the Law. Such
thoughts are foreign to this kind of exposition. The expositor wishes to
emphasize that the Law is a gracious gift from God to Israel, a signal mark of
his favour; and that the possession of it carries with it God's presence in a
unique manner and degree.

172

Siphre Numbers, Shelah, 115, 35a

The Law is a precious gift, and presupposes God's redemption of his
people.

Why is the Exodus from Egypt mentioned in connection with every
single commandment? The matter can be compared to a king, the
son of whose friend was taken prisoner. The king ransomed him, not
as son, but as slave, so that, if at any time he should disobey the king,
5 the latter could say, 'You are my slave.' So, when he came back, the
king said, 'Put on my sandals for me, take my clothes to the bath
house.' Then the man protested. The king took out the bill of sale,
and said, 'You are my slave.' So when God redeemed the children of
Abraham his friend, he redeemed them, not as children, but as slaves,
10 so that if he imposed upon them decrees, and they obeyed not, he
could say, 'Ye are my slaves.' When they went into the desert, he
began to order them some light and some heavy commands, e.g.
Sabbath and incest commands, and fringes and phylacteries. They
began to protest. Then God said, 'You are my slaves. On this
15 condition I redeemed you, that I should decree, and you should fulfil.'
[Nevertheless, God's slaves are unlike man's slaves. God's ways are
not like those of 'flesh and blood'. For a man acquires slaves that they
may look after and sustain *him*, but God acquires slaves that He may
look after and sustain *them*].

173

Kiddushin 30*b*

> The words of the Law are likened to a medicine of life. Like a king
> who inflicted a big wound upon his son, and he put a plaster upon
> his wound. He said, 'My son, so long as this plaster is on your wound,
> eat and drink what you like, and wash in cold or warm water, and
> 5 you will suffer no harm. But if you remove it, you will get a bad
> boil.' So God says to the Israelites, 'I created within you the evil
> *yetzer*, but I created the Law as a drug. As long as you occupy
> yourselves with the Law, the *yetzer* will not rule over you. But if
> you do not occupy yourselves with the Torah, then you will be
> 10 delivered into the power of the *yetzer*, and all its activity will be
> against you.'

l. 2   *Put a plaster*; derived from Deut. 11. 18 by a pun in Hebrew.

l. 7   *Yetzer.* See **158**, and note on *l.* 3.

Feasts and Festivals

After the Law itself, nothing did more to preserve the unity and uniqueness
of Israel than the due celebration of the festivals prescribed in the Law.
They were noted in Palestine and the Dispersion alike, but the three great
pilgrim feasts (Passover, Pentecost, and Booths or Tabernacles) could only
be fully observed in Palestine. This added so much more importance to
the Sabbath, which everywhere distinguished Jews from their neighbours;
nevertheless, Jews flocked to Jerusalem in great numbers to take part in
the pilgrim feasts.

SABBATH

Like all other commandments, the Sabbath was regarded as a gracious gift
of God, and was to the pious Israelite no burden but an occasion of
rejoicing. The best clothes were worn, the best food eaten. Worship was
held in the synagogue.

174

Mekilta on Exodus 31. 13 (109*b*)

> The Sabbath is given over to you, not you to the Sabbath.

175

Tamid 7. 4

This was the singing which the Levites used to sing in the Temple. On the first day they sang *The earth is the Lord's and all that therein is, the round world and they that dwell therein* (Ps. 24); on the second day they sang *Great is the Lord and highly to be praised in the city of our*
5 *God, even upon his holy hill* (Ps. 48); on the third day they sang *God standeth in the congregation of God, he is a judge among the gods* (Ps. 82); on the fourth day they sang *O Lord God to whom vengeance belongeth, thou God to whom vengeance belongeth, show thyself* (Ps. 94); on the fifth day they sang *Sing we merrily unto God our strength, make a*
10 *cheerful noise unto the God of Jacob* (Ps. 81); on the sixth day they sang *The Lord is king, and hath put on glorious apparel* (Ps. 93). On the Sabbath they sang *A Psalm: a Song for the Sabbath Day* (Ps. 92); a Psalm, a song for the time that is to come, for the day that shall be all Sabbath and rest in the life everlasting.

l. 13 *The day that shall be all Sabbath*. The Sabbath was so great a delight that it was used as a type of the Age to Come.

176

Shabbath 7. 1f.

A great general rule have they laid down concerning the Sabbath: whosoever, forgetful of the principle of the Sabbath, committed many acts of work on many Sabbaths, is liable only to one Sin-offering; but if, mindful of the principle of the Sabbath, he yet
5 committed many acts of work on many Sabbaths, he is liable for every Sabbath [which he profaned]. If he knew that it was the Sabbath and he yet committed many acts of work on many Sabbaths, he is liable for every main class of work [which he performed]; if he committed many acts of work of one main class, he is liable only to
10 one Sin-offering.
   The main classes of work are forty save one: sowing, ploughing, reaping, binding sheaves, threshing, winnowing, cleansing crops, grinding, sifting, kneading, baking, shearing wool, washing or beating or dyeing it, spinning, weaving, making two loops, weaving
15 two threads, separating two threads, tying [a knot], loosening [a knot], sewing two stitches, tearing in order to sew two stitches, hunting a gazelle, slaughtering or flaying or salting it or curing its skin, scraping it or cutting it up, writing two letters, erasing in order to write two letters, building, pulling down, putting out a fire,
20 lighting a fire, striking with a hammer and taking out aught from one domain into another. These are the main classes of work: forty save one.

l. 2   *The principle of the Sabbath.* 'Principle' translates עִיקָר ('*iqqar*), literally, 'root'. The point seems to be that he who is unaware of the fundamental principle of Sabbath observance incurs guilt only in respect of this one (fundamental) ignorance, or forgetfulness. The man who knows and remembers the Law, but forgets the Sabbath day and thus commits breaches of the Sabbath law is responsible for each act of forgetting and the consequent breach. The Law was a delight; but the Law had to be kept.

177

Shabbath 2. 7

Three things must a man say within his house when darkness is falling on the eve of Sabbath; Have ye tithed? Have ye prepared the *Erub*? and, Light the lamp. If it is in doubt whether darkness has already fallen or not, they may not set apart Tithes from what is
5   known to be untithed, or immerse utensils or light the lamps; but they may set aside Tithes from *demai*-produce and prepare the *Erub* and cover up what is to be kept hot.

l. 2   *Have ye tithed?* Food intended for use on the Sabbath had to be tithed before the Sabbath began.

Have ye prepared the Erub? The Rabbis insisted upon the observance of the Sabbath, but all possible steps were taken to see that observance was reasonably possible. For example, the law against 'going out' (based on Exod. 16. 29 and interpreted as referring to 'going out' of one domain (e.g. one's own residence) into another (see above, **176**) was mitigated by means of the '*Erub* (עירוב). This word means literally 'interweaving', 'mixture', and was used to denote various means by which movement on the Sabbath might be liberated. The most important means are given by M. Jastrow (*A Dictionary of the Targumim, etc.* (1926), 1075*b*, 1076*a*) thus: "*Erub*, a symbolical act by which the legal fiction of community or continuity is established, e.g. (*a*) with reference to Sabbath limits: a person deposits, before the Sabbath (or the Holy Day), certain eatables to remain in their place over the next day, by which act he transfers his abode to that place, and his movements on the Sabbath are measured from it as the centre; (*b*) with reference to buildings with a common court: the inmates contribute their share towards a dish which is deposited in one of the dwellings, by which act all the dwellings are considered as common to all, and the carrying of objects on the Sabbath from one to the other and across the court is permitted; (*c*) with reference to preparing meals for the Sabbath on a Holy Day occurring on a Friday: a person prepares a dish on Thursday and lets it lie over until the end of the Sabbath, by which fiction all the cooking for the Sabbath which he does on the Holy Day (Friday) is merely a continuation of the preparation begun on Thursday.'

l. 3   *Light the lamp.* The practice of lighting a lamp on Sabbath eve is very ancient. It may have had its origin in the fact that it was forbidden to kindle a fire on the Sabbath itself, but it has long been interpreted in terms of the joy of Sabbath.

l. 6   *Demai-produce*, produce on which it is uncertain whether tithe has been paid, e.g. produce acquired from an ʿ*am ha-ʾaretz* (see **195**).

PASSOVER

The yearly feast of Passover brought multitudes of pilgrims to Jerusalem. The feast commemorated the deliverance of Israel from Egypt, a deliverance in which each participating Jew was bidden to feel that he had personally shared; and it pointed forward to a future act of deliverance by God, that is, it was eschatological as well as commemorative.

178

Pesahim 10. 1, 3ff.

On the eve of Passover, from about the time of the Evening Offering, a man must eat naught until nightfall. Even the poorest in Israel must not eat unless he sits down to table, and they must not give them less than four cups of wine to drink, even if it is from the [Paupers']
5   Dish. . . .

When [food] is brought before him he eats it seasoned with lettuce, until he is come to the breaking of bread; they bring before him unleavened bread and lettuce and the *haroseth*, although *haroseth* is not a religious obligation. R. Eliezer b. R. Zadok [second century AD]
10   says: It is a religious obligation. And in the Holy City they used to bring before him the body of the Passover-offering.

They then mix him the second cup. And here the son asks his father (and if the son has not enough understanding his father instructs him [how to ask]), 'Why is this night different from other
15   nights? For on other nights we eat seasoned food once, but this night twice; on other nights we eat leavened or unleavened bread, but this night all is unleavened; on other nights we eat flesh roast, stewed, or cooked, but this night all is roast.' And according to the understanding of the son his father instructs him. He begins with the disgrace and
20   ends with the glory; and he expounds from *A wandering Aramean was my father* . . . until he finishes the whole section [Deut. 26. 5–9].

Rabban Gamaliel used to say: Whosoever has not said [the verses concerning] these three things at Passover has not fulfilled his obligation. And these are they: Passover, unleavened bread, and
25   bitter herbs: 'Passover'—because God passed over the houses of our fathers in Egypt; 'unleavened bread'—because our fathers were redeemed from Egypt; 'bitter herbs'—because the Egyptians embittered the lives of our fathers in Egypt. In every generation a man must so regard himself as if he came forth himself out of Egypt, for
30   it is written. *And thou shalt tell thy son in that day saying, It is because*

of that which the Lord did for me when I came forth out of Egypt (Exod.
13. 8). Therefore are we bound to give thanks, to praise, to glorify,
to honour, to exalt, to extol, and to bless him who wrought all these
wonders for our fathers and for us. He brought us out from bondage
35 to freedom, from sorrow to gladness, and from mourning to a
Festival-day, and from darkness to great light, and from servitude to
redemption; so let us say before him the *Hallelujah.*

l. 3   *He sits down to table,* that is, in the manner of the *triclinium* (reclining rather
than sitting). The Passover was a feast of *freedom*; reclining was the attitude
of free men.

l. 4   *The* [*Paupers'*] *Dish,* the *tamḥuy,* or daily charitable distribution. All Israelites,
however poor, had a share in God's act of redemption.

l. 7   *The breaking of bread (parper 'eth ha-path)*; other texts read *parpereth,* the bread
condiment, or bitter herbs. The breaking of the bread would refer to the
distribution of the unleavened bread with which the Passover had to be
eaten, the *parpereth* to the sauce in which the unleavened bread was dipped.
The difference in meaning (with regard to the course of the meal) is therefore
not great.

l. 8   *Ḥaroseth,* a sauce made of nuts, fruit, and vinegar.

l. 10   *In the Holy City.* After the destruction of the Temple in AD 70 the lamb (or
kid) could no longer be eaten.

l. 19   *He begins with the disgrace and ends with the glory*; as in the narrative of Deut.
26. 5–9. This theme, which of course turns upon the salvation wrought by
God, is the keynote of the Passover.

l. 37   *The Hallelujah*: The 'Hallel', Pss. 113–18.

179

Oholoth 18. 7–10

If a man bought a field in Syria that lies close to the Land of Israel
and he can enter it in cleanness, it is clean, and it is subject to the laws
of Tithes and Seventh Year produce; but if he cannot enter it in
cleanness it is deemed unclean, yet it is still subject to the laws of
5   Tithes and Seventh Year produce. The dwelling-places of gentiles are
unclean. How long must a gentile have lived in them so that
examination becomes needful? Forty days, even though he had no
woman with him; but if a slave or [an Israelitish] woman watched
over the dwelling, no examination is needful.

10   What do they examine? The deep drains and the foul water. The
School of Shammai say: Also the dunghill and loose earth. The
School of Hillel say: Wheresoever a pig or weasel can penetrate no
examination is needful.

The rules about the dwelling-places of gentiles do not apply to
15 colonnades. R. Simeon b. Gamaliel says: The rules about the dwelling-

places of gentiles do not apply to a city of the gentiles that is in ruins. The east side of Kesrin and the west side of Kesrin are graveyards. The east side of Acre was in doubt, but the Sages have declared it clean. Rabbi and his court voted on Keni and declared it clean.

20   To ten places the rules about the dwelling-places of gentiles do not apply: the tents of the Arabs, field-huts, simple tents, fruit-shelters, summer houses, a gate-house, the open space in a courtyard, a bath-house, an armoury, and the camping-grounds of the legions.

l. 2   *It is clean*; that is, on the assumption that its owner can enter it without passing over gentile land.

l. 5   *The dwelling-places of gentiles are unclean.* This passage has been included because of its bearing on John 18. 28. As the context shows, gentiles' houses were suspected of uncleanness because their owners were believed to throw abortions down the drains.

ll. 11, 12   *The School of Shammai . . . the School of Hillel.* See **154**.

l. 17   *Kesrin*, Caesarea on Sea.
        Kesrin; there is a variant Kesarion, Casesarea Philippi.

PENTECOST

This feast, held seven weeks (fifty days) after Passover, retained its primitive character as a harvest festival. Passover marked the beginning, Pentecost the end, of the ingathering. In the second century Pentecost was interpreted as the feast of the giving of the Law. In some traditions the Law was offered from Sinai to all nations in their own languages. If this legend could be traced to the first half of the first century it might be thought an important source of the narrative of Acts 2; but such an early origin is improbable.

180

Pesahim 68b

R. Eleazar [*c*. AD 270] said: Pentecost . . . the day on which the Law was given.

BOOTHS

When 'the Feast' is mentioned without the addition of a name, the feast of Booths or 'Tabernacles' is generally referred to. Like Passover this feast attracted great multitudes to Jerusalem, but it could be kept anywhere by the devout Jew who was prepared to live in a *Sukkah*, or leafy booth (as prescribed in Lev. 23. 42), for eight days. There were, however, special celebrations in the Temple.

181

Sukkah 4. 1, 5–7, 9; 5. 1–3

[The rites of] the *Lulab* and the Willow-branch [continue] six days and sometimes seven days; the *Hallel* and the rejoicing, eight days; the *Sukkah* and the Water-libation, seven days; the Flute-playing, sometimes five and sometimes six days . . .

5   How was the rite of the Willow-branch fulfilled? There was a place below Jerusalem called Motza. Thither they went and cut themselves young willow-branches. They came and set these up at the sides of the Altar so that their tops were bent over the Altar. They then blew [on the *shofar*] a sustained, a quavering and then
10   another sustained blast. Each day they went in procession a single time around the Altar, saying, *Save now, we beseech thee, O Lord: We beseech thee, O Lord, send now prosperity!* (Ps. 118. 25). R. Judah says: '*Ani waho!* save us we pray! *Ani waho!* save us we pray!' But on that day they went in procession seven times around the Altar. When
15   they departed what did they say? 'Homage to thee, O Altar! Homage to thee, O Altar!' R. Eliezer says: 'To the Lord and to thee, O Altar! To the Lord and to thee, O Altar!'

As was the rite on a week-day so was the rite on a Sabbath, save that they gathered [the willow-branches] on the eve of the Sabbath
20   and set them in gilded troughs that they might not wither. R. Johanan b. Baroka says: They used to bring palm tufts and beat them on the ground at the sides of the Altar, and that day was called, 'The day of beating the palm tufts'.

Straightway the children used to cast away their *Lulabs* and eat
25   their citrons . . .

'The Water-libation, seven days'—what was the manner of this? They used to fill a golden flagon holding three *logs* with water from Siloam. When they reached the Water Gate they blew [on the *shofar*] a sustained, a quavering and another sustained blast. [The priest
30   whose turn of duty it was] went up the [Altar-] Ramp and turned to the right where were two silver bowls. R. Judah says: They were of plaster, but their appearance was darkened because of the wine. They had each a hole like to a narrow snout, one wide and the other narrow, so that both bowls emptied themselves together. The bowl
35   to the west was for water and that to the east was for wine. But if the flagon of water was emptied into the bowl for wine, or the flagon of wine into the bowl for water, that sufficed. R. Judah says: With one *log* they could perform the libations throughout eight days. To the priest who performed the libation they used to say, 'Lift up thine
40   hand!' for once a certain one poured the libation over his feet, and all the people threw their citrons at him . . .

'The Flute-playing, sometimes five and sometimes six days'—this is the flute-playing at the Beth ha-She'ubah, which overrides neither

a Sabbath nor a Festival-day. They have said: He that never has seen
45 the joy of the Beth ha-She'ubah has never in his life seen joy.

At the close of the first Festival-day of the Feast they went down
to the Court of the Women where they had made a great amendment.
There were golden candlesticks there with four golden bowls on the
top of them and four ladders to each candlestick, and four youths of
50 the priestly stock and in their hands jars of oil holding a hundred and
twenty *logs* which they poured into all the bowls.

They made wicks from the worn out drawers and girdles of the
priests and with them they set the candlesticks alight, and there was
not a courtyard in Jerusalem that did not reflect the light of the Beth
55 ha-She'ubah.

l. 1   *The Lulab.* Properly a palm-branch; but the *lulab* carried and shaken in the
Temple at this feast was made of palm-, myrtle-, and willow-branches.

l. 13   *Ani waho.* 'We beseech thee, O Lord' is in Hebrew אנא יהוה, *'na' YHWH.*
In order to avoid the use of the sacred name there was substituted אני והו
(*'ani waho*); other forms are given, including *'ani w'hu*, 'I and he'—an
expression which has been given mystical interpretations.

l. 25   *Their citrons.* Citrons were used in fulfilment of Lev. 23. 40.

l. 27   *Three logs.* A *log* is rather less than a pint.

l. 41   *The people threw their citrons at him.* According to Josephus (*Ant.* xiii. 372)
the offending priest was Alexander Jannaeus (see **125**), but he was pelted for
his general unpopularity.

l. 43   *Beth ha-She'ubah,* בית השאובה, sometimes written בית השואבה, *Beth ha-
Sho'ebah.* The root שאב (*sh-'-b*) means 'to draw (water)', and the expression
in the text very probably means 'house of water-drawing'. This rite has been
thought to be connected with John 7. 37f.

l. 47   *A great amendment.* The women's gallery was refitted with rails.

l. 54   *The light of the Beth ha-She'ubah.* This has been thought to be connected with
the pronouncement of John 8. 12.

THE DAY OF ATONEMENT

The Day of Atonement is not a feast but a fast—the only one in the Jewish
calendar. It is fully described in the Mishnah tractate *Yoma*, from which
the following quotations are taken. The Mishnah only elaborates the Old
Testament regulations for the Temple ceremonies.

182

Yoma 3. 8

> He came to his bullock and his bullock was standing between the
> Porch and the Altar, its head to the south and its face to the west; and
> he set both his hands upon it and made confession. And thus used he
> to say: 'O God, I have committed iniquity, transgressed, and sinned
> 5 before thee, I and my house. O God, forgive the iniquities and
> transgressions and sins which I have committed and transgressed and
> sinned before thee, I and my house, as it is written in the Law of thy
> servant Moses, *For on this day shall atonement be made for you to cleanse*
> *you; from all your sins shall ye be clean before the Lord* (Lev. 16. 30)'.
> 10 And they answered after him, 'Blessed be the name of the glory of
> his kingdom for ever and ever!'

l. 1   *He came to his bullock.* The high priest was obliged first of all to offer sacrifice
on account of his own sins.

183

Yoma 5. 1ff

Before this passage opens the high priest has offered a second bullock on
account of the sins of the people.

> They brought out to him the ladle and the fire-pan and he took his
> two hands full [of incense] and put it in the ladle, which was large
> according to his largeness [of hand], or small according to his
> smallness [of hand]; and such [alone] was the prescribed measure of
> 5 the ladle. He took the fire-pan in his right hand and the ladle in his
> left. He went through the Sanctuary until he came to the space
> between the two curtains separating the Sanctuary from the Holy of
> Holies. And there was a cubit's space between them. R. Jose says:
> Only one curtain was there, for it is written, *And the veil shall divide*
> 10 *for you between the holy place and the most holy* (Exod. 26. 33). The
> outer curtain was looped up on the south side and the inner one on
> the north side. He went along between them until he reached the
> north side; when he reached the north he turned round to the south
> and went on with the curtain on his left hand until he reached the
> 15 Ark. When he reached the Ark he put the fire-pan between the two
> bars. He heaped up the incense on the coals and the whole place
> became filled with smoke. He came out by the way he went in, and
> in the outer space he prayed a short prayer. But he did not prolong
> his prayer lest he put Israel in terror.
> 20   After the Ark was taken away a stone remained there from the
> time of the early prophets, and it was called 'Shetiyah'. It was higher

than the ground by three fingerbreadths. On this he used to put [the fire-pan].

He took the blood from him that was stirring it and entered
25 [again] into the place where he had entered and stood [again] on the place whereon he had stood, and sprinkled [the blood] once upwards and seven times downwards, not as though he had intended to sprinkle upwards or downwards but as though he were wielding a whip. And thus used he to count: One, one and one, one and two,
30 one and three, one and four, one and five, one and six, one and seven. He came out and put it on the golden stand in the Sanctuary.

l. 19 *Lest he put Israel in terror*—fearing lest evil should have befallen him in the Holy of Holies.
l. 20 *The Ark was taken away*—at the Babylonian captivity.

184
Yoma 6. 1, 2

5. 4–7 describes the sacrifice of one of the pair of goats.

The two he-goats of the Day of Atonement should be alike in appearance, in size, and in value, and have been bought at the same time. Yet even if they are not alike they are valid, and if one was bought one day and the other on the morrow they are valid. If one
5 of them died before the lot was cast, a fellow may be bought for the other; but if after the lot was cast, another pair must be brought and the lots cast over them anew. And if that cast for the Lord died, he [the high priest] should say, 'Let this on which the lot "For the Lord" has fallen stand in its stead'; and if that cast for Azazel died, he should
10 say, 'Let this on which the lot "For Azazel" has fallen stand in its stead.' The other is left to pasture until it suffers a blemish, when it must be sold and its value falls to the Temple fund; for the Sin-offering of the congregation may not be left to die. R. Judah says: It is left to die. Moreover R. Judah said: If the blood was poured away
15 the scapegoat is left to die; if the scapegoat died the blood is poured away.

He then came to the scapegoat and laid his two hands upon it and made confession. And thus used he to say: 'O God, thy people, the House of Israel, have committed iniquity, transgressed, and sinned
20 before thee. O God, forgive, I pray, the iniquities and transgressions and sins which thy people, the House of Israel, have committed and transgressed and sinned before thee; as it is written in the Law of thy servant Moses, *For on this day shall atonement be made for you to cleanse you; from all your sins shall ye be clean before the Lord*' (Lev. 16. 30).
25 And when the priests and the people which stood in the Temple Court heard the Expressed Name come forth from the mouth of the High Priest, they used to kneel and bow themselves and fall down

on their faces and say, 'Blessed be the name of the glory of his kingdom for ever and ever!'

l. 26　The Expressed Name. The sacred name of God, of which the consonants are יהוה (YHWH), was uttered with the proper vowels only by the high priest on the Day of Atonement.

185

Yoma 7. 1

Then the High Priest came to read. If he was minded to read in the linen garments he could do so; otherwise he would read in his own white vestment. The minister of the synagogue used to take a scroll of the Law and give it to the chief of the synagogue, and the chief of 5　the synagogue gave it to the Prefect, and the Prefect gave it to the High Priest, and the High Priest received it standing and read it standing. And he read *After the death . . .* (Lev. 16) and *Howbeit on the tenth day . . .* (Lev. 23. 26–32). Then he used to roll up the scroll of the Law and put it in his bosom and say, 'More is written here than I 10　have read out before you.' *And on the tenth . . .* (Num. 29. 7–11) which is in the Book of Numbers, he recited by heart. Thereupon he pronounced eight Benedictions: for the Law, for the Temple-Service, for the Thanksgiving, for the Forgiveness of Sin, and for the Temple separately, and for the Israelites separately, and for the priests 15　separately; and for the rest a [general] prayer.

l. 5　The Prefect, הסגן *(ha-sagan)*; the full title was סגן הכהנים *(sᵉgan ha-kohᵃnim)*, the prefect of the priests. He was a high dignitary set over the building and services of the Temple.

186

Yoma 8. 1

On the Day of Atonement, eating, drinking, washing, anointing, putting on sandals, and marital intercourse are forbidden. A king or a bride may wash their faces and a woman after childbirth may put on sandals. So R. Eliezer. But the Sages forbid it.

The Synagogue

The Temple and its services were, even at the great Festivals when Jerusalem was thronged with worshippers, for the few. The majority of Jews found corporate practice of their religion in the Synagogue, where the Law and the Prophets were read, and the community engaged in common prayer. There follow several selections from the Eighteen

Benedictions (*Sh^emoneh 'Esreh*), one of the oldest parts of the synagogue service. For another of these Benedictions see below, **200**.

187

Benediction 1

Blessed art thou, O Lord our God and God of our fathers, God of Abraham, God of Isaac, and God of Jacob, the great, mighty and revered God, the most high God, who bestowest loving-kindnesses, and possessest all things; who rememberest the pious deeds of the
5 patriarchs, and in love wilt bring a redeemer to their children's children for thy name's sake.

O King, Helper, Saviour and Shield. Blessed art thou, O Lord, the Shield of Abraham.

188

Benediction 2

Thou, O Lord, art mighty for ever, thou quickenest the dead, thou art mighty to save.

Thou sustainest the living with loving-kindness, quickenest the dead with great mercy, supportest the falling, healest the sick, loosest
5 the bound, and keepest thy faith to them that sleep in the dust. Who is like unto thee, lord of mighty acts, and who resembleth thee, O King, who killest and quickenest, and causest salvation to spring forth?

Yea, faithful art thou to quicken the dead. Blessed art thou, O
10 Lord, who quickenest the dead.

189

Benediction 6

Forgive us, O our Father, for we have sinned; pardon us, O our King, for we have transgressed; for thou dost pardon and forgive. Blessed art thou, O Lord, who art gracious, and dost abundantly forgive.

190

Benediction 7

Look upon our affliction and plead our cause, and redeem us speedily for thy name's sake; for thou art a mighty redeemer. Blessed art thou, O Lord, the Redeemer of Israel.

191

Benediction 9

> Bless this year unto us, O Lord our God, together with every kind of the produce thereof, for our welfare; give a blessing upon the face of the earth. O satisfy us with thy goodness, and bless our year like other good years. Blessed art thou, O Lord, who blessest the years.

192

Benediction 10

> Sound the great horn for our freedom; lift up the ensign to gather our exiles, and gather us from the four corners of the earth. Blessed art thou, O Lord, who gatherest the banished ones of thy people Israel.

193

Benediction 14

> And to Jerusalem, thy city, return in mercy, and dwell therein as thou hast spoken; rebuild it soon in our days as an everlasting building, and speedily set up therein the throne of David.
> Blessed art thou, O Lord, who rebuildest Jerusalem.

194

The Qaddish Prayer

> Magnified and sanctified be his great name in the world which he hath created according to his will. May he establish his kingdom during your life and during your days, and during the life of all the house of Israel, even speedily and at a near time, and say ye, Amen.
> 5   Let his great name be blessed for ever and to all eternity.

l. 1   *Sanctified,* יתקדש, *yithqaddash, from which the name of the prayer is derived. It occurs in longer forms.*

Ḥaber and ʿAm ha-ʾaretz

The social and religious commandments by which the written and oral Law regulated Jewish life were so numerous and far-reaching as to produce marked social distinctions between the scrupulous and the careless. Those who were most punctilious in their observance of the laws of purity and tithing banded themselves together into groups of *ḥᵃberim* (חברים), or 'associates'. These associates met for religious and charitable purposes, but their main aim was to observe the levitical rules, and a man was admitted to their company only on his undertaking to do this. At the other extreme were the *'amme ha'aretz* (עמי הארץ) or 'people of the land', those who were known to be lax in their obedience to the Law. Intercourse between the two groups was limited, but by no means impossible. The scrupulous desired the lax to join their number, and the famous R. Akiba, for example, was in early life an *'am ha-'aretz* (see above, **157**). That ill-feeling between the extreme religious classes existed cannot be denied; but it probably varied much from place to place and time to time, and allowance must be made for the hyperbole of some Rabbinic sayings on the subject.

195
Demai 2. 2ff.

The corresponding passage in the Tosephta contains more details about the relations between *ḥᵃberim* and *'amme ha-'aretz*.

He that undertakes to be trustworthy must give tithe from what he eats and from what he sells and from what he buys [to sell again]; and he may not be the guest of an *'am ha-'aretz*. R. Judah says: Even he that is the guest of an *'am ha-'aretz* may still be reckoned
5 trustworthy. They replied: He would not be trustworthy in what concerns himself; how then could he be trustworthy in what concerns others?

He that undertakes to be an Associate may not sell to an *'am ha-'aretz* [foodstuff that is] wet or dry, or buy from him [foodstuff that
10 is] wet; and he may not be the guest of an *'am ha-'aretz* nor may he receive him as a guest in his own raiment. R. Judah says: Nor may he rear small cattle or be profuse in vows or levity or contract uncleanness because of the dead, but he should minister in the House of Study. They said to him: These things come not within the scope
15 of the subject [of the Associate].

If [they that undertake to be Associates are] bakers, the Sages lay upon them only the duty of setting apart [from *demai*-produce] enough for Heave-offering of Tithe and Dough-offering. If [they are] shopkeepers, they may not sell *demai*-produce. All that deal in
20 large quantities may sell *demai* produce. Who are they that deal in large quantities? The like of wholesale merchants and dealers in grain.

l. 1 *He that undertakes to be trustworthy*; not (it seems) a member of a society of *ḥᵃberim*, but 'one who can be relied upon in matters of tithes and *Tᵉrumah*' (Jastrow, *s.v.* נאמן).

l. 9 *Wet.* Wetness predisposes foodstuffs to uncleanness.

l. 11 *R. Judah* by his additional requirements changes the character of associateship; the majority however insist that it remains primarily levitical and ceremonial.

l. 17 *Demai.* See **177**.

196

Kelim 1. 1, 2

> These Fathers of Uncleanness, [namely] a [dead] creeping thing, male semen, he that has contracted uncleanness from a corpse, a leper in his days of reckoning, and Sin-offering water too little in quantity to be sprinkled, convey uncleanness to men and vessels by contact and
> 5 to earthenware vessels by [presence within their] air-space; but they do not convey uncleanness by carrying.
>
> They are exceeded by carrion and by Sin-offering water sufficient in quantity to be sprinkled, for these convey uncleanness to him that carries them, so that he, too, conveys uncleanness to garments by
> 10 contact, but the garments do not become unclean by contact [alone].

l. 1 *Fathers of Uncleanness*, objects or persons capable of causing uncleanness in other objects or persons. The laws of cleanness and uncleanness are extremely complicated and difficult. It would take a great deal of space to explain fully the few lines quoted here.

l. 3 *Days of reckoning.* Lev. 14. 8.

Proselytes

The missionary activity of Judaism is attested in the gospels (Matt. 23. 15), and in Acts we meet not only proselytes (2. 10; 6. 5; 13. 43), but also devout persons (σεβόμενοι, 13. 43, 50; 16. 14; 17. 4, 17; 18. 7; cf. **148**) who were attracted by the worship, theology, and ethics of the synagogue but had not become proselytes by taking the final step of circumcision, by which they would have cut themselves off from their own people and race. Non-Jewish authors, and Roman laws against circumcision, also attest the practice of proselytization.

In general (there are a few exceptions) the Rabbinic literature is friendly to proselytes. See **154** above. Their courage and faith in joining the ranks of Israel were esteemed.

197

Numbers Rabbah 8. 3

> The Holy One loves the proselytes exceedingly. To what is the matter like? To a king who had a number of sheep and goats which went forth every morning to the pasture, and returned in the evening

to the stable. One day a stag joined the flock and grazed with the
5 sheep, and returned with them. Then the shepherd said to the king,
'There is a stag which goes out with the sheep and grazes with them,
and comes home with them.'And the king loved the stag exceedingly.
And he commanded the shepherd, saying: 'Give heed unto this stag,
that no man beat it'; and when the sheep returned in the evening, he
10 would order that the stag should have food and drink. Then the
shepherds said to him, 'My Lord, thou hast many goats and sheep and
kids, and thou givest us no directions about these, but about this stag
thou givest us orders day by day.' Then the king replied: 'It is the
custom of the sheep to graze in the pasture, but the stags dwell in the
15 wilderness, and it is not their custom to come among men in the
cultivated land. But to this stag who has come to us and lives with
us, should we not be grateful that he has left the great wilderness,
where many stags and gazelles feed, and has come to live among us?
It behoves us to be grateful.' So too spoke the Holy One: 'I owe great
20 thanks to the stranger, in that he has left his family and his father's
house, and has come to dwell among us; therefore I order in the
Law: "Love ye the stranger"' (Deut. 10. 19).

198

Yebamoth 47a, b

For the admission of a male proselyte there were required circumcision,
baptism, and (before the destruction of the Temple) sacrifice.

One who comes to be made a proselyte in the present time is to be
asked: 'Why dost thou come to be made a proselyte? Dost thou not
know that at this time Israel is afflicted, buffeted, humiliated and
harried, and that sufferings and sore trials come upon them?' If he
5 answer: 'I know this, and am not worthy,' they are to accept him
immediately.
Then they are to instruct him in some of the lighter and some of
the weightier commandments; and inform him as to the sins in
regard to the corner of the field, the forgotten sheaf, the gleaning,
10 and the tithe for the poor. Then shall they teach him the penalties for
transgression: 'Know well that up until the time that thou hast come
hither thou hast eaten the forbidden fat of cattle without incurring
the sentence of excommunication; that thou hast profaned the
Sabbath without incurring the penalty of lapidation. But from now
15 on if thou eat the forbidden fat of cattle thou wilt be excommunicated;
if thou profanest the Sabbath thou wilt be stoned.' In the same way
as they instruct him about the penalties of transgression shall they
teach him the rewards for the observance of the commandments and
shall say to him: 'Know thou that the world to come was made only

20 for the righteous, but Israel at this present time may not experience
very great good or very great afflictions.' Yet one must not multiply
words or go too much into detail.

If he accept, he is to be circumcised immediately and received. In
case of the discovery of any defect as to [a previous] circumcision, he
25 is to be circumcised over again, and when healed brought to baptism
immediately.

Two men learned in the Law shall stand near him and instruct
him as to some of the lighter and some of the weightier
commandments. He immerses himself and when he comes up he is
30 in all respects an Israelite.

Heretics

A word commonly used to describe a heretic or sceptic is אפיקורוס
(*'appiqoros*). The origin of the word is uncertain, but even if it was derived
from a Hebrew root the coincidence of its sound with the name of the
Greek thinker Epicurus must have played no small part in the development
of its meaning.

199

Sanhedrin 10. 1

All Israelites have a share in the world to come, for it is written, *Thy
people also shall be all righteous, they shall inherit the land for ever; the
branch of my planting, the work of my hands that I may be glorified* (Isa.
60. 21). And these are they that have no share in the world to come:
5 he that says that there in no resurrection of the dead prescribed in the
Law, and [he that says] that the Law is not from heaven, and an
Epicurean. R. Akiba says: Also he that reads the heretical books, or
that utters charms over a wound and says, *I will put none of the diseases
upon thee which I have put upon the Egyptians: for I am the Lord that
10 healeth thee* (Exod. 15. 26). Abba Saul says: Also he that pronounces
the Name with its proper letters.

l. 5   He that says there is no resurrection . . . Cf. the beliefs of the Sadducees, **135**.

l. 11   The Name. See above, **184** and note.

Of particular interest are the persons described as *Minim*. They at least
include Jewish Christians, and the term may have been originally the
name of that party, the corresponding abstract noun *Minuth* standing for
their faith. There are many Rabbinic passages which refer to these sectaries;
here we may quote only the twelfth of the *Eighteen Benedictions* (see above,
187–193). This was drawn up towards the close of the first century AD as

a 'test benediction'; it was one which no heretic could pronounce (like the anathemas at the end of a creed) and therefore had the effect of banning heretics from the synagogue. It has taken various forms under the activity of Christian censors of the Jewish Prayer Book. The following is probably very close to the original wording.

200

Benediction 12

> For the renegades let there be no hope, and may the arrogant kingdom soon be rooted out in our days, and the Nazarenes and the *minim* perish as in a moment and be blotted out from the book of life and with the righteous may they not be inscribed. Blessed art thou,
> 5 O Lord, who humblest the arrogant.

l. 1   *The arrogant kingdom.* Perhaps Rome.

l. 2   *And the Nazarenes,* והנוצרים, *wᵉha-notzrim.* This may not have been part of the original text.

Theology

The theology and religion of Rabbinism cannot be sketched or illustrated within short compass. Fundamentally both were derived from the Old Testament, but they were developed on lines which, though paralleled elsewhere in Judaism, were characteristic. Pursuit of the details of this development is the task of a lifetime; here a few more characteristic quotations from the tractate Aboth are given. See also **153–8, 171–3**.

201

Aboth 3. 1

> Akabya b. Mahalaleel [first century AD] said: Consider three things and thou wilt not fall into the hands of transgression. Know whence thou art come and whither thou art going and before whom thou art about to give account and reckoning. 'Whence thou art come'—
> 5 from a putrid drop; 'and whither thou art going'—to the place of dust, worm, and maggot; 'and before whom thou art to give account and reckoning'—before the King of kings of kings, the Holy One, blessed is he.

202

Aboth 4. 2

> Ben Azzai [first half of second century AD] said: Run to fulfil the lightest duty even as the weightiest, and flee from transgression; for

one duty draws another duty in its train, and one transgression draws
another transgression in its train; for the reward of a duty [done] is a
5 duty [to be done], and the reward of one transgression is [another]
transgression.

203

Aboth 4. 16f.

R. Jacob [perhaps the teacher of R. Judah the Patriarch—see **155**]
said: This world is like a vestibule before the world to come: prepare
thyself in the vestibule that thou mayest enter into the banqueting
hall.
5   He used to say: Better is one hour of repentance and good works
in this world than the whole life of the world to come; and better is
one hour of bliss in the world to come than the whole life of this
world.

204

Aboth 5. 10f.

There are four types among men: he that says, 'What is mine is mine'
and what is thine is thine'—this is the common type, and some say
that this is the type of Sodom; [he that says,] 'What is mine is thine
and what is thine is mine'—he is an ignorant man (*'am ha-'aretz*); [he
5 that says,] 'What is mine is thine and what is thine is thine own'—he
is a saintly man; [and he that says,] 'What is thine is mine, and what
is mine is mine own'—he is a wicked man.
      There are four types of character: easy to provoke and easy to
appease—his loss is cancelled by his gain; hard to provoke and hard
10 to appease—his gain is cancelled by his loss; hard to provoke and
easy to appease—he is a saintly man; easy to provoke and hard to
appease—he is a wicked man.

205

Aboth 5. 16

If love depends on some [transitory] thing, and the [transitory] thing
passes away, the love passes away too; but if it does not depend on
some [transitory] thing it will never pass away. Which love depended
on some [transitory] thing? This was the love of Amnon and Tamar.
5 And which did not depend on some [transitory] thing? This was the
love of David and Jonathan.

206

Aboth 5. 20

> Judah b. Tema [end of the second century AD] said: Be strong as the
> leopard and swift as the eagle, fleet as the gazelle and brave as the lion
> to do the will of thy Father which is in heaven. He used to say: The
> shameless are for Gehenna and the shamefast for the Garden of Eden.
> 5 May it be thy will, O Lord our God and the God of our fathers, that
> the Temple be built speedily in our days, and grant us our portion in
> thy Law with them that do thy will.

Judicial Procedure

Legislation regarding the constitution and conduct of courts, their
procedure in civil and criminal cases, their competence, authority, and
sentences, is detailed and large in bulk. Here only a few specimen
regulations are given. It must be remembered that conditions and
regulations were not static, and that occasionally the best-intentioned rules
might be disregarded. New Testament interests suggest that some rules
for capital trials, the law of blasphemy, and the method of execution by
stoning should be quoted.

207

Sanhedrin 4. 1, 3–5*a*; 5. 1

> Non-capital and capital cases are alike in examination and inquiry,
> for it is written, *Ye shall have one manner of law* (Lev. 24. 22). In what
> do non-capital cases differ from capital cases? Non-capital cases [are
> decided] by three and capital cases by three and twenty [judges].
> 5 Non-capital cases may begin either with reasons for acquittal or for
> conviction, but capital cases must begin with reasons for acquittal
> and may not begin with reasons for conviction. In non-capital cases
> they may reach a verdict either of acquittal or of conviction by the
> decision of a majority of one; but in capital cases they may reach a
> 10 verdict of acquittal by the decision of a majority of one, but a verdict
> of conviction only by the decision of a majority of two. In non-
> capital cases they may reverse a verdict either [from conviction] to
> acquittal or [from acquittal] to conviction; but in capital cases they
> may reverse a verdict [from conviction] to acquittal but not [from
> 15 acquittal] to conviction. In non-capital cases all may argue either in
> favour of acquittal or of conviction; but in capital cases all may argue
> in favour of acquittal but not in favour of conviction. In non-capital
> cases he that had argued in favour of conviction may afterward argue
> in favour of acquittal, or he that had argued in favour of acquittal

20 may afterward argue in favour of conviction; in capital cases he that
had argued in favour of conviction may afterward argue in favour
of acquittal, but he that had argued in favour of acquittal cannot
afterward change and argue in favour of conviction. In non-capital
cases they hold the trial during the daytime and the verdict may be
25 reached during the night; in capital cases they hold the trial during
the daytime and the verdict also must be reached during the daytime.
In non-capital cases the verdict, whether of acquittal or of conviction,
may be reached the same day; in capital cases a verdict of acquittal
may be reached on the same day, but a verdict of conviction not
30 until the following day. Therefore trials may not be held on the eve
of a Sabbath or on the eve of a Festival-day . . .

The Sanhedrin was arranged like the half of a round threshing-
floor so that they all might see one another. Before them stood the
two scribes of the judges, one to the right and one to the left, and
35 they wrote down the words of them that favoured acquittal and the
words of them that favoured conviction. R. Judah says: There were
three: one wrote down the words of them that favoured acquittal,
and one wrote down the words of them that favoured conviction,
and the third wrote down the words both of them that favoured
40 acquittal and of them that favoured conviction.

Before them sat three rows of disciples of the Sages, and each knew
his proper place. If they needed to appoint [another as a judge], they
appointed him from the first row, and one from the second row
came into the first row, and one from the third row came into the
45 second; and they chose yet another from the congregation and set
him in the third row. He did not sit in the place of the former, but
he sat in the place that was proper for him.

How did they admonish the witnesses in capital cases? They
brought them in and admonished them, [saying,] 'Perchance ye will
50 say what is but supposition or hearsay or at secondhand, or [ye may
say in yourselves], We heard if from a man that was trustworthy. Or
perchance ye do not know that we shall prove you by examination
and inquiry? Know ye, moreover, that capital cases are not as non-
capital cases: in non-capital cases a man may pay money and so make
55 atonement, but in capital cases the witness is answerable for the blood
of him [that is wrongfully condemned] and the blood of his posterity
[that should have been born to him] to the end of the world . . .'

They used to prove witnesses with seven inquiries: In what week
of years? In what year? In what month? On what date in the month?
60 On what day? In what hour? In what place? (R. Jose says: [They
asked only,] On what day? In what hour? In what place?) [Moreover
they asked:] Do ye recognize him? Did ye warn him? If a man had
committed idolatry [they asked the witnesses], What did he worship?
and, How did he worship it?

l. 1   *Non-capital cases.* 'Literally "cases concerning property"; it includes all charges not entailing penalty by death' (Danby, ad loc.).

l. 15   *All may argue,* even those who are not judges. The general effect of these regulations is to favour the man accused of a capital offence.

l. 30   *Trials may not be held . . . on the eve of a Festival-day.* Nevertheless there were occasions when, for special reasons, Festivals were chosen for trials. Cf. *Sanhedrin* 11. 4.

208

Sanhedrin 7. 5

'The blasphemer' is not culpable unless he pronounces the Name itself. R. Joshua b. Karha [*c.* AD 150] says: On every day [of the trial] they examined the witnesses with a substituted name, [such as] 'May Jose smite Jose'. When sentence was to be given they did not declare
5 him guilty of death [on the grounds of evidence given] with the substituted name, but they sent out all the people and asked the chief among the witnesses and said to him, 'Say expressly what thou heardest', and he says it; and the judges stand up on their feet and rend their garments, and they may not mend them again. And the
10 second witness says, 'I also heard the like', and the third says, 'I also heard the like'.

l. 1   *The Name.* See **184** and note.

209

Sanhedrin 6. 1–4

When sentence [of stoning] has been passed they take him forth to stone him. The place of stoning was outside [far away from] the court, as it is written, *Bring forth him that hath cursed outside the camp* (Lev. 24. 14). One man stands at the door of the court with a towel
5 in his hand, and another, mounted on a horse, far away from him [but near enough] to see him. If [in the court] one said, 'I have somewhat to argue in favour of his acquittal', that man waves the towel and the horse runs and stops him [that was going forth to be stoned]. Even if he himself said, 'I have somewhat to argue in favour
10 of my acquittal', they must bring him back, be it four times or five, provided that there is aught of substance in his words. If then they found him innocent they set him free; otherwise he goes forth to be stoned. A herald goes out before him [calling], 'Such-a-one, the son of such-a-one, is going forth to be stoned for that he committed such
15 or such an offence. Such-a-one and such-a-one are witnesses against him. If any man knoweth aught in favour of his acquittal let him come and plead it'.

When he was about ten cubits from the place of stoning they used to say to him, 'Make thy confession', for such is the way of them that
20 have been condemned to death to make confession, for every one that makes his confession has a share in the world to come. For so have we found it with Achan. Joshua said to him, *My son, give, I pray thee, glory to the Lord, the God of Israel, and make confession unto him, and tell me now what thou hast done; hide it not from me. And Achan*
25 *answered Joshua and said, Of a truth I have sinned against the Lord, the God of Israel, and thus and thus have I done* (Joshua 7. 19). Whence do we learn that his confession made atonement for him? It is written, *And Joshua said, Why hast thou troubled us? the Lord shall trouble thee this day* (Joshua 7. 25)—*this day* thou shalt be troubled, but in the
30 world to come thou shalt not be troubled. If he knows not how to make his confession they say to him, 'Say, May my death be an atonement for all my sins'. R. Judah says: If he knew that he was condemned because of false testimony he should say, 'Let my death be an atonement for all my sins excepting this sin'. They said to him:
35 If so, every one would speak after this fashion to show his innocence.

When he was four cubits from the place of stoning they stripped off his clothes. A man is kept covered in front and a woman both in front and behind. So R. Judah. But the Sages say: A man is stoned naked but a woman is not stoned naked.
40 The place of stoning was twice the height of a man. One of the witnesses knocked him down on his loins; if he turned over on his heart the witness turned him over again on his loins. If he straightway died that sufficed; but if not, the second [witness] took the stone and dropped it on his heart. If he straightway died, that sufficed; but if
45 not, he was stoned by all Israel, for it is written, *The hand of the witnesses shall be first upon him to put him to death and afterward the hand of all the people* (Deut. 17. 7). All that have been stoned must be hanged. So R. Eliezer. But the Sages say: None is hanged save the blasphemer and the idolator. A man is hanged with his face to the
50 people and a woman with her face towards the gallows. So R. Eliezer. But the Sages say: A man is hanged but a woman is not hanged. R. Eliezer said to them: Did not Simeon b. Shetah hang women in Ashkelon? They answered: He hanged eighty women, whereas two ought not to be judged in one day. How did they hang a man? They
55 put a beam into the ground and a piece of wood jutted from it. The two hands [of the body] were brought together and [in this fashion] it was hanged. R. Jose says: The beam was made to lean against a wall and one hanged the corpse thereon as the butchers do. And they let it down at once; if it remained there overnight a negative command is
60 thereby transgressed, for it is written, *His body shall not remain all night upon the tree, but thou shalt surely bury him the same day; for he that is hanged is a curse against God* (Deut. 21. 23); as if to say: Why

was this one hanged? Because he blessed the Name, and the Name of Heaven was found profaned.

l. 11   *If then they found him innocent.* Bias in favour of the accused is again inculcated.

l. 52   *Did not Simeon b. Shetah . . .?* Later tradition justified Simeon's departure from the Law by saying 'The time demanded it'. It would be wrong to suggest that such a device was often used to cover illegal action; but it is at least possible that on other occasions (for example, on some recorded in the New Testament) what was believed to be the spirit of the Law was obeyed rather than the safeguarding letter.

l. 63   *He blessed the Name*; a euphemism for 'he cursed . . .'.

9 Qumran

The story of the discoveries made at and in the neighbourhood of Qumran, on the Dead Sea, from 1947 onwards, has now been often told, and it will not be repeated here. There have been found Biblical manuscripts, manuscripts of non-canonical Jewish texts, and many other objects of archaeological interest. Texts and artifacts together have made it possible to study the religious group that settled in this region, but it cannot be claimed that agreed results have been reached regarding their history or even their name; they are often described as Essenes, but the name does not occur in the texts that have been discovered and published, and at least for the present it is wise not to identify them too confidently with the Essenes described by Philo and Josephus (see above, **135–7**), though without question there is a close relation between them. Their importance for the understanding of the New Testament was often exaggerated in the years immediately after they were discovered, but there is no doubt at all that they have greatly increased our knowledge of Judaism more or less contemporary with the New Testament. Judaism was a much less uniform structure than was sometimes supposed, and a better knowledge of Judaism in its variety and in its eccentricities cannot fail to be helpful to the student of the New Testament.

Any attempt to sketch the history, beliefs, and practices of the Qumran community within a page or two could lead only to deceptive over-simplification. Some of the events in the community's story, and aspects of its theology and discipline, are illustrated in the passages that follow. The best introduction in English to the study of the Qumran literature has been provided by G. Vermes, in his translation of the non-biblical texts (*The Dea Sea Scrolls in English*, first published in 1962) and in his general survey (*The Dead Sea Scrolls: Qumran in Perspective*, 1977), though some older works, such as those of Millar Burrows (*The Dead Sea Scrolls*, 1956; *More Light on the Dead Sea Scrolls*, 1958) and M. Black (*The Scrolls and Christian Origins*, 1961) are still of great value. The original texts of the most important manuscripts, together with a German translation, are conveniently given by E. Lohse (*Die Texte aus Qumran*, 1964).

The Community and its Story

On archaeological grounds it seems probable that the Qumran community came into existence, or at least took up residence at Qumran, some time in the second century BC (or possibly early in the first). The Scrolls contain a reference to a migration to the 'land of Damascus' (CD 6. 5); the meaning of this is unclear, and disputed. Damascus may be a symbolical name for Qumran (cf. Rev. 11. 8), or may have been chosen because at the time of the migration Qumran was under the same civil authority as Damascus. The migration was in part voluntary, a protest against what the sect regarded as corrupt administration of Judaism at its heart in Jerusalem, and especially in the Temple, but may also in part have been forced by repressive measures on the part of the authority; it is easy to combine the two causes. Occupation of the site at Qumran seems to have been interrupted for a time by an earthquake.

The aim of the sect was absolute purity in terms of its own understanding of the Torah; it was firmly governed and rigidly disciplined. The structure of its hierarchy is not clear; some of the evidence is given below. Strict discipline was enforced, with punishments for the disobedient.

210

Community Rule (1QS) 5. 1—6. 8

> And this is the Rule for the men of the Community who have freely pledged themselves to be converted from all evil and to cling to all His commandments according to His will.
>
> They shall separate from the congregation of the men of falsehood
> 5 and shall unite, with respect to the Law and possessions, under the authority of the sons of Zadok, the Priests who keep the Covenant, and of the multitude of the men of the Community who hold fast to the Covenant. Every decision concerning doctrine, property, and justice shall be determined by them.
> 10 They shall practise truth and humility in common, and justice and uprightness and charity and modesty in all their ways. No man shall walk in the stubbornness of his heart so that he strays after his heart and evil inclination, but he shall circumcise in the Community the foreskin of evil inclination and of stiffness of neck that they may lay
> 15 a foundation of truth for Israel, for the Community of the everlasting Covenant. They shall atone for those in Aaron who have freely pledged themselves to holiness, and for those in Israel who have freely pledged themselves to the House of Truth, and for those who join them to live in community and to take part in the trial and
> 20 judgement and condemnation of all those who transgress the precepts.
>
> On joining the Community, this shall be their code of behaviour with respect to all these precepts.
>
> Whoever approaches the Council of the Community shall enter the Covenant of God in the presence of all who have freely pledged
> 25 themselves. He shall undertake by a binding oath to return with all

his heart and soul to every commandment of the Law of Moses in accordance with all that has been revealed of it to the sons of Zadok, the Keepers of the Covenant and Seekers of His will, and to the multitude of the men of their Covenant who together have freely
30 pledged themselves to His truth and to walking in the way of His delight. And he shall undertake by the Covenant to separate from all the men of falsehood who walk in the way of wickedness.

For they are not reckoned in His Covenant. They have neither inquired nor sought after Him concerning His laws that they might
35 know the hidden things in which they have sinfully erred; and matters revealed they have treated with insolence. Therefore Wrath shall rise up to condemn, and Vengeance shall be executed by the curses of the Covenant, and great chastisements of eternal destruction shall be visited on them, leaving no remnant. They shall not enter
40 the water to partake of the pure Meal of the saints, for they shall not be cleansed unless they turn from their wickedness: for all who transgress His word are unclean. Likewise, no man shall mix with him with regard to his work or property lest he be burdened with the guilt of his sin. He shall indeed keep away from him in all things;
45 as it is written, *Keep away from all that is false* (Exod. 23. 7). No member of the Community shall follow them in matters of doctrine and justice, or eat or drink anything of theirs, or take anything from them except for a price; as it is written, *Keep away from the man in whose nostrils is breath, for wherein is he counted?* (Isa. 2. 22). For all
50 those not reckoned in His Covenant are to be set apart, together with all that is theirs. None of the saints shall lean upon the works of vanity: for they are all vanity who know not His Covenant, and He will blot from the earth all them that despise His word. All their deeds are defilement before Him, and all their possessions unclean.

55   But when a man enters the Covenant to walk according to all these precepts that he may join the holy congregation, they shall examine his spirit in community with respect to his understanding and practice of the Law, under the authority of the sons of Aaron who have freely pledged themselves in the Community to restore
60 His Covenant and to heed all the precepts commanded by Him, and of the multitude of Israel who have freely pledged themselves in the Community to return to His Covenant. They shall inscribe them in the order, one after another, according to their understanding and their deeds, that every one may obey his companion, the man of
65 lesser rank obeying his superior. And they shall examine their spirit and deeds yearly, so that each man may be advanced in accordance with his understanding and perfection of way, or moved down in accordance with the offences committed by him.

They shall rebuke one another in truth, humility, and charity. Let
70 no man address his companion with anger, or ill-temper, or obduracy,

or with envy prompted by the spirit of wickedness. Let him not hate him [in the wickedness of an uncircumcised] heart, but let him rebuke him on the very same day lest he incur guilt because of him. And furthermore, let no man accuse his companion before the
75 Congregation without having first admonished him in the presence of witnesses.

These are the ways in which all of them shall walk, each man with his companion, wherever they dwell.

The man of lesser rank shall obey the greater in matters of work
80 and money.

They shall eat in common and pray in common and deliberate in common.

Wherever there are ten men of the Council of the Community there shall not lack a Priest among them. And they shall all sit before
85 him according to their rank and shall be asked their counsel in all things in that order. And when the table has been prepared for eating, and the new wine for drinking, the Priest shall be the first to stretch out his hand to bless the first-fruits of the bread and new wine.

And where the ten are, there shall never lack a man among them
90 who shall study the Law continually, day and night, concerning the right conduct of a man with his Companion. And the Congregation shall watch in community for a third of every night of the year, to read the Book and to study Law and to pray together.

ll. 1, 2   *Community . . . to be converted.* These words are reminiscent of some that are used in the New Testament, notably in Acts. *Community* (*yaḥad*, יחד) is thought by some to be parallel to ἐπὶ τὸ αὐτό (e.g. Acts 2. 27) and *converted* to ἐπιστρέφειν (e.g. Acts 3. 19).

l. 4   *The men of falsehood*, those who had, wrongfully in the opinion of the sect, gained control of the Temple.

l. 13   *Evil inclination, yeṣer,* יצר. See **158**.

l. 23   *The Council of the Community.* Cf. 8.1, In the Council of the Community there shall be twelve men and three priests.

211

Community Rule (1QS) 8. 1–19

In the Council of the Community there shall be twelve men and three priests, perfectly versed in all that is revealed of the Law, whose works shall be truth, righteousness, justice, lovingkindness, and humility. They shall preserve the faith in the Land with steadfastness
5 and meekness and shall atone for sin by the practice of justice and by suffering the sorrows of affliction. They shall walk with all men according to the standard of truth and the rule of the time.

When these are in Israel, the Council of the Community shall be established in truth. It shall be an Everlasting Plantation, a House of

10 Holiness for Israel, an Assembly of Supreme Holiness for Aaron. They shall be witnesses to the truth at the Judgement, and shall be the elect of Goodwill who shall atone for the Land and pay to the wicked their reward. It shall be that tried wall, that *precious corner-stone* (Isa. 28. 16). It shall be a Most Holy Dwelling for Aaron, with
15 everlasting knowledge of the Covenant of justice, and shall offer up sweet fragrance. It shall be a House of Perfection and Truth in Israel that they may establish a Covenant according to the everlasting precepts. And they shall be an agreeable offering, atoning for the Land and determining the judgement of wickedness, and there shall
20 be no more iniquity. When they have been confirmed for two years in perfection of way by the authority of the Community, they shall be set apart as holy within the Council of the men of the Community. And the Interpreter shall not conceal from them, out of fear of the spirit of apostasy, any of those things hidden from Israel which have
25 been discovered by him.

And when these become members of the Community in Israel according to all these rules, they shall separate from the habitation of ungodly men and shall go into the wilderness to prepare the way of Him; as it is written, *Prepare in the wilderness the way of . . . make*
30 *straight in the desert a path for our God* (Isa. 40. 3). This (path) is the study of the Law which He commanded by the hand of Moses, that they may do according to all that has been revealed from age to age, and as the Prophets have revealed by His Holy Spirit.

And no man among the members of the Covenant of the
35 Community who deliberately, on any point whatever, turns aside from all that is commanded, shall touch the pure Meal of the men of holiness or know anything of their counsel until his deeds are purified from all falsehood and he walks in perfection of way. And then, according to the judgement of the Congregation, he shall be admitted
40 to the Council and shall be inscribed in his rank. This rule shall apply to whoever enters the Community.

l. 1   *Twelve men and three priests.* It is not clear whether this means that there shall be a total of twelve men, of whom three shall be priests, or whether there shall be fifteen in all.

ll. 5, 12   *Atone . . . atone.* The Hebrew words are not the same (*raṣṣoth,* רצת . . . *kapper,* כפר). The former, which is related to the word goodwill (in *the elect of Goodwill*) probably gives the sense in which the latter was understood: to appease, propitiate.

l. 23   *The Interpreter.* It is not certain that this (literally, the man who studies) refers to a special person.

l. 29   *The way of . . . .* The holy name of God, which might not be pronounced, is represented in the manuscript by four dots.

l. 31   *The study of the Law.* The sect's understanding of their obligation and of the will of God is clear.

l. 36 *The pure Meal of the men of holiness.* Literally, the purity of the men . . . The interpretation is quite probably correct.

212

Damascus Rule (CD) I. I—2. I3

Hear now, all you who know righteousness, and consider the works of God; for He has a dispute with all flesh and will condemn all those who despise Him.

For when they were unfaithful and forsook Him, He hid His face
5 from Israel and His Sanctuary and delivered them up to the sword. But remembering the Covenant of the forefathers, He left a remnant to Israel and did not deliver it up to be destroyed. And in the age of wrath, three hundred and ninety years after He had given them into the hand of king Nebuchadnezzar of Babylon, He visited them, and
10 He caused a root of planting to spring from Israel and Aaron to inherit His Land and to prosper on the good things of His earth. And they perceived their iniquity and recognized that they were guilty men, yet for twenty years they were like blind men groping for the way.
15 And God observed their deeds, that they sought Him with a whole heart, and He raised for them a Teacher of Righteousness to guide them in the way of His heart. And he made known to the latter generations that which God had done to the latter generation, the congregation of traitors, to those who departed from the way. This
20 was the time of which it is written, *Like a stubborn heifer thus was Israel stubborn* (Hos. 4. 16), when the Scoffer arose who shed over Israel the waters of lies. He led them astray in a wilderness without way by bringing low the everlasting hills, and by causing them to depart from the paths of righteousness, and by removing the bound
25 with which the forefathers had marked out their inheritance, that he might call down on them the curses of His Covenant and deliver them up to the avenging sword of the Covenant. For they sought smooth things and preferred illusions (Isa. 30. 10) and they watched for breaks (Isa. 30. 13) and chose the fair neck; and they justified the
30 wicked and condemned the just, and they transgressed the Covenant and violated the Precept. They banded together against the life of the righteous (Ps. 94. 21) and loathed all who walked in perfection; they pursued them with the sword and exulted in the strife of the people. And the anger of God was kindled against their congregation so that
35 He ravaged all their multitude; and their deeds were defilement before Him.

Hear now, all you who enter the Covenant, and I will unstop your ears concerning the ways of the wicked.

God loves knowledge. Wisdom and understanding He has set
40 before Him, and prudence and knowledge serve Him. Patience and

much forgiveness are with Him towards those who turn from transgression; but power, might, and great flaming wrath by the hand of all the Angels of Destruction towards those who depart from the way and abhor the Precept. They shall have no remnant or
45 survivor. For from the beginning God chose them not; He knew their deeds before ever they were created and He hated their generations, and He hid His face from the Land until they were consumed. For He knew the years of their coming and the length and exact duration of their times for all ages to come and throughout
50 eternity. He knew the happenings of their times throughout all the everlasting years. And in all of them He raised for Himself men called by name, that a remnant might be left to the Land, and that the face of the earth might be filled with their seed. And He made known His Holy Spirit to them by the hand of His anointed ones,
55 and He proclaimed the truth (to them). But those whom He hated He led astray.

l. 8   *Three hundred and ninety years.* This brings us to something like 200 BC. But, as Lohse says, the figures are 'apocalyptic' rather than historical in any strict sense.

l. 16   *A Teacher of Righteousness,* that is, a 'right teacher', one who taught the truth. This was after twenty years of 'groping'. The Teacher must count as the true founder of the sect.

l. 21   *The Scoffer.* See **221**, where he is called The Liar (or Man of Lies).

l. 29   *Chose the fair neck.* This appears to be an allusion to Hos. 10. 11.

l. 39   *God loves knowledge, da'ath* (דעת). Much has been made of the apparent relation to the Scrolls to Gnosticism, but, as the context shows, it is on the whole the Old Testament concept of wisdom that is in mind here.

213

Damascus Rule (CD) 4. 2—6. 11

The *Priests* are the converts of Israel who departed from the land of Judah, and (the *Levites* are) those who joined them. The *sons of Zadok* are the elect of Israel, the men called by name who shall stand at the end of days. Behold the exact list of their names according to their
5 generations, and the time when they lived, and the number of their trials, and the years of their sojourn, and the exact list of their deeds . . .

(They were the first men) of holiness whom God forgave, and who justified the righteous and condemned the wicked. And until
10 the age is completed, according to the number of those years, all who enter after them shall do according to that interpretation of the Law in which the first were instructed. According to the Covenant which God made with the forefathers, forgiving their sins, so shall He forgive their sins also. But when the age is completed, according to

15 the number of those years, there shall be no more joining the house
of Judah, but each man shall stand on his watch-tower: *The wall is
built, the boundary far removed* (Mic. 7. 11).

During all those years Satan shall be unleashed against Israel, as he
spoke by the hand of Isaiah, son of Amoz, saying, *Terror and the pit*
20 *and the snare are upon you, O inhabitant of the land* (Isa. 24. 17).
Interpreted, these are the three nets of Satan with which Levi son of
Jacob said that he catches Israel by setting them up as three kinds of
righteousness. The first is riches, the second is fornication, and the
third is profanation of the Temple. Whoever escapes the first is
25 caught in the second, and whoever saves himself from the second is
caught in the third (Isa. 24. 18).

The builders of the wall (Ezek. 13. 10) who have followed after
'Precept'—'Precept' was a spouter of whom it is written, *They shall
surely spout* (Mic. 2. 6)—shall be caught in fornication twice by
30 taking a second wife while the first is alive, whereas the principle of
creation is, *Male and female created He them* (Gen. 1. 27). Also, those
who entered the Ark went in two by two. And concerning the
prince it is written, *He shall not multiply wives to himself* (Deut.
17. 17); but David had not read the sealed book of the Law which
35 was in the ark (of the Covenant), for it was not opened in Israel from
the death of Eleazar and Joshua, and the elders who worshipped
Ashtoreth. It was hidden and (was not) revealed until the coming of
Zadok. And the deeds of David rose up, except for the murder of
Uriah, and God left them to him.

40 Moreover, they profane the Temple because they do not observe
the distinction (between clean and unclean) in accordance with the
Law, but lie with a woman who sees her bloody discharge.

And each man marries the daughter of his brother or sister,
whereas Moses said, *You shall not approach your mother's sister; she is*
45 *your mother's near kin* (Lev. 18. 13). But although the laws against
incest are written for men, they also apply to women. When,
therefore, a brother's daughter uncovers the nakedness of her father's
brother, she is (also his) near kin.

Furthermore, they defile their holy spirit and open their mouth
50 with a blaspheming tongue against the laws of the Covenant of God
saying, 'They are not sure.' They speak abominations concerning
them; *they are all kindlers of fire and lighters of brands* (Isa. 50. 11), *their
webs are spiders' webs and their eggs are vipers' eggs* (Isa. 59. 5). No man
that approaches them shall be free from guilt; the more he does so,
55 the guiltier shall he be, unless he is pressed. For (already) in ancient
times God visited their deeds and His anger was kindled against their
works; *for it is a people of no discernment* (Isa. 27. 11), *it is a nation void
of counsel inasmuch as there is no discernment in them* (Deut. 32. 28).
For in ancient times, Moses and Aaron arose by the hand of the

60 Prince of Lights and Satan in his cunning raised up Jannes and his
brother when Israel was first delivered.

And at the time of the desolation of the Land there arose removers
of the bound who led Israel astray. And the land was ravaged because
they preached rebellion against the commandments of God given by
65 the hand of Moses and of His holy anointed ones, and because they
prophesied lies to turn Israel away from following God. But God
remembered the Covenant with the forefathers, and He raised from
Aaron men of discernment and from Israel men of wisdom, and He
caused them to hear. And they dug the Well: *the well which the princes*
70 *dug, which the nobles of the people delved with the stave* (Num. 21. 18).

The *Well* is the Law, and those who dug it were the converts of
Israel who went out of the land of Judah to sojourn in the land of
Damascus. God called them all *princes* because they sought Him, and
their renown was disputed by no man. The *Stave* is the Interpreter
75 of the Law of whom Isaiah said, *He makes a tool for his work* (Isa.
54. 16); and the *nobles of the people* are those who come to dig the
Well with the staves with which the *Stave* ordained that they should
walk in all the age of wickedness—and without them they shall find
nothing—until he comes who shall teach righteousness at the end
80 of days.

ll. 1, 2   *Priests . . . Levites . . . sons of Zadok.* The writer is interpreting Ezek. 44. 15.

l. 18   *Satan shall be unleashed.* Events at 'the end of days' are being described.

l. 21   *Interpreted, pishro,* literally, its interpretation. The word *pesher,* interpretation,
is very characteristic of the scrolls.

ll. 27–39   The strict teaching of the scrolls regarding divorce and remarriage is
strikingly reminiscent of that of the Gospels. David can be partly, but not
wholly, excused on the ground of ignorance.

l. 71   *The* Well *is the Law.* Again, a characteristic form of interpretation.

l. 79   *He . . . who shall teach righteousness at the end of days.* Probably the Teacher of
Righteousness (**212**). The sect believed itself to be living at or near the end,
when eschatological hopes and promises were about to be fulfilled.

214

Damascus Rule (CD) 10. 14—12. 6a

Concerning the Sabbath to observe it according to its law
No man shall work on the sixth day from the moment when the
sun's orb is distant by its own fulness from the gate (wherein it sinks);
for this is what he said, *Observe the Sabbath day to keep it holy* (Deut.
5 5. 12). No man shall speak any vain or idle word on the Sabbath day.
He shall make no loan to his companion. He shall make no decision
in matters of money and gain. He shall say nothing about work or
labour to be done on the morrow.

No man shall walk abroad doing his pleasure on the Sabbath. He
10 shall not walk more than one thousand cubits beyond his town.

No man shall eat on the Sabbath day except that which is already
prepared. He shall eat nothing lying in the fields. He shall not drink
except in the camp. If he is on a journey and goes down to bathe, he
shall drink where he stands, but he shall not draw water into a vessel.
15 He shall send no stranger to do his pleasure on the Sabbath day.

No man shall wear soiled garments, or garments brought to the
store, unless they have been washed with water or rubbed with
incense.

No man shall willingly mingle (with others) on the Sabbath.

20 No man shall walk more than two thousand cubits after a beast to
pasture it outside his town. He shall not raise his hand to strike it
with his fist. If it is stubborn he shall not take it out of his house.

No man shall take anything out of the house or bring anything in.
He shall not open a sealed vessel on the Sabbath.

25 No man shall carry perfumes on himself whilst going and coming
on the Sabbath. He shall lift neither sand nor dust in his dwelling.
No foster-father shall carry a child whilst going and coming on the
Sabbath.

No man shall chide his manservant or maidservant or labourer on
30 the Sabbath.

No man shall assist a beast to give birth on the Sabbath day. And
if it should fall into a cistern or pit, he shall not lift it out on the
Sabbath.

No man shall spend the Sabbath on a place near to Gentiles on the
35 Sabbath.

No man shall profane the Sabbath for the sake of riches or gain on
the Sabbath day. But should any man fall into water or fire, let him
be pulled out with the aid of a ladder or rope or (some such) tool.

No man on the Sabbath shall offer anything on the altar except
40 the Sabbath burnt-offerings; for it is written thus: *Except your*
Sabbath offerings (Lev. 23. 38).

No man shall send to the altar any burnt-offering, or cereal
offering, or incense, or wood, by the hand of one smitten with any
uncleanness, permitting him thus to defile the altar. For it is written,
45 *The sacrifice of the wicked is an abomination, but the prayer of the just is*
as an agreeable offering (Prov. 15. 8).

No man entering the house of worship shall come unclean and in
need of washing. And at the sounding of the trumpets for assembly,
he shall go there before or after (the meeting), and shall not cause the
50 whole service to stop, for it is a holy service.

No man shall lie with a woman in the city of the Sanctuary, to
defile the city of the Sanctuary with their uncleanness.

Every man who preaches apostasy under the dominion of the
spirits of Satan shall be judged according to the law relating to those

55   possessed by a ghost or familiar spirit (Lev. 20. 27). But no man who
      strays so as to profane the Sabbath and the feasts shall be put to death;
      it shall fall to men to keep him in custody. And if he is healed of his
      error, they shall keep him in custody seven years and he shall
      afterwards approach the Assembly.

l. 10   *One thousand cubits.* This was a strict law; the rabbinic limit was 2000 cubits
       (*Erubin* 4. 3; *Sotah* 5. 3).

l. 32   *He shall not lift it out on the Sabbath.* Again the Qumran rule was stricter than
       that observed elsewhere; cf. Luke 14. 5.

Faith and Practice

It was pointed out above (p. 219) that the aim of the sect was to achieve a
life of perfect purity in conformity with its own understanding of the
requirements of Torah. In order to achieve this, strict discipline was
imposed upon its members. Admission to the community was not easily
granted and probation was severe. The upper ranks of the hierarchy
exercised absolute authority over the lower, with power of exclusion, a
harsher punishment than might appear since the excluded member no
longer had access to the only food that his vows permitted him to eat. The
community had strict rules and they had to be strictly observed. It would
however be wrong to suppose that its religion was merely formal. It is
impossible to read not only the Hymns but also many other parts of the
Qumran literature without being aware of a warm and genuine piety.
The member of the sect was deeply penitent for his own personal sins and
for those of his people, in which he could not but share. For forgiveness
he depended wholly upon the mercy of God; in this however he knew
that he might trust, because God was loving, and because he shared in the
covenant that God had made with the fathers of the race and in the
renewal of this covenant effected by the founders and leaders of the
community and annually re-enacted. He could speak also of the
righteousness of God and of his justification; how far his understanding of
these terms coincided with Paul's is a matter of dispute. He looked forward
to life in the presence of God after death, as well as to a glorious future for
his people, or at least for the elect and righteous among them. And he did
not fail to thank God for his mercies.

215

Community Rule (1QS) 11. 2–22

As for me,
 my justification is with God.
In His hand are the perfection of my way
 and the uprightness of my heart.
5 He will wipe out my transgression
 through his righteousness.

For my light has sprung
 from the source of his knowledge;
my eyes have beheld his marvellous deeds,
10 and the light of my heart, the mystery to come.
He that is everlasting
 is the support of my right hand;
the way of my steps is over stout rock
 which nothing shall shake;
15 for the rock of my steps is the truth of God
 and His might is the support of my right hand.
From the source of His righteousness
 is my justification,
and from His marvellous mysteries
20 is the light in my heart.
My eyes have gazed
 on that which is eternal,
on wisdom concealed from men,
 on knowledge and wise design
25 (hidden) from the sons of men;
on a fountain of righteousness
 and on a storehouse of power,
on a spring of glory
 (hidden) from the assembly of flesh.
30 God has given them to His chosen ones
 as an everlasting possession,
and has caused them to inherit
 the lot of the Holy Ones.
He has joined their assembly
35 to the Sons of Heaven
to be a Council of the Community,
a foundation of the Building of Holiness,
an eternal Plantation throughout all ages to come.

 As for me,
40 I belong to wicked mankind,
 to the company of ungodly flesh.

My iniquities, rebellions, and sins,
   together with the perversity of my heart,
belong to the company of worms
45   and to those who walk in darkness.
For mankind has no way,
   and man is unable to establish his steps
since justification is with God
   and perfection of way is out of his hand.
50 All things come to pass by His knowledge;
He establishes all things by His design
   and without Him nothing is done.

As for me,
   if I stumble, the mercies of God
55   shall be my eternal salvation.
If I stagger because of the sin of flesh,
   my justification shall be
   by the righteousness of God which endures for ever.
When my distress is unleashed
60   He will deliver my soul from the Pit
   and will direct my steps to the way.
He will draw me near by His grace,
   and by His mercy will He bring my justification.
He will judge me in the righteousness of His truth
65   and in the greatness of His goodness
He will pardon all my sins.
Through His righteousness He will cleanse me
   of the uncleanness of man
   and of the sins of the children of men,
70 that I may confess to God His righteousness,
   and His majesty to the Most High.

Blessed art Thou, my god,
   who openest the heart of Thy servant to knowledge!
Establish all his deeds in righteousness,
75 and as it pleases Thee to do for the elect of mankind,
   grant that the son of Thy handmaid
may stand before Thee for ever.

For without Thee no way is perfect,
   and without Thy will nothing is done.
80 It is thou who hast taught all knowledge
   and all things come to pass by Thy will.
There is none beside Thee to dispute Thy counsel
   or to understand all Thy holy design,
   or to contemplate the depth of Thy mysteries
85   and the power of Thy might.

Who can contain Thy glory,
  and what is the son of man
  in the midst of Thy wonderful deeds?
What shall one born of woman
90 be accounted before Thee?
Kneaded from the dust,
  his abode is the nourishment of worms.
He is but a shape, but moulded clay,
  and inclines towards dust.
95 What shall hand-moulded clay reply?
  What counsel shall it understand?

l. 2 *Justification.* This translates *mishpaṭ* (מֹשׁפֹט), which might be rendered *judgement.* So far as favourable judgement is implied the thought is not remote from Paul's though the Qumran word is not the most natural way to express it.

l. 6 *Through his righteousness;* here the word is more akin to Paul's—*ṣidqothaw* (צדקותו), though the plural is used, presumably with the meaning *righteous acts.* In *l.* 17 however the singular is used.

l. 41 *Ungodly flesh, basar* (בשׁר): another possible contact with Paul.

216

Community rule (1QS) 6. 8b—7. 25

This is the rule for an Assembly of the congregation
Each man shall sit in his place: the Priests shall sit first, and the elders second, and all the rest of the people according to their rank. And thus shall they be questioned concerning the Law, and concerning
5 any counsel or matter coming before the Congregation, each man bringing his knowledge to the Council of the Community.
  No man shall interrupt a companion before his speech has ended, nor speak before a man of higher rank; each man shall speak in his turn. And in an Assembly of the Congregation no man shall speak
10 without the consent of the Congregation, nor indeed of the Guardian of the Congregation. Should any man wish to speak to the Congregation, yet not be in a position to question the Council of the Community, let him rise to his feet and say: 'I have something to say to the Congregation.' If they command him to speak, he shall speak.
15 Every man, born of Israel, who freely pledges himself to join the Council of the Community, shall be examined by the Guardian at the head of the Congregation concerning his understanding and his deeds. If he is fitted to the discipline, he shall admit him into the Covenant that he may be converted to the truth and depart from all
20 falsehood; and he shall instruct him in all the rules of the Community. And later, when he comes to stand before the Congregation, they shall all deliberate his case, and according to the decision of the

Council of the Congregation he shall either enter or depart. After he has entered the Council of the Community he shall not touch the
25 pure Meal of the Congregation until one full year is completed, and until he has been examined concerning his spirit and deeds; nor shall his property be mingled with that of the Congregation. Then when he has completed one year within the Community, the Congregation shall deliberate his case with regard to his understanding and
30 observance of the Law. And if it be his destiny, according to the judgement of the Priests and the multitude of the men of their Covenant, to enter the company of the Community, his property and earnings shall be handed over to the Bursar of the Congregation who shall register it to his account and shall not spend it for the
35 Congregation. He shall not touch the Drink of the Congregation until he has completed a second year among the men of the Community. But when the second year has passed, he shall be examined, and if it be his destiny, according to the judgement of the Congregation, to enter the Community, then he shall be inscribed
40 among his brethren in the order of his rank for the Law, and for justice, and for the pure Meal; his property shall be mingled and he shall offer his counsel and judgement to the community.

These are the rules by which they shall judge at a Community (Court of) Inquiry
45 If one of them has lied deliberately in matters of property, he shall be excluded from the pure Meal of the Congregation for one year and shall do penance with respect to one quarter of his food.

Whoever has answered his companion with obstinacy, or has addressed him impatiently, going so far as to take no account of the
50 dignity of his fellow by disobeying the order of a brother inscribed before him, he has taken the law into his own hand; therefore he shall do penance for one year [and shall be excluded].

Whoever has uttered the Name of the [Most] Venerable Being [shall be put to death]. But if he has blasphemed when frightened by
55 affliction or for any other reason whatever, while reading the Book or praying, he shall be set apart and shall return to the Council of the Community no more.

If he has spoken in anger against one of the Priests inscribed in the Book, he shall do penance for one year and shall be excluded for his
60 soul's sake from the pure Meal of the Congregation. But if he has spoken unwittingly, he shall do penance for six months.

Whoever has deliberately lied shall do penance for six months.

Whoever has deliberately insulted his companion unjustly shall do penance for one year and shall be excluded.
65 Whoever has deliberately deceived his companion by word or by deed shall do penance for six months.

If he has been careless with regard to his companion, he shall do penance for three months. But if he has been careless with regard to the property of the Community, thereby causing its loss, he shall
70 restore it in full. And if he is unable to restore it, he shall do penance for sixty days.

Whoever has borne malice against his companion unjustly shall do penance for six months/one year; and likewise, whoever has taken revenge in any matter whatever.

75 Whoever has spoken foolishly: three months.

Whoever has interrupted his companion whilst speaking: ten days.

Whoever has lain down to sleep during an Assembly of the Congregation: thirty days. And likewise, whoever has left, without reason, an Assembly of the Congregation as many as three times
80 during one Assembly, shall do penance for ten days. But if he has departed whilst they were standing he shall do penance for thirty days.

Whoever has gone naked before his companion, without having been obliged to do so, he shall do penance for six months.

85 Whoever has spat in an Assembly of the Congregation shall do penance for thirty days.

Whoever has been so poorly dressed that when drawing his hand from beneath his garment his nakedness has been seen, he shall do penance for thirty days.

90 Whoever has guffawed foolishly shall do penance for thirty days.

Whoever has drawn out his left hand to gesticulate with it shall do penance for ten days.

Whoever has gone about slandering his companion shall be excluded from the pure Meal of the Congregation for one year and
95 shall do penance. But whoever has slandered the Congregation shall be expelled from among them and shall return no more.

Whoever has murmured against the authority of the Community shall be expelled and shall not return. But if has murmured against his companion unjustly, he shall do penance for six months.

100 Should a man return whose spirit has so trembled before the authority of the Community that he has betrayed the truth and walked in the stubbornness of his heart, he shall do penance for two years. During the first year he shall not touch the pure Meal of the Congregation, and during the second year he shall not touch the
105 Drink of the Congregation and shall sit below all the men of the Community. Then when his two years are completed, the Congregation shall consider his case, and if he is admitted he shall be inscribed in his rank and may then question concerning the Law.

If, after being in the Council of the Community for ten full years,
110 the spirit of any man has failed so that he has betrayed the Community and departed from the Congregation to walk in the stubbornness of his heart, he shall return no more to the Council of the Community.

Moreover, if any member of the Community has shared with him
his food or property which . . . of the Congregation his sentence shall
115 be the same; he shall be ex[pelled].

l. 2   *The Priests, hak-koh⁴nim* (הכוהנים), who would have carried out their
functions in the Temple had they not disapproved of those who administered
it.
    The elders, haz-z⁴qenim (הזקנים).

l. 10   *The Guardian, ham-m⁴baqqer* (המבקר). Some have seen in this officer the
prototype of the Christian bishop.

l. 25   *Pure Meal,* literally *purity*; see on **211**.

l. 73   *One year.* These words are written over the line, presumably as a correction
of the previously written text.

217

Hymns (1QH) 1. 1–27a.

Thou art long-suffering in Thy judgements
    and righteous in all Thy deeds.
By Thy wisdom [all things exist from] eternity,
    and before creating them Thou knewest their works for ever and
        ever.
  5 [Nothing] is done [without Thee]
    and nothing is known unless Thou desire it.
Thou hast created all the spirits
    [and hast established a statute] and law for all their works.
Thou hast spread the heavens for Thy glory
 10   and hast [appointed] all [their hosts] according to Thy will;
the mighty winds according to their laws
    before they became angels [of holiness]
        . . . and eternal spirits in their dominions;
the heavenly lights to their mysteries,
 15   the stars to their paths,
[the clouds] to their tasks,
    the thunderbolts and lightnings to their duty,
and the perfect treasuries (of snow and hail)
    to their purposes,
 20 . . . to their mysteries.
Thou hast created the earth by Thy power
    and the seas and deeps [by Thy might].
Thou hast fashioned [all] their [inhabi]tants
    according to Thy wisdom,
 25 and hast appointed all that is in them
    according to Thy will.
[And] to the spirit of man
    which Thou hast formed in the world,
[Thou hast given dominion over the works of Thy hands]

30   for everlasting days and unending generations.
    . . . in their ages
Thou hast allotted to them tasks
    during all their generations,
and judgement in their appointed seasons
35   according to the rule [of the two spirits.
For Thou hast established their ways]
    for ever and ever,
[and hast ordained from eternity]
    their visitation for reward and chastisements;
40 Thou hast allotted it to all their seed
    for eternal generations and everlasting years . . .
In the wisdom of Thy knowledge
    Thou didst establish their destiny before ever they were.
All things [exist] according to [Thy will]
45   and without Thee nothing is done.
These things I know
    by the wisdom which comes from Thee,
for Thou hast unstopped my ears
    to marvellous mysteries.
50 And yet I, a shape of clay
    kneaded in water,
a ground of shame
    and a source of pollution,
a melting-pot of wickedness
55   and an edifice of sin,
a straying and perverted spirit
    of no understanding,
    fearful of righteous judgements,
what can I say that is not foreknown,
60   and what can I utter that is not foretold?
All things are graven before Thee
    on a written Reminder
    for everlasting ages,
and for the numbered cycles
65   of the eternal years
    in all their seasons;
they are not hidden or absent from Thee.

What shall a man say
    concerning his sin?
70 And how shall he plead
    concerning his iniquities?
And how shall he reply
    to righteous judgement?
For Thine, O God of knowledge,

75   are all righteous deeds
        and the counsel of truth;
    but to the sons of men is the work of iniquity
        and deeds of deceit.

218

Hymns (1QH) 4. 22b–40

    Clinging to Thee, I will stand.
    I will rise against those who despise me
        and my hand shall be turned
        against those who deride me;
 5 for they have no esteem for me
    [that Thou mayest] manifest Thy might through me.
    Thou hast revealed Thyself to me in Thy power
        as perfect Light,
        and Thou hast not covered my face with shame.
10 All those who are gathered in Thy Covenant
        inquire of me,
    and they hearken to me who walk in the way of Thy heart,
        who array themselves for Thee
        in the Council of the holy.
15 Thou wilt cause their law to endure for ever
        and truth to go forward unhindered,
    and Thou wilt not allow them to be led astray
        by the hand of the damned
        when they plot against them.
20 Thou wilt put the fear of them into Thy people
        and (wilt make of them) a hammer
        to all the peoples of the lands,
    that at the Judgement they may cut off
        all those who transgress Thy word.

25 Through me Thou hast illumined
        the face of the Congregation
        and hast shown Thine infinite power.
    For Thou hast given me knowledge
        through Thy marvellous mysteries,
30 and hast shown Thyself mighty within me
        in the midst of Thy marvellous Council.
    Thou hast done wonders before the Congregation
        for the sake of Thy glory,
    that they may make known Thy mighty deeds
35   to all the living.
    But what is flesh (to be worthy) of this?
    What is a creature of clay

for such great marvels to be done,
whereas he is in iniquity from the womb
40   and in guilty unfaithfulness until his old age?
Righteousness, I know, is not of man,
     nor is perfection of way of the son of man:
to the Most High God belong all righteous deeds.
The way of man is not established
45   except by the spirit which God created for him
     to make perfect a way for the children of men,
that all His creatures might know
     the might of His power,
and the abundance of His mercies
50   towards all the sons of His grace.

As for me, shaking and trembling seize me
     and all my bones are broken;
my heart dissolves like wax before fire
     and my knees are like water
55   pouring down a steep place.
For I remember my sins
     and the unfaithfulness of my fathers.
When the wicked rose against Thy Covenant
     and the damned against Thy word,
60 I said in my sinfulness,
     'I am forsaken by Thy Covenant.'
But calling to mind the might of Thy hand
     and the greatness of Thy compassion,
I rose and stood,
65   and my spirit was established
     in face of the scourge.
I lean on Thy grace
     and on the multitude of Thy mercies,
for Thou wilt pardon iniquity,
70   and through Thy righteousness
     [Thou wilt purify man] of his sin.
Not for his sake wilt Thou do it,
     [but for the sake of Thy glory].
For Thou hast created the just and the wicked
   . . .

ll. 41, 42   *Man . . . son of man.* The parallelism of the two synonymous expressions
will be observed.

219

Hymns (1QH) 6. 29–35

And then at the time of Judgement
     the Sword of God shall hasten,

And all the sons of His truth shall awake
        to [overthrow] wickedness;
5   all the sons of iniquity shall be no more.
    The Hero shall bend his bow;
    the fortress shall open on to endless space
    and the everlasting gates shall send out weapons of war.
    They shall be mighty
10   from end to end [of the earth
    and there shall be no escape]
        for the guilty of heart [in their battle];
    they shall be utterly trampled down
        without any [remnant.
15 There shall be no] hope
        in the greatness [of their might],
        no refuge for the mighty warriors;
    for [the battle shall be] to the Most High God
        . . .
20 Hoist a banner,
        O you who lie in the dust!
    O bodies gnawed by worms,
        raise up an ensign for [the destruction of wickedness]!
    [The sinful shall] be destroyed
25   in the battles against the ungodly.

l. 6   *The Hero, gibbor* (גבור). There is no article in the Hebrew, but the reference
is presumably to God; cf. Isa. 9. 5.

220

Hymns (1QH) 11. 3–14

I thank Thee, my God,
        for Thou hast dealt wondrously to dust,
        and mightily towards a creature of clay!
    I thank Thee, I thank Thee!

5   What am I, that Thou shouldst [teach] me
        the counsel of Thy truth,
    and give me understanding
        of Thy marvellous works;
    that Thou shouldst lay hymns of thanksgiving
10   within my mouth
        and [praise] upon my tongue,
    and that of my circumcised lips
        (Thou shouldst make) a seat of rejoicing?

    I will sing Thy mercies,
15   and on Thy might I will meditate all day long.
    I will bless Thy name evermore.

I will declare thy glory in the midst of the sons of men
    and my soul shall delight in Thy great goodness.
I know that Thy word is truth,
20   and that righteousness is in Thy hand;
that all knowledge is in thy purpose,
    and that all power is in Thy might,
    and that every glory is Thine.

In Thy wrath are all chastisements,
25   but in Thy goodness is much forgiveness
    and Thy mercy is towards the sons of thy goodwill.
For thou hast made known to them
    the counsel of Thy truth,
and hast taught them Thy marvellous mysteries.

30 For the sake of thy glory
    Thou hast purified man of sin
that he may be made holy for Thee,
    with no abominable uncleanness
    and no guilty wickedness;
35 that he may be one [with] the children of Thy truth
    and partake of the lot of Thy Holy Ones;
that bodies gnawed by worms may be raised from the dust
    to the counsel [of Thy truth],
and that the perverse spirit (may be lifted)
40   to the understanding [which comes from Thee];
that he may stand before Thee
    with the everlasting host
    and with [Thy] spirits [of holiness],
to be renewed together with all the living
45   and to rejoice together with them that know.

l. 37 *That bodies gnawed by worms may be raised from the dust.* The Qumran sect accepted fully the notion of resurrection. Cf. Dan. 12. 2.

Biblical Exegesis

The interpretation of the Old Testament was of vital importance to the Qumran sect, for two reasons. In the first place, it had to show that its understanding of Torah, over against that of the authorities in Jerusalem, from whom it had separated, was correct. In the second place, it had to show that the words of the prophets had truly been fulfilled in its own history, that the members of the sect were the elect to whom the promises had been made and in, for, and among whom they were being fulfilled. It is especially this latter necessity that brings Qumran exegesis close to early Christian exegesis, for the Christians also believed not only that they were correct interpreters of Scripture but that they had witnessed the fulfilment of Scripture in Christ and continued to witness its fulfilment in themselves and in their experience.

The most characteristic term used in interpreting the Old Testament is *pēsher* (פשר). 'This word occurs once only in the Old Testament (Eccles. 8. 1), and does not appear to have been used by the rabbis as a technical exegetical term. The Aramaic equivalent is hardly more common. There is no doubt that the general meaning is *interpretation*, but only from the context can the method and manner of the interpretation be determined. A separate *pēsher* is supplied for each small unit of text. Paragraphs are not interpreted as wholes, though it occasionally happens that clauses are combined in defiance of the original connection (or lack of it). Continuity is thus provided not by the original sense and context, but by the new historical context into which the biblical material is introduced and in terms of which it is explained. Within the several units of text the allegorical method is used in order to apply the passage quoted to its new historical setting. The use of allegory is a fairly clear indication that the commentator has in fact begun with historical circumstances, and convictions regarding them, known to himself, and has imposed them on his text.' (*The Cambridge History of the Bible* I (1970), pp. 388f.)

There follows here the whole of what remains (apart from a few lines too broken to be worth quoting) of the Qumran commentary on Habakkuk. It seemed better to give one extended piece of exegesis than to pick out passages from a number of texts.

221

Commentary on Habakkuk (1 Q pHab)

> *[Behold the nations and see, marvel and be astonished; for I accomplish a deed in your days but you will not believe it when]* told (Hab. 1. 5).
>
> [Interpreted, this concerns] those who were unfaithful together with the Liar, in that they [did] not [listen to the word received by]
> 5 the Teacher of Righteousness from the mouth of God. And it concerns the unfaithful of the New [Covenant] in that they have not believed in the Covenant of God [and have profaned] His holy Name. And likewise, this saying is to be interpreted [as concerning those who] will be unfaithful at the end of days. They, the men of
> 10 violence and the breakers of the Covenant, will not believe when they hear all that [is to happen to] the final generation from the Priest [in whose heart] God set [understanding] that he might interpret all the words of His servants the Prophets, through whom he foretold all that would happen to His people and [His land].
> 15 *For behold, I rouse the Chaldeans, that [bitter and hasty] nation* (1. 6a).

Interpreted, this concerns the Kittim [who are] quick and valiant in war, causing many to perish. [All the world shall fall] under the dominion of the Kittim, and the wicked . . . they shall not believe in 20 the laws of [God . . .]

[Who march through the breadth of the earth to take possession of dwellings which are not their own] (i. 6b).

. . . they shall march across the plain, smiting and plundering the cities of the earth. For it is as He said, *To take possession of dwellings* 25 *which are not their own.*

They are fearsome and terrible; their justice and grandeur proceed from themselves (i. 7).

Interpreted, this concerns the Kittim who inspire all the nations with fear [and dread]. All their evil plotting is done with intention 30 and they deal with all the nations in cunning and trickery.

Their horses are swifter than leopards and fleeter than evening wolves. Their horses step forward proudly and spread their wings; they fly from afar like an eagle avid to devour. All of them come for violence; the look on their faces is like the east wind (i. 8–9a).

35 [Interpreted, this] concerns the Kittim who trample the earth with their horses and beasts. They come *from afar,* from the islands of the sea, to devour all the peoples *like an eagle* which cannot be satisfied, and they address [all the peoples] with anger and [wrath and fury] and indignation. For it is as He said, *The look on their faces is like the* 40 *east wind.*

. . .

They scoff [at kings], and princes are their laughing-stock (i. 10a).

Interpreted, this means that they mock the great and despise the venerable; they ridicule kings and princes and scoff at the mighty 45 host.

They laugh at every fortress; they pile up earth and take it (i. 10b).

Interpreted, this concerns the commanders of the Kittim who despise the fortresses of the peoples and laugh at them in derision. To capture them, they encircle them with a mighty host, and out of fear 50 and terror they deliver themselves into their hands. They destroy them because of the sins of their inhabitants.

The wind then sweeps on and passes; and they make of their strength their god (i. 11).

Interpreted, [this concerns] the commanders of the Kittim who, 55 on the counsel of [the] House of Guilt, pass one in front of the other; one after another [their] commanders come to lay waste the earth. *[And they make] of their strength their god*: interpreted, this concerns [. . . all] the peoples . . .

[Art Thou not from everlasting, O Lord, my God, my Holy One? We 60 *shall not die.] Thou hast ordained them, [O Lord], for judgement; Thou hast established them, O Rock, for chastisement. Their eyes are too pure to behold evil; and Thou canst not look on distress* (i. 12–13a).

Interpreted, this saying means that God will not destroy His people
by the hand of the nations; God will execute the judgement of the
65 nations by the hand of his elect. And through their chastisement all
the wicked of His people shall expiate their guilt who keep His
commandments in their distress. For it is as He said, *Too pure of eyes*
to behold evil: interpreted, this means that they have not lusted after
their eyes during the age of wickedness.

70 *O traitors, why do you stare and stay silent when the wicked swallows*
up one more righteous than he? (1. 13b).

Interpreted, this concerns the House of Absalom and the members
of its council who were dumb at the time of the chastisement of the
Teacher of Righteousness and gave him no help against the Liar who
75 flouted the Law in the midst of the whole [congregation].

Thou dealest with men like the fish of the sea, like crawling creatures, to
rule over them. They draw [them all up with a fish-hook], and drag them
out with their net, and gather them in [their seine. Therefore they sacrifice]
to their net. Therefore they rejoice [and exult and burn incense to their
80 *seine; for by them] their portion is fat [and their sustenance rich]* (1. 14–
16).

. . . the Kittim and they shall gather in their riches, together with
all their booty, *like the fish of the sea*. And as for that which He said,
Therefore they sacrifice to their net and burn incense to their seine:
85 interpreted, this means that they sacrifice to their standards and
worship their weapons of war. *For through them their portion is fat and*
their sustenance rich: interpreted, this means that they divide their
yoke and their tribute—*their sustenance*—over all the peoples year
by year, ravaging many lands.

90 *Therefore their sword is ever drawn to massacre nations mercilessly*
(1. 17).

Interpreted, this concerns the Kittim who cause many to perish by
the sword—youths, grown men, the aged, women and children—
and who even take no pity on the fruit of the womb.

95 *I will take my stand to watch and will station myself upon my fortress.*
I will watch to see what He will say to me and how [He will answer] my
complaint. And the Lord answered [and said to me, 'Write down the vision
and make it plain] upon the tablets, that [he who reads] may read it
speedily' (2. 1–2).

100 . . . and God told Habakkuk to write down that which would
happen to the final generation, but He did not make known to him
when time would come to an end. And as for that which He said,
That he who reads may read it speedily, interpreted this concerns the
Teacher of Righteousness, to whom God made known all the
105 mysteries of the words of His servants the Prophets.

For there shall be yet another vision concerning the appointed time. It
shall tell of the end and shall not lie (2. 3a).

Interpreted, this means that the final age shall be prolonged, and
shall exceed all that the prophets have said; for the mysteries of God
110 are astounding.

If it tarries, wait for it, for it shall surely come and shall not be late
(2. 3b).

Interpreted, this concerns the men of truth who keep the Law,
whose hands shall not slacken in the service of truth when the final
115 age is prolonged. For all the ages of God reach their appointed end as
He determines for them in the mysteries of His wisdom.

Behold, [his soul] is puffed up and is not upright (2. 4a).

Interpreted, this means that [the wicked] shall double their guilt
upon themselves [and it shall not be forgiven] when they are judged
120 ...

[But the righteous shall live by his faith] (2. 4b).

Interpreted, this concerns all those who observe the Law in the
House of Judah, whom God will deliver from the House of
Judgement because of their suffering and because of their faith in the
125 Teacher of Righteousness.

Moreover, the arrogant man seizes wealth without halting. He widens
his gullet like Hell and like Death he has never enough. All the nations
are gathered to him and all the peoples are assembled to him. Will they not
all of them taunt him and jeer at him saying, 'Woe to him who amasses
130 *what does not belong to him! How long will he load himself up with*
pledges?' (2. 5–6).

Interpreted, this concerns the Wicked Priest who was called by
the name of truth when he first arose. But when he ruled over Israel
his heart became proud, and he forsook God and betrayed the
135 precepts for the sake of riches. He robbed and amassed the riches of
the men of violence who rebelled against God, and he took the
wealth of the peoples, heaping sinful iniquity upon himself. And he
lived in the ways of abominations amidst every unclean defilement.

Shall not your oppressors suddenly arise and your torturers awaken;
140 *and shall you not become their prey? Because you have plundered many*
nations, all the remnant of the peoples shall plunder you (2. 7–8a).

[Interpreted, this concerns] the Priest who rebelled [and violated]
the precepts [of God ... to command] his chastisement by means of
the judgements of wickedness. And they inflicted horrors of evil
145 diseases and took vengeance upon his body of flesh. And as for that
which He said, *Because you have plundered many nations, all the remnant*
of the peoples shall plunder you, interpreted this concerns the last Priests
of Jerusalem, who shall amass money and wealth by plundering the
peoples. But in the last days, their riches and booty shall be delivered
150 into the hands of the army of the Kittim, for it is they who shall be
the *remnant of the peoples.*

Because of the blood of men and the violence done to the land, to the city,
and to all its inhabitants (2. 8b).

Interpreted, this concerns the Wicked Priest whom God delivered
155 into the hands of his enemies because of the iniquity committed
against the Teacher of Righteousness and the men of his Council,
that he might be humbled by means of a destroying scourge, in
bitterness of soul, because he had done wickedly to His elect.

Woe to him who gets evil profit for his house; who perches his nest high
160 *to be safe from the hand of evil! You have devised shame to your house; by*
cutting off many peoples you have forfeited your own soul. For the [stone]
cries out [from] the wall [and] the beam from the woodwork replies (2. 9–
11).

[Interpreted, this] concerns the [Priest] who ... that its stones
165 might be laid in oppression and the beam of its woodwork in
robbery. And as for that which He said, *By cutting off many peoples*
you have forfeited your own soul, interpreted this concerns the
condemned House whose judgement God will pronounce in the
midst of many peoples. He will bring him thence for judgement and
170 will declare him guilty in the midst of them, and will chastise him
with fire of brimstone.

Woe to him who builds a city with blood and founds a town upon
falsehood! Behold, is it not from the Lord of Hosts that the peoples shall
labour for fire and the nations shall strive for naught? (2. 12–13).
175 Interpreted, this concerns the Spouter of Lies who led many astray
that he might build his city of vanity with blood and raise a
congregation on deceit, causing many thereby to perform a service
of vanity for the sake of its glory, and to be pregnant with [works]
of deceit, that their labour might be for nothing and that they might
180 be punished with fire who vilified and outraged the elect of God.

For as the waters cover the sea, so shall the earth be filled with the
knowledge of the glory of the Lord (2. 14).

Interpreted, [this means that] when they return ... the lies. And
afterwards, knowledge shall be revealed to them abundantly, like the
185 waters of the sea.

Woe to him who causes his neighbours to drink; who pours out his
venom to make them drunk that he may gaze on their feasts! (2. 15).

Interpreted, this concerns the Wicked Priest who pursued the
Teacher of Righteousness to the house of his exile that he might
190 confuse him with his venomous fury. And at the time appointed for
rest, for the Day of Atonement, he appeared before them to confuse
them, and to cause them to stumble on the Day of Fasting, their
Sabbath of repose.

You have filled yourself with ignominy more than with glory. Drink
195 *also, and stagger! The cup of the Lord's right hand shall come round to you*
and shame shall come on your glory (2. 16).

Interpreted, this concerns the priest whose ignominy was greater
than his glory. For he did not circumcise the foreskin of his heart,

and he walked in the ways of drunkenness that he might quench his
200 thirst. But the cup of the wrath of God shall confuse him, multiplying
his . . . and the pain of . . .

[For the violence done to Lebanon shall overwhelm you, and the
destruction of the beasts] shall terrify you, because of the blood of men and
the violence done to the land, the city, and all its inhabitants (2. 17).

205 Interpreted, this saying concerns the Wicked Priest, inasmuch as
he shall be paid the reward which he himself tendered to the poor.
For *Lebanon* is the Council of the Community; and the *beasts* are the
Simple of Judah who keep the Law. As he himself plotted the
destruction of the Poor, so will God condemn him to destruction.
210 And as for that which He said, *Because of the blood of the city and the*
violence done to the land: interpreted, *the city* is Jerusalem where the
Wicked Priest committed abominable deeds and defiled the temple
of God. *The violence done to the land*: these are the cities of Judah
where he robbed the Poor of their possessions.

215 *Of what use is an idol that its maker should shape it, a molten image, a*
fatling of lies? For the craftsman puts his trust in his own creation when
he makes dumb idols (2. 18).

Interpreted, this saying concerns all the idols of the nations which
they make so that may serve and worship them. But they shall not
220 deliver them on the Day of Judgement.

Woe [to him who says] to wood, 'Awake', and to dumb [stone, 'Arise'!
Can such a thing give guidance? Behold, it is covered with gold and silver
but there is no spirit within it. But the Lord is in His holy Temple]: let all
the earth be silent before Him! (2. 19–20).

225 Interpreted, this concerns all the nations which serve stone and
wood. But on the Day of Judgement, God will destroy from the
earth all idolatrous and wicked men.

l. 4 *The Liar.* The identification of the various persons referred to under a
number of sobriquets in this Commentary is one of the major historical
problems presented by the Scrolls, and no attempt can be made here to
discuss them or even to mention the various suggestions that have been
made. Presumably the Liar is either to be identified with the Wicked Priest
or should be thought of as a colleague or ally of his.

l. 5 *The Teacher of Righteousness.* This person was evidently the 'good' counterpart
of the Wicked Priest, and led the secession which was the origin of the
Qumran sect. He was the *right* teacher; there is no reason to think that there
existed a specific office that bore this title. The Teacher of Righteousness was
probably a priest (see *l.* 11).

l. 17 *The Kittim* (כתים). The term appears several times in the Old Testament
(e.g. Isa. 23.1; Jer. 2. 10; Dan. 11. 30), and refers properly to the Cypriotes,
but later to inhabitants of the Mediterranean coastlands in general. Here
non-Jewish enemies are in mind; probably Romans; cf. among others lines
36, 47–50, 85.

l. 61   *Their eyes* . . . The Hebrew text is the same as that which is more usually translated, Thou who art of purer eyes . . .

l. 72   *The House of Absalom* presumably describes Jewish authorities who if they did not actually support the Wicked Priest against the Teacher of Righteousness failed to protest against his action.

l. 73   *The chastisement of the Teacher of Righteousness.* The founder of the sect was made to suffer for his stand against authority. See further lines 155, 189.

l. 104   *To whom God made known all the mysteries.* The Teacher of Righteousness was able to expound Old Testament Scripture, apparently claiming that it was in part fulfilled in the events of his time.

l. 124   *Their faith in* . . . , or perhaps 'their faithfulness to . . .'.

l. 147   *The last Priests.* The triumph of the opponents of the sect would be only temporary; the present generation of wicked priests would be the last.

l. 175   *The Spouter of Lies.* Cf. the Liar (*l.* 4).

ll. 188–193   These lines clearly refer to a venomous attack on the Teacher of Righteousness, but it is impossible confidently to reconstruct a picture of what happened. *Confuse* might be rendered 'to swallow up', but this gives no clearer understanding of the scene.

The War

One considerable text in the Qumran library is devoted to 'the war of the sons of light against the sons of darkness'. It is such as to raise the question whether it refers to a literal war about to be fought with material weapons by Qumranite Jews against Gentiles and renegade (that is, non-Qumranite) Jews, or a spiritual conflict, a 'wrestling not against flesh and blood but against principalities and powers', the last stand of the spiritual forces of darkness before the establishing of the rule of God. It is probably fair to say that the question thus put is mis-stated. What are expressed as alternatives were probably seen as opposite sides of the same coin. The supreme adversary of God and his people is the devil, and spiritual conflict there must be before the devil is overthrown and God is seen to be victorious. But the devil has human agents and they must be dealt with on their own terms, and if they have swords, spears, and shields, the people of God must have swords, spears, and shields too. Thus there will be real, that is, military, fighting to do, but in it the Qumranite soldier will have complete confidence in God who wins his own spiritual victory and enables his troops to win theirs.

222

War Rule (1 QM) 1. 1–12a

> *For the M[aster. The Rule of] War on the unleashing of the attack of the sons of light against the company of the sons of darkness, the army of*

Satan: against the band of Edom, Moab, and the sons of Ammon, and
[against the army of the sons of the East and] the Philistines, and against
5 *the bands of the Kittim of Assyria and their allies the ungodly of the*
Covenant.

The sons of Levi, Judah, and Benjamin, the exiles in the desert, shall battle against them in . . . all their bands when the exiled sons of light return from the Desert of the Peoples to camp in the Desert of
10 Jerusalem; and after the battle they shall go up from there (to Jerusalem?).

[The king] of the Kittim [shall enter] into Egypt, and in his time he shall set out in great wrath to wage war against the kings of the north, that his fury may destroy and cut off the horn of [the nations].
15 This shall be a time of salvation for the people of God, an age of dominion for all the members of His company, and of everlasting destruction for all the company of Satan. The confusion of the sons of Japheth shall be [great] and Assyria shall fall unsuccoured. The dominion of the Kittim shall come to an end and iniquity shall be
20 vanquished, leaving no remnant; [for the sons] of darkness there shall be no escape. [The seasons of righteous]ness shall shine over all the ends of the earth; they shall go on shining until all the seasons of darkness are consumed and, at the season appointed by God, His exalted greatness shall shine eternally to the peace, blessing, glory,
25 joy, and long life of all the sons of light.

On the day when the Kittim fall, there shall be battle and terrible carnage before the God of Israel, for that shall be the day appointed from ancient times for the battle of destruction of the sons of darkness. At that time, the assembly of gods and the hosts of men shall battle,
30 causing great carnage; on the day of calamity, the sons of light shall battle with the company of darkness amid the shouts of a mighty multitude and the clamour of gods and men to (make manifest) the might of God. And it shall be a time of [great] tribulation for the people which God shall redeem; of all its afflictions none shall be as
35 this, from its sudden beginning until its end in eternal redemption.

l. 3 *Edom, Moab, etc.* It does not seem possible to find precise and distinct interpretations for all the different Old Testament names that are added to that of the Kittim. They represent the gentile enemy.

l. 5 *The ungodly of the Covenant,* the Jewish enemy, those who have not entered into and renewed the covenant as the Qumran sect had done.

l. 23 *The season appointed by God.* The sect shared the common apocalyptic belief that the future, including the turn of events in favour of God's people, had already been determined by God.

223

War Rule (1 QM) 5. 3—6.17

The rule for the ordering of the battle divisions to complete a front formation
when their host had reached its full number

The formation shall consist of one thousand men ranked seven lines deep, each man standing behind the other.

5   They shall all hold shields of bronze burnished like mirrors. The shield shall be edged with an interlaced border and with inlaid ornament, a work of art in pure gold and silver and bronze and precious stones, a many-coloured design worked by a craftsman. The length of the shield shall be two and a half cubits and its width one
10   and a half cubits.

In their hands they shall hold a spear and a sword. The length of the spear shall be seven cubits, of which the socket and spike shall measure half a cubit. The socket shall be edged with three embossed interlaced rings of pure gold and silver and bronze, a work of art.
15   The inlaid ornaments on both edges of the ring shall be bordered with precious stones—a many-coloured design worked by a craftsman—and (embossed) with ears of corn. Between the rings, the socket shall be embossed with artistry like a pillar. The spike shall be made of brilliant white iron, the work of a craftsman; in its centre,
20   pointing towards the tip, shall be ears of corn in pure gold.

The swords shall be made of pure iron refined by the smelter and blanched to resemble a mirror, the work of a craftsman; on both sides (of their blades) pointing towards the tip, figured ears of corn shall be embossed in pure gold, and they shall have two straight
25   borders on each side. The length of the sword shall be one and a half cubits and its width four fingers. The width of the scabbard shall be four thumbs. There shall be four palms to the scabbard (from the girdle), and it shall be attached (to the girdle) on both sides for a length of five palms (?). The hilt of the sword shall be pure horn
30   worked by a craftsman, with a many-coloured design in gold and silver and precious stones . . .

. . . seven times and shall return to their positions.

And after them, three divisions of foot-soldiers shall advance and shall station themselves between the formations, and the first division
35   shall hurl seven javelins of war towards the enemy formation. On the point of the javelins they shall write, *Shining Javelin of the Power of God*; and on the darts of the second division they shall write, *Bloody Spikes to bring down the Slain by the Wrath of God*; and on the javelins of the third division they shall write, *Flaming Blade to devour*
40   *the Wicked struck down by the Judgement of God*. All these shall hurl their javelins seven times and shall afterwards return to their positions.

Then two divisions of foot-soldiers shall advance and shall station themselves between the two formations. The first division shall be armed with a spear and a shield, and the second with a shield and a
45   sword, to bring down the slain by the judgement of God, and to bend the enemy formation by the power of God, to pay the reward of their wickedness to all the nations of vanity. And sovereignty shall

be to the God of Israel, and He shall accomplish mighty deeds by the saints of His people.

50 Seven troops of horsemen shall also station themselves to right and to left of the formation; their troops shall stand on this (side) and on that, seven hundred horsemen on one flank and seven hundred horsemen on the other. Two hundred horsemen shall advance with the thousand men of the formation of foot-soldiers; and they shall

55 likewise station themselves on both [flanks] of the camp. Altogether there shall be four thousand six hundred (men), and one thousand cavalrymen with the men of the army formations, fifty to each formation. The horsemen, together with the cavalry of the army, shall number six thousand; five hundred to each tribe.

60 The horses advancing into battle with the foot-soldiers shall all be stallions; they shall be swift, sensitive of mouth, and sound of wind, and of the required age, trained for war, and accustomed to noise and to every (kind of) sight. Their riders shall be gallant fighting men and skilled horsemen, and their age shall be from thirty to forty-five

65 years. The horsemen of the army shall be from forty to fifty years old. They [and their mounts shall wear breast-plates,] helmets, and greaves; they shall carry in their hands bucklers, and a spear [eight cubits] long. [The horsemen advancing with the foot-soldiers shall carry] bows and arrows and javelins of war. They shall all hold

70 themselves prepared . . . of God and to spill the blood of the wicked.

l. 1   *The rule for the ordering of the battle divisions.* It is hard to believe that all the detailed instructions given here had no more than allegorical significance; real warfare was in mind. It is however almost equally hard to believe that all the troops were equipped with such elaborate and richly ornamented weapons. Equipment and tactics seem to owe something to Roman example.

224

War Rule (1 QM) 11. 1—12. 18

Truly, the battle is Thine! Their bodies are crushed by the might of Thy hand and there is no man to bury them.

Thou didst deliver Goliath of Gath, the mighty warrior, into the hands of David Thy servant, because in place of the sword and in

5 place of the spear he put his trust in Thy great Name; for Thine is the battle. Many times, by Thy great Name, did he triumph over the Philistines. Many times hast Thou also delivered us by the hand of our kings through Thy lovingkindness, and not in accordance with our works by which we have done evil, nor according to our

10 rebellious deeds.

Truly the battle is Thine and the power from Thee! It is not ours. Our strength and the power of our hands accomplish no mighty deeds except by Thy power and by the might of Thy great valour.

This Thou hast taught us from ancient times, saying, *A star shall come*
15   *out of Jacob, and a sceptre shall rise out of Israel. He shall smite the temples*
of Moab and destroy all the children of Sheth. He shall rule out of Jacob
and shall cause the survivors of the city to perish. The enemy shall be his
possession and Israel shall accomplish mighty deeds (Num. 24 17–19).

By the hand of Thine anointed, who discerned Thy testimonies,
20   Thou hast revealed to us the [times] of the battles of Thy hands that
Thou mayest glorify Thyself in our enemies by levelling the hordes
of Satan, the seven nations of vanity, by the hand of Thy poor whom
Thou hast redeemed [by Thy might] and by the fulness of Thy
marvellous power. (Thou hast opened) the door of hope to the
25   melting heart: Thou wilt do to them as Thou didst to Pharaoh, and
to the captains of his chariots in the Red Sea. Thou wilt kindle the
downcast of spirit and they shall be a flaming torch in the straw to
consume ungodliness and never to cease till iniquity is destroyed.

From ancient times Thou hast fore [told the hour] when the might
30   of Thy hand (would be raised) against the Kittim, saying, *Assyria*
shall fall by the sword of no man, the sword of no mere man shall devour
him (Isa. 31. 8). For Thou wilt deliver into the hands of the poor the
enemies from all the lands, to humble the mighty of the peoples by
the hand of those bent to the dust, to bring upon the [head of Thine
35   enemies] the reward of the wicked, and to justify Thy true judgement
in the midst of all the sons of men, and to make for Thyself an
everlasting Name among the people [whom Thou hast redeemed]
. . . of battles to be magnified and sanctified in the eyes of the remnant
of the peoples, that they may know . . . when Thou chastisest Gog
40   and all his assembly gathered about him . . .

For Thou wilt fight with them from heaven . . . For the multitude
of the Holy Ones [is with Thee] in heaven, and the host of the Angels
is in Thy holy abode, praising Thy Name. And Thou hast established
in [a community] for Thyself the elect of Thy holy people. [The list]
45   of the names of all their host is with Thee in the abode of Thy
holiness; [the reckoning of the saints] is in Thy glorious dwelling-
place. Thou hast recorded for them, with the graving-tool of life, the
favours of [Thy] blessings and the Covenant of Thy peace, that Thou
mayest reign [over them] for ever and ever and throughout all the
50   eternal ages. Thou wilt muster the [hosts of] thine [el]ect, in their
Thousands and Myriads, with Thy Holy Ones [and with all] Thine
Angels that they may be mighty in battle, [and may smite] the rebels
of the earth by Thy great judgements, and that [they may triumph]
together with the elect of heaven.

55   For Thou art [terrible], O God, in the glory of Thy kingdom, and
the congregation of Thy Holy Ones is among us for everlasting
succour. We will despise kings, we will mock and scorn the mighty;
for our Lord is holy, and the King of Glory is with us together with

the Holy Ones. Valiant [warriors] of the angelic host are among our
60 numbered men, and the Hero of war is with our congregation; the
host of His spirits is with our foot-soldiers and horsemen. [They are
as] clouds, as clouds of dew (covering) the earth, as a shower of rain
shedding righteousness on all that grows on the earth.

Rise up, O Hero!
65 Lead off Thy captives, O Glorious One!
Gather up Thy spoils, O Author of Mighty deeds!
Lay Thine hand on the neck of Thine enemies
    and Thy feet on the pile of the slain!
Smite the nations, Thine adversaries,
70   and devour the flesh of the sinner with Thy sword!
Fill thy land with glory
    and Thine inheritance with blessing!
Let there be a multitude of cattle in Thy fields,
    and in Thy palaces silver and gold and precious stones!

75 O Zion, rejoice greatly!
O Jerusalem, show thyself amidst jubilation!
Rejoice, all you cities of Judah;
keep your gates ever open
    that the hosts of the nations
80   may be brought in!

Their kings shall serve you
    and all your oppressors shall bow down before you;
    [they shall lick] the dust [of your feet].
Shout for joy, [O daughters of] my people!
85 Deck yourselves with glorious jewels
    and rule over [the kingdoms of the nations!
Sovereignty shall be to the Lord]
    and everlasting dominion to Israel.

l. 1   *The battle is Thine.* This conviction is no more inconsistent with the military
preparations for battle described elsewhere than the same conviction with
David's sling (*l.* 4).

l. 19 *Thine anointed.* The word is in the plural (מְשִׁיחֶיכָה) and apparently refers
to the prophets.

l. 39 *Gog.* See Ezek. 38; 39: another 'biblical' way of describing the enemy.

Philo is the only Jew contemporary with the origins of Christianity who is well known to us from his own writings. The dates of his birth and death cannot be given with precision, but his life must have covered approximately the period 20 BC–AD 45. During the greater part of this time he seems to have lived quietly in Alexandria. He was wealthy and belonged to one of the leading Jewish families in Alexandria; in his old age he was employed in an important mission on behalf of his fellow-countrymen; see **48, 149**. The rest of his life was, so far as we know, uneventful; and it is certain that the production of his extensive philosophical works must have required a good deal of learned leisure. There is however no reason to doubt that Philo was sufficiently acquainted with at least the religious activities of his fellow-Jews in Alexandria. For his account of the Essenes and Therapeutae see **136–7**.

It is in his writings, not his life, that the interest of Philo for the student of early Christianity lies. These fall roughly into two parts. One set of treatises is devoted to an allegorical and homiletical exposition, discursive but, within the limits of Philo's methods, systematic, of a considerable part of the Greek text of Genesis. In substance, Philo's ideas are often far removed from his biblical text, but formally he offers us here a solid piece of verse by verse exegesis. The other set of treatises is less homogeneous, and less closely bound to the text of Scripture. It contains biographies (for example, of Moses); books on particular Old Testament laws (for example, the Decalogue); more strictly philosophical writings, and two historical works.

Philo's Faithfulness to the Law

Philo, as a philosophical writer, made much use of non-Jewish material; yet, unlike some Hellenistic Jews, he never ceased to be a Jew, and to maintain the strict observance of the national laws.

225

De Migratione Abrahami 89–93

> There are some who, regarding laws in their literal sense in the light of symbols of matters belonging to the intellect, are overpunctilious

about the latter, while treating the former with easy-going neglect.
Such men I for my part should þlame for handling the matter in too
5 easy and off-hand a manner: they ought to have given careful
attention to both aims, to a more full and exact investigation of what
is not seen and in what is seen to be stewards without reproach. As it
is, as though they were living alone by themselves in a wilderness, or
as though they had become disembodied souls, and knew neither city
10 nor village nor household nor any company of human beings at all,
overlooking all that the mass of men regard, they explore reality in
its naked absoluteness. These men are taught by the sacred word to
have thought for good repute, and to let go nothing that is part of
the customs fixed by divinely empowered men greater than those of
15 our time.

It is quite true that the Seventh Day is meant to teach the power of
the Unoriginate and the non-action of created beings. But let us not
for this reason abrogate the laws laid down for its observance, and
light fires or till the ground or carry loads or institute proceedings in
20 court or act as jurors or demand the restoration of deposits or recover
loans, or do all else that we are permitted to do as well on days that
are not festival seasons. It is true also that the Feast is a symbol of
gladness of soul and of thankfulness to God, but we should not for
this reason turn our backs on the general gatherings of the year's
25 seasons. It is true that receiving circumcision does indeed portray the
excision of pleasure and all passions, and the putting away of the
impious conceit, under which the mind supposed that it was capable
of begetting by its own power: but let us not on this account repeal
the law laid down for circumcising. Why, we shall be ignoring the
30 sanctity of the Temple and a thousand other things, if we are going
to pay heed to nothing except what is shown us by the inner meaning
of things. Nay, we should look on all these outward observances as
resembling the body, and their inner meanings as resembling the
soul. It follows that, exactly as we have to take thought for the body,
35 because it is the abode of the soul, so we must pay heed to the letter
of the laws. If we keep and observe these, we shall gain a clearer
conception of those things of which these are the symbols; and
besides that we shall not incur the censure of the many and the
charges they are sure to bring against us.

l. 1 *There are some . . .* Thus Philo was not alone in his allegorical treatment of
the Pentateuch; and some of his fellow-allegorists went further than he did,
and disregarded the literal sense of the laws.

l. 2 *Matters belonging to the intellect.* Philo is here using Platonic language; the
laws literally understood belong to the world of phenomena, while their
inward meaning belongs to the world of ideas. But Philo has no intention of
belittling the phenomenal world.

l. 12 *The sacred word (λόγος).* The plain meaning of the laws must not be neglected because men live in society. The 'sacred word' here means primarily the Scriptures, but it moves over to a wider meaning, and the 'divinely empowered' men (primarily Moses) are spoken of in terms of the Stoic sage, who lives according to reason (λόγος).

l. 16 *The power of the Unoriginate.* The Sabbath is really a witness to the eternal activity of God (cf. John 5. 17 and contrast the notion that God himself keeps the Sabbath, e.g. Jubilees 2. 19).

l. 22 *The Feast.* Philo does not say which feast he means, and it is possible that the word should be translated 'The keeping of feasts'. In Rabbinic usage 'the feast' commonly means Tabernacles. If the reference is not general, one of the 'Pilgrim Feasts' (see **178–81** and notes) is probably meant.

l. 25 *Circumcision.* In the somewhat later Judaism which is clearly known from the Rabbinic sources circumcision was demanded of all proselytes, but it is possible that earlier the demand was sometimes waived. In Josephus *Antiquities* xx. 17ff. a conversion to Judaism is recorded in which circumcision was not required; in *Yebamoth 46a* there is a discussion (which may be dated at about AD 100) on the question whether baptism without circumcision, or circumcision without baptism availed to make a proselyte, but the almost universal view was that both were necessary.

l. 30 *Temple.* It is worth noting the provincial Jew's interest in the Temple which he so rarely saw.

l. 38 *The censure of the many.* It may be inferred that both the allegorists and those who resisted their treatment of Scripture were fairly numerous. Philo characteristically seeks to mediate between these two extreme positions.

His Philosophical Eclecticism

Perhaps more influential in Philo's day than any strongly marked philosophical system was the eclectic method which was fostered by the mixing of nations and the flux of ideas in the early Empire. Platonism, Stoicism, and Neo-Pythagoreanism contributed complementary elements to the general intellectual atmosphere of the time; they can hardly be regarded as rivals for the whole-hearted allegiance of thinking men. Philo, with no great discrimination, selects from his knowledge of pagan thought any argument that will serve his turn.

PLATONISM

226

De Opificio Mundi 15f.

> [Philo is writing of the first day of creation.] We must recount as many as we can of the elements embraced in it. To recount them all would be impossible. Its pre-eminent element is the intelligible

world, as is shown in the treatise dealing with the 'One'. For God,
5 being God, assumed that a beautiful copy would never be produced
apart from a beautiful pattern, and that no object of perception
would be faultless which was not made in the likeness of an original
discerned only by the intellect. So when he willed to create this
visible world he first fully formed the intelligible world, in order
10 that he might have the use of a pattern wholly God-like and
incorporeal in producing the material world, as a later creation, the
very image of an earlier, to embrace in itself objects of perception of
as many kinds as the other contained objects of intelligence.

l. 3   *The intelligible world.* The adjective is used by Plato, and the phrase signifies
the world of ideas, of which, according to Plato, the phenomenal world (the
objects of perception, *l.* 12) is but a copy. It is important to note that Philo
professes to find this world of ideas in Gen. 1.

l. 4   *The 'One'.* This treatise is not extant.

l. 11   *Incorporeal.* The Platonic doctrine which Philo is handling in this paragraph
led very quickly to an ethical dualism between matter and spirit. Philo's firm
adherence to an essentially realist Judaism shielded him to some extent from
this kind of dualism.

227

Legum Allegoriae i. 70–3

In this paragraph Philo describes the soul as threefold, a division
thoroughly Platonic; cf. Plato, *Timaeus* 69C, *Republic* iv. 439D. He
proceeds with a mythical picture of the chariot of the soul which is taken
directly from *Phaedrus* 246ff., while the location of the various faculties in
parts of the body is borrowed from *Timaeus* 69E, 90A, though it is not
without parallels in the psychological language of the Old Testament.

[Philo is allegorizing the rivers of Gen. 2. 10–14.] It is worth
inquiring why courage is mentioned in the second place, self-mastery
in the third, and prudence in the first, and why he has not set forth a
different order of the virtues. We must observe, then, that our soul is
5 threefold, and has one part that is the seat of reason, another that is
the seat of high spirit, and another that is the seat of desire. And we
discover that the head is the place and abode of the reasonable part,
the breast of the passionate part, the abdomen of the lustful part; and
that to each of the parts a virtue proper to it has been attached;
10 prudence to the reasonable part, for it belongs to reason to have
knowledge of the things we ought to do and of the things we ought
not; courage to the passionate part; and self-mastery to the lustful
part. For it is by self-mastery that we heal and cure our desires. As,
then, the head is the first and highest part of the living creature, the
15 breast the second, and the abdomen the third, and again of the soul

the reasoning faculty is first, the high-spirited second, the lustful third: so too of the virtues, first is prudence which has its sphere in the first part of the soul which is the domain of reason, and in the first part of the body, namely the head; and second is courage, for it
20 has its seat in high spirit, the second part of the soul, and in the breast, the corresponding part of the body; and third self-mastery, for its sphere of action is the abdomen, which is of course the third part of the body, and the lustful faculty, to which has been assigned the third place in the soul.
25 '*The fourth river*', he says, '*is Euphrates*'. 'Euphrates' means 'fruitfulness', and is a figurative name for the fourth virtue, justice, a virtue fruitful indeed and bringing gladness to the mind. When, then, does it appear? When the three parts of the soul are in harmony. Harmony for them is the dominance of the more excellent; for
30 instance, when the two, the high-spirited and the lustful, are guided by the reasoning faculty as horses by their driver, then justice emerges; for it is justice for the better to rule always and everywhere, and for the worse to be ruled: and the reasoning faculty is better, the lustful and the high-spirited the inferior. Whenever, on the other
35 hand, high spirit and desire turn restive and get out of hand, and by the violence of their impetus drag the driver, that is the reason, down from his seat and put him under the yoke, and each of these passions gets hold of the reins, injustice prevails. For it cannot but be that owing to the badness and want of skill of the driver, the team is
40 swept down precipices and gullies, just as by experience and skill it must needs be brought safely through.

ll. 2f.   The virtues prudence, courage, and self-mastery are fancifully derived from the names of the rivers Pheison, Geon, and Tigris (which flows over against the Assyrians). These three (together with justice, *l.* 26) are the cardinal virtues of Platonism.

l. 25   '*Euphrates*' *means* '*fruitfulness*'. See below (p. 261 and **231**) on Philo's use of etymological arguments. Here his etymology is almost certainly wrong.

STOICISM

Much of Philo's ethical teaching, and from time to time his anthropology also, shows clear traces of Stoic origins. The passages printed below are perhaps even more significant, for they show the interpretation of a fundamental element of Judaism—Law—in terms of a fundamental concept of Stoicism, Nature, the vital and regulative power of the universe.

228

De Opificio Mundi 3, 8f.

His exordium is one that excites our admiration in the highest
degree. It consists of an account of the creation of the world, implying
that the world is in harmony with the Law, and the Law with the
world, and that the man who observes the Law is constituted thereby
5 a loyal citizen of the world, regulating his doings by the purpose and
will of Nature, in accordance with which the entire world itself also
is administered. . . .

Moses, both because he had attained the very summit of philosophy,
and because he had been divinely instructed in the greater and most
10 essential part of Nature's lore, could not fail to recognize that the
universal must consist of two parts, one part active Cause and the
other passive object; and that the active Cause is the perfectly pure
and unsullied Mind of the universe, transcending virtue, transcending
knowledge, transcending the good itself and the beautiful itself;
15 while the passive part is in itself incapable of life and motion, but,
when set in motion and shaped and quickened by Mind, changes into
the most perfect masterpiece, namely this world. Those who assert
that this world is unoriginate unconsciously eliminate that which of
all incentives to piety is the most beneficial and the most indispensable,
20 namely providence.

l. 1 *His exordium.* The *de Opificio Mundi* is the first work in Philo's systematic
exposition of Genesis (see above), and in it he comments upon the seven days
of creation, adding notes on Gen. 2. 4–7. Unlike some lawgivers, Moses (he
says) begins his code with a cosmogony—a very significant fact, according
to Philo, for it shows that the detailed laws which follow are not arbitrary
but arise out of the fundamental Natural Law.

l. 5 *Citizen of the world*—a very characteristic Stoic term; see **81** and note.
Regulating his doings by the purpose and will of Nature. This was the Stoic ideal
of the wise and virtuous life. Philo—always ready to identify Judaism with
the best wisdom of the Greeks—asserts that the man who practises the Law
of Moses achieves the ideal of the Stoic sage.

l. 8 *Moses.* The giver of the Law, obedience to which means living according to
Nature, is naturally presented as the greatest of philosophers.

l. 11 *Active Cause . . . passive object.* The distinction between cause and object
belongs to the Stoic view of the universe; it should be compared with the
use we have already seen Philo making of the Platonic framework of ideal
and phenomenal.

l. 13 *Mind (*νοῦς*).* One of Philo's most frequent terms for God; it allowed a
rapprochement between the Stoic and Platonic categories mentioned in the
last note, and also led to the doctrine of providence (πρόνοια) which was
equally important in Stoicism and Judaism.

NEO-PYTHAGOREANISM

Philo's indebtedness to this school of thought is perhaps less deep than his relation to Platonism and Stoicism, which seem to have affected the substance of his thinking. But from time to time at least the form of his writing has been moulded by Neo-Pythagorean methods; note especially his fantastic discussions of the significance of numbers.

229

De Opificio Mundi 99f.

[Philo is discussing the significance of the number 7.] So august is the dignity inherent by nature in the number 7, that it has a unique relation distinguishing it from all the other numbers within the decade: for of these some beget without being begotten, some are
5   begotten but do not beget, some do both these, both beget and are begotten: 7 alone is found in no such category. We must establish this assertion by giving proof of it. Well then, 1 begets all the subsequent numbers while it is begotten by none whatever: 8 is begotten by twice 4, but begets no number within the decade: 4
10 again holds the place of both, both of parents and of offspring; for it begets 8 by being doubled, and is begotten by twice 2. It is the nature of 7 alone, as I have said, neither to beget nor to be begotten. For this reason other philosophers liken this number to the motherless and virgin Nike, who is said to have appeared out of the head of Zeus,
15 while the Pythagoreans liken it to the chief of all things: for that which neither begets nor is begotten remains motionless; for creation takes place in movement, since there is movement both in that which begets and in that which is begotten, in the one that it may beget, in the other that it may be begotten. There is only one thing that
20 neither causes motion nor experiences it, the original Ruler and Sovereign. Of him 7 may be fitly said to be a symbol. Evidence of what I say is supplied by Philolaus in these words: 'There is, he says, a supreme Ruler of all things, God, ever One, abiding, without motion, himself [alone] like unto himself, different from all others'.

l. 4   *Beget . . . begotten.* That is, they may be factorized; or (*or*, and) are themselves factors of numbers in the first decade.

l. 16 *Motionless.* The freedom of God from all motion, and thus from all experience or passibility, was a doctrine common to Platonism and Pythagoreanism.

l. 22 *Philolaus.* A Pythagorean philosopher of the fifth century BC.

EPICUREANISM

On Philo's objection to the Epicurean philosophy see the next passage, **230**.

The Allegorical Method

It has already been pointed out that one of Philo's principal aims was to read the doctrines of Hellenistic religious philosophy out of the canonical documents of Judaism. This could hardly be the easiest of tasks, since the doctrines Philo wished to find were not contained in the sources in which he sought them. They existed in Philo's mind, and the means by which he transferred them from their place of origin to the place where he hoped to find them was Allegory.

Allegorical exegesis, which was by no means confined to Judaism, was widely practised in the Hellenistic age. It arose partly out of the undoubted fact that some of the earlier philosophers had written with intentional obscurity; partly out of the longing of somewhat enervated minds for the authority of the great ones of the past; and partly out of the conviction that philosophy was superior to narrative, and that the reputation of Homer and other poets must be salvaged by finding hidden meanings in their sometimes all too vulgar stories. When Philo wished to fashion the Old Testament into something its authors had not intended, the allegorical tool lay ready to hand; and it must be admitted that he used it with skill, and that sometimes the results are pleasing and effective, though quite unconvincing as exegesis.

230

De Posteritate Caini 1–11

> '*And Cain went out from the face of God, and dwelt in the land of Naid, over against Eden*' (Gen. 4. 6). Let us here raise the question whether in the books in which Moses acts as God's interpreter we ought to take his statements figuratively, since the impression made by the
> 5 words in their literal sense is greatly at variance with truth. For if the Existent Being has a face, and he that wishes to quit its sight can with perfect ease remove elsewhere, what ground have we for rejecting the impious doctrines of Epicurus, or the atheism of the Egyptians, or the mythical plots of play and poem of which the world is full?
> 10 For a face is a piece of a living creature, and God is a whole not a part, so that we shall have to assign to him the other parts of the body as well, neck, breasts, hands, feet, to say nothing of the belly and genital organs, together with the innumerable inner and outer organs. And if God has human forms and parts, he must needs also have human

15 passions and experiences. For in the case of these organs, as in all other
cases, Nature has not made idle superfluities, but aids to the weakness
of those furnished with them. And she adjusts to them, according to
their several needs, all that enables them to render their own special
services and ministries. But the Existent Being is in need of nothing,
20 and so, not needing the benefit that parts bestow, can have no parts
at all.

And whence does Cain 'go out'? From the palace of the Lord of
all? But what dwelling apparent to the senses could God have, save
this world, for the quitting of which no power or device avails? For
25 all created things are enclosed and kept within itself by the circle of
the sky. Indeed the particles of the deceased break up into their
original elements and are again distributed to the various forces of
the universe out of which they were constituted, and the loan which
was lent to each man is repaid, after longer or shorter terms, to
30 Nature his creditor, at such time as she may choose to recover what
she herself had lent.

Again he that goes out from someone is in a different place from
him whom he leaves behind. [If, then, Cain goes out from God], it
follows that some portions of the universe are bereft of God. Yet
35 God has left nothing empty or destitute of himself, but has completely
filled all things.

Well, if God has not a face, transcending as he does the peculiarities
that mark all created things; if he is to be found not in some particular
part only, seeing that he contains all and is not himself contained by
40 anything; if it is impossible for some part of this world to remove
from it as from a city, seeing that nothing has been left over outside
it; the only thing left for us to do is to make up our minds that none
of the propositions put forward is literally intended and to take the
path of figurative interpretation so dear to philosophical souls. Our
45 argument must start in this way. If it is a difficult thing to remove
out of sight of a mortal monarch, must it not be a thousandfold more
difficult to quit the vision of God and be gone, resolved henceforth
to shun the sight of him; in other words to become incapable of
receiving a mental picture of him through having lost the sight of
50 the soul's eye? Men who have suffered this loss under compulsion,
overwhelmed by the force of an inexorable power, deserve pity
rather than hatred. But those who have of their own free choice
turned away and departed from the Existent Being, transcending the
utmost limit of wickedness itself—for no evil could be found
55 equivalent to it—these must pay no ordinary penalties, but such as
are specially devised and far beyond the ordinary. Now no effort of
thought could hit upon a penalty greater and more unheard of than
to go forth into banishment from the Ruler of the Universe.

Adam, then, is driven out by God; Cain goes out voluntarily.
60 Moses is showing us each form of moral failure, one of free choice,

the other not so. The involuntary act, not owing its existence to our deliberate judgment, is to obtain later on such healing as the case admits of, '*for God shall raise up another seed in place of Abel whom Cain slew*' (Gen. 4. 25). This seed is a male offspring, Seth or 'Watering',
65 raised up to the soul whose fall did not originate in itself. The voluntary act, inasmuch as it was committed with forethought and of set purpose, must incur woes for ever beyond healing. For even as right actions that spring from previous intention are of greater worth than those that are involuntary, so, too, among sins those which are
70 involuntary are less weighty than those which are voluntary.

l. 4 *Figuratively* (τροπικώτερον). The word is a common one in Philo for his own method of treating the biblical text. He proceeds to give the principal ground for this treatment: the text as it stands is nonsense. God has not a face, and it is impossible to 'go out from' him. Consequently, Moses, the inspired sage, must have meant something other than he appeared to have said. It was in precisely this way that the Hellenistic writers allegorized the anthropomorphisms of Homer.

l. 8 *The impious doctrines of Epicurus.* Philo means his anthropomorphism. It is doubtful whether he is fair in his judgement of Epicurus, but he always mentions him unfavourably. Cf. p. 210.
The atheism of the Egyptians. The Egyptians were frequently blamed by philosophical writers for their worship of animals. But if we say, or imply, that God has a face how are we better than those who see him in a cat?

l. 19 *The Existent Being* (τὸ ὄν). This philosophical term for God is probably connected in Philo's mind with Exod. 3. 14 (see below, p. 291).

l. 44 *The path of figurative interpretation so dear to philosophical souls.* Philo certainly does not think of himself as a pioneer in allegorical work; he has predecessors and colleagues.

l. 59 *Adam, then, . . . Cain goes out voluntarily.* It is important to note that the use Philo makes of his allegorical method, once he has justified it, is ethical rather than metaphysical. This is often so; his allegorizing is akin to the Rabbinic Haggadah (see p. 184).

Etymological Arguments

These should perhaps be regarded as a special case of allegory. The question whether they reveal ignorance or knowledge of Hebrew is hardly capable of an answer. The etymologies are often very fanciful, and quite incorrect, but so sometimes are those of the Rabbis, who undoubtedly knew Hebrew.

231
De Abrahamo 81ff.

What has been said is attested by the alteration and change in his name, for his original name was Abram, but afterwards he was

addressed as Abraham [*Greek*, Abraam]. To the ear there was but the
duplication of one letter, alpha, but in fact and in the truth conveyed
5 this duplication showed a change of great importance. Abram is by
interpretation 'uplifted father'; Abraham, 'elect father of sound'. The
former signifies one called astrologer and meteorologist, one who
takes care of the Chaldean tenets as a father would of his children.
The latter signifies the Sage, for he uses 'sound' as a figure for spoken
10 thought and 'father' for the ruling mind, since the inward thought is
by its nature father of the uttered, being senior to it, the secret
begetter of what it has to say. 'Elect' signifies the man of worth, for
the worthless character is random and confused, while the good is
elect, chosen out of all for his merits.

ll. 2f.   *Abram . . . Abraham.* The reference is to Gen. 17. 5. An etymology is given
in the biblical text ('father of a multitude of nations'), but it is certainly
mistaken. It is probably wrong to seek any difference in meaning at all; the
longer name seems to be an orthographical variant of the shorter.

l. 6   *Uplifted father.* The true meaning of Abram seems to be 'My father (a divine
title) is exalted', or 'My father is the Exalted One' (both divine titles).
Elect father of sound. How Philo derived this meaning from Abraham is not
clear; possibly he was using traditional material.

l. 7   *Astrologer.* The Rabbinic literature also knows a tradition that Abraham
before he was called by God was an astrologer (see e.g. *Shabbath* 156a).

l. 9   *Spoken thought* (τὸν προφορικὸν λόγον). For Philo's conception of the Logos
see below. The relation of the outgoing word, or spoken thought, to the
inward word or reason (ἐνδιάθετος λόγος), or mind (νοῦς), is here made very
clear. In the present passage, mind, inward thought, and outward word are
all human. But if the νοῦς becomes the mind which creates and upholds all
things, then the προφορικὸς λόγος naturally undergoes a corresponding
transformation into the divine Word.

Philo's Doctrine of the Logos and other intermediate Beings

To speak of Philo's 'doctrine' of the Logos is certainly misleading if by
doctrine is meant an articulated and thoroughly thought-out system. The
background of his thought, and therefore the thought itself, is not simple.
The Logos played a considerable part in the Stoic account of the universe
(see p. 65), and there can be no doubt that Philo writes under the influence
of Stoic ideas. Not that these can be defined with precision: the Stoics
speak of a λόγος σπερματικός (seminal reason) which is the life-giving,
constitutive factor in all existence, through which alone plants, animals
and men have the life proper to them; they speak also of a λόγος ἐνδιάθετος
(immanent reason; see above) and a λόγος προφορικός (expressed reason;
see above). These last may belong to God (so far as the Stoic system may

be said to have a God), or to men. Men themselves think, and may express their thought to others; and it is this very faculty that relates them to God (or the universe). This Stoic Logos, then, is a quasi-physical principle of life, which is capable of being crystallized into concrete expressions of life. There is also, however, a Platonic element in Philo's use of Logos, which comes to particularly clear expression in the account of creation at *de Opif. M.* 24f., where the thought is as follows. When man surveys the physical universe there rises to his mind the thought of an ideal universe, of which the phenomenal world is but a copy. This ideal universe is called the κόσμος νοητός (since it exists in the mind, νοῦς). But, Philo urges, this ideal universe has an existence prior to our thought of it; it is in fact the thought of the divine mind which was before the creation of the visible world and was the means by which the visible world was made. This 'archetypal seal' (ἀρχέτυπος σφραγίς) may be called ὁ τοῦ θεοῦ λόγος, the Logos of God. In this identification Philo was no doubt influenced by the biblical cosmogony, in which creation is effected by the powerful word (or speech) of God. Here Philo's thought is in close contact with Jewish speculation about Wisdom; see pp. 298–303.

The passage now to be quoted is one of very many; it is perhaps more biblical than most of Philo's references to the Logos.

232

Quis Rerum divinarum Heres? 205f.

To his Word, his chief messenger, highest in age and honour, the Father of all has given the special prerogative, to stand on the border and separate the creature from the Creator. This same Word both pleads with the immortal as suppliant for afflicted mortality and acts
5 as ambassador of the ruler to the subject. He glories in this prerogative and proudly describes it in these words '*and I stood between the Lord and you*', that is neither uncreated as God, nor created as you, but midway between the two extremes, a surety to both sides; to the parent, pledging the creature that it should never altogether rebel
10 against the rein and choose disorder rather than order; to the child, warranting his hopes that the merciful God will never forget his own work. For 'I am the harbinger of peace to creation from that God whose will is to bring wars to an end, who is ever the guardian of peace.'

l. 1 *Chief messenger*, literally, *archangel*. The word seems to be of biblical origin; that is, Philo is identifying his Logos with the Old Testament 'angel of the Lord'.

l. 2 *To stand on the border*. The Logos is mediator; he mediates between creature and Creator both ontologically (since he is neither created nor creating) and epistemologically (since he brings to men knowledge of God, and of their relation to God).

l. 4   Suppliant. This description of the Logos recalls several New Testament statements about both Christ and the Holy Spirit, who make intercession for men. But it must be inferred from the following lines that the Logos is able to evoke God's mercy as being in himself a proof that men, who partake in him, are ultimately rational and will not altogether revolt from God.

l. 6   I stood between the Lord and you (Deut. 5. 5). Philo ignores the fact that these words were spoken by Moses. It is true that in the Targum of Onkelos the verse is paraphrased, 'I stood between the Memra (word) of the Lord and you', but in this form the text is even further from what Philo wishes it to mean.

The Logos is not the only intermediate being in Philo's view of the universe. Subordinate to him there are also the Powers (δυνάμεις). If it is difficult to make precise statements about the personality and functions of the Logos it is impossible to make them about the Powers. They are partly personifications of divine attributes, partly emanations from God's being; but they derive substance, as it were, from the common belief of antiquity in angels and demons.

In the following passage Philo allegorizes the narrative (Gen. 18) of the three travellers entertained by Abraham.

233

De Abrahamo 119–22

Here we may leave the literal exposition and begin the allegorical. Spoken words contain symbols of things apprehended by the understanding only. When, then, as at noontide God shines around the soul, and the light of the mind fills it through and through and 5 the shadows are driven from it by the rays which pour all around it, the single object presents to it a triple vision, one representing the reality, the other two the shadows reflected from it. Our life in the light which our senses perceive gives us a somewhat similar experience, for objects standing or moving often cast two shadows at 10 once. No one, however, should think that the shadows can be properly spoken of as God. To call them so is loose speaking, serving merely to give a clearer view of the fact which we are explaining, since the real truth is otherwise. Rather, as anyone who has approached nearest to the truth would say, the central place is held 15 by the Father of the Universe, who in the sacred scriptures is called he that IS as his proper name, while on either side of him are the senior potencies, the nearest to him, the creative and the kingly. The title of the former is God, since it made and ordered the All; the title of the latter is Lord, since it is the fundamental right of the maker to 20 rule and control what he has brought into being. So the central Being

with each of his potencies as his squire presents to the mind which has vision the appearance sometimes of one, sometimes of three: of one, when that mind is highly purified and passing beyond not merely the multiplicity of other numbers, but even the dyad which
25 is next to the unit, presses on to the ideal form which is free from mixture and complexity, and being self-contained needs nothing more; of three, when, as yet uninitiated into the highest mysteries, it is still a votary of the minor rites and unable to apprehend the Existent alone by itself and apart from all else, but only through its
30 actions, as either creative or ruling.

l. 1   *The allegorical.* The literal exposition drew out the example of Abraham's hospitality. Philo now seeks the underlying truth.

l. 6   *A triple vision.* Philo's similitude is not happy; it has been made to fit his exposition. Two of the travellers, he means, are but shadows of the third. He goes on to point out that the shadows (which later he will call Powers) are not to be spoken of as God.

l. 16   *He that IS.* See above, **230,** *l.* 19, where however the neuter, and therefore less personal form is used, as it is below (*l.* 29, the Existent).

ll. 18f.   *God . . . Lord* (θεός . . . κύριος). Philo of course knows well that these two names are used in the Greek Old Testament; but while all names are inadequate, ὁ ὤν (He that IS) is that which best expresses God in his absoluteness. 'God' and 'Lord' reveal him to men in his functions and attributes. 'God' describes God's creative and ordering power (ἡ ποιητικὴ δύναμις); 'Lord' suggests his sovereign power (ἡ βασιλικὴ δύναμις).

l. 27   *The highest mysteries.* For this metaphorical language see below, **236–7.**

Philo's own Religion and Ethics

It is possible to criticize Philo's theology and philosophy, especially on grounds of consistency; but it is impossible to mistake the sincere piety without which none of his works would have been written. Moral exhortation is thrown out on page after page of his works,
5 and it would be difficult to illustrate in short compass the Stoic–Jewish ethics which were the guide of his life. It must be sufficient to quote two passages which illustrate, first, the ideal of humble dependence upon God which is certainly the noblest contribution Philo makes to the history of religion, and, second, the moments of
10 ecstatic illumination which brought him into communion with God and inspired his literary activity.

234

Quis Rerum divinarum Heres? 24–9

[Philo is interpreting Gen. 15 2.] He who says, 'Master, what wilt thou give me?' virtually says no less than this, 'I am not ignorant of

thy transcendent sovereignty; I know the terrors of thy power; I
come before thee in fear and trembling, and yet again I am confident.
5 For thou hast vouchsafed to bid me fear not; thou hast given me a
tongue of instruction that I should know when I should speak (Isa.
50. 4), my mouth that was knitted up thou has unsewn, and when
thou hadst opened it, thou didst strengthen its nerves for speech; thou
hast taught me to say what should be said, confirming the oracle "I
10 will open thy mouth and teach thee what thou shalt speak" (Exod.
4. 12). For who was I, that thou shouldst impart speech to me, that
thou shouldst promise me something which stood higher in the scale
of goods than "gift" or grace, even a "reward"? Am I not a wanderer
from my country, an outcast from my kinsfolk, an alien from my
15 father's house? Do not all men call me excommunicate, exile,
desolate, disfranchised? But thou, Master, art my country, my
kinsfolk, my paternal hearth, my franchise, my free speech, my great
and glorious and inalienable wealth. Why then shall I not take
courage to say what I feel? Why shall I not inquire of thee and claim
20 to learn something more? Yet I, who proclaim my confidence,
confess in turn my fear and consternation, and still the fear and
confidence are not at war within me in separate camps, as one might
suppose, but are blended in a harmony. I find then a feast which does
not cloy in this blending, which has schooled my speech to be neither
25 bold without caution, nor cautious without boldness. For I have
learnt to measure my own nothingness, and to gaze with wonder on
the transcendent heights of thy loving-kindnesses. And when I
perceive that I am earth or cinders or whatever is still more worthless,
it is just then that I have confidence to come before thee, when I am
30 humbled, cast down to the clay, reduced to such an elemental state,
as seems not even to exist.'

235

De Migratione Abrahami 34f.

I feel no shame in recording my own experience, a thing I know
from its having happened to me a thousand times. On some occasions,
after making up my mind to follow the usual course of writing on
philosophical tenets, and knowing definitely the substance of what I
5 was to set down, I have found my understanding incapable of giving
birth to a single idea, and have given it up without accomplishing
anything, reviling my understanding for its self-conceit, and filled
with amazement at the might of him that IS to whom is due the
opening and closing of the soul-wombs. On other occasions, I have
10 approached my work empty and suddenly become full, the ideas
falling in a shower from above and being sown invisibly, so that
under the influence of the divine possession I have been filled with

corybantic frenzy and been unconscious of anything, place, persons present, myself, words spoken, lines written. For I obtained language,
15 ideas, an enjoyment of light, keenest vision, pellucid distinctness of objects, such as might be received through the eyes as the result of clearest shewing.

Finally, an attempt may be made to show briefly some of the evidence on which it has been held that Philo constructed out of Judaism a sort of mystery religion (see Chapter 6). There are not a few passages in which Philo makes wholesale use of language drawn from the mystery cults. The following is representative.

236

De Cherubin 48f.

These thoughts, ye initiated, whose ears are purified, receive into your souls as holy mysteries indeed and babble not of them to any of the profane. Rather as stewards guard the treasure in your own keeping, not where gold and silver, substances corruptible, are stored,
5 but where lies that most beautiful of all possessions, the knowledge of the Cause and of virtue, and, besides these two, of the fruit which is engendered by them both. But, if ye meet with any of the initiated, press him closely, cling to him, lest knowing of some still newer secret he hide it from you; stay not till you have learnt its full lesson.
10 I myself was initiated under Moses the God-beloved into his greater mysteries, yet when I saw the prophet Jeremiah and knew him to be not only himself enlightened, but a worthy minister of the holy secrets, I was not slow to become his disciple.

l. 1 *Ye initiated* . . . Almost all the words in this sentence are technical.

l. 10 *Greater mysteries.* At Eleusis there were 'greater' and 'lesser' mysteries. Here Philo distinguishes the greater mysteries of Moses from the lesser mysteries of the prophets—an interesting comment upon the state of the Old Testament canon in Philo's time.

l. 11 *I saw the prophet Jeremiah.* This kind of language is sufficient to show that throughout the present passage Philo is speaking metaphorically; it is unnecessary therefore to assume that he is turning Judaism into a real mystery cult.

l. 12 *Not only himself enlightened* . . . *holy secrets.* Once more the language is technical.

Philo's own view of the pagan mysteries was not likely to cause him to produce a rival to them.

237

De Specialibus Legibus i. 319f.

He banishes from the sacred legislation the lore of occult rites and
mysteries and all such imposture and buffoonery. He would not have
those who were bred in such a commonwealth as ours take part in
mummeries and clinging on to mystic fables despise the truth and
5 pursue things which have taken night and darkness for their province,
discarding what is fit to bear the light of day. Let none, therefore, of
the followers and disciples of Moses either confer or receive initiation
to such rites. For both in teacher and taught such action is gross
sacrilege. For tell me, ye mystics, if these things are good and
10 profitable, why do you shut yourselves up in profound darkness and
reserve their benefits for three or four alone, when by producing
them in the midst of the market-place you might extend them to
every man and thus enable all to share in security a better and happier
life?

l. 1 *He banishes.* The subject is Moses, and the ground for Philo's statement is the
LXX text of Deut. 23. 17(18).

l. 9 *For tell me* . . . This argument is borrowed from contemporary philosophy,
where it appears frequently.

11 Josephus

Josephus the son of Matthias, a Jew of Palestine, was born shortly after the Crucifixion and lived till about the end of the first century. He lived through, and participated in, the great revolt and war of AD 66–70, and had the unusual privilege of seeing them from both the Jewish and the Roman side. He makes much (see below) of his distinguished ancestry and of his personal gifts; and the latter indeed were not small. He wrote the history of his people from the Creation to his own times, and, though it is not free from faults, his story is one of the most valuable ancient records extant. He defended his race and his religion against attack, and was in fact one of the first apologists. There is no doubt that in his literary compositions he received assistance, especially in the writing of Greek, which was not his native tongue; and it is equally certain that his actions were sometimes guided by the motives of self-preservation rather than by loyalty to his cause. But the historian of the first century before and the first century after Christ may well be grateful to Josephus both for his personal observation and for the, often important, sources he incorporates.

The extant works of Josephus are:

1 *The Jewish War*. This work was originally written, immediately after the close of the war, in Aramaic, for the inhabitants of Upper Syria (*War* i. 3). Its aim was to urge upon these orientals the futility of further conflict with Rome, a piece of propaganda no doubt emanating from Josephus's Roman patrons (see below, **241**). Later an expanded version was drawn up in Greek, with the aid of literary assistants.

2 *The Antiquities of the Jews*. This much longer book, which begins with a paraphrase of the biblical narrative of creation, carries the history of the Jews from the earliest times up to the period of the *War*. It was published *c.* AD 93–4. It is possible to distinguish in it the work of several different assistants, who must have put Josephus's material into shape.

3 *The Life*. This autobiography seems to have been added to a second edition of the *Antiquities* (see *Ant.* xx. 259, 266f.). It was written in reply to a rival history, drawn up by Justus of Tiberias, who not only claimed that his history was superior to all others, Josephus's included, but also made allegations against Josephus himself. Josephus replies by recapitulating his version of the story. It appears incidentally (*Life* 359f.) that Justus's history, and therefore also the *Life*, was not written till after AD 100.

4 *Against Apion*. This book of Jewish apologetics was written because

Josephus found that the *Antiquities* was discredited by reason of the calumnies which certain persons were spreading about the Jews. Josephus makes a reply to this anti-semitic propaganda, writing, probably, in the first years of the second century.

5 There are indications that Josephus wrote, or intended to write, several other works, but not even fragments of them survive.

Biographical Material

It has already been indicated that we possess materials for a long and detailed life of Josephus. Here only the following essential points may be brought out.

238

Life 7–12

Distinguished as he was by his noble birth, my father Matthias was even more esteemed for his upright character, being among the most notable men in Jerusalem, our greatest city. Brought up with Matthias, my own brother by both parents, I made great progress in
5 my education, gaining a reputation for an excellent memory and understanding. While still a mere boy, about fourteen years old, I won universal applause for my love of letters; insomuch that the chief priests and leading men of the city used constantly to come to me for precise information on some particular of our ordinances. At
10 about the age of sixteen I determined to gain personal experience of the several sects into which our nation is divided. These, as I have frequently mentioned, are three in number—the first that of the Pharisees, the second that of the Sadducees, and the third that of the Essenes. I thought that, after a thorough investigation, I should be in
15 a position to select the best. So I submitted myself to hard training and laborious exercises and passed through the three courses. Not content, however, with the experience thus gained, on hearing of one named Bannus, who dwelt in the wilderness, wearing only such clothing as trees provided, feeding on such things as grew of
20 themselves, and using frequent ablutions of cold water, by day and night, for purity's sake, I became his devoted disciple. With him I lived for three years and, having accomplished my purpose, returned to the city. Being now in my nineteenth year I began to govern my life by the rules of the Pharisees, a sect having points of resemblance
25 to that which the Greeks call the Stoic school.

l. 1   *Noble birth.* Josephus has already (*Life* 2) claimed that his family was descended from the Hasmoneans; on whom see **118–26** and notes.

l. 7   *Universal applause.* It was at about the age of fourteen that a Jewish boy entered fully upon the responsibilities of Judaism. Josephus may exaggerate his precocity, but there is no reason to doubt it altogether.

l. 11   *The several sects.* See the descriptions in *War* ii. 119; *Ant.* xiii. 171; xviii. 11; and **135.** In trying to make the 'sects' (αἱρέσεις) intelligible to his Greek and Roman readers Josephus has to some extent distorted them (see below), but his descriptions are of great value; he knew them all at first hand.

l. 18   *Bannus* was clearly an ascetic; not an Essene, because he was a solitary, yet similar to the Essenes in some of his practices, especially his repeated lustrations. His desert life also calls to mind John the Baptist, but the differences also must be remembered. Bannus baptized himself, not converts, and he did not (so far as Josephus tells us) preach either the practice of righteousness or the advent of judgement and the kingdom of God.

l. 25   *The Stoic school.* The similarity between Pharisees and Stoics is in fact slight. Both groups were earnest seekers after the virtuous life, and both believed in some kind of destiny which could override man's choice; but between them lay the difference between a personal predestinating God, and an impersonal fatalism.

When Josephus was not quite thirty his career was interrupted by the outbreak of the Jewish war, in AD 66. Both in the *War* and in the *Life* he gives a detailed account of the part he played—and according to his own narrative it was a prominent one—in the campaigns, first on the one side, then on the other. He was soon entrusted with an important mission to Galilee.

239

Life 28f.

> After the defeat of Cestius, already mentioned, the leading men in Jerusalem, observing that the brigands and revolutionaries were well provided with arms, feared that, being without weapons themselves, they might be at the mercy of their adversaries, as in fact eventually
> 5 happened. Being informed, moreover, that the whole of Galilee had not yet revolted from Rome, and that a portion of it was still tranquil, they dispatched me with two other priests, Joazar and Judas, men of excellent character, to induce the disaffected to lay down their arms and to impress upon them the desirability of reserving these for the
> 10 picked men of the nation. The latter, such was the policy determined on, were to have their weapons constantly in readiness for future contingencies, but should wait and see what action the Romans would take.

l. 1   *Cestius Gallus* was governor of the Roman province of Syria. When the Jewish revolutionary movement first made head he marched with his forces to put down the disturbances, but, after preliminary successes, he was disastrously defeated at the pass of Bethhoron (*War* ii. 546; November 66), to the regret of Josephus and his friends, who had no desire for a struggle with Rome (though it is perhaps not unfair to suggest that had the war turned out differently they would have had no objection to taking advantage of a Jewish victory).

l. 2   *The brigands* (λῇστας) *and revolutionaries.* These were the nationalist group who were really enthusiastic in the prosecution of the war, and as Josephus says in this passage, ultimately gained control of Jewish policy and overcame the resistance of the moderates.

l. 7   *Two other priests.* Josephus was himself a priest. It has already been noted that Josephus was descended from the Hasmoneans, the priest-kings of the previous century. It is worth noting that unlike many of the priests he was a Pharisee (see above, **238**).

l. 12   *What action the Romans would take.* The official Jewish policy was opportunist. A greater measure of independence was desirable, but it was not worth while to take too many risks.

Josephus's activity as a Jewish general, though skilful and resourceful (as he tells us), did not last long. He was besieged in Jotapata (a town in Galilee); and in spite of his successful use of many stratagems, the town was captured by the Romans. Josephus and a few others escaped.

240

War iii. 392–408

Having thus survived both the war with the Romans and that with his own friends, Josephus was brought by Nicanor into Vespasian's presence. The Romans all flocked to see him, and from the multitude crowding around the general arose a hubbub of discordant voices:
5   some exulting at his capture, some threatening, some pushing forward to obtain a nearer view. The more distant spectators clamoured for the punishment of their enemy, but those close beside him recalled his exploits and marvelled at such a reversal of fortune. Of the officers there was not one who, whatever his past resentment, did not then
10 relent at the sight of him. Titus in particular was specially touched by the fortitude of Josephus under misfortunes and by pity for his youth. As he recalled the combatant of yesterday and saw him now a prisoner in his enemy's hands, he was led to reflect on the power of fortune, the quick vicissitudes of war, and the general instability of
15 human affairs. So he brought over many Romans at the time to share his compassion for Josephus, and his pleading with his father was the main influence in saving the prisoner's life. Vespasian, however, ordered him to be guarded with every precaution, intending shortly to send him to Nero.
20   On hearing this, Josephus expressed a desire for a private interview with him. Vespasian having ordered all to withdraw except his son Titus and two of his friends, the prisoner thus addressed him: 'You

imagine, Vespasian, that in the person of Josephus you have taken a
mere captive; but I come to you as a messenger of greater destinies.
25 Had I not been sent on this errand by God, I knew the law of the
Jews and how it becomes a general to die. To Nero do you send me?
Why then? Think you that [Nero and] those who before your
accession succeed him will continue? You will be Caesar, Vespasian,
you will be Emperor, you and your son here. Bind me then yet more
30 securely in chains and keep me for yourself; for you, Caesar, are
master not of me only, but of land and sea and the whole human
race. For myself, I ask to be punished by stricter custody, if I have
dared to trifle with the words of God.' To this speech Vespasian, at
the moment, seemed to attach little credit, supposing it to be a trick
35 of Josephus to save his life. Gradually, however, he was led to believe
it, for God was already rousing in him thoughts of empire and by
other tokens foreshadowing the throne. He found, moreover, that
Josephus had proved a veracious prophet in other matters. For one of
the two friends present at the private interview remarked: 'If these
40 words are not a nonsensical invention of the prisoner to avert the
storm which he has raised, I am surprised that Josephus neither
predicted the fall of Jotapata to its inhabitants nor his own captivity.'
To this Josephus replied that he had foretold to the people of Jotapata
that their city would be captured after forty-seven days and that he
45 himself would be taken alive by the Romans. Vespasian, having
privately questioned the prisoners on these statements and found
them true, then began to credit those concerning himself. While he
did not release Josephus from his custody or chains, he presented him
with raiment and other precious gifts, and continued to treat him
50 with kindness and solicitude, being warmly supported by Titus in
these courtesies.

l. 1   *Both the war with the Romans*, the Roman attack on Jotapata.
And that with his own friends. A number of Jewish soldiers, including Josephus,
took refuge in a cave. His suggestion of surrender to the Romans so enraged
his compatriots that they were for killing him. From this course he cleverly
dissuaded them, and urged them instead to agree to kill one another, drawing
lots to determine who should be killed first. As the lot fell out ('should one
say by fortune or by the providence of God?' asks Josephus) he was in the
end left alive with one other man, whom he was able to persuade to surrender
with him.

l. 2   *Vespasian*, sent by Nero to undertake the Jewish war in AD 66/67, himself
became emperor in AD 69. See **15**.

l. 10   *Titus*, Vespasian's son, who succeeded him in AD 79.

l. 12   *His youth*. It was now AD 67, and Josephus was thirty.

l. 19   *Nero*, the Emperor. See **11–14**. Josephus evidently thought that if he were
sent to Rome his prospects of safety would be small.

l. 28 *You will be Caesar.* The family name Caesar had already become a title of the reigning emperor. This prophecy is reported also by Suetonius, *Vespasian* 5, and by Dio Cassius (*Epitome* lxvi. 1).

l. 37 *By other tokens.* Cf. Tacitus, *Histories* i. 10; ii. 1. A belief (for which see Tacitus, *Hist.* v. 13, and Suetonius, *Vesp.* 4) had become current that 'persons proceeding from Judaea were to become masters of the world'.

In due course Josephus's prediction was fulfilled, and he was now secure in the imperial favour. He lived at Rome under the protection first of Vespasian, then of Titus. For some further information about the subsequent activities of Josephus see the short account of his literary works above. The following description of his career in Rome is given in the *Life*.

241

Life 422–30

When Titus had quelled the disturbances in Judaea, conjecturing that the lands which I held at Jerusalem would be unprofitable to me, because a Roman garrison was to be quartered there, he gave me another parcel of ground in the plain. On his departure for Rome, he
5 took me with him on board, treating me with every mark of respect. On our arrival in Rome I met with great consideration from Vespasian. He gave me a lodging in the house which he had occupied before he became Emperor; he honoured me with the privilege of Roman citizenship; and he assigned me a pension. He continued to
10 honour me up to the time of his departure from this life, without any abatement in his kindness towards me.

My privileged position excited envy and thereby exposed me to danger. A certain Jew, named Jonathan, who had promoted an insurrection in Cyrene, occasioning the destruction of two thousand
15 of the natives, whom he had induced to join him, on being sent in chains by the governor of the district to the Emperor, asserted that I had provided him with arms and money. Undeceived by this mendacious statement, Vespasian condemned him to death, and he was delivered over to execution. Subsequently, numerous accusations
20 against me were fabricated by persons who envied me my good fortune; but, by the providence of God, I came safe through all. Vespasian also presented me with a considerable tract of land in Judaea.

At this period I divorced my wife, being displeased at her
25 behaviour. She had borne me three children, of whom two died; one, whom I named Hyrcanus, is still alive. Afterwards I married a woman of Jewish extraction who had settled in Crete. She came of very distinguished parents, indeed the most notable people in that country. In character she surpassed many of her sex, as her subsequent

30 life showed. By her I had two sons, Justus the elder, and then
Simonides, surnamed Agrippa. Such is my domestic history.

The treatment which I received from the Emperors continued
unaltered. On Vespasian's decease Titus, who succeeded to the empire,
showed the same esteem for me as did his father, and never credited
35 the accusations to which I was constantly subjected. Domitian
succeeded Titus and added to my honours. He punished my Jewish
accusers, and for a similar offence gave orders for the chastisement of
a slave, a eunuch and my son's tutor. He also exempted my property
in Judaea from taxation—a mark of the highest honour to the
40 privileged individual. Moreover, Domitia, Caesar's wife, never ceased
conferring favours upon me.

Such are the events of my whole life; from them let others judge
as they will of my character.

Having now, most excellent Epaphroditus, rendered you a
45 complete account of our antiquities, I shall here for the present
conclude my narrative.

l. 13 *Jonathan.* Another, and somewhat fuller, account of this man's plots is given
in the *War* vii. 437–50. His revolt was part of the widespread activity of the
Sicarii after AD 70. The revolt was put down by Catullus and Jonathan burnt
alive.

l. 24 *I divorced my wife, being displeased at her behaviour.* This was Josephus's second
wife. He had previously married at the order of Vespasian (*Life* 414f.), but
his wife, one of the women taken captive by the Romans at Caesarea, soon
left him. For the Jewish law of divorce see Deut. 24. 1–4, and for its
interpretation by the School of Hillel and the School of Shammai see **154**
and note. Josephus does not tell us whether he was displeased with his wife
on moral or other grounds.

l. 35 *Domitian,* emperor AD 81–96.

l. 36 *My Jewish accusers.* Josephus's unpopularity with his compatriots is plain, and
understandable.

l. 44 *Epaphroditus.* The *Life*, the work *Against Apion*, and the *Antiquities* are all
dedicated to Epaphroditus, who appears to have succeeded after the death of
Domitian to the position of Josephus's imperial patrons. Josephus's
Epaphroditus may have been the grammarian of that name, but this is quite
uncertain.

Josephus on John the Baptist, Jesus Christ, and James

A small quantity of the valuable historical material given by Josephus
appears in other parts of this book (see especially Chapter 7). It is
unnecessary to give a further selection here, but it will be convenient to
add his famous and important references to John the Baptist, Jesus, and
James the Just.

242

Antiquities xviii. 116–19

Josephus's reference to the Baptist arises almost casually out of his account
of the affairs of Herod Antipas.

> Some of the Jews thought that Herod's army had been destroyed by
> God as a just punishment for his treatment of John called the Baptist.
> Herod killed him, though he was a good man and commanded the
> Jews to practise virtue, by exercising justice towards one another and
> 5 piety towards God, and to come together to baptism. For the baptism
> would be acceptable to God if they used it, not for the putting away
> of certain sins, but for the purification of the body, the soul having
> previously been cleansed by righteousness. Now when the rest
> crowded together to him (for they were greatly moved by hearing
> 10 his words) Herod was afraid lest John's great influence over the
> people might lead to a revolt; for they seemed ready to do anything
> he advised. He therefore thought it much the better course to
> anticipate any rebellion that might arise from him by destroying
> him, than be involved in difficulties through an actual revolution
> 15 and then regret it. So John, a victim to Herod's suspicion, was sent to
> Machaerus (the fortress metnioned above), and there killed.

l. 1   *Herod's army had been destroyed by God.* The Herod in question is Herod
Antipas, a son of Herod the Great and tetrarch of Galilee (see e.g. Luke 3. 1).
His army had been destroyed by Aretas, king of the Nabataean Arabs, who
had been enraged by Herod's treatment of his (Aretas's) daughter, to whom
he was married. Herod, who wished to marry Herodias, his brother's wife,
planned to divorce the daughter of Aretas; she however heard of his plans
and escaped to her father, who collected an army and destroyed Herod's
forces. This narrative does not agree in all particulars with that of Mark 6.
14–29; there is also a difficulty regarding its date. The defeat of Herod by
Aretas took place not long before the death of Tiberius in March AD 37,
which is long after any date that can be reasonably deduced from the Gospels
for the death of John. Nevertheless, Aretas may have lacked an earlier
opportunity and his anger may have continued to smoulder for seven years
or more.

l. 2   *John called the Baptist.* It is possible that the title was interpolated from a
Christian source; but Josephus has not a little to say about John's practice of
baptizing and it is not impossible that his use of the name is independent.
The general picture of John that he presents is different from that of the
Christian sources; the eschatological and messianic element is lacking (but
see note on *l.* 4).

l. 3   *Herod killed him.* Josephus does not relate the 'bazaar story' of Mark 6. His
interests and tastes were different from those of the primitive Christian
communities.

l. 4   *To practise virtue.* The evangelists (Matt. 3. 7–10 = Luke 3. 7ff.; Luke 3. 10–
14) provide some account of John's moral teaching; but their primary

interest was in his prediction of the Coming One. Josephus, writing in Rome, would no doubt find it convenient to avoid the discussion of such matters (a Christian interpolator would not have omitted them); but in point of fact his later references to Herod's fear of a revolutionary movement show that the Baptist was concerned in messianic activity which either was, or showed the possibility of becoming, political and military.

l. 5   *Baptism ... baptism.* Josephus uses two words, one of which (βαπτισμός) is rare in the New Testament, while the other (βάπτισις) does not occur at all. This fact does not suggest Christian influence or interpolation.

l. 6   *Not for the putting away of certain sins, but for the purification of the body.* Josephus's account hardly makes sense. The multitudes who were baptized by John did not go to Jordan to wash. There may be anti-Christian propaganda here; but compare Josephus's remark on the baptisms of the Essenes and of Bannus; see **135, 238**.

l. 8   *The rest.* The expression is awkward, and emendations have been proposed. The Latin *perplurima multitudo*, a very numerous multitude, gives the sense. It does not seem to be correct to distinguish between a company of ascetics who before John's ministry had practised virtue and the 'rest' who subsequently joined the movement.

l. 16   *Machaerus.* The Gospels do not name the place where John was killed. It is sometimes said that Herod's birthday feast would not have been held in a gloomy fortress like Machaerus; but compare *War* vii. 175 '. . . a palace with magnificently spacious and beautiful apartments'.

243
Antiquities xviii. 63f.

The authenticity of Josephus's reference to Jesus as it now stands is very questionable. The passage is found in all the MSS. of the *Antiquities* (but none of these is older than the eleventh century), and was known to Eusebius (fourth century); but Origen (first half of the third century) does not seem to have read it, at least in its present form, since he says plainly that Josephus did not believe Jesus to be the Christ. It does not however follow from this fact that the whole passage is spurious. It will be indicated in the notes that several clauses could not have been written by Josephus; but when these are removed there remains a notice of Jesus comparable with that of John the Baptist, a notice from which all messianic and eschatological claims have been suppressed. It is, moreover, possible that Christian omissions as well as Christian interpolations should be allowed for; Christian writers, adding material in praise of Jesus, may quite well have omitted what they thought derogatory to his person.

About this time arose Jesus, a wise man, if indeed it be lawful to call him a man. For he was a doer of wonderful deeds, and a teacher of men who gladly receive the truth. He drew to himself many both of the Jews and of the Gentiles. He was the Christ; and when Pilate, on

5 the indictment of the principal men among us, had condemned him
to the cross, those who had loved him at the first did not cease to do
so, for he appeared to them again alive on the third day, the divine
prophets having foretold these and ten thousand other wonderful
things about him. And even to this day the race of Christians, who
10 are named from him, has not died out.

l. 1   *About this time.* Josephus has just described two disturbances made by the
Jews under the provocation of Pilate who had (*a*) brought into Jerusalem
military standards bearing images of the emperor, (*b*) diverted Temple funds
for the building of an aqueduct. The immediately preceding passage ends,
'And so the disturbance (στάσις, cf. Mark 15. 7, *et al.*) came to an end.' It is in
such a context as this that Josephus might be expected to refer to the messianic
disturbances which accompanied the execution of Jesus.

    A wise man. This does not seem to be a Christian description of Jesus.
Josephus is probably 'civilizing' Jesus as he did John.

    If indeed it be lawful to call him a man. This, on the other hand, is almost
certainly a Christian addition. One who was not a Christian would have no
hesitation in calling Jesus a man.

l. 3   *Many . . . of the Gentiles.* Either this is a Christian interpolation, or Josephus
is writing out of his knowledge of the composition of the Church of his day.

l. 4   *He was the Christ.* This must be a Christian interpolation; it is quite
impossible to make Josephus's words mean, 'He was believed to be the
Christ.'

l. 5   *On the indictment . . . condemned him to the cross.* This agrees sufficiently with
the narratives of the gospels, but it is not necessarily to be ruled out as an
interpolation, especially as 'those who loved him at the first' is not a
specifically Christian phrase.

l. 7   *He appeared to them . . . about him.* These words must have been written by a
Christian.

l. 9   *The race of Christians.* The expression (φῦλον) is not found in the earliest
Christian literature, though in the second century Christians are spoken of as
a 'new (i.e. neither Jewish nor Gentile) race (γένος)' (*Epistle to Diognetus* 1).

244

Antiquities xx. 200

Like the reference to John the Baptist, Josephus's allusion to James the
brother of Jesus arises out of his account of the political history of the time.
It is repeated by Eusebius (*HE* II, xxiii. 22), who also cites in the same
passage another paragraph which he (in company with Origen) attributes
to Josephus but which is not in our MSS., and Hegesippus's, somewhat
divergent, narrative of James's death.

    Ananus, therefore, being of this character, and supposing that he had
a favourable opportunity on account of the fact that Festus was dead,
and Albinus was still on the way, called together the Sanhedrin, and

brought before them the brother of Jesus, the so-called Christ, James
5 by name, together with some others, and accused them of violating
the law, and condemned them to be stoned.

l. 1   *Ananus, being of this character.* He was a son of the Annas mentioned in the
Gospels as participating in the arraignment of Jesus; Josephus has in the
context described him as exceptionally bold and reckless.

ll. 2f.   *Festus ... Albinus* were successive procurators of Judaea. The latter was
particularly rapacious and unscrupulous, and did much to provoke the revolt
of AD 66; he took office in AD 62, which accordingly will be the date of this
incident.

l. 4   *The so-called Christ.* This seems to be the best rendering of the phrase in the
MSS. of Josephus (τοῦ λεγομένου Χριστοῦ). It is noteworthy that Eusebius
transposes the words so as to read τοῦ Χριστοῦ λεγομένου, perhaps with the
intention of giving the sense, 'who was called Christ'.

l. 6   *To be stoned.* This was the normal punishment for blasphemy and certain
other offences; see *Sanhedrin* 7. 4. Hegesippus has a different and more
circumstantial account which it is worth while to compare with *Sanhedrin*
9. 6.

Josephus as Apologist

The Jews were perhaps the most favoured and the most hated race in the
Roman Empire. Their peculiarities led to incessant friction with other
races, yet they also, unlike other nations, were constantly active in
commending their religious practices to others. Their self-defence and
their zeal for their faith led to a fairly considerable literary output, of
which little remains to us. Philo (see Chapter 10) may be regarded as a
propagandist at the higher level; he was a thinker concerned to show the
unity of his own faith with the best of Greek philosophy, and to set it
forth in terminology which the Greek mind could understand and accept.
Josephus works at a lower level; he rebuts slanders, demonstrates the
antiquity of his faith, and commends the piety and virtue which it
engenders. The whole of the *Antiquities* is a kind of apology; but the work
Against Apion shows him most clearly as an apologist. The following
passages bring out characteristic arguments.

245
Against Apion i. 69–72

Josephus introduces his argument for the antiquity of his race. The
Egyptians reproached the Greeks as a youthful race; Josephus would show
that the Jews were younger than neither of these peoples.

> Suppose that we were to presume to dispute the antiquity of the
> Greek nation and to base our contention on the absence of any

mention of them in our literature. Would they not undoubtedly laugh us to scorn? They would, I imagine, offer the very reasons
5 which I have just given for such silence, and produce the neighbouring nations as witnesses to their antiquity. Well, that is just what I shall endeavour to do. As my principal witnesses I shall cite the Egyptians and Phoenicians, whose evidence is quite unimpeachable; for the Egyptians, the whole race without exception, and among the
10 Phoenicians the Tyrians, are notoriously our bitterest enemies. Of the Chaldaeans I could not say the same, because they are the original ancestors of our race, and this blood-relationship accounts for the mention which is made of the Jews in their annals. After producing the evidence supplied by these nations, I shall then bring forward
15 those Greek historians who have spoken of the Jews, in order to deprive our jealous enemies of even this pretext for controversy.

l. 4   Reasons which I have just given. The principal reasons given by Josephus for the paucity of references to the Jews in Greek authors are that the cities of the Jews lay inland, and that as a people they gave themselves rather to the cultivation of their land and the education of their children than to such activities as piracy or military aggrandizement, which might have made them better known.

l. 7   Egyptians. Josephus draws his evidence from Manetho, an Egyptian priest of about 300 BC. Josephus takes over from him the well known (though inaccurate) identification of the Israelites with the Hyksos, who lived in Egypt in the second millennium BC.

l. 8   Phoenicians. Here Josephus's evidence is more varied. He draws it from the archives of Tyre; a certain Dius, 'an accurate historian of Phoenicia', and Menander of Ephesus.

l. 11   Chaldaeans. Josephus cites Berosus, a priest of the temple of Bel at Babylon, about 300 BC.

l. 15   Greek historians. Josephus mentions and quotes Pythagoras, Theophrastus, Herodotus, Choerilus, Aristotle (as quoted by Clearchus), Hecataeus, and Agatharcides; then lists a number more, whose briefer allusions he does not trouble to record.

We may next take examples of the way in which Josephus rebuts slanders made against his people and their religion.

246

Against Apion ii. 79–85

I am no less amazed at the proceedings of the authors who supplied him with his materials, I mean Posidonius and Apollonius Molon. On the one hand they charge us with not worshipping the same gods as other people; on the other, they tell lies and invent absurd
5 calumnies about our Temple, without showing any consciousness of

impiety. Yet to high-minded men nothing is more disgraceful than a lie, of any description, but above all on the subject of a Temple of world-wide fame and commanding sanctity.

10 Within this sanctuary Apion has the effrontery to assert that the Jews kept an ass's head, worshipping that animal and deeming it worthy of the deepest reverence; the fact was disclosed, he maintains, on the occasion of the spoliation of the Temple by Antiochus Epiphanes, when the head, made of gold and worth a high price, was discovered. On this I will first remark that, even if we did possess any 15 such object, an Egyptian should be the last person to reproach us; for an ass is no worse than the cats, he-goats, and other creatures which in his country rank as gods. Next, how did it escape him that the facts convict him of telling an incredible lie? Throughout our history we have kept the same laws, to which we are eternally faithful. Yet, 20 notwithstanding the various calamities which our city, like others, has undergone, when the Temple was occupied by successive conquerors, [Antiochus] the Pious, Pompey the Great, Licinius Crassus, and most recently Titus Caesar, they found there nothing of the kind, but the purest type of religion, the secrets of which we may 25 not reveal to aliens. That the raid of Antiochus Epiphanes on the Temple was iniquitous, and that it was impecuniosity which drove him to invade it, when he was not an open enemy, that he attacked us, his allies and friends, and that he found there nothing to deserve ridicule; these facts are attested by many sober historians. Polybius of 30 Megalopolis, Strabo the Cappadocian, Nicolas of Damascus, Timagenes, Castor the chronicler, and Apollodorus all assert that it was impecuniosity which induced Antiochus, in violation of his treaties with the Jews, to plunder the Temple with its stores of gold and silver. There is the evidence which Apion should have considered, 35 had he not himself been gifted with the mind of an ass and the impudence of the dog, which his countrymen are wont to worship. An outsider can make no sense of his lies.

l. 2 *Him*, that is Apion, Josephus's adversary.
Posidonius, the famous Stoic philosopher; see **71–2**.
Apollonius Molon, a teacher of rhetoric in the first century BC; he seems to have made a point of attacking the Jews, and Josephus several times replies to his charges.

l. 12 *The spoliation of the temple by Antiochus Epiphanes*. For this, cf. *Ant.* xii. 248; *War* i. 32; 1 Macc. 1; 2 Macc. 5; and see **117, 118**. It took place *c.* 168 BC.

l. 22 *[Antiochus] the Pious.* The reference must be to Antiochus VII Eusebes (or Pious), who received his title from his behaviour at the siege of Jerusalem in 135 BC (*Ant.* xiii. 244). The MSS. of Josephus (in Latin only at this point) read Dius, probably by confusion with Antiochus VI Theos (in Latin, Diuus). *Pompey the Great* captured Jerusalem in 63 BC. See **126**.

l. 22   *Licinius Crassus* took the city in 54–53 BC.

l. 23   *Titus Caesar*, the victor of AD 70. See **142**.

247

Against Apion ii. 91–6

    Apion, who is here the spokesman of others, asserts that:
Antiochus found in the Temple a couch, on which a man was
reclining, with a table before him laden with a banquet of fish of the
sea, beasts of the earth, and birds of the air, at which the poor fellow
5 was gazing in stupefaction. The king's entry was instantly hailed by
him with adoration, as about to procure him profound relief; falling
at the king's knees, he stretched out his right hand and implored him
to set him free. The king reassured him and bade him tell him who
he was, why he was living there, what was the meaning of his
10 abundant fare. Thereupon, with sighs and tears, the man, in a pitiful
tone, told the tale of his distress. He said that he was a Greek and that,
while travelling about the province for his livelihood, he was
suddenly kidnapped by men of a foreign race and conveyed to the
Temple; there he was shut up and seen by nobody, but was fattened
15 on feasts of the most lavish description. At first these unlooked for
attentions deceived him and caused him pleasure; suspicion followed,
then consternation. Finally, on consulting the attendants who waited
upon him, he heard of the unutterable law of the Jews, for the sake
of which he was being fed. The practice was repeated annually at a
20 fixed season. They would kidnap a Greek foreigner, fatten him up
for a year, and then convey him to a wood, where they slew him,
sacrificed his body with their customary ritual, partook of his flesh,
and, while immolating the Greek, swore an oath of hostility to the
Greeks. The remains of their victim were then thrown into a pit.
25 The man (Apion continues) stated that he had now but a few days
left to live, and implored the king, out of respect for the gods of
Greece, to defeat this Jewish plot upon his life-blood and to deliver
him from his miserable predicament.

l. 2   *Antiochus*, that is, Antiochus Epiphanes. See **116–18**.

l. 22 *Partook of his flesh ... swore an oath of hostility to the Greeks.* How many
intelligent non-Jews believed slanders of this kind it is difficult to estimate.
Behind it lie, it appears, a perversion of the Passover ritual, and the undoubted
aloofness of the Jews from the whole range of pagan life. Socially and in
religion the Jews refused the ordinary tolerant give and take of the
cosmopolitan life of the Mediterranean world. Their motives were not
understood, and it is not altogether surprising that such tales as these,
ridiculous as they are, were disseminated.

l. 28 *His miserable predicament.* So far Josephus quotes Apion. His reply is
interesting, but so long that it must be summarized rather than quoted. The

story, he points out, is simply ridiculous. Why should only Greeks be murdered? For how few Jews would the body of one Greek suffice! Why did Antiochus never produce the man? But the strongest argument lies in a plain and positive account of the Temple and its management, which are such as to make the allegations quite impossible. Josephus's account of the Temple has considerable value apart from its apologetic purpose.

Lastly we may hear Josephus at his best, extolling the religion and virtue practised among his fellow-countrymen.

248

Against Apion ii. 164–71

There is endless variety in the details of the customs and laws which prevail in the world at large. To give but a summary enumeration: some peoples have entrusted the supreme political power to monarchs, others to oligarchies, yet others to the masses. Our lawgiver, however,
5 was attracted by none of these forms of polity, but gave to his constitution the form of what—if a forced expression be permitted—may be termed a 'theocracy' placing all sovereignty and authority in the hands of God. To him he persuaded all to look, as the author of all blessings, both those which are common to all mankind, and those
10 which they had won for themselves by prayer in the crises of their history. He convinced them that no single action, no secret thought, could be hid from him. He represented him as one, uncreated and immutable to all eternity; in beauty surpassing all mortal thought, made known to us by his power, although the nature of his real
15 being passes knowledge.
That the wisest of the Greeks learnt to adopt these conceptions of God from principles with which Moses supplied them, I am not now concerned to urge; but they have borne abundant witness to the excellence of these doctrines, and to their consonance with the nature
20 and majesty of God. In fact, Pythagoras, Anaxagoras, Plato, the Stoics who succeeded him, and indeed nearly all the philosophers appear to have held similar views concerning the nature of God. These, however, addressed their philosophy to the few, and did not venture to divulge their true beliefs to the masses who had their own
25 preconceived opinions; whereas our lawgiver, by making practice square with precept, not only convinced his own contemporaries, but so firmly implanted this belief concerning God in their descendants to all future generations that it cannot be moved. The cause of his success was that the very nature of his legislation made it
30 [always] far more useful than any other; for he did not make religion a department of virtue, but the various virtues—I mean, justice, temperance, fortitude, and mutual harmony in all things between the members of the community—departments of religion. Religion

governs all our actions and occupations and speech; none of these
35 things did our lawgiver leave unexamined or indeterminate.

l. 7 *Theocracy* (θεοκρατία). Liddell and Scott quote no other use of the word, and
it seems from Josephus's own language that he has coined it. The thought
that God alone is the true ruler of Israel is, of course, common in the Old
Testament.

l. 17 *Principles with which Moses supplied them.* The notion that the best of Greek
philosophy was plagiarized from Moses was current long before Josephus
(e.g. in the Jewish apologist Aristobulus, *apud* Eusebius, *Praep. Ev.* xiii, xii.),
and was taken up by the Christians (e.g. Justin, *Apol.* i. 60). There is no
evidence that the Greek writers were in any way familiar with the
Pentateuch.

l. 31 *Justice, temperance, fortitude, and mutual harmony.* These are the four cardinal
virtues of the Platonists, except that here mutual harmony takes the place of
understanding.

l. 33 *Departments of religion.* If Josephus has above quite misrepresented the relation
between Greek and Jewish thought (since Hellenistic Jewish thought at least
was much indebted to the philosophers) he has here seized upon a profound
truth of biblical theology.

Josephus as Interpreter of Scripture

Especially in his account of *Jewish Antiquities* (see above, p. 269) Josephus
was obliged to make considerable use of the Old Testament, often
paraphrasing it and thereby to some extent revealing the text in which he
read it and the way he interpreted it. It is clear that he was able to read it
in both Hebrew and Greek, and he claims to have been trained as a
Pharisee; he must therefore have been familiar with early rabbinic
exegesis. He does not use the Old Testament, as Philo did, in the manner
of a philosopher and theologian; the following passages give some
examples of the way in which he drew upon it for mainly historical
purposes.

249

Antiquities i. 27–39

In the beginning God created the heaven and the earth. The earth
had not come into sight, but was hidden in thick darkness, and a
breath from above sped over it, when God commanded that there
should be light. It came, and, surveying the whole of matter, He
5 divided the light from the darkness, calling the latter night and the
former day, and naming morning and evening the dawn of the light
and its cessation. This then should be the first day, but Moses spoke

of it as 'one' day; I could explain why he did so now, but, having
promised to render an account of the causes of everything in a special
10 work, I defer till then the explanation of this point also. After this,
on the second day, He set the heaven above the universe, when He
was pleased to sever this from the rest and to assign it a place apart,
congealing ice about it and withal rendering it moist and rainy to
give the benefit of the dews in a manner congenial to the earth. On
15 the third day He established the earth, pouring around it the sea; and
on the self-same day plants and seeds sprang forthwith from the soil.
On the fourth He adorned the heaven with sun and moon and the
other stars, prescribing their motions and courses to indicate the
revolutions of the seasons. The fifth day He let loose in the deep and
20 in the air the creatures that swim or fly, linking them in partnership
and union to generate and to increase and multiply their kind. The
sixth day He created the race of four-footed creatures, making them
male and female: on this day also He formed man. Thus, so Moses
tells us, the world and everything in it was made in six days in all;
25 and on the seventh God rested and had respite from His labours, for
which reason we also pass this day in respose from toil and call it the
sabbath, a word which in the Hebrew language means 'rest'.

And here, after the seventh day, Moses begins to interpret nature,
writing on the formation of man in these terms: 'God fashioned man
30 by taking dust from the earth and instilled into him spirit and soul.'
Now this man was called Adam, which in Hebrew signifies 'red',
because he was made from the red earth kneaded together; for such
is the colour of the true virgin soil. And God brought before Adam
the living creatures after their kinds, exhibiting both male and
35 female, and gave them the names by which they are still called to this
day. Then seeing Adam to be without female partner and consort
(for indeed there was none), and looking with astonishment at the
other creatures who had their mates, He extracted one of his ribs
while he slept and from it formed woman; and when she was
40 brought to him Adam recognized that she was made from himself.
In the Hebrew tongue woman is called *essa*; but the name of that
first woman was Eve, which signifies 'mother of all (living)'.

Moses further states that God planted eastward a park, abounding
in all manner of plants, among them being the tree of life and another
45 of the wisdom by which might be distinguished what was good and
what was evil.

---

l. 1   The parallels between Josephus and the Old Testament, especially the LXX
version, are too evident to be pointed out; the differences are worth study—
for example the fact that he writes *created* (ἔκτισεν) rather than *made*
(ἐποίησεν).

l. 3   *A breath*: the word is πνεῦμα, often translated spirit.

l. 9   *A special work.* Passages such as *Ant.* iv. 198; xx. 268 suggest that Josephus may have begun this work, which he intended to write after completing the *Antiquities*, but it is not extant and was probably never completed and published.

ll. 31, 32   *Adam . . . red . . . red earth.* Earth is in Hebrew *'ªdamah* (אדמה), but Josephus' etymological connections are almost certainly wrong.

l. 35   *And gave them the names.* This translation is strictly correct, since Josephus gives no hint of a change of subject, so that the subject of *gave* will be that of *brought.* But it may well be that Josephus in fact thought as Genesis does that Adam named the creatures, but expressed himself inaccurately.

l. 41   *Essa:* Hebrew *ishshah,* אשה.

l. 42   *Eve, which signifies 'mother of all (living).'* Some MSS omit *living* (τῶν ζώντων). *Eve* means *life; mother of all living* is an interpretation of the name.

250

Antiquities iii. 83–92

Such was their mood when suddenly Moses appeared, radiant and high-hearted. The mere sight of him rid them of their terrors and prompted brighter hopes for the future; the air too became serene and purged of its recent disturbances on the arrival of Moses.
5 Thereupon he summoned the people to assembly to hear what God had said to him, and, when all were collected, he stood on an eminence whence all might hear him and 'Hebrews', said he, 'God, as of yore, has received me graciously and, having dictated for you rules for a blissful life and an ordered government, is coming Himself into
10 the camp. In His name, then, and in the name of all that through Him has already been wrought for us, scorn not the words now to be spoken, through looking only on me, the speaker, or by reason that it is a human tongue that addresses you. Nay, mark but their excellence and ye will discern the majesty of Him who conceived
15 them and, for your profit, disdained not to speak them to me. For it is not Moses, son of Amaram and Jochabad, but He who constrained the Nile to flow for your sake a blood-red stream and tamed with divers plagues the pride of the Egyptians, He who opened for you a path through the sea, He who caused meat to descend from heaven
20 when ye were destitute, water to gush from the rock when ye lacked it, He thanks to whom Adam partook of the produce of land and sea, Noah escaped the deluge, Abraham our forefather passed from wandering to settle in the land of Canaan, He who caused Isaac to be born of aged parents, Jacob to be graced by the virtues of twelve
25 sons, Joseph to become lord of the Egyptians' might—He it is who favours you with these commandments, using me for interpreter. Let them be had by you in veneration: battle for them more jealously than for children and wives. For blissful will be your life, do ye but follow these: ye will enjoy a fruitful earth, a sea unvext by tempest,

30 a breed of children born in nature's way, and ye will be redoubtable
to your foes. For I have been admitted to a sight of God, I have
listened to an immortal voice: such care hath He for our race and for
its perpetuation.'

That said, he made the people advance with their wives and
35 children, to hear God speak to them of their duties, to the end that
the excellence of the spoken words might not be impaired by human
tongue in being feebly transmitted to their knowledge. And all heard
a voice which came from on high to the ears of all, in such wise that
not one of those ten words escaped them which Moses has left
40 inscribed on the two tables. These words it is not permitted us to
state explicitly, to the letter, but we will indicate their purport.

The first word teaches us that God is one and that He only must
be worshipped. The second commands us to make no image of any
living creature for adoration, the third not to swear by God on any
45 frivolous matter, the fourth to keep every seventh day by resting
from all work, the fifth to honour our parents, the sixth to refrain
from murder, the seventh not to commit adultery, the eighth not to
steal, the ninth not to bear false witness, the tenth to covet nothing
that belongs to another.

l. 41 *To the letter.* There seems to be no parallel to this rule that the wording of
the Ten Commandments is to be kept secret. It is reminiscent of the rule that
the Tetragrammaton must not be pronounced.

251

Antiquities viii. 111–121

When the king had thus spoken to the crowd, he looked again
toward the temple and, raising his right hand up to heaven, said, 'Not
by deeds is it possible for men to return thanks to God for the benefits
they have received, for the Deity stands in need of nothing and is
5 above any such recompense. But with that (gift of speech), O Lord,
through which we have been made by Thee superior to other
creatures, we cannot but praise Thy greatness and give thanks for
Thy kindnesses to our house and the Hebrew people, for with what
other thing is it more fitting for us to appease Thee when wrathful,
10 and, when ill disposed, to make Thee gracious than with our voice,
which we have from the air, and know to ascend again through this
element? And so, with my voice I render thanks to Thee, first for
my father's sake, whom Thou didst raise from obscurity to such great
glory, and next on my own behalf, for whom unto the present day
15 Thou hast done all that Thou didst foretell. And I beseech Thee
henceforth to grant whatever God has power to bestow on men
esteemed by Thee, and to increase our house for ever, as Thou didst
promise David, my father, both in his lifetime and when he was near

death, saying that the kingship should remain among us and that his
20 descendants should transmit it to numberless successors. These things,
therefore, do Thou grant us, and to my sons give that virtue in which
Thou delightest. Beside these things I entreat Thee also to send some
portion of Thy spirit to dwell in the temple, that Thou mayest seem
to us to be on earth as well. For to Thee even the whole vault of
25 heaven and all its host is but a small habitation—how much less this
poor temple! Nonetheless I pray Thee to guard it for ever from
sacking by our enemies, as Thine own temple, and to watch over it
as Thine own possession. And if ever the people sin and then because
of their sin are smitten by some evil from Thee, by unfruitfulness of
30 the soil or a destructive pestilence or any such affliction with which
Thou visitest those who transgress any of the sacred laws, and if they
all gather to take refuge in the temple, entreating Thee and praying
to be saved, then do Thou hearken to them as though Thou wert
within, and pity them and deliver them from their misfortunes. And
35 this help I ask of Thee not alone for the Hebrews who may fall into
error, but also if any come even from the ends of the earth or from
wherever it may be and turn to Thee, imploring to receive some
kindness, do Thou hearken and give it them. For so would all men
know that Thou Thyself didst desire that this house should be built
40 for Thee in our land, and also that we are not inhumane by nature
nor unfriendly to those who are not of our country, but wish that all
men equally should receive aid from Thee and enjoy Thy blessings.'

Having spoken in these words, he threw himself upon the ground
and did obeisance for a long time; then he arose and brought sacrifices
45 to the altar, and, when he had heaped it with whole victims, he knew
that God was gladly accepting the sacrifice, for a fire darted out of
the air and, in the sight of all the people, leaped upon the altar and,
seizing on the sacrifice, consumed it all. When this divine
manifestation occurred, all the people supposed it to be a sign that
50 God would thereafter dwell in the temple, and with joy they fell
upon the ground and did obeisance. But the king began to bless God
and urged the multitude to do the like, seeing that they now had
tokens of God's good will toward them, and to pray that such would
be His treatment of them always and that their minds might be kept
55 pure from all evil as they continued in righteousness and worship
and in observance of the commandments which God had given them
through Moses; for thus would the Hebrew nation be happy and the
most blessed of all the races of men. And he exhorted them to
remember that in the same way in which they had acquired their
60 present blessings they would also preserve them surely and would
make them greater and more numerous. For, he said, they ought to
realize that not only had they received them because of their piety
and righteousness, but that they would also maintain them through

these same qualities, and that it is not so great a thing for men to
65 acquire something which they have not had before as to preserve
what is given them and be guilty of nothing which may harm it.

l. 1   *The king . . . the temple*; King Solomon at the inauguration of the temple in
Jerusalem.

l. 2   *Heaven* is a conjecture, based on the Old Testament; the MSS of Josephus
read *to the crowd* (Greek ὄχλον, not οὐρανόν). The Old Testament does not
refer to the *right* hand. Perhaps in both cases we should adopt the text that
makes Josephus differ from the scriptural wording.

l. 4   *In need of nothing* (ἀπροσδεές), a Stoic belief about God, reflected also in Acts
17. 25 (God is not worshipped by human hands, as if he were in need (προσ–
δεόμενος) of anything). *The Deity* (τὸ θεῖον, neuter, *l.* 4) also recalls Acts 17.
29.

l. 10   *Voice*. Josephus is sensitive about the use of material sacrifices, though he
cannot deny that they were offered. He prefers the sacrifice of praise and
thanksgiving.

ll. 23, 24   *. . . to send some portion of Thy spirit to dwell in the temple, that Thou
mayest seem to us to be on earth as well*. As with material sacrifice so also with
the notion that God is in any sense localized in the temple Josephus feels some
difficulty and tends to rationalize. Cf. Acts 7. 47–50.

What Christians call the Old Testament was and is the sacred book of the Jews. In antiquity many, perhaps most, Jews were able to read it in the Hebrew in which by far the greater part of it was written. There were however some who could not understand Hebrew, and for their benefit it was early translated into the two languages most widely used at and beyond the eastern end of the Mediterranean, Greek and Aramaic. The earliest Greek translation is known as the Septuagint on account of the tradition (see below) that it was made by seventy (two) translators. The tradition is in most respects false, although here and there it shows glimpses of what appears to be the truth. The Jewish community in Egypt, and particularly in Alexandria, was both numerous and influential (see **48, 148–9**); and it was Greek-speaking. Probably as early as the second century BC this community felt the need of a version of its sacred books in what was its every-day tongue, the dialect of vernacular Greek current in those parts. The translation was made, and the tradition, though false, clearly reveals the popularity of the new text and the veneration in which it was held. It is not probable that the whole of the Old Testament was translated at the same time; first came the Pentateuch, next the prophets, and last the books that were the latest to be received into the Jewish canon. More books were in fact translated into Greek than were ultimately received and authorized in Hebrew; the excess of material which the LXX contains in comparison with the Hebrew Bible constitutes what are known as the Old Testament apocrypha.

The importance of this book, which was the Bible of the apostolic Church, is beyond all exaggeration. In it the first Christians sought the prophecies that justified their interpretation of the life and death of Jesus, and sometimes the Greek text was more accommodating than the Hebrew. Thus Isa. 7. 14 in Greek spoke of a *virgin*, while in Hebrew it spoke of a *young woman* who might well be married and bearing a child in the course of nature. Again, at Acts 15. 16ff. James is represented as basing an argument upon a passage in Amos (9. 11f.) as read in the LXX but not in the Hebrew text. Justin's *Dialogue with Trypho* illustrates the textual disputes which inevitably arose between Church and Synagogue. Even more significant however than this use of the LXX is the fact that the characteristic theological terminology of the New Testament can again and again be shown to rest, in great part, upon the usage of the LXX. That this should be so is not surprising, and is due not simply to the fact that the minds of many of the early Christian writers had been formed upon the LXX. They succeeded to a task in which the LXX translators had been pioneers. Jewish Christianity, like the parent religion, Judaism itself, was a Semitic faith maintaining and propagating itself in the Hellenistic world. Its basic thoughts, as well as their expression in language, had to be translated from one world into another, and the earliest Christian writers found their work in part done for them by those who had already adapted the Greek language to express the faith of the Old Testament.

In the LXX a double interaction of Greek and Hebrew thought took place. On the one hand, Greek ideas were occasionally introduced into Old Testament passages which originally were innocent of them. The clearest example of this process is at Exod. 3. 14, where אהיה אשר אהיה (I am that I am; *or*, I will be that I will be) becomes ἐγώ εἰμι ὁ ὤν (I am the Self-Existent); in general it is confined to the removal of anthropomorphisms, e.g. Exod. 24. 10, They saw the place where the God of Israel stood, for They saw the God of Israel. The extent to which Hebrew ideas were, on the other hand, read into Greek words that did not originally contain them is a matter of dispute and cannot be seriously discussed here. It must be remembered that whereas the modern student will work with both Hebrew and Greek texts open in front of him, the LXX came into being for the benefit of those who were unable to use the Hebrew. Thus when the student reading the LXX meets the word νόμος, *law*, he will recall that it translates תורה (*torah*), which often means simply *teaching, instruction*, and will be likely to find this sense in the Greek word. But the ancient user of the LXX when he encountered the word νόμος would take it to mean—νόμος, *law*, though recollection of the contexts in which the word was used may have modified his understanding to some extent.

The LXX is also a very important witness to the original text of the Old Testament.

A translation of the Old Testament into Aramaic is known as a Targum. In many synagogues the reading of Torah, and of the accompanying Haftarah, or prophetic lection, was followed by a translation into Aramaic, a *targum* made by a *methurgeman*. These renderings were in theory made *ex tempore*, but there is no doubt that translators found ways of reminding themselves on paper of suitable translations of difficult passages, and in due course written targums appeared. The oldest that we have is probably the Neofiti Targum; later are the Targum of Onqelos and the Targum of Pseudo-Jonathan. In addition there are the so-called Fragment Targum (fragments of a Palestinian Targum) and the fragments from the Cairo Geniza. These in their present form do not go further back than the third century AD, but they may contain much older traditional translations and interpretations, for on the whole the Targums are free renderings and contain extensive interpretative material.

In addition to Greek and Aramaic the Old Testament was translated into other languages, notably Latin, Syriac, and Coptic. In the following paragraphs the linguistic and textual importance of the LXX will not be treated. First the tradition of the origin of the LXX will be illustrated and criticized; next, certain aspects of LXX thought and writing, not represented or only slightly represented in the Hebrew canon, will be presented. Some characteristic Targum passages will then be quoted. Of these the first two are taken from J. Bowker, *The Targums and Rabbinic Literature* (Cambridge 1969), the best introduction to the subject.

The Traditional Origin of the Septuagint

The tradition regarding the origin of the LXX is given in the simplest and briefest form by Philo; it is given at great length in the so-called *Epistle of Aristeas*, of which a fairly extensive paraphrase and summary is given by Josephus (*Ant.* xii. 11–118; cf. i. 10ff.; *Against Apion* ii. 45ff.), and alluded to by Aristobulus (*apud* Eusebius *Praep. Ev.* xiii, xii. 2). All these sources agree in ascribing the design of translating the Jewish Scriptures to the Alexandrian king Ptolemy Philadelphus, who ruled 283–245 BC. Philo and Josephus wrote, of course, in the first century AD; the *Epistle of Aristeas* claims to have been written by a contemporary of the events it records; in fact it is undoubtedly pseudonymous, and was probably written between 140 and 100 BC. The passage in Philo runs as follows.

252

Philo, *de Vita Mosis* ii. 26–42

> In ancient times the laws were written in the Chaldean tongue, and remained in that form for many years, without any change of language, so long as they had not yet revealed their beauty to the rest of mankind. But, in course of time, the daily, unbroken regularity of
> 5 practice exercised by those who observed them brought them to the knowledge of others, and their fame began to spread on every side. For things excellent, even if they are beclouded for a short time through envy, shine out again under the benign operation of nature when their time comes. Then it was that some people, thinking it a
> 10 shame that the laws should be found in one half only of the human race, the barbarians, and denied altogether to the Greeks, took steps to have them translated. In view of the importance and public utility of the task, it was referred not to private persons or magistrates, who were very numerous, but to kings, and amongst them to the king of

15 highest repute. Ptolemy, surnamed Philadelphus, was the third in succession to Alexander, the conqueror of Egypt....

This great man, having conceived an ardent affection for our laws, determined to have the Chaldean translated into Greek, and at once dispatched envoys to the high priest and king of Judaea, both offices
20 being held by the same person, explaining his wishes and urging him to choose by merit persons to make a full rendering of the Law into Greek. The high priest was naturally pleased, and, thinking that God's guiding care must have led the king to busy himself in such an undertaking, sought out such Hebrews as he had of the highest
25 reputation, who had received an education in Greek as well as in their native lore, and joyfully sent them to Ptolemy. When they arrived, they were offered hospitality, and, having been sumptuously entertained, requited their entertainer with a feast of words full of wit and weight. For he tested the wisdom of each by propounding
30 for discussion new instead of the ordinary questions, which problems they solved with happy and well-pointed answers in the form of apophthegms, as the occasion did not allow of lengthy speaking.

After standing this test, they at once began to fulfil the duties of their high errand. Reflecting how great an undertaking it was to
35 make a full version of the laws given by the voice of God, where they could not add or take away or transfer anything, but must keep the original form and shape, they proceeded to look for the most open and unoccupied spot in the neighbourhood outside the city. For, within the walls, it was full of every kind of living creatures,
40 and consequently the prevalence of diseases and deaths, and the impure conduct of the healthy inhabitants, made them suspicious of it. In front of Alexandria lies the island of Pharos, stretching with its narrow strip of land towards the city, and enclosed by a sea not deep but mostly consisting of shoals, so that the loud din and booming of
45 the surging waves grows faint through the long distance before it reaches the land. Judging this to be the most suitable place in the district, where they might find peace and tranquillity and the soul could commune with the laws with none to disturb its privacy, they fixed their abode there; and, taking the sacred books, stretched them
50 out towards heaven with the hands that held them, asking of God that they might not fail in their purpose. And he assented to their prayers, to the end that the greater part, or even the whole, of the human race might be profited and led to a better life by continuing to observe such wise and truly admirable ordinances.
55   Sitting here in seclusion with none present save the elements of nature, earth, water, air, heaven, the genesis of which was to be the first theme of their sacred revelation, for the laws begin with the story of the world's creation, they became as it were possessed, and, under inspiration, wrote, not each several scribe something different,

60 but the same word for word, as though dictated to each by an invisible prompter. Yet who does not know that every language, and Greek especially, abounds in terms, and that the same thought can be put in many shapes by changing single words and whole phrases and suiting the expression to the occasion? This was not the
65 case, we are told, with this law of ours, but the Greek words used corresponded literally with the Chaldean, exactly suited to the things they indicated. . . . The clearest proof of this is that, if Chaldeans have learned Greek, or Greeks Chaldean, and read both versions, the Chaldean and the translation, they regard them with awe and
70 reverence as sisters, or rather one and the same, both in matter and words, and speak of the authors not as translators but as prophets and priests of the mysteries, whose sincerity and singleness of thought has enabled them to go hand in hand with the purest of spirits, the spirit of Moses.
75   Therefore, even to the present day, there is held every year a feast and general assembly in the island of Pharos, whither not only Jews but multitudes of others cross the water, both to do honour to the place in which the light of that version first shone out, and also to thank God for the good gift so old yet ever young. But, after the
80 prayers and thanksgivings, some fixing tents on the seaside and others reclining on the sandy beach in the open air feast with their relations and friends, counting that shore for the time a more magnificent lodging than the fine mansions in the royal precincts.

l. 17   *This great man.* Ptolemy Philadelphus, who succeeded Ptolemy Soter, who himself was one of the successors of Alexander the Great. The omitted passage represents him as the most distinguished of the Ptolemies. Aristeas also ascribed to him the initiative in the translation of the Law, and the tradition appears also in Rabbinic writings, e.g. *Megillah 9a* (see below, note on *l.* 69).

l. 19   *Both offices being held by the same person.* The high priest, according to Aristeas (33), followed by Josephus, was Eleazar. On his place in the succession of high priests see Josephus, *Ant.* xii 43f., and Appendix B in Vol. VII of the Loeb edition of Josephus (R. Marcus). At this period the high priest was also the secular head of the Jewish state, but not a 'king'.

l. 24   *Sought out such Hebrews as he had of the highest reputation.* In Aristeas (46) the high priest selects six elders from each of the twelve tribes; the seventy-two names are given. By this means the Greek translation is given the full sanction and approval of Palestinian Judaism; and indeed some such connection is not impossible.

l. 25   *Who had received an education in Greek.* That there were such persons need not be doubted. It was much later that Judaism shut the door against Greek learning and influence. Both the earlier attitude to Greek studies and the later are well expressed in the Mishnah (*Sotah* 9. 14: During the war of Titus (*v. l.* Quietus, governor of Judaea AD 117) they forbade . . . that a man should teach his son Greek). For further evidence see below on *l.* 69.

l. 27 Having been sumptuously entertained. Aristeas gives further details, especially of the 'feast of words'. In such passages it becomes very clear that the Epistle of Aristeas is an apology for, and praise of, Judaism, put, for effect, into the mouth of a Gentile.

l. 42 The island of Pharos was connected with the mainland by a sea-wall nearly a mile in length (the 'Heptastadion') which divided the harbour into two parts. Neither Aristeas nor Josephus mentions the name Pharos, but it is clear that they thought of this place as the scene of the translators' labours.

l. 60 The same word for word. It is evident that Philo believes that he is describing a miracle. The translators wrote 'under inspiration' (προεφήτευον). A different view is given by Aristeas (followed by Josephus); no miraculous agreement was involved, but the translators compared their work so as to produce an agreed result. The development of the tradition in Philo well illustrates the veneration felt in his day for the LXX. On this see the next note.

l. 69 They regard them with awe and reverence as sisters. Note that Philo is able to think of Greeks who have learned Chaldean (Hebrew) and Hebrews who have learned Greek. In his day there were such bilingual Jews, though later the learning of Greek was frowned upon (see note on *l.* 25). This changing attitude to Greek was reflected in a changing attitude to the LXX. In the early period it was allowed. Thus *Megillah* 1. 8: ... the Books may be written in any language . . . Rabban Simeon b. Gamaliel [before AD 70] says: The Books, too, they have only permitted to be written in Greek [in addition to Hebrew]. Both a changing attitude and the old tradition appear in *Megillah* 9a: R. Judah [*c.* AD 150] said: When our teachers permitted the Holy Scriptures to be written in Greek they permitted it only in respect of the book of the Law [i.e. the Pentateuch], and on account of the incident of King Ptolemy. For it is taught in a *baraita*: King Ptolemy brought together seventy-two elders, whom he led into seventy-two closets, without telling them for what purpose he had assembled them. Then he went into each and said to them, Write out for me the Law of Moses your teacher. God gave each one counsel in his heart, so that they all agreed in every point. This statement appears to agree with Philo's; but a difference in tone should be observed. Here the point is that translations are never desirable but that the Greek Pentateuch may be justified on account of a special miracle. The developed attitude which prevailed after the Church had appropriated the LXX is found in *Sepher Torah* 1, §8: Seventy elders wrote the Law in Greek, writing for King Ptolemy, and that day was as bad for Israel as the day on which they made the calf, for the Law could not be translated in a way corresponding to all requirements. When the LXX fell out of favour (to a great extent because of its use by Christians) its place was taken among Greek-speaking Jews by more literal renderings, those of Aquila, Symmachus and Theodotion.

l. 75 A feast and general assembly. This festival Philo must have known himself, and there is no need to doubt its existence in his day, though no other evidence for its celebration is known. It does not of course prove a historical connexion between the island and the LXX.

Only a small part of the long *Epistle of Aristeas* can be quoted here.

253

Epistle of Aristeas, 301–16

Three days later Demetrius took the men and passing along the sea-
wall, seven stadia long, to the island, crossed the bridge and made for
the northern districts [of Pharos]. There he assembled them in a
house, which had been built upon the sea-shore, of great beauty and
5 in a secluded situation, and invited them to carry out the work of
translation, since everything that they needed for the purpose was
placed at their disposal. So they set to work comparing their several
results and making them agree, and whatever they agreed upon was
suitably copied out under the direction of Demetrius. And the session
10 lasted until the ninth hour; after this they were set free to minister to
their physical needs. Everything they wanted was furnished for them
on a lavish scale. In addition to this Dorotheus made the same
preparations for them daily as were made for the king himself—for
thus he had been commanded by the king. In the early morning they
15 appeared daily at the Court, and after saluting the king went back to
their own place. And as is the custom of all the Jews, they washed
their hands in the sea and prayed to God and then devoted themselves
to reading and translating the particular passage [upon which they
were engaged], and I put the question to them, Why it was that they
20 washed their hands before they prayed? And they explained that it
was a token that they had done no evil (for every form of activity is
wrought by means of the hands) since in their noble and holy way
they regard everything as a symbol of righteousness and truth.

As I have already said, they met together daily in the place which
25 was delightful for its quiet and its brightness and applied themselves
to their task. And it so chanced that the work of translation was
completed in seventy-two days, just as if this had been arranged of set
purpose.

When the work was completed, Demetrius collected together the
30 Jewish population in the place where the translation had been made,
and read it over to all, in the presence of the translators, who met
with a great reception also from the people, because of the great
benefits which they had conferred upon them. They bestowed warm
praise upon Demetrius, too, and urged him to have the whole law
35 transcribed and present a copy to their leaders.

After the books had been read, the priests and the elders of the
translators and the Jewish community and the leaders of the people
stood up and said, that since so excellent and sacred and accurate a
translation had been made, it was only right that it should remain as
40 it was and no alteration should be made in it. And when the whole
community expressed their approval, they bade them pronounce a
curse in accordance with their custom upon any one who should

make any alteration either by adding anything or changing in any
way whatever any of the words which had been written or making
45 any omission. This was a very wise precaution to ensure that the
book might be preserved for all the future time unchanged.

When the matter was reported to the king, he rejoiced greatly, for
he felt that the design which he had formed had been safely carried
out. The whole book was read over to him and he was greatly
50 astonished at the spirit of the lawgiver. And he said to Demetrius,
'How is it that none of the historians or the poets have ever thought
it worth their while to allude to such a wonderful achievement?'
And he replied, 'Because the law is sacred and of divine origin. And
some of those who formed the intention [of dealing with it] have
55 been smitten by God and therefore desisted from their purpose.' He
said that he had heard from Theopompus that he had been driven
out of his mind for more than thirty days because he intended to
insert in his history some of the incidents from the earlier and
somewhat unreliable translations of the law. When he had recovered
60 a little, he besought God to make it clear to him why the misfortune
had befallen him. And it was revealed to him in a dream, that from
idle curiosity he was wishing to communicate sacred truths to
common men, and that if he desisted he would recover his health. I
have heard, too, from the lips of Theodectes, one of the tragic poets,
65 that when he was about to adapt some of the incidents in the book
for one of his plays, he was affected with cataract in both his eyes.
And when he perceived the reason why the misfortune had befallen
him, he prayed to God for many days and was afterwards restored.

l. 1 *Three days later,* that is, after the banquet at which the king entertained the
translators.
Demetrius, according to Aristeas (9), was at this time president of the king's
library. This is almost certainly a mistake, and a proof that the Epistle was
not written by a contemporary of Ptolemy II Philadelphus. Demetrius of
Phalerum was brought to Alexandria by Ptolemy I Soter to supervise his
library. He fell into disfavour, however, towards the end of this king's reign
because he supported the claim to succession of the elder son, Keraunos,
against those of his brother Philadelphus. He was sent into exile and died
c. 283 BC.

l. 3 *The northern districts of Pharos.* Pharos is not named in the Greek text but is
clearly intended.

l. 12 *Dorotheus* is mentioned at 182 as having charge of the entertainment of the
Jewish translators.

l. 16 *As is the custom of all the Jews, they washed their hands* . . . Cf. Mark 7. 3; but it
should be noted that this is not a washing before eating, but in the early
morning and before prayer. This seems to be the earliest evidence for the
custom of washing before morning prayer.

l. 21   *A token that they had done no evil.* This of course was not the true origin and meaning of Jewish ablutions; but it is quite possible that Alexandrian Jews so explained their practices to their heathen neighbours.

l. 27   *In seventy-two days,* as there were seventy-two translators.

l. 30   *The Jewish population.* It is noteworthy that, though Aristeas represents the translation as due to the initiative of the king and his librarian, and as commissioned by them, yet when the work is completed it is presented not to the royal patron but to the Jewish people. It may be that Aristeas here unwittingly allows us to see a glimpse of the truth. In all probability it was the Jewish community in Alexandria that needed and produced the LXX.

l. 39   *It should remain as it was.* Probably a secondary purpose of the Epistle (which is to be regarded as primarily a piece of Jewish propaganda) was to commend and insist upon the authority of a standard LXX text.

l. 51   *How is it that none of the historians or the poets* . . . ? This question implies what is expressly stated in *l.* 58 (and perhaps in Aristeas 30 also), namely, that earlier translations had been made, even though they had proved unsatisfactory. This supports the suggestion of the last note. The question itself is of some interest, since there is in fact little trace of the LXX in non-Jewish Greek authors (the most notable exception being certain tractates of the *Corpus Hermeticum*; see pp. 93–103). The primary reasons for this neglect are to be found not, as Aristeas suggests, in the divine origin of the Law, but in the general dislike for the Jews and their religion, and in the extreme barbarity of LXX Greek.

Selections from the Septuagint

Peculiar difficulty accompanies the selection of passages from the LXX itself. No attempt is made in this book to describe the history and theology of the Old Testament, though they are both elements of fundamental importance in the background of the New Testament, and it has already been pointed out that a comparison of the Hebrew and Greek texts of the Old Testament is particularly instructive. Certain parts of the Greek Old Testament are quoted elsewhere (see **116–24; 260, 273**) for special purposes; here three passages only will be given. They will be drawn from parts of the LXX which have no canonical Hebrew equivalent, and they will illustrate ideas which are important in the development of Hellenistic Judaism but are only scantily represented, or not represented at all, in the Hebrew Old Testament.

THE DIVINE WISDOM

Already in the later parts of the Hebrew Old Testament Wisdom (חכמה, *ḥokmah*) is recognized as one of the good gifts of God to men. The word means, at first, practical good sense; the ability to live life intelligently, virtuously, and successfully (e.g. Prov. 1. 2ff.). Whether this view of Wisdom was a native Jewish development or was borrowed from foreign sources is a question we need not here examine. Since however this Wisdom was naturally spoken of as the Wisdom *of God* (for from what other source could it spring?) it came to be thought of in a new way, once more, perhaps, under the pressure of foreign influence as well as inward development. Wisdom belonged to the stuff of the universe, and therefore, since God was the Creator of the universe, it stood in a double relationship to God and to the universe. Wisdom was not merely an attribute of wise men, or even an attribute of God himself; it had a more or less independent, a more or less personal, existence. It is necessary here to use terms of considerable vagueness since precision is one of the least evident characteristics of the Wisdom literature, and it is probably not correct to describe Wisdom as portrayed there as, in any strict sense, a hypostasis. We are moving in the realm of poetical and imaginative description, not of metaphysics, and it is certainly not one single view of Wisdom that we find in the Wisdom books, or even within any one of them.

It is possible that the Jewish conception of Wisdom, and the literary form which it sometimes took, were influenced by the contemporary belief in the goddess Isis (on this see the notes below); and possible also that the figure of Wisdom is related to the Stoic conception of the Logos (see **64–6, 232–3**). Probably, however, the influence of these external factors was in general secondary; that is, the Jewish writers employed the language of Hellenistic religion or philosophy as a means of commending their own faith.

It seems very probable that the Wisdom of Solomon is to be regarded as a composite work. For the doctrine of Wisdom the most significant section (part of which is quoted below) is 7. 1 (or 6. 1)—9. 18. This discourse upon, and prayer for, Wisdom is put into the mouth of Solomon. It may be dated before the time of Philo, probably in the first century BC.

254

Wisdom of Solomon 7. 1—8. 1

> I myself also am mortal, like to all,
> And am sprung from one born of the earth, the man first formed,
> And in the womb of a mother was I moulded into flesh in the time of ten months,
> Being compacted in blood of the seed of man and pleasure that came with sleep.
> 5 And I also, when I was born, drew in the common air,
> And fell upon the kindred earth,
> Uttering, like all, for my first voice, the self-same wail:

In swaddling clothes was I nursed, and with watchful cares.
For no king had any other first beginning;
10 But all men have one entrance into life, and a like departure.
For this cause I prayed, and understanding was given me:
I called upon God, and there came to me a spirit of wisdom.
I preferred her before sceptres and thrones,
And riches I esteemed nothing in comparison of her.
15 Neither did I liken to her any priceless gem,
Because all the gold of the earth in her sight is but a little sand,
And silver shall be accounted as clay before her.
Above health and comeliness I loved her,
And I chose to have her rather than light,
20 Because her bright shining is never laid to sleep.
But with her there came to me all good things together,
And in her hands innumerable riches;
And I rejoiced over them all because wisdom leadeth them;
Though I knew not that she was the mother of them.
25 As I learned without guile, I impart without grudging;
I do not hide her riches.
For she is unto men a treasure that faileth not,
And they that use it obtain friendship with God,
Commended to him by the gifts which come through discipline.
30 But to me may God give to speak with judgement,
And to conceive thoughts worthy of what hath been given me;
Because himself is one that guideth even wisdom and correcteth the
wise.
For in his hand are both we and our words;
All understanding, and all acquaintance with divers crafts.
35 For he hath given me an unerring knowledge of the things that are,
To know the constitution of the world, and the operation of the
elements;
The beginning and end and middle of times,
The alternations of the solstices and the changes of seasons,
The circuits of years and the positions of stars;
40 The natures of living creatures and the ragings of wild beasts,
The powers of spirits and the thoughts of men,
The diversities of plants and the virtues of roots:
All things that are either secret or manifest I learned,
For she that is the artificer of all things taught me, even wisdom.
45 For there is in her a spirit quick of understanding, holy,
Alone in kind, manifold,
Subtil, freely moving,
Clear in utterance, unpolluted,
Distinct, that cannot be harmed,
50 Loving what is good, keen, unhindered,

Beneficent, loving toward man,
Steadfast, sure, free from care,
All-powerful, all-surveying,
And penetrating through all spirits
55 That are quick of understanding, pure, subtil:
For wisdom is more mobile than any motion;
Yea, she pervadeth and penetrateth all things by reason of her
   pureness.
For she is a breath of the power of God,
And a clear effluence of the glory of the Almighty;
60 Therefore can nothing defiled find entrance into her,
For she is an effulgence from everlasting light
And an unspotted mirror of the working of God,
And an image of his goodness.
And she, though but one, hath power to do all things;
65 And remaining in herself, reneweth all things:
And from generation to generation passing into holy souls
She maketh them friends of God and prophets.
For nothing doth God love save him that dwelleth with wisdom.
For she is fairer than the sun,
70 And above all the constellations of the stars:
Being compared with light, she is found to be before it;
For to the light of day succeedeth night,
But against wisdom evil doth not prevail;
But she reacheth from one end of the world to the other with full
   strength,
75 And ordereth all things well.

l. 1 *I myself also am mortal.* Solomon speaks. King though he is, he shares in the
   common descent of men from Adam, the man first formed of the dust of the
   earth. Wisdom is therefore for him no natural possession; he must pray for
   it, if he is to be the 'understanding king' who is 'tranquillity to his people'
   (6. 24).

l. 11 *I prayed.* The author recalls 1 Kings 3. 4–15; 2 Chron. 1. 7–13.

ll. 11f. *Understanding . . . spirit of wisdom* (φρόνησις . . . πνεῦμα σοφίας). The two
   expressions are used in parallelism without difference of meaning. The spirit
   of wisdom is wisdom itself (see *l.* 45, and cf. Isa. 11. 2), and wisdom is here
   meant in the sense of practical wisdom.

l. 13 *I preferred her before sceptres and thrones.* This preference, which is expanded
   in the following lines, rests primarily upon the choice of Solomon in his
   prayer (1 Kings 3. 9; 2 Chron. 1. 10), but it is one which occurs frequently,
   and is frequently elaborated, in the Wisdom books; see e.g. Prov. 3. 14f.;
   8. 10f.; 16. 16; Job 28. 15–19; Eccles. 7. 11f.

l. 19 *Light.* Cf. *ll.* 61f., 69–72, and the note on *l.* 61.

l. 24 *The mother of them.* Once more the writer is dependent not so much on his
   own thought about wisdom and its value as on the Old Testament; see 1
   Kings 3. 13; 2 Chron. 1. 12.

l. 36   *The constitution of the world.* The writer proceeds in the next lines to parade his knowledge of astronomy, zoology, and medicine; but there is no reason to suppose that it was more than superficial, or that he knew more of Greek science than the imposing phrases he uses. Cf. 1 Kings 4. 33, and the frequent allusions to the natural world in Proverbs.

l. 41   *The powers of spirits.* A possible translation would be 'the forces of winds'; but in view of the widespread tradition that Solomon enjoyed unusual powers over spirits and demons the translation in the text is more probable.

l. 44   *The artificer of all things.* Wisdom is no longer mere pious common sense but, metaphorically at least, a person. The description of Wisdom as artificer (τεχνῖτις) of all things probably rests upon Prov. 8. 30 (LXX ἁρμόζουσα), though it is doubtful whether the corresponding Hebrew word (אָמוֹן) means 'master workman' (EV). To suppose that this description of Wisdom means that our author was thinking in terms of either a Platonic pattern of the universe or a Stoic world-soul is to press his language a great deal too far; but he probably means to show that Judaism also is able to produce a mediator at once cosmological and revelatory. Cf. *l.* 61 and note.

l. 45   *There is in her a spirit.* See the note on *ll.* 11f. above. There follows a list of twenty-one adjectives, by which Wisdom is described. It many be recalled that Philo (*de Conf. Ling.* 146) speaks of the Logos as 'many-named'; also that the multiplication of titles is not unusual in addresses to divine persons, not least in addresses to Isis. The author of Wisdom is probably following non-Jewish models; this is confirmed by the fact that some of his adjectives are certainly of non-Jewish background and origin.

Quick of understanding. This translation hardly succeeds in bringing out the sense of νοερόν a Stoic word which means rather 'pertaining to the intellect (νοῦς)'. The κόσμος itself was described by Zeno (von Arnim, op. cit. i. 32) as ἔμψυχος, νοερός, and λογικός (living, rational, and spiritual).

l. 46   *Alone in kind, manifold.* Like the Stoic world-soul, Wisdom is one, yet expresses itself in many forms.

l. 54   *Penetrating through all spirits.* This is expanded and justified in *l.* 57, where Wisdom is said to pervade all things; *a fortiori* it will pervade all rational beings. The Stoic concept of the Logos is parallel to the thought here; Logos is everywhere, but is pre-eminently to be found in those wise and virtuous souls which live according to Logos.

l. 59   *Effluence,* or emanation. The thought is far from clear; but Wisdom seems here to be a distinct being, derived from God but differentiated from him. This definitely theistic conception is Platonic rather than Stoic, though it is not suggested that the author is himself consciously combining the two schools.

l. 61   *Effulgence.* This is the natural meaning of the word ἀπαύγασμα (cf. Heb. 1. 3); but in view of the next line some prefer to render 'reflection'. The frequent use of the imagery of light is noteworthy, but perhaps too natural to demand belief that it has been borrowed from Hellenistic sources. Yet, here and elsewhere, it is doubtless true that the author means to say to his readers, 'All those properties which you ascribe to νοῦς [Mind] and λόγος [Reason], the divine Wisdom which I have to proclaim to you also possesses, and is indeed even more glorious' (Fichtner, *ad loc.*).

l. 67 *Friends of God and prophets.* Abraham was the friend of God (Isa. 41. 8; 2
Chron. 20. 7; James 2. 23; cf. John 15. 14); but it seems probable that the
author is here dependent on the Hellenistic description of the wise man as
the friend of God. Many references could be given: e.g. Xenophon,
Memorabilia II, i. 33 where Virtue (ἀρετή) claims to make men friends of
God; Plato, *Laws* iv. 716 D. Philo also took up the notion; e.g. *de Abra.* 273,
of Abraham. Similarly the inspired prophet is a common enough figure in
the Old Testament, but an attempt is made here to combine the Old
Testament prophet with the Hellenistic wise man. Cf. Cicero, *de Divinatione*
ii. 63 (129). There is a close approximation between Spirit, Wisdom, and
Logos.

l. 75 *Ordereth all things well.* The word and thought are both Platonic and Stoic.
Cf. Plato, *Phaedrus* 246 C; Diogenes Laertius 133: the Stoics said that the
cosmos was ordered according to Mind and Providence; which need not be
greatly different from the statement that all things are ordered by the
Wisdom of God.

ETHICAL PARAENESIS

The conception of Wisdom, though in origin practical, may be regarded
as an expression of the speculative activity of Judaism. A more characteristic
feature of Judaism is however its deep-rooted interest in ethics, and this
interest is reflected in the later LXX books, where moral paraenesis is a
not uncommon literary form. The book of Tobit in particular may be
described as an ethical romance designed to teach the practice of virtue
and to demonstrate God's providential care for the righteous, especially
for righteous Israelites. Its date is difficult to estimate since the story seems
to have been known in a number of different forms; the earliest of these
was probably not much later than 200 BC. In the passage quoted here the
aged Tobit gives parting advice (most of which needs no explanation) to
his son Tobias.

255

Tobit 4. 3–19

And he called Tobias his son and he came unto him and he said unto
him, Bury me well, and honour thy mother; and forsake her not all
the days of her life, and do that which is pleasing before her, and
grieve not her spirit in any matter. Remember her, child, that she
5 hath experienced many dangers for thee in her womb; and when she
is dead, bury her by me in one grave. My child, be mindful of the
Lord all thy days, and let not thy will be set to sin and to transgress
his commandments: do acts of righteousness all the days of thy life,
and walk not in the ways of unrighteousness. For if thou doest the
10 truth, success shall be in thy works, and so it shall be unto all that do

righteousness. Give alms of thy substance: turn not away thy face
from any poor man, and the face of God shall not be turned away
from thee. As thy substance is, give alms of it according to thine
abundance: if thou have much, according to the abundance thereof,
15 give alms; if thou have little bestow it, and be not afraid to give alms
according to that little: for thou layest up a good treasure for thyself
against the day of necessity: because alms delivereth from death, and
suffereth not to come into darkness. Alms is a good offering in the
sight of the Most High for all that give it. Beware, my child, of all
20 whoredom, and take first a wife of the seed of thy fathers, take not a
strange wife, which is not of thy father's tribe; for we are the sons of
the prophets. Noah, Abraham, Isaac, Jacob, our fathers of old time,
remember, my child, that they all took wives of their kinsmen, and
were blessed in their children, and their seed shall inherit the land.
25 And now, my child, love thy brethren, and scorn not in thy heart
thy brethren and the sons and the daughters of thy people so as not
to take one of them; for in scornfulness is destruction and much
trouble, and in idleness is decay and great want, for idleness is the
mother of famine. Let not the wages of any man, which shall work
30 for thee, tarry with thee, but render it unto him out of hand: and if
thou serve God, recompense shall be made unto thee. Take heed to
thyself, my child, in all thy works, and be discreet in all thy
behaviour. And what thou thyself hatest, do to no man. Drink not
wine unto drunkenness, and let not drunkenness go with thee on thy
35 way. Give of thy bread to the hungry, and of thy garments to them
that are naked: of all thine abundance give alms; and let not thine
eye be grudging when thou givest alms. Pour out thy bread and thy
wine on the tomb of the just, and give not to sinners. Ask counsel of
every man that is wise, and despise not any counsel that is profitable.
40 And bless the Lord thy God at all times, and ask of him that thy ways
may be made straight, and that all thy paths and thy counsels may
prosper: for every nation hath not good counsel; but the Lord will
give to them all good things; and whom he will the Lord humbleth
unto the nethermost Hades. And now, child, remember these
45 commandments, and let them not be blotted out of thy heart.

l. 2   *Bury me well.* Care for the dead is a primary moral obligation in Judaism.
Tobit himself had made a practice of burying those whose bodies would
otherwise have been neglected (1. 17; cf. 2. 4–8), and was rewarded for
doing so (cf. 12. 12). Cf. Matt. 8. 21; Luke 9. 59; 16. 22; 1 Enoch 22. 10.
Honour thy mother. Cf Exod. 20. 12. For examples of the honouring of
parents (and especially mothers) in late Judaism, see C. G. Montefiore and H.
Loewe, *A Rabbinic Anthology*, 500–4.

l. 9   *If thou doest the truth.* Cf. John 3. 21; 1 John 1. 6. Here it means 'to act
faithfully', in obedience to the law.

ll. 11, 13   *Give alms.* Another primary obligation, for which many examples can be given both in Jewish literature and the New Testament. *Turn not away thy face from any poor man*: cf. Matt. 5. 42; Luke 6. 30. *Thou layest up a good treasure*: cf. Matt. 6. 19ff.; Luke 12. 33f.; Mark 10.21, *et al.*

l. 18   *Suffereth not to come into darkness.* Cf. 14. 10: See, child, what things Nadab did unto Ahikar that brought him up! Was he not brought down alive into the earth? and God recompensed the shame upon his face, and Ahikar came forth into the light, and Nadab went into the eternal darkness, because he had sought to slay Ahikar. Because I did alms, he came forth from the snare of death which Nadab had set for him, and Nadab fell into the snare of death, and it destroyed him. Tobit, certainly in ch. 14 and probably in ch. 4, refers to the legend of Ahikar and his enemy Nadab. See R. H. Charles, *Apocrypha and Pseudepigrapha*, ii. 724–84.

l. 21   *A strange wife.* It is not clear whether Tobit insists upon marriage within the tribe, or, more generally, within the race. The patriarchs (here called prophets) fall within the scope of the former regulation only if later traditions are taken into account (Jubilees 4. 33). The reference to 'thy brethren' suggests the latter alternative.

l. 25   *Love thy brethren.* Cf. Lev. 19. 18. The fellow-Jew is meant; but hatred of the enemy, or non-Jew, is not implied; cf. Matt. 5. 43.

l. 29   *Let not the wages of any man . . . tarry with thee.* Cf. James 5. 4.

l. 33   *What thou thyself hatest, do to no man.* Cf. Matt. 7. 12; Luke 6. 31. Tobit states the Golden Rule in its negative from; this is how it usually appears, for example in the teaching of Hillel and Akiba.

l. 37   *Pour out thy bread and thy wine on the tomb of the just.* This seems to be the original text. The zeugma by which 'pour' is applied to bread as well as wine is harsh, but readily comprehensible. Again we have a parallel with the Ahikar legend; see the Arabic text 2. 13 (Pour out thy wine on the tombs of the just, and drink not with ignorant, contemptible people), and the Syriac A text 2. 10 (Pour out thy wine on the graves of the righteous, rather than drink it with evil men; Charles, op. cit., ii. 730f.). The practice referred to may be of pagan origin, and the words taken from a non-Jewish literary source; but the fact that such a reference can be made throws a surprising light upon the fervent Jewish piety which produced the book of Tobit. Judaism was more open to foreign influences than is often supposed; more open, perhaps, than it supposed itself to be.

MARTYRDOM AND THE FUTURE LIFE

The development of Judaism as a religion of obedience to the written Law, and the recurring misfortunes which befell the national life of the Jews, provoked new experiences and fresh thinking. The attack upon Judaism by Antiochus IV Epiphanes (see **116–19**), though it was directed against the nation and the national religion, fell in the first instance upon those who were, in their own consciences, confronted with the question whether they should or should not continue to be obedient to the Law. The question was not, as once it had been, whether the whole nation should remain in its own land or be carried away to Babylon, but whether a particular man should remain faithful to the religion in which he had been reared, and receive death by torture as his reward, or should compromise, and live. In these circumstances martyrdoms took place, perhaps for the first time in religious history. But (men began to ask) what was to be the ultimate fate of the martyrs? Were their suffering and death to be the last word? This was an intolerable thought, and the notion of a blessed personal future life, to which doubtless other sources contributed, was fostered by the faith and the sufferings of those who gave their lives for the Law.

The Second Book of Maccabees is an epitome of a longer work; so much the book itself tells us (2. 23: . . . this [the things concerning Judas Maccabaeus and his brothers], recounted by Jason in five books, we will try to compress into a single volume). Who Jason was, when he lived, and who was his epitomist, are questions which cannot be precisely answered. Probably the origins of the book go back into the second century BC, and they reveal both a Pharisaic kind of piety and the influence of Hellenistic Judaism. The seventh chapter (quoted below) is a vignette of the persecution which took place when Antiochus IV Epiphanes attempted to make the Jews surrender their religious rites and legal observances.

256

2 Maccabees 7

It also came to pass that seven brothers and their mother were arrested and shamefully lashed with whips and scourges, by the king's orders, that they might be forced to taste the abominable swine's flesh. But one of them spoke up for the others and said, Why question
5　us? What wouldst thou learn from us? We are prepared to die sooner than transgress the laws of our fathers. Then the king, in his exasperation, ordered pans and cauldrons to be heated, and when they were heated immediately, ordered the tongue of the speaker to be torn out, had him scalped and mutilated before the eyes of his
10　brothers and mother, and then had him put on the fire, all maimed and crippled as he was, but still alive, and set to fry in the pan. And as the vapour from the pan spread abroad, they and their mother exhorted one another to die nobly, uttering these words: The Lord God beholdeth this, and truly hath compassion on us, even as Moses
15　declared in his song which testifieth against them to their face, saying,
　　And he shall have compassion on his servants.
And when the first had died after this manner, they brought the second to the shameful torture, tearing off the skin of his head with

the hair and asking him, Wilt thou eat, before we punish thy body
20 limb by limb? But he answered in the language of his fathers and
said to them, No. So he too underwent the rest of the torture, as the
first had done. And when he was at the last gasp, he said, Thou cursed
miscreant! Thou dost dispatch us from this life, but the King of the
world shall raise us up, who have died for his laws, and revive us to
25 life everlasting. And after him the third was made a mocking-stock.
And when he was told to put out his tongue, he did so at once,
stretching forth his hands courageously, with the noble words, These
I had from heaven; for his name's sake I count them naught; from
him I hope to get them back again. So much so that the king himself
30 and his company were astounded at the spirit of the youth, for he
thought nothing of his sufferings. And when he too was dead, they
tortured the fourth in the same shameful fashion. And when he was
near his end, he said: 'Tis meet for those who perish at men's hands
to cherish hope divine that they shall be raised up by God again; but
35 thou—thou shalt have no resurrection to life. Next they brought the
fifth and handled him shamefully. But he looked at the king and said,
Holding authority among men, thou doest what thou wilt, poor
mortal; but dream not that God hath forsaken our race. Go on, and
thou shalt find how his sovereign power will torture thee and thy
40 seed! And after him they brought the sixth. And when he was at the
point of death he said, Deceive not thyself in vain! We are suffering
this on our own account, for sins against our own God. That is why
these awful horrors have befallen us. But think not thou shalt go
unpunished for daring to fight against God! The mother, however,
45 was a perfect wonder; she deserves to be held in glorious memory,
for, thanks to her hope in God, she bravely bore the sight of seven
sons dying in a single day. Full of noble spirit and nerving her weak
woman's heart with the courage of a man, she exhorted each of them
in the language of their fathers, saying, How you were ever conceived
50 in my womb, I cannot tell! 'Twas not I who gave you the breath of
life or fashioned the elements of each! 'Twas the creator of the world
who fashioneth men and deviseth the generating of all things, and he
it is who in mercy will restore to you the breath of life even as you
now count yourselves naught for his laws' sake. Now Antiochus felt
55 that he was being humiliated, but, overlooking the taunt of her
words, he made an appeal to the youngest brother, who still survived,
and even promised on oath to make him rich and happy and a Friend
and a trusted official of State, if he would give up his fathers' laws. As
the young man paid no attention to him, he summoned his mother
60 and exhorted her to counsel the lad to save himself. So, after he had
exhorted her at length, she agreed to persuade her son. She leant over
to him, and, befooling the cruel tyrant, spoke thus in her fathers'
tongue: My son, have pity on me. Nine months I carried thee in my

womb, three years I suckled thee; I reared thee and brought thee up
65 to this age of thy life. Child, I beseech thee, lift thine eyes to heaven
and earth, look at all that is therein, and know that God did not make
them out of the things that existed. So is the race of men created. Fear
not this butcher, but show thyself worthy of thy brothers, and accept
thy death, that by God's mercy I may receive thee again together
70 with thy brothers. Ere she had finished, the young man cried, What
are you waiting for? I will not obey the king's command, I will obey
the command of the law given by Moses to our fathers. But thou,
who hast devised all manner of evil against the Hebrews, thou shalt
not escape the hands of God. We are suffering for our own sins, and
75 though our living Lord is angry for a little, in order to rebuke and
chasten us, he will again be reconciled to his own servants. But thou,
thou impious wretch, vilest of all men, be not vainly uplifted with
thy proud, uncertain hopes, raising thy hand against the heavenly
children; thou hast not yet escaped the judgement of the Almighty
80 God who seeth all. These our brothers, after enduring a brief pain,
have now drunk of everflowing life, in terms of God's covenant, but
thou shalt receive by God's judgement the just penalty of thine
arrogance. I, like my brothers, give up body and soul for our fathers'
laws, calling on God to show favour to our nation soon, and to make
85 thee acknowledge, in torments and plagues, that he alone is God, and
to let the Almighty's wrath, justly fallen on the whole of our nation,
end in me and in my brothers. Then the king fell into a passion and
had him handled worse than the others, so exasperated was he at
being mocked. Thus he also died unpolluted, trusting absolutely in
90 the Lord. Finally after her sons the mother also perished.

Let this suffice for the enforced sacrifices and the excesses of
barbarity.

l. 14 *Moses declared in his song.* Deut. 32. 36.

l. 23 *The King of the world shall raise us up, who have died for his laws, and revive us
to life everlasting.* See the introductory note above and cf. Dan. 12. 2 (written
at the time to which 2 Macc. 7 refers).

l. 29 *I hope to get them back again.* The resurrection will be a resurrection of the
body.

l. 35 *Thou shalt have no resurrection to life.* The resurrection will be a resurrection
of the righteous. The fate of the wicked is not clear. This passage might
suggest annihilation; but *l.* 39 (His sovereign power will torture thee and
thy seed) and *l.* 43 (Think not thou shalt go unpunished), punishment.

l. 57 *A Friend.* The title of a high official at court.
Passim: it seems almost certain that the author of Heb. 11 had this chapter in mind.
See especially Heb. 11. 3, 34ff.: cf. 11. 26f.

Selections from Targums

The first two passages are taken from the Targum of Pseudo-Jonathan (Jerusalem I) to the Pentateuch, the third from the Targum of Jonathan to the Prophets.

257
Genesis 1

At the beginning *God created the heaven and the earth.*
And the earth was waste and void, desolate without the sons of men, and empty of animals. *And darkness was upon the face of the deep: and the spirit of* mercies from before God blew *upon the face of the waters.*
5 *And God said, 'Let there be light* to lighten the world'. *And* immediately there was light.
And God saw the light, that it was good: and God divided the light from the darkness.
And God called the light Day, and he made it so that the dwellers on
10 the earth might labour during it; *and the darkness he called Night*, and he made it so that the creatures might have rest during it. *And there was evening and there was morning, one day.*
And God said, 'Let there be a firmament in the midst of the waters, and let it divide the waters above *from the waters* below'.
15 *And God made the firmament*, its thickness being three fingers between the limits of the heavens and the waters of the ocean. *And he divided the waters which were under the firmament from the waters which were above* in the vault of *the firmament: and it was so.*
And God called the firmament Heaven. And there was evening and there
20 *was morning, a second day.*
And God said, 'Let the lower *waters* which are left over *under the heaven* be for a single place, *and let* the earth be dried up that *the dry land* may be visible'. *And it was so.*
And God called the dry land Earth; and the assembly *of the waters called*
25 *he Seas: and God saw that it was good.*
And God said, 'Let the earth increase putting forth the herb whose seed produces seed, and the tree, fruit *bearing fruit after its kind, wherein is the seed thereof, upon the earth'. And it was so.*
And the earth brought forth the herb whose seed produces seed (*after its*
30 *kind*), *and tree bearing fruit, wherein is the seed thereof, after its kind: and God saw that it was good.*
And there was evening and there was morning, a third day.
And God said, 'Let there be lights in the firmament of the heaven to divide the day from the night; and let them be for signs and for seasons of festivals
35 and for numbering by them the reckoning of days, and for sanctifying

by them the new moon days and the new year days, the intercalations
of the months and the intercalations of the years, the solstices of the
sun and the appearance of the new moon, and the solar cycles:
and let them be for lights in the firmament of the heaven to give light upon
40   *the earth'.*
And it was so.
And God made the two great lights, and they were equal in glory for
21 years less 672 parts of an hour. Then the moon reported against
the sun a false report, and was diminished. And he separated the sun
45   to be *the greater light to rule the day, and* the moon to be *the lesser light,*
and *the stars.*
And God set them in their courses *in the firmament of the heaven to give
light upon the earth,*
and to rule over the day and over the night, and to divide the light of day
50   *from the darkness* of night: *and God saw that it was good.*
And there was evening and there was morning, a fourth day.
And God said, 'Let the miry lakes of *the waters* swarm forth swarms
of living creatures, and the bird which flies, and makes its nest on the
earth, and let the day of its flight be through the air of the *firmament*
55   *of heaven.'*
And God created the great tannins, the leviathan and its mate which
were made for the day of consolation, *and every living creature* which
swarms, *which the* clear *waters brought forth abundantly, after their
kinds,* the kinds which are clean and the kinds which are not clean,
60   and every bird flying with wings *after its kind,* the kinds which are
clean and the kinds which are not clean: *and God saw that it was good.*
*And God blessed them, saying, 'Be fruitful, and multiply, and fill the
waters in the seas, and let fowl multiply in the earth.'*
And there was evening and there was morning, a fifth day.
65   *And God said, 'Let the* fragments of *earth bring forth the living creature
after its kind,* the kinds which are clean and the kinds which are not
clean, *cattle, and creeping thing, and the beast of the earth after its kind.'*
And it was so.
And God made the living creature *of the earth after its kind,* the kinds
70   which are clean and the kinds which are not clean, *and the cattle after
their kind, and every thing that creepeth upon the ground after its kind,*
the kinds which are clean and the kinds which are not clean: *and God
saw that it was good.*
And God said to the angels who minister before him and who were
75   created on the second day of the creation of the world, '*Let us make
man in our image, after our likeness: and let them have dominion over the
fish of the sea, and over the fowl of the air* of heaven, *and over the cattle,
and over all the earth, and over every creeping thing that creepeth upon the
earth.'*
80   *And God created man in his own* likeness, *in the image of God created he*

him with 248 members and 365 sinews, and he laid skin over them, and filled it with flesh and blood: *male and female* in their way *created he them.*

And God blessed them, and said unto them, 'Be fruitful, and multiply, and
85 fill the earth with sons and daughters, *and subdue it; and have dominion over the fish of the sea, and over the fowl of the* heaven, *and over every living thing that moveth upon the earth.'*

And God said, 'Behold I have given you every herb yielding seed, which is upon the face of all the earth, and every tree unfruitful for the purposes
90 of building and for burning; (and every tree) *in the which is the fruit of a tree yielding seed: to you it shall be for meat:*

and to every living creature *of the earth, and to every fowl* of the heaven, *and to every thing that creepeth upon the earth, wherein there is life, (I have given) every green herb for meat.' And it was so.*
95 *And God saw everything that he had made, and, behold, it was very good. And there was evening and there was morning, the sixth day.*

l. 1   *At the beginning.* In this passage and the next (both taken from J. Bowker, op. cit.), words are italicized which are in agreement with the Hebrew text. The first three words are in roman type presumably because they could equally well, or better, be rendered, *from the beginning.*

l. 2   *Desolate without the sons of men.* Here and elsewhere the Targum simply fills out the original text with straightforward explanatory expansion.

l. 15   *Three fingers.* The firmament is a thin shell between heaven and the lower world.

l. 43   *The moon reported against the sun a false report.* The strange behaviour of the moon gave rise to many speculations. Another is to be found in the Greek Apocalypse of Baruch 9. There (v. 7) the moon's fault is that 'when the first Adam sinned, it was near Sammael when he took the serpent as a garment. And it did not hide itself away; and God was angry with it and punished it, and shortened its days.'

l. 56   *The great tannins.* The same word is used at Isa. 27. 1, so that it is probably correct here to take it to refer to the great sea-monsters, though it is also used to mean snake (Exod. 7. 9, 12).

l. 74   *God said to the angels.* The Targum thus accounts for the plural, Let *us* make, which Christians used as a proof of the Trinity.

258

Genesis 22

And it came to pass after these things, that Isaac and Ishmael were disputing. Ishmael said: 'It is right for me to be the heir of my father, since I am his first-born son.' But Isaac said: 'It is right for me to be the heir of my father, since I am the son of Sarah his wife, but you
5 are the son of Hagar, the handmaid of my mother.' Ishmael answered and said: 'I am more righteous than you because I was circumcised

when thirteen years old; and if it had been my wish to refuse I would not have handed myself over to be circumcised.' Isaac answered and said: 'Am I not now thirty-seven years old? If the Holy One, blessed
10 be he, demanded all my members I would not hesitate.' Immediately, these words were heard before the Lord of the universe, and immediately, the word of the Lord tested *Abraham, and said unto him,* '*Abraham*'; *and* he said, 'Here am I.'

And he said, 'Take now thy son, thine only son, whom thou lovest, even
15 *Isaac, and get thee into the land of* worship; *and offer him there for a burnt offering upon one of the mountains which I will tell thee of.'*

And Abraham rose early in the morning and he saddled his ass, and took two of his young men, Eliezer and Ishmael, *with him, and Isaac his son; and he clave the wood* of the olive and the fig and the palm which are
20 proper *for the burnt offering, and rose up, and went unto the place of which* the Lord *had told him.*

On the third day Abraham lifted up his eyes, and saw the cloud of glory smoking on the mountain, and he recognised it *afar off.*

And Abraham said unto his young men, 'Abide ye here with the ass, and I
25 *and the lad will go yonder* to find if what I was assured—"so shall thy seed be"—will be established; *and we will worship* the Lord of the universe, *and come again to you.'*

And Abraham took the wood of the burnt offering, and laid it upon Isaac his son; and he took in his hand the fire and the knife; and they went both
30 *of them together.*

And Isaac spoke unto Abraham his father, and said, 'My father:' and he said, 'Here am I, my son.' And he said, 'Behold the fire and the wood: but where is the lamb for a burnt offering?'

And Abraham said: 'The Lord will choose for himself the lamb for a
35 burnt offering my son.' *So they went both of them* with a single heart together.

And they came to the place which God had told him of; and Abraham built the altar there which Adam had built, which had been destroyed by the waters of the flood and which Noah had rebuilt. It had been
40 destroyed in the generation of the division. And he *laid the wood in order, and bound Isaac his son, and laid him on the altar, upon the wood.*

And Abraham stretched forth his hand, and took the knife to slay his son. Isaac answered and said to his father: 'Bind me well that I may not struggle at the anguish of my soul, and that a blemish may not be
45 found in your offering, and that I may not be cast into the depth of destruction.' The eyes of Abraham looked at the eyes of Isaac, but the eyes of Isaac looked at the angels on high: Isaac saw them but Abraham did not see them. The angels on high answered, 'Come and see these two unique men in the earth; the one slaughters and the
50 other is slaughtered. The one who slaughters does not hesitate, the one to be slaughtered stretches out his neck.'

And the angel of the Lord called to him out of heaven, and said to him, 'Abraham, Abraham': and he said, 'Here am I.'

And he said, 'Lay not thine hand upon the lad, neither do thou anything
55 evil *unto him: for now* it is revealed before me *that thou fearest the Lord, seeing thou hast not withheld thy son, thine only son, from me.'*

And Abraham lifted up his eyes, and looked, and behold, that one ram which was created in the evening of the completion of the world *caught in the thicket* of a tree *by his horns: and Abraham went and took*
60 *the ram, and offered him up for a burnt offering in the stead of his son.*

And Abraham gave thanks and prayed there in *that place,* and said: 'When I prayed for mercy from before you, O Lord, it was revealed before you that there was no deviousness in my heart, and I sought to perform your decree with joy, that when the descendants of Isaac,
65 my son, shall come to the hour of distress, you may remember them, and answer them, and deliver them; and that all generations to come may say, In this mountain Abraham bound Isaac, his son, and there the Shekina of the Lord was revealed to him.'

And the angel of the Lord called to Abraham a second time out of heaven
70 *and said,* 'By my word *have I sworn, saith the Lord, because thou hast done this thing, and hast not withheld thy son, thine only son:*
that in blessing I will bless thee, and in multiplying I will multiply thy seed as the stars of heaven, and as the sand which is upon the sea shore; and thy sons' sons *shall possess the* cities of their *enemies;*
75 *and* because of the merit of your sons *shall all the nations of the earth be blessed; because thou hast obeyed my voice.'*

And the angels on high led Isaac and brought him to the school of Shem the great, and he was there three years. And on the same day *Abraham returned unto his young men, and they rose up and went together*
80 *to Beer-sheba; and Abraham dwelt at Beer-sheba.*

l. 1 *Isaac and Ishmael were disputing.* The Targum is concerned to find some moral ground for the strange story of attempted human sacrifice that follows, and also to emphasize the righteousness of Isaac, whose 'binding' played an important part in Jewish thought (see H. J. Schoeps, *Paulus* (Tübingen 1959), pp. 144–152; G. Vermes, *Scripture and Tradition in Judaism* (Leiden 1961), pp. 193–227).

l. 25 *To find if what I was assured will be established.* The command to sacrifice Isaac seemed to threaten the promise of numerous descendants through Isaac.

ll. 34, 35 Bowker (op. cit.) rightly draws attention to the ambiguity of the Hebrew: is *my son* vocative ('The Lord will choose the lamb, my son'), or appositive accusative ('The Lord will choose a lamb, namely my son'). In the Targum it is implied that Isaac now knows that it is God's will that he should be sacrificed, and he is as willing as Abraham to be obedient.

ll. 38, 39 *Which Adam had built. . . which Noah had rebuilt.* The effect of this is to emphasize the continuity and unity of the Old Testament.

l. 43 Bind me well. The willingness and obedience of Isaac in suffering himself to be bound and offered is once more underlined. See above.

ll. 65, 66 . . . you may remember them, and answer them, and deliver them. This is to be the effect of the 'binding' of Isaac.

l. 68 Shekina, the glorious presence of God.

l. 70 By my word. 'Word' is the Aramaic *memra* (מימרא), which is sometimes almost personified; hardly so here, where it refers to what God has spoken.

l. 75 Because of the merit of your sons. The merit (*zᵉkuth*, זכות) of the (Israelite) children of Abraham is capable of being transferred to the nations, for their benefit.

259

Isaiah 52. 13—53. 12

Behold, my servant, the Anointed One (or, *the Messiah*), shall prosper; he shall be exalted, and increase, and be very strong. As the house of Israel hoped (or, *waited*) for him many days, for his (text, *their*) appearance was wretched among the nations, and his (text,
5 *their*) countenance beyond that of the sons of men: so shall he scatter many nations; kings shall be silent because of him (or, *it*); they shall set their hands upon their mouths: for the things which had not been told them have they seen, and that which they had not heard have they perceived.
10   Who hath believed these our tidings? and to whom hath the power of the mighty arm of the Lord been so revealed? And the righteous shall grow up before him even as budding shoots; and as a tree that sendeth forth its roots by streams of water, so shall the holy generations increase in the land that was in need of him: his
15 appearance shall not be that of a common man, nor the fear of him that of an ordinary man; but his countenance (or, *complexion*) shall be a holy countenance, so that all who see him shall regard him earnestly. Then shall the glory of all the kingdoms be despised and come to an end; they shall be infirm and sick even as a man of
20 sorrows and as one destined for sicknesses, and as when the presence of the Shekinah was withdrawn from us, they (or, *we*) *shall be* despised and of no account. Then he shall pray on behalf of our transgressions and our iniquities shall be pardoned for his sake, though we were accounted smitten, stricken from before the Lord,
25 and afflicted. But he shall build the sanctuary that was polluted because of our transgressions *and* given up because of our iniquities; and by his teaching shall his peace be multiplied upon us, and by our devotion to his words our transgressions shall be forgiven us. All we like sheep had been scattered; we had wandered off each on his own
30 way; but it was the Lord's good pleasure to forgive the transgressions

of us all for his sake. He was praying, and he was answered, and
before he opened his mouth he was accepted; the mighty ones of the
peoples shall he deliver up like a lamb to the slaughter, and as a ewe
that before her shearers is dumb, and there shall be none before him
35 opening his mouth or speaking a word. Out of chastisements and
punishment shall he bring our exiles near, *and* the wondrous things
that shall be wrought for us in his days who shall be able to recount?
For he shall take away the dominion of the peoples from the land of
Israel, *and* the sins which my people sinned shall he transfer unto
40 them. And he shall deliver the wicked into Gehinnam, and those that
are rich in possessions which they have obtained by violence unto
the death of destruction, that those who commit sin may not be
established, nor speak deceits with their mouth. And it was the Lord's
good pleasure to refine and to purify the remnant of his people, in
45 order to cleanse their soul from sin: they shall look upon the kingdom
of their Anointed One (or, *Messiah*), they shall multiply sons and
daughters, they shall prolong days, and they that perform the law of
the Lord shall prosper in his good pleasure. From the subjection of
the peoples shall he deliver their soul; they shall look upon the
50 punishment of them that hate them; they shall be satisfied with the
spoil of their kings: by his wisdom shall he justify the just, in order
to subject many to the law; and for their transgressions shall he make
intercession. Then will I divide unto him the spoil of many peoples
and the riches of strong cities; he shall divide the booty, because he
55 delivered his soul unto death, and subjected the rebellious to the law;
and he shall make intercession for many transgressions, and the
rebellious shall be forgiven for his sake.

l. 1   *My servant* is identified with the Anointed One, by which almost certainly
the Messiah is intended.

ll. 4, 5   *Their . . . their.* There seems to be no reason why the plural of the text
should not be retained. Throughout this Servant Song the Targum removes
features of suffering and disgrace from the Servant, applying them most
often to his enemies, sometimes to the disobedient in Israel, for whom he
secures forgiveness. It would be inconsistent here to say that the Servant's
appearance was wretched. It is unnecessary here to draw attention to all the
subtle (and unsubtle) variations that the translator has made; it is easy enough
to detect them. They may have been made because the Christians had made
their own use of the Song of the Suffering Servant, and it was found necessary
to counter their interpretation with another.

13   Apocalyptic

The roots of Jewish and Christian apocalyptic are in Old Testament prophecy, though not a few non-Jewish influences helped to shape its development. On the general question of the relation between prophecy and apocalyptic, see H. H. Rowley, *The Relevance of Apocalyptic*, Ch. 1. Here it may simply be emphasized that while both prophecy and apocalyptic were concerned with the future they conceived it in different ways. Prophets and apocalyptists alike believed that the future lay entirely within the prevision and control of God; but whereas the former saw the future developing continuously out of the present, good and evil bearing their own fruit and reaping their own reward, the latter saw the future as essentially discontinuous with the present. History would, as it were, take a leap to a new level, on which the judgements of God would be more plainly visible; or, better, God would, by entering history, either personally or through a representative, introduce into it a new factor which would revolutionize its course. A prophet might announce the captivity or restoration of his people; the apocalyptist announces the end of the age. The apocalyptists 'foreshorten' history even more radically than the prophets, and for them the last days are almost always at hand. This is not simply because the apocalyptic writers believed they could see the signs of the times in the growing evil of their age and that God must surely act speedily if he was to act at all. 'Apocalypse' means revealing, the disclosing of secrets; and the secrets were not only secrets of what was to be. They included also secrets of what already was, but was concealed in heaven. Out of their knowledge of these heavenly realities grew their awareness of what would in due course take place on earth; and since the heavenly beings stood ready for action their manifestation could not be long delayed.

This awareness of persons and events belonging to an upper world means that apocalypticism is related to mysticism, man's immediate consciousness of the supernatural. This aspect of apocalypticism has been emphasized in recent years, notably by C. Rowland, in *The Open Heaven* (London 1982), though the practical 'Platonism' of apocalyptic was noted as long ago as 1953 (*Scottish Journal of Theology* 6, pp 138f.); *The Background of the New Testament and its Eschatology, Studies in Honour of C. H. Dodd* (Ed. W.D. Davies and D. Daube; Cambridge 1956), pp 363–393). Speculation regarding the supreme God and his revelation of himself to men led also to the development of belief in mediating divine beings to such an extent that it seemed at times to threaten Jewish monotheism. These matters are illustrated below. Just as no sharp dividing line can be drawn between Jewish apocalyptists and Jewish mystics, so it is impossible to make a sharp distinction between apocalypticism and Pharisaism (see W.D. Davies, *Christian Origins and Judaism* (London 1962), pp 19–30). Rabbis included apocalyptic elements in their teaching, and the apocalyptists were eager that the law should be observed.

The widespread influence of apocalyptic in the period of primitive Christianity hardly needs demonstration; not only can most of the apocalypses which are still extant be dated within that period, many other documents also, not primarily apocalyptic, bear clear traces of apocalyptic in their style and matter. This is true both of Jewish literature and of Christian, for though there is in the New Testament only one Apocalypse, apocalyptic material is to be found in almost every book.

The Literary Forms of Apocalyptic

Most of the apocalypses reveal almost stereotyped forms of construction and expression.

PSEUDONYMITY

The Christian Apocalypse is noteworthy in that it makes no claim to be the work of a famous hero of the past; in the Church, prophecy flourished again, and in the presence of direct inspiration there was no need to claim antiquity as a source of authority. Nearly every Jewish apocalypse however is attributed to some ancient worthy; and a corollary of this pseudonymity is the necessity of finding some means of explaining why the book had not become known before its actual date of publication.

260

Daniel 12

Daniel was written at the time of the attempt of Antiochus Ephiphanes to impose Hellenism upon the Jews (see **116–21**), i.e., *c.* 167 BC.

> And at that time shall Michael stand up, the great prince which standeth for the children of thy people: and there shall be a time of trouble, such as never was since there was a nation even to that same time: and at that time thy people shall be delivered, everyone that
> 5 shall be found written in the book. And many of them that sleep in the dust of the earth shall awake, some to everlasting life, and some to shame and everlasting contempt. And they that be wise shall shine

as the brightness of the firmament; and they that turn many to
righteousness as the stars for ever and ever. But thou, O Daniel, shut
10   up the words, and seal the book, even to the time of the end: many
shall run to and fro, and knowledge shall be increased. Then I Daniel
looked, and, behold, there stood other two, the one on the brink of
the river on this side, and the other on the brink of the river on that
side. And one said to the man clothed in linen, which was above the
15   waters of the river, How long shall it be to the end of these wonders?
And I heard the man clothed in linen, which was above the waters
of the river, when he held up his right hand and his left hand unto
heaven, and sware by him that liveth for ever that it shall be for a
time, times, and a half; and when they have made an end of breaking
20   in pieces the power of the holy people, all these things shall be
finished. And I heard, but I understood not: then said I, O my lord,
what shall be the issue of these things? And he said, Go thy way,
Daniel: for the words are shut up and sealed till the time of the end.
Many shall purify themselves, and make themselves white, and be
25   refined; but the wicked shall do wickedly; and none of the wicked
shall understand: but they that be wise shall understand. And from
the time that the continual burnt-offering shall be taken away, and
the abomination that maketh desolate set up, there shall be a thousand
two hundred and ninety days. Blessed is he that waiteth, and cometh
30   to the thousand three hundred and five and thirty days. But go thy
way till the end be: for thou shalt rest, and shalt stand in thy lot, at
the end of the days.

l. 5   *Many of them that sleep . . . shall awake.* The notion of a resurrection, not
found in the older parts of the Old Testament, is common in the apocalypses,
where supernatural occurrences are common.

l. 9   *Shut up the words, and seal the book.* Daniel seems to have been the name of a
legendary figure of famous wisdom and virtue (cf. Ezek. 14. 14, 20; 28. 3).
In the book of Daniel he is represented as having lived in the time of the
Exile and having received his visions then. To account for the fact that his
writings did not appear till the age of Antiochus Epiphanes the author uses a
literary device common in the apocalypses. Daniel had been bidden to seal
his writings; they were to be released only when the 'end' was imminent—
as the author of Daniel believed it to be. Cf. *l.* 23.

261

4 *Ezra* (otherwise 2 *Esdras*) 14. 1–17

4 Ezra is a composite work, but the greater part of it was written in the
first century AD. Christian additions were made, and the whole edited, at
a later time.

And it came to pass after the third day, while I sat under the oak, lo!
there came a voice out of a bush over against me; and it said, Ezra,

Ezra! And I said: Here am I, Lord. And I rose upon my feet. Then
said he unto me: I did manifestly reveal myself in the bush, and
5 talked with Moses when my people were in bondage in Egypt: and
I sent him, and led my people out of Egypt, and brought them to
Mount Sinai; and I held him by me for many days.

   I told him many wondrous things,
      showed him the secrets of the times,
10   declared to him the end of the seasons:
   Then I commanded him saying:
   These words shalt thou publish openly, but these keep secret,
And now I do say to thee:
   The signs which I have shewed thee,
15   The dreams which thou hast seen,
      and the interpretations which thou hast heard—
lay them up in thy heart! For thou shalt be taken up from among
men, and henceforth thou shalt remain with my Son, and with such
as are like thee, until the times be ended.
20   For the world has lost its youth,
      The times begin to wax old.
For the world-age is divided into twelve parts; nine parts of it are
passed already, and the half of the tenth part; and there remain of it
two parts, besides the half of the tenth part.
25   Now, therefore, set in order thy house,
      and reprove thy people;
         Comfort the lowly among them,
         and instruct those that are wise.
   Now do thou renounce the life that is corruptible,
30   let go from thee the cares of mortality;
   cast from thee the burdens of man,
      put off now the weak nature;
   lay aside thy burdensome cares,
      and hasten to remove from these times!
35   For still worse evils than those which thou hast seen happen shall
yet take place. For the weaker the world grows through age, so much
more shall evils increase upon the dwellers on earth.
   Truth shall withdraw further off,
      and falsehood be nigh at hand:
40 for already the Eagle is hastening to come whom thou sawest in
vision.

l. 2   *Ezra, Ezra.* Ezra in Jewish tradition was the great continuator of the work of
Moses, the example and model of the scribes. To ascribe an apocalypse to
him was to claim the shelter not merely of a respectable antiquity but also of
the Law itself.

l. 12   *These words shalt thou publish openly,* that is, the Law.
      These keep secret. This refers to the apocalyptic tradition, some at least of
which was ascribed to Moses. The oral Law (see **153** and note on *l.* 1) as well

as the written was ascribed to Moses; here his authority is claimed for the apocalyptic material also. It had not been published earlier because Moses had been forbidden to make it known.

l. 17 *Lay them up in thy heart.* These revelations are not for Ezra's own time.

l. 18 *With my Son.* The Messiah, who, as God's Son, is already pre-existent in heaven.

l. 22 *The world-age is divided into twelve parts.* See below on the Two Ages.

l. 35 *Still worse evils.* Before the messianic age must come the messianic afflictions; see **271–2**.

l. 40 *The Eagle.* See 4 Ezra 11(**264**).

262

1 *Enoch* 1. 1f.

The words of the blessing of Enoch, wherewith he blessed the elect and righteous, who will be living in the day of tribulation, when all the wicked and godless are to be removed. And he took up his parable and said—Enoch a righteous man, whose eyes were opened
5 by God, saw the vision of the Holy One in the heavens, which the angels showed me, and from them I heard everything, and from them I understood as I saw, but not for this generation, but for a remote one which is for to come.

HISTORY IN ALLEGORICAL FORM

The apocalyptist very commonly conveys his meaning by portraying contemporary history in symbolic form, and continuing the symbolic narrative so as to include the supernatural events which he believes to be close at hand. This method often permits the dating of apocalypses; the point at which the history loses precision and accuracy is the moment of writing.

263

Psalms of Solomon 2. 1–6, 24–35

The Psalms of Solomon were written about the middle of the first century BC, and seem to have come from the Pharisaic party within Judaism (see **135**). In this Psalm the history is scarcely concealed, except that names are not mentioned.

When the sinner waxed proud, with a battering-ram he cast down
    fortified walls,
      And thou didst not restrain him.
Alien nations ascended thine altar,

5   They trampled it proudly with their sandals;
Because the sons of Jerusalem had defiled the holy things of the Lord,
    Had profaned with iniquities the offerings of God.
Therefore he said: Cast them far from me;
    It was set at naught before God,
10   It was utterly dishonoured;
The sons and the daughters were in grievous captivity,
    Sealed was their neck, branded was it among the nations. . . .

And I saw and entreated the Lord and said,
    Long enough, O Lord, has thine hand been heavy on Israel, in
15   bringing the nations upon them.
For they have made sport unsparingly in wrath and fierce anger;
    And they will make an utter end, unless thou, O Lord, rebuke
      them in thy wrath.
For they have done it not in zeal, but in lust of soul,
20   Pouring out their wrath upon us with a view to rapine.
Delay not, O God, to recompense them on their heads,
    To turn the pride of the dragon into dishonour.
And I had not long to wait before God showed me the insolent
    one slain on the mountains of Egypt,
25   Esteemed of less account than the least, on land and sea;
His body, too, borne hither and thither on the billows with much
    insolence,
      With none to bury him, because he had rejected him with
      dishonour.
30 He reflected not that he was man,
    And reflected not on the latter end;
He said: I will be lord of land and sea;
    And he recognized not that it is God who is great,
    Mighty in his great strength.
35 He is king over the heavens,
    And judgeth kings and kingdoms.
It is he who setteth me up in glory,
    And bringeth down the proud to eternal destruction in dishonour,
Because they knew him not.

l. 1 *With a battering-ram.* This, and other details in the passage, correspond closely
to the siege of Jerusalem by Pompey in 63 BC. Cf. Josephus, *War* i. 147
(Pompey ... brought up the battering engines which had been conveyed
from Tyre), 150 (Many of the priests, seeing the enemy advancing sword in
hand, calmly continued their sacred ministrations, and were butchered in the
act of pouring libations and burning incense).

l. 19 *Not in zeal.* It was indeed God's purpose to punish Israel, but the Roman
soldiers were not acting with this in mind.

l. 22 *The dragon.* Probably the 'insolent one' of the next line; that is, Pompey.

l. 24   *The mountains of Egypt.* After the battle of Pharsalia (48 BC) Pompey escaped, but when he landed in Egypt he was at once killed. The word 'mountains' does not seem apt in reference to Egypt and may be an error for 'rivers' or 'borders'.

l. 33   *It is God who is great.* This is probably an allusion to Pompey's name Magnus, the Great.

264

4 *Ezra* 11

The vision of this chapter, the well known Eagle Vision, is based on Daniel 7. The eagle represents the fourth kingdom seen by Daniel in the vision of ch. 7; but here it stands for the Roman Empire, whereas in Daniel it stands for the Greek.

And it came to pass the second night that I saw a dream: and lo! there came up from the sea an eagle which had twelve feathered wings, and three heads. And I beheld, and lo! he spread his wings over the whole earth, and all the winds of heaven blew on him, and

5 the clouds were gathered together unto him. And I beheld, and lo! out of his wings there grew anti-wings; and they became wings petty and small. But his heads were at rest; the middle head was greater than the other heads, yet it rested with them. And I beheld, and lo! the eagle flew with his wings to reign over the earth and over them

10 that dwell therein. And I beheld how all things under heaven were subject unto him, and no one spake against him—not even one of the creatures upon earth. And I beheld, and lo! the eagle rose upon his talons, and uttered his voice to his wings, saying, Watch not all at once: sleep every one in his place, and watch by course: but let the

15 heads be preserved for the last. And I beheld, and lo! the voice proceeded not from his heads, but from the midst of his body. And I numbered his anti-wings, and lo! there were eight.

And I beheld, and lo! [on the right side] there arose one wing, and reigned over the whole earth. And it came to pass that, after it had

20 reigned, it came to its end and disappeared, so that the place of it was not visible. Then arose the second and reigned, and this bare rule for a long time. And it came to pass that, after it had reigned, it also came to its end, so that it disappeared even as the first. And lo! a voice sounded which said to it: Hear, thou that hast borne rule over the

25 earth so long a time; this I proclaim unto thee before thou shalt disappear—After thee shall none bear rule the length of thy time, nay not even the half of it! Then the third lifted itself up and held the rule even as the former, and it also disappeared. And so it fell to all the wings [in turn] to rule and then disappear. And I beheld, and

30 lo! in process of time the little wings also were set up [upon the right
    side] that they also might hold the rule; and some of them bare rule
    but disappeared suddenly: and some of them were set up but did not
    hold the rule. After this I beheld, and lo! the twelve wings
    disappeared, and two little wings; and nothing was left in the eagle's
35 body save only the three heads that were at rest, and six little wings.
    And I beheld, and lo! from the six little wings two detached
    themselves, and remained under the head that was upon the right
    side: but four remained in their place. And I beheld, and lo! one was
    set up, but immediately disappeared; a second also, and this
40 disappeared more quickly than the first. And I beheld, and lo! the
    two that remained thought also in themselves to reign; and while
    they were thinking thus, lo! one of the heads that were at rest—it,
    namely, that was in the midst—awoke; for this one was greater than
    the two [other] heads. And I beheld how it allied itself with the two
45 other heads; and lo! the head was turned with them that were with
    it, and did eat up the two under-wings that thought to have reigned.
    This head bare rule over the whole earth, and exercised lordship over
    the dwellers therein with much oppression; [and it wielded more
    power over the inhabited world than all the wings that had been.]
50 And after this I beheld, and lo! the middle head suddenly disappeared,
    even as the wings. But there remained the two heads which also
    reigned over the earth, and over the inhabitants therein. And I
    beheld, and lo! the head upon the right side devoured that which
    was upon the left. Then I heard a voice, which said unto me: Look
55 before thee, and consider what thou seest. And I beheld, and lo! as it
    were a lion, roused out of the wood, roaring; and I heard how he
    uttered a man's voice against the eagle; and he spake, saying: Hear,
    thou Eagle—I will talk with thee; the Most High saith to thee: Art
    thou not it that remainest of the four beasts which I made to reign in
60 my world, that the end of my times might come through them?
    Thou, however, the fourth, who art come, hast overcome all the
    beasts that are past;
        Thou hast wielded power over the world with great terror,
            and over all the inhabited earth with grievous oppression;
65   Thou hast dwelt so long in the civilized world with fraud,
            and hast judged the earth, but not with faithfulness:
        For thou hast afflicted the meek,
            and oppressed the peaceable;
        Thou hast hated the upright,
70   and loved liars;
        Thou hast destroyed the strongholds of the fruitful,
            and laid low the walls of such as did thee no harm—
        And so thine insolence hath ascended to the Most High,
            and thy pride to the Mighty One.

75   Then the Most High regarded his times—
        And lo! they were ended:
     And his ages—
        and they were fulfilled.
     Therefore shalt thou disappear, O thou Eagle,
80   and thy horrible wings,
        and thy little wings most evil,
        thy harm-dealing heads,
        thy hurtful talons,
        and all thy worthless body!
85   And so the whole earth, freed from thy violence, shall be refreshed
again, and hope for the judgement and mercy of him that made her.

l. 2   *An eagle which had twelve feathered wings, and three heads.* For a similar
portrayal of an empire and its rulers cf. Rev. 13. 1. The twelve wings are the
Emperors up to Vitellius, with Julius Caesar, Vindex, Nymphidius and Piso;
the three heads Vespasian, Titus and Domitian.

l. 6   *Anti-wings.* This obscure expression probably means rivals to the Emperors.
They are eight in number (see *l.* 17).

l. 21   *This bare rule for a long time.* This refers to Augustus, who ruled (from the
battle of Actium, 31 BC) forty-five years; Tiberius ruled twenty-three, no
other Emperor so long.

l. 34   *Two little wings.* Perhaps Mucianus, proconsul of Syria, and Tiberius
Alexander, prefect of Egypt.

l. 48   *And it wielded more power . . .* This may be an addition by a later editor who
thought that the middle head represented Trajan; its original meaning was
Vespasian.

l. 53   *The head upon the right side devoured . . .* Domitian was believed to have
compassed the death of his brother and predecessor Titus.

l. 56   *A lion.* In the time of Domitian the Messiah arises, and the eagle is destroyed.
It is noteworthy that though Ezra is manifestly dependent upon Dan. 7 he
does not (at this point) identify the 'one like unto a son of man' (Dan. 7. 13)
with the Messiah; a fresh figure is introduced. From this point the apocalypist
has no more exact information; naturally, since he is now writing about the
future.

l. 85   *The . . . earth . . . shall be refreshed again.* A very brief and bare description of
the messianic age.

VISION AND PARABLE

It is impossible to carry through a rigid distinction of these two forms,
and they have already been illustrated incidentally (see especially 4 Ezra
11). The visions described by the apocalyptists were undoubtedly
influenced in form by a literary tradition. It is impossible to think that the
whole of the last passage, for example, was seen and remembered in a

dream. On the other hand, it is quite unnecessary to suppose that, because the apocalyptists edited their visions and gave them literary order, they never received real visionary experiences. It is very probable that they did receive such visions, reflected upon them, and produced thereby the parables and allegories which we now read.

265

4 *Ezra* 13. 1–13

This is the sixth vision of this book. A long interpretation follows, from which some notes are taken here. Almost every detail is interpreted allegorically.

And it came to pass after seven days that I dreamed a dream by night: [and I beheld,] and lo! there arose a violent wind from the sea, and stirred all its waves. And I beheld, and lo! [The wind caused to come up out of the heart of the seas as it were the form of a man. And I
5 beheld, and lo!] this Man flew with the clouds of heaven. And wherever he turned his countenance to look everything seen by him trembled; and whithersoever the voice went out of his mouth, all that heard his voice melted away, as the wax melts when it feels the fire. And after this I beheld, and lo! there was gathered together from
10 the four winds of heaven an innumerable multitude of men to make war against the Man that came up out of the sea. And I beheld, and lo! he cut out for himself a great mountain and flew up upon it. But I sought to see the region or place from whence the mountain had been cut out; and I could not. And after this I beheld, and lo! all who
15 were gathered together against him were seized with great fear; yet they dared to fight. And lo! when he saw the assault of the multitude as they came he neither lifted his hand, nor held spear nor any warlike weapon; but I saw only how he sent out of his mouth as it were a fiery stream, and out of his lips a flaming breath, and out of his
20 tongue he shot forth a stream of sparks. And these were all mingled together—the fiery stream, the flaming breath, and the ... storm, and fell upon the assault of the multitude which was prepared to fight, and burned them all up, so that suddenly nothing more was to be seen of the innumerable multitude save only dust of ashes and
25 smell of smoke. When I saw this I was amazed. Afterwards I beheld the same Man come down from the mountain, and call unto him another multitude which was peaceable. Then he drew nigh unto him the faces of many men, some of whom were glad, some sorrowful; while some were in bonds, some brought others who
30 should be offered.

l. 1   *After seven days,* from the Eagle vision of chs. 11f.; see **264**.
      I dreamed. Cf. 11. 1 and many other passages. The dream is a regular form of revelation, going back to Daniel, and beyond.

l. 4   The form of a man . . . this Man flew with the clouds of heaven. The passage 'the wind . . . and lo!' is not in the Latin VS. from which the translation in the English Apocrypha was made; it is in the Syriac and was omitted probably by error. The description of the Man flying with the clouds, and the phrase 'the form of a man', recall the vision of Dan. 7. 13 ('one like unto a son of man'), and it is very probable that Ezra is dependent upon the earlier work. But the strange expression 'son of man' has disappeared, and it is now said that the Man rises from a storm-tossed sea. In the interpretation it is explained that the Man represents God's son, the Messiah, whom God has kept in readiness through many ages; he is a pre-existent Messiah. The sea may be merely a picturesque detail; more probably it is drawn from some earlier speculation regarding the primal Man, or Saviour, or from a recollection of the agitated deep of Gen. 1. 2, out of which came the first creation.

l. 10   To make war against the Man. Cf. the description in Dan.7 of the four beasts who persecute the people of God (represented by the human figure of the one like a son of man). Ezra elsewhere attests the common belief that the bliss of the messianic age would be ushered in by a period of conflict and woe. See **271–2**.

l. 12   A great mountain. The picture may be derived from Dan. 2. 45, but the use made of it is fresh.

l. 17   Nor held spear nor any warlike weapon. The victory of the Messiah is supernatural. In the interpretation the fire by which the Man slays his enemies is said to be the Law.

l. 26   Another multitude. After the destruction of his adversaries the Messiah assembles his holy people (note that the Man is now wholly distinguished from the people; whether this is so in Dan. 7 is disputed). The description of the peaceable multitude is not in all respects clear. Jews are being brought together from the dispersion; and some of them, it seems, have passed through great tribulation.

266

1 *Enoch* 90. 28–42

1 Enoch 85–90 is a long allegorical account of the history of Israel from the Creation to the messianic age. There is some mixing of metaphor, but in general men, Israelites and others, are represented by various kinds of animals. The present passage is the close of the allegory, which was written probably in or not long after the time of the Maccabees (see the notes and **116–123**).

And I stood up to see till they folded up that old house; and carried off all the pillars, and all the beams and ornaments of the house were at the same time folded up with it, and they carried it off and laid it in a place in the south of the land. And I saw till the Lord of the sheep
5   brought a new house greater and loftier than that first, and set it up in the place of the first which had been folded up: all its pillars were new, and its ornaments were new and larger than those of the first,

the old one which he had taken away, and all the sheep were within it.

10   And I saw all the sheep which had been left, and all the beasts on the earth, and all the birds of the heaven, falling down and doing homage to those sheep and making petition to and obeying them in every thing. And thereafter those three who were clothed in white and had seized me by my hand [who had taken me up before], and
15   the hand of that ram also seizing hold of me, they took me up and set me down in the midst of those sheep before the judgement took place. And those sheep were all white, and their wool was abundant and clean. And all that had been destroyed and dispersed, and all the beasts of the field, and all the birds of the heaven, assembled in that
20   house, and the Lord of the sheep rejoiced with great joy because they were all good and had returned to his house. And I saw till they laid down that sword, which had been given to the sheep, and they brought it back into the house, and it was sealed before the presence of the Lord, and all the sheep were invited into that house, but it held
25   them not. And the eyes of them all were opened, and they saw the good, and there was not one among them that did not see. And I saw that that house was large and broad and very full.

And I saw that a white bull was born, with large horns, and all the beasts of the field and all the birds of the air feared him and made
30   petition to him all the time. And I saw till all their generations were transformed, and they all became white bulls; and the first among them became a lamb, and that lamb became a great animal and had great black horns on its head; and the Lord of the sheep rejoiced over it and over all the oxen. And I slept in their midst: and I awoke and
35   saw everything. This is the vision which I saw while I slept, and I awoke and blessed the Lord of righteousness and gave him glory. Then I wept with a great weeping and my tears stayed not till I could no longer endure it: when I saw, they flowed on account of what I had seen; for everything shall come and be fulfilled, and all the deeds
40   of men in their order were shown to me. On that night I remembered the first dream, and because of it I wept and was troubled—because I had seen that vision.

l. 1   *That old house.* The old Jerusalem is to be replaced by a new one which God himself will establish. The idea of a new Jerusalem, or new Temple, is fairly common in apocalyptic writings; cf. Rev. 21. 2.

l. 4   *The Lord of the sheep.* The faithful of Israel are described as sheep; cf. Ezek. 34, a chapter to which the author of this vision is much indebted.

l. 8   *All the sheep were within it.* A variant reading, giving what is a frequent description of the Temple in the last days, runs, 'the Lord of the sheep was within it.'

l. 10   *The sheep which had been left.* The preceding section of the allegory or vision (90. 20–7) has described a judgement and destruction of apostate 'sheep'.

l. 10   *All the beasts . . . all the birds,* that is, the Gentiles. Cf. Dan. 4. 12, 21f.; Ezek. 31. 6, 13. The Gentiles will be converted and become servants of Israel. The apocalypses differ widely regarding the fate of the Gentiles.

l. 13   *Those three who were clothed in white.* Cf. 1 Enoch 87. 3; they are three arch-angels.

l. 15   *That ram,* probably Elijah; cf. 1 Enoch 89. 52, where, however, he is not called a ram. In 89. 42ff. the ram is first Saul, then those who succeed him as kings.

l. 22   *That sword, which had been given to the sheep.* 1 Enoch 90. 19. The reference is to the fierce and successful resistance made by Israel under the Maccabees, which the author seems to regard as foreshadowing, or even ushering in, the messianic age.

l. 28   *A white bull was born.* The Messiah. It is to be noted that he is born after the Judgement, the establishment of faithful Israel in the new Jerusalem and the conversion of the Gentiles. He is therefore a somewhat otiose figure, for whom the author's evident admiration for Judas Maccabaeus left little room. Adam was represented by a white bull at 85. 3.

l. 31   *The first among them became a lamb, and that lamb became . . .* This is a possible restoration of a corrupt text, which runs: The first among them became (*or,* became among them) a word, and the word became . . . But even with the emendation the text is too corrupt to yield a satisfactory sense.

l. 34   *I slept.* The author speaks in the person of Enoch. This long and highly wrought allegory cannot possibly be regarded as a real dream.

The Essential Notions of Apocalyptic

It would not be wrong to say that the one essential notion of apocalyptic is not (as has too often been supposed) the conviction that the end is near, but that God wills to reveal himself to chosen men, whom he authorizes (or occasionally does not authorize—e.g. Dan. 12. 9; Rev. 10. 4) to communicate the revelation to his people. Various aspects of this divine self-communication will be illustrated below. It is certainly true that apocalyptic often includes the belief that the time is short: God is about to bring his final purposes to pass. Those who have been warned must take appropriate action. Predictions of the future are inevitably various; there never was or could be an apocalyptic orthodoxy. Indeed some apocalyptic writers were decidedly unorthodox, not least those whose interest in the future was minimal.

THE TWO AGES

The apocalyptists inherited the feeling for history which was characteristic of the prophets, and accordingly their thought was cast in a chronological mould. The line drawn between the secret and the manifest activity of God was a line in time, which separated the Present Age from the Age to

Come. The present age witnessed the usurpation of God's authority by evil powers; in the Age to Come God alone would be the supreme ruler, and his perfect will would be perfectly seen and done. This distinction between two ages is no peculiarity of the apocalypses; it was current also among the Rabbis; see **158**.

267

4 Ezra 7. 45–61

And I answered and said: O Lord, I said even then and say now: Blessed are they who come into the world and keep thy commandments.

But concerning those for whom my prayer was offered: who is
5 there of those who have come into the world that has not sinned? Or who of the earth-born is there that has not transgressed thy covenant? And now I see that the coming Age shall bring delight to few, but torment unto many. For the evil heart has grown up in us which has estranged us from God,
10 and brought us into destruction;
And has made known to us the ways of death,
And showed us the paths of perdition,
and removed us far from life;
and that not a few only, but well nigh all that have been created!
15 And he answered me and said:
Hear me, and I will instruct thee,
and a second time will admonish thee:
For this cause the Most High has made not one Age but two.
And whereas thou hast said that the righteous are not many but few,
20 while the ungodly abound—hear the answer to this: Suppose thou have choice stones, in number exceeding few; wilt thou set [place] with them lead and clay?
And I said: Lord, how should it be possible?
And he said unto me: Not only so, but
25 Ask the earth, and she shall tell thee;
Speak to her, and she shall declare it unto thee.
Say to her: Thou bringest forth gold and silver and brass—and also iron and lead and clay: but silver is more abundant than gold, and brass than silver, and iron than brass, lead than iron, and clay
30 than lead. Do thou, then, consider which things are precious and to be desired: that which is abundant or that which is rare?
And I said: O Lord my Lord, that which is plentiful is of less worth, but that which is more rare is precious.
And he answered me and said: Weigh within thyself what thou
35 hast thought! For he that has what is rare rejoices beyond him that has what is plentiful.

So also shall be my promised judgment; I will rejoice over the few
that shall be saved, inasmuch as they it is that make my glory prevail
now already and through them my name is now already named
40   [with praise].
And I will not grieve over the multitude of them that perish: for
they it is who now
are made like vapour,
counted as smoke,
45   are comparable unto the flame:
They are fired, burn hotly, are extinguished!

l. 2   *Blessed are they who come (into the world) and keep thy commandments.* The
words in brackets are added because the phrase 'those who come into the
world' is a common one for 'the human race'. Ezra is appalled by a problem
which appears also in the New Testament. The Law is given as a condition,
or means, of salvation. Few or none observe the Law perfectly; what of the
remainder of mankind? Ezra's evident distress at the fewness of those who
should be saved is illuminating, but he cannot give so hopeful an answer as
Paul.

l. 7   *The coming Age.* See below, where the two Ages are contrasted.

l. 8   *The evil heart,* that is, the evil inclination. See **158** and note.

l. 18   *For this cause the Most High has made not one Age but two,* that is, in order to
redress the wickedness and ill of the present Age. Evil men cannot be allowed
for ever to dominate over the good; there is a just reward for the godly.

l. 37   *So also shall be my promised judgement.* The coming Age will be inaugurated
by the judgement, the separation of good from evil. It may be noted that
though God is said to save the righteous few, it is from their misfortunes, not
from their sins, that he saves them. The apocalyptists in general take the
somewhat naive view that there *are* righteous and there *are* wicked, white
and black; we do not hear of the reclamation and conversion of the wicked.

l. 46   *They are fired, burn hotly, are extinguished!* A period of torment followed by
annihilation seems to be intended.

268

2 Baruch 83. 4–9

Let none therefore of these present things ascend into your hearts,
but above all let us be expectant, because that which is promised to
us shall come. And let us not now look unto the delights of the
Gentiles in the present, but let us remember what has been promised
5   to us in the end. For the ends of the times and of the seasons and
whatsoever is with them shall assuredly pass by together. The
consummation, moreover, of the age shall then show the great might
of its ruler, when all things come to judgement. Do ye therefore
prepare your hearts for that which before ye believed, lest ye come

10 to be in bondage in both worlds, so that ye be led away captive here and be tormented there. For that which exists now, or which has passed away, or which is to come, in all these things, neither is the evil fully evil, nor again the good fully good.

l. 2   Let us be expectant. Baruch (another pseudonym, of course) is dealing with the religious attitude proper to those who are looking for the speedy arrival of a new age. They must not be preoccupied with things belonging to the present world, but 'look for the kingdom of God' (cf. Mark 15. 43; Luke 2. 25; Col 3. 1f.).

l. 7   The consummation ... of the age. The end of the present order and the beginning of the new. As frequently, between the two Ages stands the judgement.

l. 10   In bondage in both worlds. To endure bondage now would be a price worth paying for bliss in the world to come. But to apostatize now would lead to the worst results in both worlds.

l. 12   Neither is the evil fully evil, nor again the good fully good. In contrast with the age to come, in which felicity and torment are unmixed. Baruch is apparently referring to the doctrine that in this Age the good receive full punishment for their few sins, that their bliss may be perfect in the Age to come, and that the wicked, for a similar reason, receive compensation for their few virtues.

JUDGEMENT AND THE KINGDOM OF GOD

Reference to a final judgement has appeared in many of the passages already quoted; it is a constant theme of apocalyptic, and a necessary event before present wrongs could be righted under the rule of God.

269

Assumption of Moses 10

This book was probably written during the lifetime of Jesus.

> And then his kingdom shall appear throughout all his creation,
> And then Satan shall be no more,
> And sorrow shall depart with him.
> Then the hands of the angel shall be filled
> 5 Who has been appointed chief,
> And he shall forthwith avenge them of their enemies.
> For the Heavenly One will arise from his royal throne,
> And he will go forth from his holy habitation
> With indignation and wrath on account of his sons.
> 10 And the earth shall tremble: to its confines shall it be shaken:
> And the high mountains shall be made low
> And the hills shall be shaken and fall.
> And the horns of the sun shall be broken and he shall be turned into darkness;

15   And the moon shall not give her light, and be turned wholly into blood.
       And the circle of the stars shall be disturbed.
       And the sea shall retire into the abyss,
       And the fountains of waters shall fail,
20   And the rivers shall dry up.
       For the Most High will arise, the Eternal God alone,
       And he will appear to punish the Gentiles,
       And he will destroy all their idols.
       Then thou, O Israel, shalt be happy,
25   And thou shalt mount upon the necks and wings of the eagle,
       And they shall be ended.
       And God will exalt thee,
       And he will cause thee to approach to the heaven of the stars,
       In the place of their habitation.
30   And thou shalt look from on high and shalt see thy enemies in Gehenna,
       And thou shalt recognize them and rejoice,
       And thou shalt give thanks and confess thy Creator.
       And do thou, Joshua the son of Nun, keep these words and this
35   book: for from my death [assumption] until his advent there shall be CCL times. And this is the course of the times which they shall pursue till they are consummated. And I shall go to sleep with my fathers. Wherefore, Joshua thou son of Nun, [be strong and] be of good courage; [for] God hath chosen [thee] to be minister in the
40   same covenant.

l. 1   *Then his kingdom shall appear.* There has probably been some dislocation in the text of this apocalypse; but it is clear that 'Moses' means that the coming of the kingdom will be preceded by a period of special affliction and distress for the people of God. This period was often called the 'travail-pains of the Messiah'; but it should be observed that in the Assumption of Moses there is no Messiah.

l. 2   *Satan shall be no more.* The establishment of God's rule necessarily means the removal of Satan who has usurped God's authority.

l. 7   *The Heavenly One will arise from his royal throne.* It becomes very clear that the 'coming of the Kingdom' is a way of expressing God's royal authority, now at length put into action.

l. 10   *The earth shall tremble.* Physical portents are particularly characteristic of apocalyptic over against prophecy; see above, p. 316.

l. 21   *The Eternal God alone.* The emphasis on the fact that God works alone excludes the notion of a Messiah, and may be intended to combat such a notion.

l. 22   *To punish the Gentiles.* 'Moses' takes a nationalist view of the kingdom of God. For a different view of the fate of the Gentiles see the next passage, **270**.

l. 25 *Mount upon ... be ended.* The text seems to be corrupt. Charles emends to:
> Thou shalt go up against the eagle
> And its necks and wings shall be destroyed.

l. 29 *In the place of their habitation.* Another corrupt passage; Charles's emendation is:
> And he will establish thy habitation among them.

l. 34 *Joshua (the son of) Nun.* This part of the apocalypse is cast in the form of an address made by Moses to Joshua. For this use of pseudonymity see above, pp. 317–20.

l. 35 *There shall be CCL times.* By 'times' are meant weeks of years, that is 1750 years altogether. This is the period between the death of Moses and the coming of the kingdom of God. We do not know the date the author would have ascribed to the death of Moses, but there can be little doubt that he thought that, in his day, the 250 times had almost elapsed. Apocalypses were written under the conviction that the end was near.

270

Sibylline Oracles iii. 767–808

In antiquity, considerable weight was attached to utterances attributed to the various Sibyls. Their oracles conveyed, for those who could understand them, divine judgements on human affairs. The production of such oracles was easy to anyone capable of writing Greek hexameter verses (their traditional medium), and Jewish writers (later, Christian also) were not slow to adopt this valuable means of propaganda. The Sibylline books as they have come down to us are not a unity, but there can be no doubt of the Jewish origin of the following verses.

> And then indeed he will raise up his kingdom for all ages over men, he who once gave a holy law to godly men, to all of whom he promised to open out the earth and the world, and the portals of the blessed, and all joys, and everlasting sense and eternal gladness.
>
> 5 And from every land they shall bring frankincense and gifts to the house of the great God: and there shall be no other house for men even in future generations to know but only that which he has given to faithful men to honour. For mortals call that alone the house of the great God. And all the paths of the plain and the sheer banks, and
>
> 10 the lofty mountains and the wild sea waves shall become easy to travel over by foot or sail in those days. For nought but peace shall come upon the land of the good: and the prophets of the Mighty God shall take away the sword. For they are the judges of mortal men and just kings. Even wealth shall be righteous among men: for
>
> 15 this is the judgement and the rule of the Mighty God.
>
> Rejoice, O virgin, and exult: for to thee the Creator of heaven and earth has given everlasting joy. And in thee shall he dwell, and thou shalt have eternal light.

And wolves and lambs together shall crop grass upon the
20 mountains, and leopards shall feed with kids. Prowling bears shall lie
with calves, and the carnivorous lion shall eat in the manger like the
ox, and the tiniest infants shall lead them in bonds, for he shall make
the beasts upon the earth incapable of harm. Serpents and asps shall
sleep with babes, and shall not harm them: for God's hand shall be
25 stretched over them.

Now I will tell thee a very evident sign, that thou mayest
understand when the end of all things is coming on the earth. When
swords in the star-lit heaven appear by night towards dusk and
towards dawn, and straightway dust is carried from heaven to earth,
30 and all the brightness of the sun fails at midday from the heavens,
and the moon's rays shine forth and come back to earth, and a sign
comes from the rocks with dripping streams of blood: and in a cloud
ye shall see a battle of foot and horse, as a hunt of wild beasts, like
unto misty clouds. This is the consummation of war which God,
35 whose dwelling is in heaven, is bringing to pass. But all must sacrifice
to the Mighty King.

l. 2   *Who once gave a holy law to godly men.* The Jewish propagandist is too subtle
to declare himself, though his meaning is apparent to the initiated.

l. 5   *From every land . . . of the great God.* The 'Sibyl' is a Jewish universalist, who
believes not in the destruction but in the conversion of the Gentiles. The
Temple in Jerusalem will become the centre of a worldwide faith and cultus.

l. 16   *O virgin.* Presumably Jersualem. The Old Testament language (e.g. 2 Kings
19. 21) would be evident to Jews, cryptic to others.

l. 19   *Wolves and lambs . . .* Probably a reference to Isa. 11. 6.

l. 26   *A very evident sign.* This interest in signs brings the author of the present
passage into the field of apocalyptic.

l. 29   *To earth . . .* 'The line is defective and emendations can only be conjectural'
(H. C. O. Lanchester in Charles, op. cit., ii. 392).

l. 34   *The consummation of war.* It is possible that the text is again corrupt; some
would read 'the end of all things'.

THE MESSIANIC WOES AND THE MESSIAH

The notion that the good Age would be preceded by a period of affliction
and trial has its roots in Old Testament prophecy and other religious
movements of the ancient East. It appears in many apocalyptic documents,
and in the New Testament, but in several different forms. Sometimes the
distress is political and military; sometimes it arises from supernatural
portents; often from a combination of both. Similarly there is no
consistency of thought about the Messiah.

271

2 *Baruch* 25–30

And he answered and said unto me: Thou too shalt be preserved till that time, till that sign which the Most High will work for the inhabitants of the earth in the end of days. This therefore shall be the sign. When a stupor shall seize the inhabitants of the earth, and they
5 shall fall into many tribulations, and again when they shall fall into great torments. And it will come to pass when they say in their thoughts by reason of their much tribulation: The Mighty One doth no longer remember the earth—yea, it will come to pass when they abandon hope, that the time will then awake.
10 And I answered and said: Will that tribulation which is to be continue a long time, and will that necessity embrace many years?

And he answered and said unto me: Into twelve parts is that time divided, and each one of them is reserved for that which is appointed for it. In the first part there shall be the beginning of commotions.
15 And in the second part there shall be slayings of the great ones. And in the third part the fall of many by death. And in the fourth part the sending of the sword. And in the fifth part famine and the withholding of rain. And in the sixth part earthquakes and terrors. [Wanting]. And in the eighth part a multitude of spectres and attacks
20 of the Shedim. And in the ninth part the fall of fire. And in the tenth part rapine and much oppression. And in the eleventh part wickedness and unchastity. And in the twelfth part confusion from the mingling together of all those things aforesaid. For these parts of that time are reserved, and shall be mingled one with another and minister one to
25 another. For some shall leave out some of their own, and receive in its stead from others, and some complete their own and that of others, so that those may not understand who are upon the earth in those days that this is the consummation of the times.

Nevertheless, whosoever understandeth shall then be wise. For the
30 measure and reckoning of that time are two parts a week of seven weeks. And I answered and said: It is good for a man to come and behold, but it is better that he should not come lest he fall. [But I will say this also: Will he who is incorruptible despise those things which are corruptible, and whatever befalls in the case of those things which
35 are corruptible, so that he might look only to those things which are not corruptible?] But if, O Lord, those things shall assuredly come to pass which thou hast foretold to me, so do thou show this also unto me if indeed I have found grace in thy sight. Is it in one place or in one of the parts of the earth that those things are come to pass, or will
40 the whole earth experience them?

And he answered and said unto me: Whatever will then befall will befall the whole earth; therefore all who live will experience

them. For at that time I will protect only those who are found in
those selfsame days in this land. And it shall come to pass when all is
45 accomplished that was to come to pass in those parts, that the Messiah
shall then begin to be revealed. And Behemoth shall be revealed
from his place and Leviathan shall ascend from the sea, those two
great monsters which I created on the fifth day of creation, and shall
have kept until that time; and then they shall be for food for all that
50 are left. The earth also shall yield its fruit tenthousandfold and on
each [?] vine there shall be a thousand branches, and each branch
shall produce a thousand clusters, and each cluster produce a thousand
grapes, and each grape produce a cor of wine. And those who have
hungered shall rejoice: moreover, also, they shall behold marvels
55 every day. For winds shall go forth from before me to bring every
morning the fragrance of aromatic fruits, and at the close of the day
clouds distilling the dew of health. And it shall come to pass at that
selfsame time that the treasury of manna shall again descend from on
high, and they will eat of it in those years, because these are they who
60 have come to the consummation of time.

And it shall come to pass after these things, when the time of the
advent of the Messiah is fulfilled, that he shall return in glory.

Then all who have fallen asleep in hope of him shall rise again.
And it shall come to pass at that time that the treasuries will be
65 opened in which is preserved the number of the souls of the righteous,
and they shall come forth, and a multitude of souls shall be seen
together in one assemblage of one thought, and the first shall rejoice
and the last shall not be grieved. For they know that the time is come
of which it is said, that it is the consummation of the times. But the
70 souls of the wicked, when they behold all these things, shall then
waste away the more. For they shall know that their torment is come
and their perdition has arrived.

l. 1   *Thou too.* That is, Baruch, who is supposed to receive the apocalypse.

l. 12   *Into twelve parts is that time divided.* This kind of cryptic chronology was
popular among those who 'calculated the end'. See for example the passage
from *Ass. Mos.* 10 quoted above (**269**).

l. 18   *Terrors.* Reference to the seventh part of the time has fallen out of the text.

ll. 27–9   *So that those may not understand ... shall then be wise.* The author
distinguishes between himself and his friends, who can discern the signs of
the times, and those who either make no calculations at all or differ from
him in their conclusions. If there are those who hold a different (and, to his
mind, incorrect) view, it is because their misapprehension has been willed
by God.

l. 30   *Two parts a week of seven weeks.* This seems unintelligible. There may have
been corruption in the text. If it is to be emended the simplest guess is that
Baruch wrote not 'two' but 'twelve parts', and meant that the whole time of

the tribulation would last a week of seven weeks (perhaps, forty-nine years). But this is no more than a guess.

ll. 32–6 *But I will say ... not corruptible.* This sentence seems to interrupt the thought and to be out of place here. It may have been displaced from a point later in the book (see 43. 2).

l. 44 *In this land.* Palestine will be an island of safety. The thought is not uncommon.

l. 45 *The Messiah shall then begin to be revealed,* that is, after the tribulation. In this apocalypse the Messiah is revealed, but is not said to do anything. He is really an unnecessary figure.

ll. 46f. *Behemoth ... and Leviathan.* These two monsters appear in the Old Testament (e.g. Job 40. 15, 25); as the context shows they belong to the creation myth. There is other evidence for the belief that they would provide food for the messianic banquet.

l. 50 *Tenthousandfold.* For this opinion also there is other evidence. The prediction was apparently ascribed to Jesus by Papias (*apud* Irenaeus, *Haer.* v. 33).

l. 58 *The treasury of manna.* This belief also is widely attested in Jewish sources, and appears in the New Testament (see Rev. 2. 17, with Charles's note for parallels).

l. 62 *He shall return in glory.* This has been taken to mean, He will, after residence on earth, return to heaven; this is however improbable. It is more likely that the resurrection would be heralded by the coming of the Messiah than by his departure. This statement may simply be parallel to 'the Messiah shall then begin to be revealed' (*l.* 45). But the use of the word 'return' suggests that we may be dealing here with a Christian interpolation.

272

Psalms of Solomon 17. 23–51

In the earlier part of the Psalm (which is to be dated soon after Pompey's capture of Jerusalem, 63 BC; see **126**) the writer laments the calamities that have befallen his people by reason of foreign invaders, and sinful Jews.

> Behold, O Lord, and raise up unto them their king, the son of David,
>   At the time in the which thou seest, O God, that he may reign
>   over Israel thy servant.
> And gird him with strength, that he may shatter unrighteous rulers,
> 5   And that he may purge Jerusalem from nations that trample her
>   down to destruction.
> Wisely, righteously he shall thrust out sinners from the inheritance,
>   He shall destroy the pride of the sinner as a potter's vessel.
> With a rod of iron he shall break in pieces all their substance,
> 10 He shall destroy the godless nations with the word of his mouth;
> At his rebuke nations shall flee before him,
>   And he shall reprove sinners for the thoughts of their heart.

And he shall gather together a holy people, whom he shall lead in righteousness,

15   And he shall judge the tribes of the people that has been sanctified by the Lord his God.

And he shall not suffer unrighteousness to lodge any more in their midst,

Nor shall there dwell with them any man that knoweth wickedness,

20   For he shall know them, that they are all sons of their God.

And he shall divide them according to their tribes upon the land,

And neither sojourner nor alien shall sojourn with them any more.

He shall judge peoples and nations in the wisdom of his righteousness. *Selah.*

25   And he shall have the heathen nations to serve him under his yoke;

And he shall glorify the Lord in a place to be seen of [?] all the earth;

And he shall purge Jerusalem, making it holy as of old:

So that nations shall come from the ends of the earth to see his glory,

30   Bringing as gifts her sons who had fainted,

And to see the glory of the Lord, wherewith God hath glorified her.

And he shall be a righteous king, taught of God, over them,

And there shall be no unrighteousness in his days in their midst,

35   For all shall be holy and their king the anointed of the Lord.

For he shall not put his trust in horse and rider and bow,

Nor shall he multiply for himself gold and silver for war,

Nor shall he gather confidence from [?] a multitude [?] for the day of battle.

40   The Lord himself is his king, the hope of him that is mighty through his hope in God.

[?] All nations shall be in fear before him,

For he will smite the earth with the word of his mouth for ever.

He will bless the people of the Lord with wisdom and gladness,

45   And he himself will be pure from sin, so that he may rule a great people.

He will rebuke rulers, and remove sinners by the might of his word;

And relying upon his God, throughout his days he will not stumble;

50   For God will make him mighty by means of his holy spirit,

And wise by means of the spirit of understanding, with strength and righteousness.

And the blessing of the Lord will be with him: he will be strong and stumble not;

55   His hope will be in the Lord: who then can prevail against him?

He will be mighty in his works, and strong in the fear of God,

He will be shepherding the flock of the Lord faithfully and righteously,

And he will suffer none among them to stumble in their pasture,
60 He will lead them all aright,
And there will be no pride among them that any among them
should be oppressed.
This will be the majesty of the king of Israel whom God knoweth;
He will raise him up over the house of Israel to correct him.
65 His words shall be more refined than costly gold, the choicest;
In the assemblies he will judge the peoples, the tribes of the
sanctified.
His words shall be like the words of the holy ones in the midst of
sanctified peoples.
70 Blessed be they that shall be in those days,
In that they shall see the good fortune of Israel which God shall
bring to pass in the gathering together of the tribes.
May the Lord hasten his mercy upon Israel!
May he deliver us from the uncleanness of unholy enemies!
75 The Lord himself is our king for ever and ever.

l. 1   *The son of David.* In 17. 5 the promise to David's family is recalled. The
Messiah of this Psalm is a warrior, who will triumph over Israel's foes.

l. 22   *Neither sojourner nor alien* . . . Palestine will be evacuated of all non-Jewish
residents. The Gentiles will be spared but will be governed by the Messiah.

l. 35   *Their king the anointed of the Lord.* A literal rendering of the Greek text is, the
Lord Messiah (Messiah = Anointed One). It is however very probable that
the Psalms were originally written in Hebrew, though they are no longer
extant in that language, and the Hebrew which 'Lord Messiah' represents
could, if unpointed, equally well be read as 'the Lord's Anointed'. It is
probable that the Greek translator is here in error, since in a similar passage
(18. 6) we have 'his (*sc.* the Lord's) anointed'. The Lord's Christ is a common
phrase, and though 'King Messiah' also is common in Rabbinic literature this
hardly supplies precedent for 'Lord Messiah'. It may be that the erring
translator was a Christian (cf. Luke 2. 11), but this is by no means necessary.

l. 36   *He shall not put his trust* . . . Cf. Deut. 17. 16f. The new king will not fall into
the errors of David's son Solomon.

l. 40   *The Lord himself is his king,* and thus the Messiah represents to his people the
kingship of God.

l. 50   *Holy Spirit.* Better, spirit of holiness. There is no reference to the Holy Spirit.
Cf. Isa. 11. 1.

l. 57   *Shepherding the flock of the Lord.* Cf. Micah 5. 4; Ezek. 34. 23.

ll. 65, 68   *His words.* The king will have some of the properties of a Pharisaic
scribe; he will be a teacher as well as a ruler.

THE SON OF MAN

No attempt will be made here to give an account of the problems raised
by the use of this term in the Gospels, much less to answer them. There

are indeed few New Testament problems that require a more extensive knowledge of Jewish and kindred literature, though when these have been ransacked it remains very doubtful whether 'the Son of man' was ever in Jewish use as a *title* for the Messiah, or for anyone else. That the Gospels use it as a *title* for Jesus seems clear; whether he used it as a *title* for himself is a matter of dispute, as is its origin. The words *Son of man*, or *the Son of man*, or *that Son of man* occur in, or are suggested by, the following passages which are often quoted in discussions of the question. It must be remembered that '(the) son of man' is a Semitic idiom for '(the) man'.

273

Daniel 7. 1–14

On the date and origin of Daniel see above, **260** and note.

In the first year of Belshazzar king of Babylon Daniel had a dream and visions of his head upon his bed: then he wrote the dream and told the sum of the matters. Daniel spake and said, I saw in my vision by night, and, behold, the four winds of the heaven brake forth upon
5   the great sea. And four great beasts came up from the sea, diverse one from another. The first was like a lion, and had eagle's wings: I beheld till the wings thereof were plucked, and it was lifted up from the earth, and made to stand upon two feet as a man, and a man's heart was given to it. And behold another beast, a second, like to a
10 bear, and it was raised up on one side, and three ribs were in his mouth between his teeth: and they said unto it, Arise, devour much flesh. After this I beheld, and lo another, like a leopard, which had upon the back of it four wings of a fowl; the beast had also four heads; and dominion was given to it. After this I saw in the night
15 visions, and behold a fourth beast, terrible and powerful, and strong exceedingly; and it had great iron teeth: it devoured and brake in pieces, and stamped the residue with his feet: and it was diverse from all the beasts that were before it; and it had ten horns. I considered the horns, and, behold, there came up among them another horn, a
20 little one, before which three of the first horns were plucked up by the roots: and, behold, in this horn were eyes like the eyes of a man, and a mouth speaking great things. I beheld till thrones were placed, and one that was ancient of days did sit: his raiment was white as snow, and the hair of his head like pure wool; his throne was fiery
25 flames, and the wheels thereof burning fire. A fiery stream issued and came forth from before him; thousand thousands ministered unto him, and ten thousand times ten thousand stood before him; the judgement was set, and the books were opened. I beheld at that time because of the voice of the great words which the horn spake; I
30 beheld even till the beast was slain, and his body destroyed, and he

was given to be burned with fire. And as for the rest of the beasts their dominion was taken away: yet their lives were prolonged for a season and a time. I saw in the night visions, and, behold, there came with the clouds of heaven one like unto a son of man, and he came
35 even to the ancient of days, and they brought him near before him. And there was given him dominion, and glory, and a kingdom, that all the peoples, nations, and languages should serve him: his dominion is an everlasting dominion, which shall not pass away, and his kingdom that which shall not be destroyed.

l. 5   *The great sea.* Cf. the reference to the sea out of which the 'Man' rises in 4 Ezra 13. 3. This is a strong indication that in this human figure we are dealing with an ancient myth, probably a cosmological myth. It may be that ultimately the 'Son of man' became simply a feature of the Jewish messianic hope, but his origin may well lie elsewhere, in speculations concerning a primal, or heavenly, man.
Four great beasts. The beasts are explained in the second part of the chapter as 'four kings'; 'four kingdoms' would have been a plainer statement. It seems that the first beast represents the Babylonian Empire, the second the Median, the third the Persian, and the fourth the Greek Empire of Alexander and his successors. The little horn represents Antiochus IV Epiphanes, whose assaults upon Judaism provoked the writing of Daniel.

l. 22   *Thrones were placed.* If this means that the Son of man is to sit on a throne beside God, it squares ill with the view (see next note) that he is no more than a personification of Israel.

l. 34   *One like unto a son of man,* that is to say, a human figure. Like the four beasts the human figure is explained in the second part of the chapter: The kingdom and the dominion, and the greatness of the kingdoms under the whole heaven, shall be given to the people of the saints of the Most High (7. 27). Thus the human figure represents Israel; his glory is the glory of the people. It must not be inferred from this that he is a mere personification; see the preceding note, and the fact that elsewhere in Daniel nations are represented by angels, real personal heavenly beings. It seems probable that the 'Man' was originally a figure in an ancient myth, was taken over by the author of Daniel for the present purpose, and by reason of his functions as representing the people of God came ultimately to have messianic status.

274

1 *Enoch* (*a*) 48 (*b*) 69. 26–9 (*c*) 71. 14–17

The central section (37–71) of 1 Enoch, generally known as the Similitudes of Enoch, contains frequent reference to a person described as the (or that) Son of man. The date of the Similitudes is disputed, but may be contemporary with the New Testament.

(*a*)   And in that place I saw the fountain of righteousness
Which was inexhaustible:
And around it were many fountains of wisdom:

And all the thirsty drank of them,
5 And were filled with wisdom,
And their dwellings were with the righteous and holy and elect.
And at that hour that Son of man was named
In the presence of the Lord of Spirits,
And his name before the Head of Days.
10 Yea, before the sun and the signs were created,
Before the stars of the heaven were made,
His name was named before the Lord of Spirits.
He shall be a staff to the righteous whereon to stay themselves and
    not fall,
15 And he shall be the light of the Gentiles,
And the hope of those who are troubled of heart,
All who dwell on earth shall fall down and worship him,
And will praise and bless and celebrate with song the Lord of Spirits.
And for this reason hath he been chosen and hidden before him,
20 Before the creation of the world and for evermore.
And the wisdom of the Lord of Spirits hath revealed him to the holy
    and righteous;
For he hath preserved the lot of the righteous,
Because they have hated and despised this world of unrighteousness,
25 And have hated all its works and ways in the name of the Lord of
    Spirits:
For in his name they are saved,
And according to his good pleasure hath it been in regard to their
    life.
30 In these days downcast in countenance shall the kings of the earth
    have become,
And the strong who possess the land because of the works of their
    hands,
For on the day of their anguish and affliction they shall not be able
35   to save themselves.
And I will give them over into the hands of mine elect:
As straw in the fire so shall they burn before the face of the righteous,
And no trace of them shall any more be found.
And on the day of their affliction there shall be rest on the earth,
40 And before them they shall fall and not rise again:
And there shall be no one to take them with his hands and raise
    them:
For they have denied the Lord of Spirits and his Anointed.
The name of the Lord of Spirits be blessed.

45 (*b*) And there was great joy amongst them,
And they blessed and glorified and extolled
Because the name of that Son of man had been revealed unto them.
And he sat on the throne of his glory,

And the sum of judgement was given unto the Son of man,
50 And he caused the sinners to pass away and be destroyed from off the
    face of the earth,
  And those who have led the world astray.
  With chains shall they be bound,
  And in their assemblage-place of destruction shall they be im-
55   prisoned,
  And all their works vanish from the face of the earth.
  And from henceforth there shall be nothing corruptible;
  For that Son of man has appeared,
  And has seated himself on the throne of his glory,
60 And all evil shall pass away before his face,
  And the word of that Son of man shall go forth
  And be strong before the Lord of Spirits.
      This is the third Parable of Enoch.

(*c*) And he came to me and greeted me with his voice, and said unto
65   me:
  This is the Son of man who is born unto righteousness,
  And righteousness abides over him,
  And the righteousness of the Head of Days forsakes him not.
  And he said unto me:
70 He proclaims unto thee peace in the name of the world to come;
  For from hence has proceeded peace since the creation of the world,
  And so shall it be unto thee for ever and for ever and ever.
  And all shall walk in his ways since righteousness never forsaketh
    him:
75 With him will be their dwelling-places, and with him their heritage,
  And they shall not be separated from him for ever and ever and ever.
  And so there shall be length of days with that Son of man,
  And the righteous shall have peace and an upright way
  In the name of the Lord of Spirits for ever and ever.

l. 1 *In that place.* Enoch sees heaven, and even God himself (described as the Lord
of Spirits, and the Head of Days). It will be remembered that the secrets
disclosed in apocalyptic are not exclusively secrets of the future.

l. 10 *Before the sun and the signs were created . . . his name was named.* Cf. *l.* 20. The
Son of man is represented as having a real pre-existence as a heavenly being.

l. 19 *Hath he been chosen and hidden before him.* The Son of man holds his office in
dependence on the will of God; but his existence is at the time of writing an
apocalyptic secret, known only to the apocalyptist and the circle to which he
discloses his visions.

l. 21 *The wisdom of the Lord of Spirits hath revealed him to the holy and righteous,* that
is, by means of Enoch and his visions. In face of sayings such as this it is
difficult to think that (in 1 Enoch) the Son of man is identified with the
righteous as a group.

l. 27 In his name they are saved. The righteous are saved by the Son of man from their affliction. There is no suggestion in 1 Enoch that the Son of man came to seek and save that which was lost (Luke 19. 10) or to save men from their sins.

l. 38 No trace of them shall any more be found. The wicked are annihilated.

l. 43 His Anointed, or, if we take the word as a technical term, his Messiah. The question whether the Son of man in 1 Enoch is thought of as Messiah is a difficult and disputed one.

l. 47 The name of that Son of man had been revealed unto them. The name of the Son of man is made generally known in the last days.

l. 49 The sum of judgement was given unto the Son of man. The Son of man acts as the judge of sinners. The 'sum of judgement' means 'all judgement'; cf. John 5. 22, 27.

l. 66 This is the Son of man who is born unto righteousness. This translation (of R. H. Charles) does not represent the text of the MSS., which give the second person, not the third: Thou art the Son of man ... (and similarly in the following verses). The scene is the final exaltation of Enoch to heaven (these are the last verses of the Similitudes); according to Charles he is shown the Son of man, about whom he has already received revelations; according to the MSS. it is revealed to Enoch, as the last secret of all, that he himself is the Son of man. Charles abandoned the MSS. because they did not seem to him intelligible; and indeed the thought they convey is very difficult. The Son of man (according to the Similitudes) has existed from eternity in heaven. Enoch, the man, came to exist on earth and after a long life is translated to heaven. We now learn that the one of these distinct characters *is* the other. This identification cannot be rationally conceived; but rationality is perhaps the last quality we should expect in an apocalypse, and the wisest course may be to suppose that there were circles in Judaism in which this strange belief was held. There are several other pieces of evidence which attest the belief that Enoch was translated to heaven to become a celestial being. If there were, in the first century AD, Jews who believed that it was possible for a man to be exalted to heaven so as to be identified with a supernatural being who was called Son of man and was to come in glory as judge and saviour, their existence and their belief can hardly fail to be relevant to the study of the Gospels.

Mysticism

To live in communion with the secrets of heaven is mysticism, and as was noted above it is never far from apocalypticism, in which the secrets of the upper world, and in close relation with them the secrets of the future, are revealed (Greek, ἀποκαλύπτειν). To some extent this intercourse with the heavenly world was a literary convention, but it was not wholly so; much of apocalyptic was based on sincere (even if sometimes misguided) religious experience.

275

1 *Enoch* 14

Compare **274**. This part of 1 Enoch may go back as far as the third century
BC.

This book is the word of righteousness and of reproof for the
Watchers who are from eternity, as the Holy and Great One
commanded in that vision. I saw in my sleep what I will now tell
with the tongue of flesh and with my breath which the Great One
5 has given to men in the mouth, that they might speak with it and
understand with the heart. As he has created and appointed men to
understand the word of knowledge, so he created and appointed me
to reprove the Watchers, the sons of heaven. And I wrote out your
petition, but in my vision thus it appeared, that your petition will
10 not be granted you for all the days of eternity; and complete
judgement has been decreed against you, and you will not have peace.
And from now on you will not ascend into heaven for all eternity,
and it has been decreed that you are to be bound in the earth for all
the days of eternity. And before this you will have seen the
15 destruction of your beloved sons, and you will not be able to enjoy
them, but they will fall before you by the sword. And your petition
will not be granted in respect of them, nor in respect of yourselves.
And while you weep and supplicate, you do not speak a single word
from the writing which I have written. And the vision appeared to
20 me as follows: Behold clouds called me in the vision, and mist called
me, and the path of the stars and flashes of lightning hastened me and
drove me, and in the vision winds caused me to fly and hastened me
and lifted me up into heaven. And I proceeded until I came near to a
wall which was built of hailstones, and a tongue of fire surrounded
25 it, and it began to make me afraid. And I went into the tongue of fire
and came near to a large house which was built of hailstones, and the
wall of that house was like a mosaic made of hailstones, and its floor
was snow. Its roof was like the path of the stars and flashes of
lightning, and among them were fiery Cherubim, and their heaven
30 was like water. And there was a fire burning around its wall, and its
door was ablaze with fire. And I went into that house, and it was hot
as fire and cold as snow, and there was neither pleasure nor life in it.
Fear covered me and trembling took hold of me, and as I was shaking
and trembling, I fell on my face. And I saw in the vision, and behold,
35 another house, which was larger than the former, and all its doors
were open before me, and it was built of a tongue of fire. And in
everything it so excelled in glory and splendour and size that I am
unable to describe to you its glory and its size. And its floor was fire,
and above were lightning and the path of the stars, and its roof also
40 was a burning fire. And I looked and I saw in it a high throne, and its

appearance was like ice and its surrounds like the shining sun and the sound of Cherubim. And from underneath the high throne there flowed out rivers of burning fire so that it was impossible to look at it. And He who is great in glory sat on it, and his raiment was
45 brighter than the sun, and whiter than any snow. And no angel could enter, and at the appearance of the face of him who is honoured and praised no creature of flesh could look. A sea of fire burnt around him, and a great fire stood before him, and none of those around him came near to him. Ten thousand times ten thousand stood before
50 him, but he needed no holy counsel. And the Holy Ones who were near to him did not leave by night or day, and did not depart from him. And until then I had a covering on my face, as I trembled. And the Lord called me with his own mouth and said to me, Come hither, Enoch, to my holy word. And he lifted me up and brought me near
55 to the door. And I looked, with my face down.

l. 2   *The Watchers* appear to be fallen angels.

l. 41   *Its surrounds like the shining sun.* The Greek version refers to the wheel(s) (of the throne). This recalls the wheels in the chariot vision of Ezekiel (1. 15–21).

Apocalyptic Judaism, like all Judaism, was based upon exegesis of a sacred text; in its mystical strand the passages most used were the creation narrative (Gen. 1; 2) and the chapters of the Chariot (Ezek. 1; 10). The latter in particular led both to mystical experience and to theological speculation, and its dangers were recognized.

276

Mishnah Hagigah 2. 1

The forbidden degrees may not be expounded before three persons, nor the Story of Creation before two, nor the chapter of the Chariot before one alone, unless he is a sage that understands of his own knowledge. Whosoever gives his mind to four things it were better
5 for him if he had not come into the world—what is above? what is beneath? what was beforetime? and what will be hereafter? And whosoever takes no thought for the honour of his Maker, it were better for him if he had not come into the world.

l. 3   *Before one alone.* There was the danger of creating an esoteric tradition if the hearer was unable to listen critically.

ll. 5, 6   *Above . . . beneath . . . aforetime . . . hereafter.* The first two words cover mystical speculation, the third and fourth apocalyptic 'history'.

277

Mishnah Megillah 4. 10

The story of Reuben is read out but not interpreted; the story of Tamar is read out and interpreted. The first story of the calf is read out and interpreted, and the second is read out but not interpreted. The Blessing of the Priests and the story of David and of Amnon are
5 read out but not interpreted. They may not use the chapter of the Chariot as a reading from the Prophets; but R. Judah permits it. R. Eliezer says: They do not use the chapter *Cause Jerusalem to know* as a reading from the Prophets.

l. 4   The story of David: 2 Sam. 11. 2–17.

Four rabbis in particular were said to have 'entered into Paradise', that is, to have seen the secrets of the heavenly world. Only one, R. Akiba, came out of the experience unharmed. The account is given here from a passage in the Tosephta; there are parallels in Babylonian Hagigah 14b; Jerusalem Hagigah 77b; Song of Songs Rabbah 1. 4.

278

Tosephta Hagigah 2. 3, 4 (ETr. C. Rowland)

Four men entered into a garden. Ben Azzai, Ben Zoma, Aher, and R. Akiba. One looked and died. One looked and was struck. One looked and cut the plants. One went up in peace and came down in peace. Ben Azzai looked and died. Concerning him scripture says, Precious
5 in the sight of the LORD is the death of his saints. Ben Zoma looked and was struck. Concerning him scripture says, Have you found honey? Eat what is sufficient for you ... Elisha looked and cut the plants. Concerning him scripture says, Do not allow your mouth to bring your flesh into sin ... R. Akiba went up in peace and came
10 down in peace. Concerning him scripture says, Draw me; we shall run after you.

l. 1   A garden. So Dr Rowland translates *pardes* (פרדס), but it seems better to retain *paradise*, since it seems clear that the word is used metaphorically (*cut the plants, l. 3*). Also *went up ... came down* (two of the parallels have *entered ... came out*) suggests going to the heavenly world.
All the rabbis named belonged to the third generation of Tannaim (approximately AD 120–140).

l. 4   Ben Azzai was highly regarded as a student: 'When Ben Azzai died there were no more diligent students' (Sotah 9. 15).

l. 5   Ben Zoma was a great preacher (Sotah 9. 15), but went mad.

l. 7   *Elisha.* The proper name of Aher was Elisha ben Abuyah; Aher means 'A.N. Other'. His name was sometimes suppressed as a kind of *damnatio memoriae* because he fell into heresy. The parallels in the Jerusalem Talmud and Song of Songs Rabbah explain *cut the plants* by the suggestion that Elisha (= Aher) interfered with children as they studied Torah, but in fact he threatened to destroy Judaism by the speculation that there were 'two powers in heaven'.

l. 9   R. Akiba was an honoured martyr.

Mysticism could thus lead to madness and to heresy. Mystical theologians asked whether God was truly one or whether there was another to share his throne. In such speculations a being called Metatron played an important part; in the following passages, drawn from the same book (which contains very early traditions, though its final redaction may be as late as the fifth century AD), positive and negative views seem to be expressed.

279

3 *Enoch* 11; 12

R. Ishmael said: The angel Metatron, Prince of the Divine Presence, said to me:

The Holy One, blessed be he, revealed to me from that time onward all the mysteries of wisdom, all the depths of the perfect
5 Torah and all the thoughts of men's hearts. All the mysteries of the world and all the orders of nature stand revealed before me as they stand revealed before the Creator. From that time onward I looked and beheld deep secrets and wonderful mysteries. Before a man thinks in secret, I see his thought; before he acts, I see his act. There is
10 nothing in heaven above or deep within the earth concealed from me.

R. Ishmael said: Metatron, Prince of the Divine Presence, said to me:

Out of the love which he had for me, more than for all the
15 denizens of the heights, the Holy One, blessed be he, fashioned for me a majestic robe, in which all kinds of luminaries were set, and he clothed me in it. He fashioned for me a glorious cloak in which brightness, brilliance, splendour, and lustre of every kind were fixed, and he wrapped me in it. He fashioned for me a kingly crown in
20 which 49 refulgent stones were placed, each like the sun's orb, and its brilliance shone into the four quarters of the heaven of 'Arabot, into the seven heavens, and into the four quarters of the world. He set it upon my head and he called me, 'The lesser YHWH' in the presence of his whole household in the height, as it is written, 'My name is in
25 him.'

ll. 9, 10   *There is nothing . . . concealed from me.* This means an omniscience that can scarcely be less than divine.

l. 21   '*Arabot*, the seventh heaven.

l. 23   *The lesser YHWH.* This is the most significant of the names applied to Metatron. It seems to imply that though less than the supreme God he nevertheless belongs to the same order of being.

280

3 Enoch 16

R. Ishmael said: The angel Metatron, Prince of the Divine Presence, the glory of highest heaven, said to me:

At first I sat upon a great throne at the door of the seventh palace, and I judged all the denizens of the heights on the authority of the
5 Holy One, blessed be he. I assigned greatness, royalty, rank, sovereignty, glory, praise, diadem, crown, and honour to all the princes of kingdoms, when I sat in the heavenly court. The princes of kingdoms stood beside me, to my right and to my left, by authority of the Holy One, blessed be he. But when 'Aḥer came to
10 behold the vision of the chariot and set eyes upon me, he was afraid and trembled before me. His soul was alarmed to the point of leaving him because of his fear, dread, and terror of me, when he saw me seated upon a throne like a king, with ministering angels standing beside me as servants and all the princes of kingdoms crowned with
15 crowns surrounding me. Then he opened his mouth and said, 'There are indeed two powers in heaven!' Immediately a divine voice came out from the presence of the Šekinah and said, 'Come back to me, apostate sons—apart from 'Aḥer!' Then 'Anapi'el YHWH, the honoured, glorified, beloved, wonderful, terrible, and dreadful
20 Prince, came at the command of the Holy One, blessed be he, and struck me with sixty lashes of fire and made me stand to my feet.

l. 9   '*Aḥer.* See **278**.

l. 18   '*Aḥer's* denial of a fundamental principle, that of the unity of God, was unforgivable.
'*Anapi'el*, an angel.

Index of References[1]

1   Old Testament

Genesis
1. —   96,100,255,346
1. 2   96, 326
1. 3   37
1. 14–18   97
1. 26f.   98
1. 27   97
2. —   346
2. 4–7   257
2. 7   37
2. 10–14   255
6. 5; 8.21   182
15. 2   266
15. 20   37
17. 5   262
18. —   264

Exodus
3. 2   36
3. 8   37
3. 14   261, 291
3. 17   37
7. 9, 12   311
13. 21f.   37
16. 29   196
20. 12   304
24. 10   291

Leviticus
14. 8   208
16. —   204
19. 18   305
21. 14   146
23. 40   201
23. 42   199

Numbers
24. 17   172

Deuteronomy
5. 5   264
6. 5   183
11. 18   194
17. 16f.   339
23. 12ff.   160
23. 17 (18)   268
24. 1–4   275
26. 5–9   198
31. 21   182
32. 36   308

Joshua
24. 31   177

2 Samuel
11. 2–17   34
22. 11   37

1 Kings
3. 4–15, 9, 13   301
4. 33   302

2 Kings
19. 21   334

1 Chronicles
28. 9; 29.18   182

2 Chronicles
1. 7–13, 10,12   301
3.11   37
20. 7   303

Job
28. 15–19   301
40. 15, 25   337

---

[1] This index does not include references to passages quoted as part of the text.

Psalms
77. 1   192
113–18. —   198

Proverbs
1. 2ff   299
3. 14 f.   301
8. —   182
8. 10 f.   301
8. 30   302
16. 16   301

Ecclesiastes
7. 11f.   301
8. 1   240

Isaiah
7. 14   290
9. 5   238
11. 1   339
11. 2   301
11. 6   334
23. 1   245
26. 3   182
27. 1   311
41. 8   303

Jeremiah
2. 10   245

Ezekiel
1. —   346
10. —   346
14. 14, 20 ; 28. 3   318
31. 6, 13   328
34. —   327
34. 23   339
38. —; 39. —   251
44. 15   226

Daniel
2. 45   326
4. 12, 21f.   328
7. —   322, 324, 326
7. 13   324, 326
7. 27   341
11. 30   245
11. 31   137
12. 2   239, 308
12. 9   328
12. 11   137

Hosea
10. 11   224

Amos
9. 11f.   290

Micah
5. 4   339

Habakkuk
2. 1   192

2   New Testament

Matthew
3. 7–10   276
5. 14   114
6. —   113
5. 42, 43; 6.19ff.;
   7.12   305
6. 22, 23   114
6. 33   113
7. 3–5   114
7. 7   113
7. 12   305
8. 21   304
10. 26   113

Matthew—*continued*
11. 27   100, 111
12. 27   34
15. 13   111
17. 24   170
19. 28   113
19. 30   113
20. 16   113
23. 15   208
27. 62–6; 28. 11–
   15   13, 15
28. 18   100

Mark

1. 15	99
1. 25	36
2. 17	111
4. 9	114
4. 14	99
4. 22	113
5. 8	36
5. 9	37
5. 22	55
6. 8, 9	31
6. 14–29	276
7. 3	297
9. 25	36
10. 21	305
10. 31	113
15. 7	278
15. 43	331

Luke

2.11	339
2. 25	331
3. 1	276
3. 7ff., 10–14	276
4. 35	36
6. 30, 31	305
6. 41, 42	114
8.17	113
9.59	304
10. 22	100, 111
11. 9, 10	113
11. 19	34
11. 34–6	114
12. 2	113
12. 33f.	305
13. 30	113
14. 5	228
16. 22	304
17. 20	114
17. 21	113, 114
19. 10	344
22. 29, 30	113
24. 13	170

John

1. 3f.	97
1. 11	100
1. 12	99
3. 21	304
4. 10	99

John—*continued*

5. 17	254
5. 20	100
5. 22	344
5. 27	100, 344
7. 37f.; 8. 12	201
8. 52	113
10. 22	141
14. 5	114
15. 14	303
17. 26	111
18. 28	199

Acts

2. —	199
2. 10; 6. 5	208
2. 27	221
3. 19	221
6. 9	54
7. 47–50	289
13. 43, 50	208
15. 16ff.	290
15. 23	29
15. 23–9	28
15. 29	29
16. 14; 17. 4, 17	208
17. 25, 29	289
17. 28	68
18. 2	14
18. 7	208
18. 12	51
19. 13	34, 36
21. 26–30	53
23. 26	29
23. 26–30	28
23. 30	29
25. 23	176

Romans

12. 1	100
16. 1	29

1 Corinthians

1. 18	99
4. 15	129

2 Corinthians

3. 1	29
13. 7	31

Galatians
4. 19 129

Ephesians
2. 14 53

Philippians
1. 21 90

Colossians
1. 19 111
2. 8 58, 92
2. 9 111
3. 1f. 331
4. 7ff. 29

1 Timothy
6. 20 92

Hebrews
1. 3 302
11. 3, 26f., 34ff. 308
13. 15 100

James
1. 1 29
2. 19 36
2. 23 303
5. 4 305

1 Peter
1. 7 36
2. 2, 5 100

1 John
1. 6 304
2. 4 93
3. 9 99

3 John
15. — 30

Revelation
2. 17 337
10. 4 328
11. 8 219
13. 1 324
17. 12–17 15
21. 2 327

3   Apocrypha and Pseudepigrapha[1]

1 Maccabees
1. — 281
1. 29 139
1. 29f. 137
1. 36 141
2. 70 139
10. 20 143
13. 50 141

2 Maccabees
2. 23 306
4. — 136
5. — 281
5. 24 139
7. — 308

Tobit
1. 17; 2. 4–8 304
4. — 305
12. 12 304
14. —; *14. 10* 305

Wisdom of Solomon
6. 24 301
7. 1 (6. 1)–9. 18 299

Jubilees
2. 19 254
4. 33 305

[1] As in R. H. Charles, *The Apocrypha and Pseudepigrapha of the Old Testament* (1913).

Epistle of Aristeas
9   297
30   298
33, 46   294
182   297

I Enoch
22. 10   304
37–71   341
85–90   326
85. 3   328
87. 3; 89. 42ff., 52; 90.
19   328
90. 20–7   327

Assumption of Moses
10   336

2 Baruch
43. 2   337

3 Baruch
9.7   311

4 Ezra
11. —   320, 324
11. 1   325
13. 3   341

Psalms of Solomon
17. 5; 18. 6   339

Ahikar
2. 10   305
2. 13   305

4   Josephus and Philo

Josephus
 Life
  2   270
  359f.   269
  414f.   275
 Against Apion
  ii. 45 ff.   292
 Jewish War
  i. 3   269
  i. 32   281
  i. 90   146
  i. 147, 150   321
  i. 388–90   151
  ii. 119   271
  ii. 129   160
  ii. 136, 159   160
  ii. 160f.   160
  ii. 162f.   182
  ii. 546   271
  v. 193f.; vi. 125   53
  vii. 175   277
  vii. 437–50   275
 Jewish Antiquities
  i. 10ff.   292
  iv. 198   286
  xii. 11–118   292
  xii. 43   178
  xii. 43f.   294
  xii. 157, 224   178

Jewish Antiquities—*continued*
  xii. 244, 246   137
  xii. 248   281
  xiii. 171   271
  xiii. 244   281
  xiii. 292, 356   146
  xiii. 372   201
  xiv. 158   150
  xv. —   148
  xv. 417   53
  xvii. 342   156
  xviii. 11   271
  xviii. 55   157
  xx.17ff.   254
  xx. 259, 266f.   269
  xx. 268   286

Philo
 De Opificio Mundi
  24f.   263
 Legum Allegoriae
  iii. 42   95
 De Confusione Linguarum
  146   302
 De Abrahamo
  273   303
 In Flaccum
  74   174
 Legatio ad Gaium
  212   53

5 Rabbinic Literature

Mishnah
 Berakoth
  9. 5 183
 Erubin
  4. 3 228
 Yoma
  5. 4–7 203
 Sukkah
  3. 12 180
 Betzah
  1. 6 185
 Taanith
  1. 1 189
 Megillah
  1. 8 295
 Ketuboth
  4. 7–12; 5. 1 191
 Sotah
  5. 3 228
  9. 14 294
  9. 15 182, 347
 Gittin
  9. 10 178
 Baba Metzia
  2. 1–6 192
 Sanhedrin
  7. 4; 9. 6 279
  11. 4 215
 Eduyoth
  4f.; 4. 1 178
 P. *Aboth*
  1. 1 181, 184
  4. 5 179

Babylonian Talmud
 Shabbath
  156a 262
 Pesahim
  49b 181
 Sukkah
  53a 179
 Megillah
  9a 294, 295
 Yebamoth
  46a 254
 Nedarim
  62a 179
 Hagigah
  14b 347

Jerusalem Talmud
 Hagigah
  77b 347

Midrash Rabbah
 Genesis
  9. 7 182
 Leviticus
  35. 1 179
 Song of Songs
  1. 4 347

Sepher Torah
  1, §8 295

6 Greek and Latin Authors

Aratus of Soli
 Phaenomena 5 68

Augustus
 Res Gestae 22. 2 8

Cicero
 Ad Atticum
  xiii. 25. 3 27
  xvi. 3. 1 27
 De Divinatione
  ii. 63 (129) 303

Corpus Hermeticum
 i. 37
 i. 7f. 97
 i. 13 100
 i. 16f. 98
 xi. 103
 xi. 15 95
 xiii. 7 95

Corpus Inscriptionum
 Graecarum
  2079 56

Corpus Inscriptionum
  Latinarum
  vi. 510   127

Dio Cassius
  Epitome lxvi. I   274

Diogenes Laertius
  133   303

Heraclitus
  Fragments
  45, 115   60

Homer
  Iliad vi. *168*   24

Horace
  Carmen Saeculare
  51f.   166

Livy
  i. 19   4
  xxix. 10   121

Lucan
  ii. 592–3   176

Plato
  Apology 19BC   87
  Republic
  iv. 439D   255
  Laws iv. *716D*   303
  Timaeus
  69C; 69E;
    90A   255

Plato—*continued*
  Phaedrus
  246ff.   255
  246C   303

Pliny
  Natural History
  xii. 104   25

Plutarch
  On the Malice of
    Herodotus 13   124

Spartian
  Hadrian 4   170

Suetonius
  Augustus 101   I
  Domitian 15   22
  Vespasian 4; 5   274
    10   22

Tacitus
  Histories
  i. 10   19, 274
  ii. 1; v. 13   274
  v. 4   176
  v. 5   176

Xenophon
  Memorabilia
  II, i. 33   303

Virgil
  Aeneid vi. 851ff.   166

7   Patristic Writings

Diognetus, Epistle to
  1. —   278
  5. 6   41

Eusebius
  Historia Ecclesiastica
  II, xxiii. 22   278
  Praeparatio Evangelica
  XIII, xii. —   284
  XIII, xii. 2   292

Gospel of Thomas
  77   113

Irenaeus
  Adversus Haereses
  iii. 11. 9   108
  v. 33   337

Justin
  Apology I. *60*   284

Index of Names and Subjects

Abomination of desolation 137, 141, 318
Abstinence 94, 127, 129
Abtalion 179
Actium 1, 4, 150, 324
Aelia Capitolina 170f.
Aeschylus 85, 88-9
Age to come (*see also* World to come) 182, 195, 328-31
Aḥer 347, 349
Ahikar 305
Akiba 170, 172, 181f., 190, 207, 210, 305, 347, 348
Albinus 163, 278f.
Alexander the Great 1, 24, 135f., 293, 294
Alexander Jannaeus 145ff., 201
Alexandra 148
Alexandria 13, 24, 33, 47-50, 84, 135, 173f., 252, 290, 293, 297
Allegory (*see also* Cave) 252f., 255f., 259-62, 320-4
Almsgiving 304f.
'*Am ha-'aretz* 181, 197, 207, 212
Ananus 278f.
Andromache 90-1
Antigone 89, 90
Antigonus of Soko 177f.
Antioch (in Syria) 12, 135
Antiochus Epiphanes 135ff., 155, 281ff., 305-8, 317, 341
Antipater 148f., 153
Antony 4, 150f.
Anubis 131f.
Apion 269f., 280f.
Apocalyptic 316-48
Apollo 2, 5, 7ff., 52, 55, 121, 125
Apollonius of Tyana 82-5
Apologetics 279-84
'*Appiqoros* 210
Apprenticeship 39f.
Archelaus 156
Aretas 148, 276
Aristo of Pella 172

Aristobulus 147f., 153
Aristophanes 85-8
Aristotle 77-8
Ascent (of the soul) 94
Asceticism 158f., 270f.
Astrology 38, 68, 96f., 262
Attis 125
Augustus 1-11, 14, 25f., 40, 48f., 129, 150f., 174, 324

Babylonia 184
Bannus 270f., 277
Baptism 102, 117, 209f., 276f.
Bar Cocheba 170, 172, 181
Baraita 184
Ben Zoma 182, 347
Benedictions 204ff., 211
Beth ha-She'ubah 201
Bethhoron 139, 271
Bethsura 141, 144
Binding of Isaac 313-14
Birth (registration of) 39
Bisexuality 96f., 98
Bithara 172
Blasphemy 213ff.
Booths, Feast of (*see also* Tabernacles) 189, 194, 199ff.

Caesarea 147, 152, 164f., 275
Cave (allegory of) 62-5
Chariot 346-7
Charms 33-7
Chrysippus 66, 68f.
Circumcision 208ff., 253f.
Claudius 13ff., 26, 47-50, 173
Cleanthes 66ff.
Community 221f., 231-4
Conflagration (Stoic) 66, 68
Coponius 156
Cosmogony 95ff.
Cosmopolitanism 1, 76f., 257
Cosmos 68, 70, 300ff.
Courts (Jewish) 213f.

Creation   284–6, 309–11
Cybele   121, 125
Cynic, Cynicism   30–1, 81f.

Day of Atonement   201–4
Dead, care for the   303ff.
Death   61f., 74–6, 79ff., 81f.
Death (registration of)   43
Dedication, Feast of   140f.
Deed of sale   44f., 55f.
Deeds of loving-kindness   177f.
Delphi   51f., 55, 61f.
Demai-produce   196f., 208
Demetrius of Phalerum   296ff.
Demiurge   96f.
Demons   34–7, 83
Destiny   9, 67f., 74, 81, 96ff., 120
Diogenes   82
Dionysus   121f., 124
Dispersion (Jewish)   56, 173ff., 194
Divination   69
Divorce   8, 41f., 178f., 275
Domitian   19–22, 46, 275, 324
Dream   325, 340
Dualism   95f., 255

Egypt   3, 4, 23ff., 30, 49, 84, 93,
   136f., 142, 147, 150, 170, 173f., 290,
   293, 321f., 324
Eleazar   168–9
Eleusinian mysteries   129
Emmaus   170
Epaphroditus   275
Ephebi   48f.
Epictetus   70–4
Epicurus   78–81, 259
Erinyes   89
'*Erub*   196
Essenes   156–61, 218, 270f., 277
Eumenides   89
Euripides   85, 90–1
Evil   68f., 74f., 97f.
Exegesis (Rabbinic)   185ff.
Exorcism   34–7, 83
Exposure (of children)   40f., 46f.
Ezra   177

Fasting   204
Fear   60ff., 73, 79f.
Feasts   55, 194–204, 253f.

Felix   28, 163
Festus   163, 278f.
Fire of Rome   15, 17
Flaccus   174f.
Flavia Domitilla   21–2
Flavius Clemens   21–2
Flesh   231
Freedom   72ff., 159, 181f., 198

Gaius (Caligula)   11ff., 173, 175
Galilee   12, 149, 271, 276
Gallio   51f.
Gamaliel II   197f.
Gehenna   332
Gemara   184
Gentiles   320f., 333, 339
Gessius Florus   163ff.
Glabrio   21–2
Gnosis, Gnosticism   58, 92–119
God-fearers   173f., 208f.
'Gospel' (Hermetic)   94, 99
Great Synagogue   177
Guardian   234

Haber   206f.
Hadrian   170ff.
Haggadah   184f., 261
Halakah   184
Hallel   198
Hanukkah see Dedication
Hasmoneans   270
Heraclitus   59f.
Hermes   93, 121, 123
Hermetica   93–103
Herod Agrippa I   156
Herod Agrippa II   156, 175
Herod Antipas   276
Herod the Great   148–53, 155, 276
Herodias   276
Hillel   178, 185, 198–9, 305
Horus   123

Ideas   62–5
Image of God   97, 181
Immortality   99, 120, 132f., 159f.
Initiation   125–30
Inspiration   265ff., 293f.
Ishmael (R.)   185
Isis   120–4, 130ff., 299, 302

Jabneh 180
James 278f., 290
Jericho 152
Jerusalem 12, 18, 21, 28, 53ff., 136ff.,
    141, 143–8, 149, 153ff., 163–8,
    170ff., 192, 197f., 199ff., 206, 270,
    274, 321, 334, 337f.
Jesus 14f., 57, 112–14, 277f.
Jews 10, 12ff., 20, 49, Chs. 7–13
    passim
Johanan b. Zakkai 180, 183, 190
John Hyrcanus 147–50
John the Baptist 114, 271, 275ff.
Jonathan 138, 142f., 145
Josephus 165, 174, 269–89, 292, 294
Jotapata 272f.
Judaea, Judah 12f., 16, 18f., 137f.,
    144, 149, 156, 171, 274f., 293
Judah the Prince 179, 181, 184, 187,
    212
Judas Maccabaeus 138–41, 143, 306,
    328
Judgement 331f.
Julius Caesar 6, 149f., 324
Justification 228–31
Justin Martyr 172, 290
Justus of Tiberias 269

Ketubah 190f.
Kingdom of God 113–14, 182,
    331ff.
Kittim 245, 247, 250
Knowledge *see* Gnosis
Kušta 117–119

Laufa 117
Law (of Moses) 49, 54f., 137f., 140,
    156, 164, 177–82, 184, 188, 192–4,
    199, 202, 203, 210, 213, 252ff.,
    256f., 268, 283, 293, 305f., 308,
    319f., 326, 330, 333
Letters (papyrus) 28–31
Life after death 306ff.
Logos 59f., 66f., 70, 72, 95f., 100,
    254, 262ff., 299, 302f.
Lucretius 78f.
Lulab 180, 200f.
Lustrations 296f.

Machaerus 276
Magic 34–8
Man (*see also* Son of man) 95, 97f.,
    325f., 340f.
Manda dḤaiyê 95, 118–19
Mandaeans 114–19
Manna 336f.
Manumission 55ff.
Marcus Aurelius 70f., 74ff.
Marriage 40f., 158f.
Martyrdom 137, 305–8
Masada 168–9
Mattathias 138f., 143
Matthias 269f.
Mediation 263f.
Meir 181, 184, 188, 190
Messiah 315, 320, 324ff., 328, 332,
    334–9, 342f.
Messianic afflictions 326, 332, 334f.
Metatron 348–9
Middoth 185
Midrash 184
Military service 43
Mind 95–8, 257, 302
Minim, Minuth 210
Miracles 190
Mishnah 179, 181, 184
Mithraism, Mithras 125f., 132–4
Modin 138
Moses 177, 286–7
Mysteries, Mystery religions 120–
    34, 265, 267f., 294
Mysticism 344–9
Myth 94, 120–5

Nag Hammadi 103–14
Nature 66, 74f., 97f., 256f.
Nazarenes 211
Nazareth 13, 15
Neo-Pythagoreanism 258
Nero 11, 15–19, 70, 272f.
New Jerusalem 327
New Temple 327
Numbers 258

Onias the Circlemaker 191f.
Oracle 33–7
Orestes 88–9
Osiris 121–4

Pain   69, 76, 81
Pairs   178
Palestine   94, 135, 170, 184, 194, 269, 337
Papyrus   23–8
Parable   188ff., 192ff., 208f., 324–8
Paradise   347
Parents, care for   303f.
Passover   185, 194, 197ff., 282
Paul   51f., 68
Pentecost   194, 199
Persecution   15ff.
Pesher   226, 240–6
Pessinus   121, 125
Petronius   11–13
Pharisees   157ff., 182, 183, 270f., 320
Phasael   149f.
Philo   95, 173ff., 252–68, 279, 292, 299
Pilgrim feasts   194
Planets   127
Plato, Platonism   60–5, 68, 253–7, 263, 284, 303
Pleasure   69, 78, 80f.
Pleroma   111
Poets, Greek   58–9, 85–91
Poimandres   94–101
Police   44f.
Pompey   6, 147f., 155, 281, 321f., 337
Pontius Pilate   16, 155–6, 278
Porta Capena   175
Posidonius   66, 69f., 280
Powers   264f.
Procurators   155ff.
Prophecy, Prophet   32f., 144, 316, 334
Proselytes   179, 208ff.
Providence   66, 71f., 257, 303
Provinces   4, 14, 52
Pseudonymity   317–20, 331, 333
Ptolemies   135
Ptolemy Philadelphus   292–5, 297
Pythagoreanism   83

Qaddish   206
Qumran   218–51

Rabbis   177–217, 261
Reason *see* Logos

Rebirth   102–3
Religion   67, 78f.
Republic (Roman)   1, 4f.
Resurrection   210, 239, 307f., 336
Revelation   93f., 99f.
Rewards   177ff., 181, 212
Rome   25, 30, 121, 129, 136, 141f., 147, 149, 274

Sabbath   155, 176, 178, 188, 194ff., 200f., 209, 214, 226–8, 253f.
Sacraments   120
Sacrifice   32, 99f.
Sadducees   157ff., 178, 183, 210, 270
Salvation   94ff., 120
Samaria, Samaritans   138, 151, 156, 164
Sanhedrin   178, 180
Satan   331f.
Saviour   120
Sebaste *see* Samaria
Secular Games   6–8
Seleucids   135f.
Senate (Roman)   1, 4, 14, 19, 21
Septuagint   24, 290–308
Servant of the Lord   314, 315
Shammai   178, 185, 198–9, 275
Shemaiah   179
Sibylline Books (Oracles)   5–7, 333
Sicarii   162f., 275
Siloam   167
Silva   168–9
Simeon b. Shetah   192, 216f.
Simeon the Just   177f.
Simon Maccabaeus   138, 142–5
Slavery, Slaves   2, 55f.
Socrates   60–2, 70, 85–7
Solomon   287–9
Son of David   337ff.
Son of God   320
Son of man (*see also* Man)   107, 237, 339–44
Sophists   60f., 87
Sophocles   85, 89, 90
Spheres   94
Spirit   300–3
Stoicism   1, 65–77, 97, 256f., 262, 265, 270, 299, 303
Stoning   213, 215ff.
Strabo   173f.

Stuff 66
Suf 117, 118
Sukkah 189, 199ff.
Synagogue 53–5, 164, 173, 204ff.
Synagogue, Ruler of 54f.
Syria 12, 19, 49, 85, 135, 143, 146ff., 150, 170, 271, 324

Tabernacles, Feast of (*see also* Booths) 141, 145
Talmud 184
Tannaim 184
Targum 291–2, 309–15
Taurobolium 125f., 134
Taxes 14, 20, 32f., 38, 44, 170, 275
Teacher of righteousness 223–4, 226, 240–6
Temple (of Jerusalem) 53, 136f., 139ff., 146f., 151, 165, 170, 180, 198, 201–4, 213, 253, 278, 280f.
Temple-service 177, 204
Theocracy 283f.
Therapeutae 161–2
Thoth 93
Tiberius 2ff., 10f., 13f., 131, 156, 175, 276, 324

Tithes 181, 196, 198, 207
Titus 18f., 165f., 272–5, 281f., 324
Tomb-breaking 13, 15
Tosephta 184
Trajan 19, 324
Trypho 290
Typhon 121–4

Uthra 119

Vespasian 15, 18f., 165f., 272–5, 324
Vestal Virgins 1, 5
Virtues 255f., 283f.
Vision 324–8, 340
Vows 190f.

Will 42
Wisdom 96, 182, 263, 298–303
Word *see* Logos
World to come (*see* Age to come) 182, 210, 212, 216

Yetzer 182, 194, 221, 330
Yoke 188

Zeno 65ff., 85, 302